MW00563823

THE
COLLEGE
PRESS
NIV
COMMENTARY

PSALMS
VOLUME 1

THE
COLLEGE
PRESS
NIV
COMMENTARY

PSALMS
VOLUME 1

S. EDWARD TESH
WALTER D. ZORN

Old Testament Series Co-Editors:

Terry Briley, Ph.D.
Lipscomb University

Paul Kissling, Ph.D.
Great Lakes Christian College

COLLEGE PRESS
PUBLISHING COMPANY
Joplin, Missouri

The publishers gratefully acknowledge permission by James E.
Smith to use his category titles for Psalms from *The Wisdom
Literature and Psalms* (Old Testament Survey Series from College
Press) in the outline of this commentary.

Library of Congress Cataloging-in-Publication Data

Tesh, S. Edward (Samuel Edward), 1911–1999.
    Psalms / S. Edward Tesh & Walter Zorn.
        p.   cm. – (The College Press NIV commentary. Old
    Testament series)
    Includes bibliographical references.
    ISBN 0-89900-887-9
    1. Bible. O.T. Psalms—Commentaries.   I. Zorn, Walter, 1943–   .
    II. Bible. O.T. Psalms. English. New International. 1995.
    III. Title.   IV. Series.
    BS1430.3.T47 1999
    223'.2077–dc21   99-23687
                                                        CIP

A WORD
FROM THE PUBLISHER

Years ago a movement was begun with the dream of uniting all Christians on the basis of a common purpose (world evangelism) under a common authority (the Word of God). The College Press NIV Commentary Series is a serious effort to join the scholarship of two branches of this unity movement so as to speak with one voice concerning the Word of God. Our desire is to provide a resource for your study of the New Testament that will benefit you whether you are preparing a Bible School lesson, a sermon, a college course, or your own personal devotions. Today as we survey the wreckage of a broken world, we must turn again to the Lord and his Word, unite under his banner and communicate the life-giving message to those who are in desperate need. This is our purpose.

ABBREVIATIONS

ANE . . . . *Ancient Near Eastern Texts Relating to the Old Testament*
ASV . . . . *American Standard Version*
BASOR . . . . . *Bulletin of the American Schools of Oriental Research*
BHS . . . . *Biblia Hebraica Stuttgartensia*
Bib . . . . *Biblica*
BT . . . . *The Bible Translator*
DOTT . . . . . . *Documents from Old Testament Times*
EJ . . . . *Encyclopedia Judaica*
EvQ . . . . *The Evangelical Quarterly*
HAR . . . . *Hebrew Annual Review*
ICC . . . . *International Critical Commentary*
IDB . . . . *Interpreter's Dictionary of the Bible*
Int . . . . *Interpretation*
JBL . . . . *The Journal of Biblical Literature*
JBR . . . . *The Journal of Bible and Religion*
JQR . . . . *The Jewish Quarterly Review*
JSOT . . . . *The Journal for the Study of the Old Testament*
JSS . . . . *The Journal of Semitic Studies*
JTS . . . . *The Journal of Theological Studies*
KJV . . . . *King James Version*
LXX . . . . *Septuagint*
MT . . . . *Masoretic Text*
NASB . . . . . . *New American Standard Bible*
NEB . . . . *New English Bible*
NIV . . . . *New International Version*
NT . . . . *New Testament*
OT . . . . *Old Testament*
RSV . . . . *Revised Standard Version*
TDNT . . . . . . *Theological Dictionary of the New Testament, Kittel*

TDOT   *Theological Dictionary of the Old Testament,*
              Butterwick & Ringgren
TWOT . . . . . *Theological Wordbook of the Old Testament*
VT . . . . *Vetus Testamentum*

Simplified Guide to Hebrew Writing

Heb. letter	Translit.	
א	’	Has no sound of its own; like smooth breathing mark in Greek
ב	b	Pronounced like English B *or* V
ג	g	Pronounced like English G
ד	d	Pronounced like English D
ה	h	Pronounced like English H
ו	w	As a consonant, pronounced like English V or German W
וּ	û	Represents a vowel sound, pronounced like English long OO
וֹ	ô	Represents a vowel sound, pronounced like English long O
ז	z	Pronounced like English Z
ח	ḥ	Pronounced like German and Scottish CH and Greek χ (chi)
ט	ṭ	Pronounced like English T
י	y	Pronounced like English Y
כ/ך	k	Pronounced like English K
ל	l	Pronounced like English L
מ/ם	m	Pronounced like English M
נ/ן	n	Pronounced like English N
ס	s	Pronounced like English S
ע	‘	Stop in breath deep in throat before pronouncing the vowel
פ/ף	p/ph	Pronounced like English P *or* F
צ/ץ	ṣ	Pronounced like English TS/TZ
ק	q	Pronounced very much like כ (k)
ר	r	Pronounced like English R
שׂ	ś	Pronounced like English S, much the same as ס
שׁ	š	Pronounced like English SH
ת	t/th	Pronounced like English T *or* TH

Note that different forms of some letters appear at the end of the word (written right to left), as in כָּפַף (*kāphaph*, "bend") and מֶלֶךְ (*melek*, "king").

Vowels in Hebrew (except where the ו is used to represent a vowel sound), are represented by "vowel points" added to the consonant. For example: הַ (*ha*, "the"). The letter *yod* (י, *y*) also becomes a *part of* certain vowel sounds, as in the conjunction כִּי (*kî*, "that"). Originally, Hebrew was written as "unpointed" text, with just the consonants. For convenience, the different vowel points are shown below on the letter Aleph (א).

אָ	ā	Pronounced not like long A in English, but like the broad A or AH sound
אַ	a	The Hebrew short A sound, but more closely resembles the broad A (pronounced for a shorter period of time) than the English short A
אֶ	e	Pronounced like English short E
אֵ	ē	Pronounced like English long A, or Greek η (eta)

אִ	i	Pronounced like English short I
אִ	î	The same vowel point is sometimes pronounced like אִי (see below)
אָ	o	This vowel point sometimes represents the short O sound
אֹ	ō	Pronounced like English long O
אֻ	u	The vowel point ֻ sometimes represents a shorter U sound and
אֻ	ū	is sometimes pronounced like the וּ (û, see above)
אֵי	ê	Pronounced much the same as אֵ
אֵי	ê	Pronounced much the same as אֵ
אִי	î	Pronounced like long I in many languages, or English long E
אְ	ə	An unstressed vowel sound, like the first E in the word "severe"
אֱ, אֲ, אֳ	ŏ, ă, ĕ	Shortened, unstressed forms of the vowels אָ, אַ, and אֶ, pronounced very similarly to אְ

PREFACE

Prof. S. Edward Tesh "went home to be with the Lord" on March 17, 1999. He was 87 years old, having been born May 28, 1911. He served for forty years at Lincoln Christian College & Seminary, first at the college (Lincoln Bible Institute) in 1949, and then in the Seminary (Lincoln Christian Seminary) beginning in 1951 when Enos Dowling became the first dean of the new graduate program. Prof. Tesh continued as the Old Testament professor for 38 years. A graduate from Johnson Bible College (1931, B.A.), he received his M.Div. from Butler University in 1948 before moving to Lincoln. Later he did some graduate work at the University of Manchester in England. Prof. Tesh lived his entire professional career in Lincoln and retired as Professor Emeritus on October 31, 1989.

In the early 1980's Bro. Don DeWelt encouraged Prof. Tesh to write a commentary on the Psalms. By 1984 a letter from Don DeWelt suggested that the first volume of two be completed within a year. Of course that never happened. Prof. Tesh continued to read and study and seemed never ready to finish the commentary. Unfortunately, Bro. DeWelt was "called home," and Prof. Tesh was diagnosed with the early stage of Parkinson's disease while in his mid-seventies. In spite of the setback, Prof. Tesh continued to work on his commentary and actually finished the first volume and was working on the second when the disease slowly but surely destroyed the gifted professor's ability to write and research. Fortunately, over half of the second volume was completed before Prof. Tesh had to cease his labor.

In 1998 Chris DeWelt invited me to edit the first volume and complete the writing of the second volume for this series. Prof. Tesh's commentary would be the first Old Testament volume in the series. The second volume would follow as soon as possible. However, Prof. Tesh had written his commentary from the King James Version and all comments were based on that version. While I was able to shift the text to NIV and all comments from that perspective, Prof. Tesh's comments have a rich vocabulary and style that mimics the KJV style which most agree has never been matched for the Psalms. It is a unique mix and I am happy to present such a volume to the Christian public at large.

While Prof. Tesh was concerned about the canonical context and exegesis, he clearly wanted to communicate to the reader or student the range of human emotional depth, height, and breadth of the Psalms. Prof. Tesh's main concern with this commentary was the *real meaning* of the text, not only to the author and his contemporaries (if that could be discerned!) but also to the Christian today. I know now what one of the anonymous quotes meant that Prof. Tesh wanted to use in his "preface." "Everyone should write a commentary on Psalms." Once you do this, you cannot remain the same. Just in the editing process of this commentary I have fallen *in love with God* in a way I never knew him before. I can only express it through a Psalm verse: *As the deer pants for streams of water, so my soul pants for you, O God* (Ps 42:1). What happened to me, I hope will happen to you, the reader, the student.

May Yahweh God be praised!

Walter D. Zorn, Ph.D., Professor of Old Testament
    and Biblical Languages
Lincoln Christian College & Seminary
Lincoln, Illinois
June, 1999

INTRODUCTION

It has been said that poetry is the language of the soul. Little wonder, then, that poetry is very much a part of Holy Scripture, for the Bible, above all else, would speak to the heart and soul of humankind. When God delivered Israel from the power of the Egyptian monarch, the event was celebrated in song (Exod 15:20,21). When Saul and Jonathan were slain in battle, David expressed his grief in an elegy of sublime pathos — "How the mighty have fallen!" (2 Sam 1:19-27). In the days of King Hezekiah, Sennacherib of Assyria threatened to destroy Jerusalem. In response to the prayers of the king the prophet Isaiah brought reassurance from God in the language of Hebrew poetry (2 Kgs 19:21-28). Altogether, fully one-third of the Old Testament is poetic in form.[1]

In the New Testament in the first two chapters of Luke are no less than three hymns in the typical Hebrew pattern (Luke 1:46-55,68-79; 2:29-32). Jesus utilized poetry in his discourses — Matt 5:3-10, for example — and it is evident that "psalms, hymns, and spiritual songs" were an important part of the daily existence of the early Christians (Eph 5:19). Elsewhere in the New Testament one may find poetic expression, including the new song of the twenty-four elders in praise of the Lamb that was slain (Rev 5:9,10).

Poetry is thus to be found throughout the entire Bible, and why not? Is there any reason why the inspired writer should not set

---

[1]Poetic books include Psalms, Job (except the prologue and the epilogue), Song of Songs, Lamentations, and much of Ecclesiastes and Proverbs. To these should be added Obadiah, Micah, Nahum, Habakkuk, Zephaniah, and numerous portions of the other prophets. In addition, poetic material is to be found to some extent in almost all of the other OT books. The Masoretes distinguished the books of Job, Proverbs, and Psalms as poetical in a particular sense, or for a particular purpose, by giving to them a special system of accents.

forth the message in exalted literary form? This would be the aim of the psalmist especially, since that which he expresses arises from deep emotional involvement in the exigencies of life.

THE POETIC NATURE OF PSALMS

RHYTHM

The poetic nature of the Psalms eludes some because there is virtually no rhyming of words to be found in Hebrew verse and no *precise* meter. Yet there is a certain rhythm of stressed syllables delineating the thought pattern. A verse may consist of a single line but usually will have two or more, each of which is called a stich (*stichos*). The following is an example of a two line verse, a *distich*.

Lísten, — O heávens, — and I will spéak;
heár, — O eárth, — the words of my moúth.

This verse from Deut 32:1 (NIV) is said to employ 3+3 meter. The translation obscures the fact that there are only six terms in the Hebrew, three in each stich. Yet the pattern of accented ideas is evident even in the English. Note that the two lines of the verse are separated by a simple pause, ending in a complete stop.

Another common meter, often used in laments and called *Qinah*, is 3+2. For example:

O Lórd, — heár — my práyer;
lísten — to my cry for mércy (Ps 143:1).

In addition there may be found 2+2, 4+4, 3+2+2, 2+2+2, and other metric variations, with a mixture appearing sometimes within a single literary unit. The morphology of the Hebrew language lends itself to the above accentual patterns, but it should be noted that the number of unaccented syllables is variable. Thus, Hebrew poetry seeks to present a *balance of ideas* in successive lines rather than a *balance of sound* or *uniformity in the number of syllables* per verse. The end result is the beautiful achievement of a rhythm of thought patterns, striking in its effect.

PARALLELISM

To a degree the rhythm of the Hebrew text is lost in translation and may entirely disappear in the English. Unmistakable, however, is the balance between verse members mentioned above. To this phenomenon Bishop Robert Lowth of Oxford gave the designation "parallelism of members" (in *De sacra poesi Hebraeorum*, 1753). The term is apt if it is properly understood. The actuality is that the second line of the verse corresponds *in some way* to the first. The balance is not restricted to, nor does it necessarily require, a correspondence of meaning. But words, phrases, ideas, parts of speech, and grammatical structure of the first member of the verse may find their *complement* or *completion* in the second. Parallelism has often been defined as saying the same thing over again in different words, but this is unduly to simplify and to restrict its significance.

Lowth identified three general types of parallelism: synonymous, antithetic, and synthetic. In reality, there are far more variations than can be subsumed under these categories,[2] but let us note examples. First, the *synonymous*, in which the thought of the first line is repeated, with variation, in the second:

> I will extol the LORD at all times:
> his praise will always be on my lips (Ps 34:1).

The *antithetic*, in which the thought of the first is contrasted:

> For the LORD watches over the way of the righteous,
> but the way of the wicked will perish (Ps 1:6).

And the *synthetic*, in which the second line enhances the first.[3]

---

[2]James Kugel, among others, has recognized that the categories of Lowth are inadequate and inexact. Kugel stresses that the second element in the parallel should be understood primarily as the completion, in some way, of the idea expressed in the first, rather than as a repetition. See *The Idea of Biblical Poetry: Parallelism and Its History* (New Haven: Yale University Press, 1981), pp. 12, 13. Also Stanley Gevirtz, *Patterns in the Early Poetry of Israel* (Chicago: University of Chicago Press, 1963), and Georg Fohrer, *Introduction to the Old Testament* (Nashville: Abingdon, 1965), pp. 43-49.

[3]One might question whether a verse of this type is truly parallel, although the synthetic relationship is obvious. Some prefer to designate this as an incomplete parallelism. See George Buchanan Gray, *The Forms of Hebrew Poetry* (New York: KTAV, 1972), a reprint of a 1915 work, p. 49.

> Oh, that I had the wings of a dove!
> I would fly away and be at rest (Ps 55:6).

A variant of the synthetic was designated as *climactic* by S.R. Driver. In such a verse the succeeding line moves beyond the first to a heightened emphasis. For example:

> If an enemy were insulting me, I could endure it;
> if a foe were raising himself against me, I could hide
>   from him.
> But it is you, a man like myself, my companion, my close
>   friend (Ps 55:12,13).

Among other suggested types of parallelism are *stair-like*, in which a word or phrase of the first line is repeated in the second as a stepping-stone to the finished statement:

> Ascribe to the LORD, O mighty ones,
> Ascribe to the LORD glory and strength (Ps 29:1).

Emblematic, consisting of a figurative comparison:

> As the deer pants for streams of water,
> So my soul pants for you, O God (Ps 42:1).

And *inverted*, or *chiastic*, in which there is an inversion of the order of words in the parallel lines:

> Have mercy on me, O God, *according to your unfailing*
>   *love;*
> *according to your great compassion* blot out my transgres-
>   sions (Ps 51:1).

The italicized words indicate the chiastic arrangement, which is after the pattern of A-B, B-A. Ps 1:6, previously quoted, is also chiastic.

These examples do not exhaust the variety of parallelisms that exists. The manner of expression in Hebrew is so varied that scholars have been able to point out numerous other types and subtypes.[4] On the other hand, it should be noted that parallelism is not

---

[4]For a comprehensive treatment of the parallelistic line, see Kugel, *Idea*, pp. 1-58. Also see A.A. Anderson, *Psalms 1-72*, The New Century Bible Commentary (Grand Rapids: Eerdmans, 1972), pp. 40-43.

always present in biblical poetry and that it may at times appear in prose. This phenomenon therefore is no certain indicator of the distinction between prose and poetry in Hebrew literature. As a matter of fact, the distinction is not always clearly discernible, since "even the prose of Israel is more or less poetic," as Pius Drijvers has observed.[5] Failure to recognize this has led some scholars to view certain *quasi-poetic* passages as corruptions of earlier poems of more precise structure. The attempt was then made needlessly to restore the poem, but the entire process was based on a false assumption. As Kugel has observed, "To see biblical style through the split lens of prose or poetry is to distort the view."[6] At times the differentiation is not all that exact. Nevertheless, we do recognize poetry in the Old Testament, all the while remembering that we must not attempt to make it conform to modern conventions.

STROPHE OR STANZA

Charles A. Briggs, early in the twentieth century, stated that the Psalms were arranged "in regular strophical organization," having concluded that such arrangement was a practical necessity for their use as songs in worship.[7] According to Briggs, almost all of the Psalms were so ordered, and his view reflected the opinion of numerous scholars of the nineteenth century, including Wilhelm DeWette, G.H. Ewald, Hermann Olshousen, T.K. Cheyne, and Franz Delitzsch. However, when it came to determining what constituted the strophes, or stanzas, there was wide divergence of opinion, for the strophic pattern was not always self-evident.

---

[5]Pius Drijvers, *The Psalms, Their Structure and Meaning* (New York: Herder and Herder, 1965), p. 25.

[6]Kugel, *Idea*, p. 85. The author also calls attention to the fact that there is no word for "poetry" in biblical Hebrew and suggests that modern critics might well use quotation marks when they write of biblical "poetry." Note should be taken that in the Dead Sea scroll 11QPs[a] all the psalms are written as prose with no indication of verse division except in Ps 119, an acrostic. However, other Psalms manuscripts from Qumran do indicate versification.

[7]Charles A. Briggs, *A Critical and Exegetical Commentary on the Book of Psalms*, ICC (Edinburgh: T & T Clark, 1906), p. xiv.

The absence of a clear arrangement was taken to indicate that the original had been obscured or destroyed by later glosses or by dislocations of the text. Consequently, various scholars attempted to reconstruct the original form of the psalm as they conjectured it to be. The supposed glosses were omitted, lines were rearranged, and the text otherwise emended, according to the judgment of the scholar. Naturally, such work was often highly speculative and the results were subjectively arrived at, at best.

Today it is recognized that a regular strophic order of metrical equivalents is not to be imposed upon the Psalms.[8] The semblance of stanza arrangement is often evident, but absolute symmetry in this regard is not found, nor should it be expected. This conclusion is indicated, in part, by analogy from the study of other ancient Near Eastern literature, especially that of Ugarit (*Ras Shamra*), discovered in 1928 and after, and dating from the fourteenth century B.C. Ugaritic is a Semitic dialect related to Hebrew, and the literature that was discovered contains parallels with the Hebrew, both in structure and in vocabulary. These parallels demonstrate that the asymmetrical pattern in the Psalms is not at all unusual, and no longer is this pattern considered to indicate a need for emendation of the text. In the words of R.K. Harrison, "It should now be fairly apparent to all scholars . . . that the text of the Hebrew Psalter is by no means as faulty or corrupt as was supposed by a great many nineteenth-century critics."[9] Apparently the psalmist intentionally varied the strophic pattern, especially near the end of a psalm to give it stress.

---

[8]As early as 1915 so prestigious a scholar as G.B. Gray suggested caution regarding the "considerable uncertainty" that "underlies the regular symmetrical forms in which certain scholars have presented the poetical parts of the Old Testament" (*Forms*, p. vi). Gray acknowledged that "at times the very existence of metre in the Old Testament has been questioned" (ibid. p. 47). For a summary of later treatment of this subject by biblical scholars, see W.O.E. Oesterley and T.H. Robinson, *An Introduction to the Books of the Old Testament* (London: SPCK, 1949), pp. 147-149.

[9]R.K. Harrison, *Introduction to the Old Testament* (Grand Rapids: Eerdmans, 1969), p. 974.

OTHER LITERARY DEVICES

A characteristic of poetry in general is the use that is made of figures of speech and other literary devices. These are found in great variety and abundance in the book of Psalms. Among such are the following:

Allegory, a figurative treatment of one subject under the image of another: "You brought a *vine* [Israel] out of Egypt; you drove out the nations and planted it" (Ps 80:8). (Isa 5:1-7 provides a more detailed use of this allegory.)

Metaphor, a comparison not to be taken literally but made to suggest a resemblance: "Since you are my rock and my fortress, for the sake of your name lead and guide me" (Ps 31:3).

Simile, the expressing of a resemblance, usually with the use of the words "like" or "as": "The righteous will flourish like a palm tree, they will grow like a cedar of Lebanon" (Ps 92:12).

Metonymy, the use of one word when another with which it is associated is really meant: "You prepare a *table* before me" (meaning *food*, Ps 23:5).

Hyperbole, an obvious exaggeration for emphasis: "Streams of tears flow from my eyes, for your law is not obeyed" (Ps 119:136).

Synecdoche, in which a part is put for the whole or the whole for a part: "You love every harmful word, O you deceitful tongue!" ("tongue" meaning *the person*, Ps 52:4).

Apostrophe, addressing either one not present, inanimate objects, or imaginary persons: "Tremble, O earth, at the presence of the Lord, at the presence of the God of Jacob" (Ps 114:7).

Personification, attributing characteristics of persons to inanimate objects: "Then all the trees of the forest will sing for joy" (Ps 96:12).

Irony, in which the actuality is the opposite of what is anticipated: "But their idols are silver and gold, made by the hands of men. They have mouths, but cannot speak, eyes, but they cannot see" (Ps 115:4,5). Or an even better example: "Their tombs will remain their houses forever, their dwellings for endless generations, though they had named lands after themselves" (Ps 49:11). See also Ps 118:22, "The stone the builders rejected has become the capstone."

Anaphora, repetition for emphasis or for dramatic effect: "All the nations surrounded me, but in the name of the LORD I cut them off. They surrounded me on every side, but in the name of the LORD I cut them off" (Ps 118:10,11).

Litotes, an understatement to increase the effect, or an emphasis of an idea by denying its opposite: "a broken and contrite heart, O God, you will not despise" (meaning "you will welcome," Ps 51:17).

Assonance, a correspondence in the sound of words in terms of their vowels and used in repetition or dominance of a single vowel sound: The "A" sound in Ps 48:7a (*rᵊʿādāh ʾăḥāzātham šām*) and the "I" sound in Ps 113:8 (*lᵊhôšîbî ʿim–nᵊdîbîm ʿim nᵊdîbê ʿammô*). There are many throughout the Psalms.

Alliteration, the repetition of letters or syllables having similar sounds: "Pray for the peace of Jerusalem" (*šaʾălû šᵊlôm Yᵊrûšālā(y)im*, Ps 122:6).

Acrostic, in which a group of verses begin each with a successive letter of the Hebrew alphabet. Psalm 34 is an example of a simple one verse, one letter acrostic while Psalm 119 is more elaborate with eight verses per Hebrew letter. Naturally, this feature is not evident in translation, since the English letters differ from the Hebrew.[10]

If one supposed the above varieties of expression to be the achievement of the *literati* of the Western world, then he or she needs to consider that the biblical writers employed them three thousand years ago! Obviously, on the part of the psalmists, divine inspiration did not preclude the utilizing of various means of expression. In our reading, it is essential that we recognize the figures of speech that they employed, in order properly to interpret and to grasp what is written.

We should also recognize the poetic style for its emotional content and for the pure joy of appreciation of the idiom.

---

[10]Psalm 119 is an acrostic in which each group of eight verses begins with the same letter of the alphabet, in succession—Aleph, Beth, Gimel, etc. Since there are twenty-two letters in the Hebrew, there are 176 verses in this psalm, making it the longest "chapter" in the Bible. English Bibles often include the Hebrew alphabet with this psalm to indicate the divisions. See the NIV text.

Prosaically one may say, "The human heart has aspirations toward God." But the psalmist cries out, "My soul thirsts for God, for the living God" (Ps 42:2). And our own heartstrings are touched as we catch the deeper significance that his words convey.

THE TITLE OF THE BOOK

Sepher Tehillim — "The Book of Praises"

Psalm 40 is a hymn of thanksgiving to God. Verse three strikes a note of exuberance: "He put a new song in my mouth, a hymn of praise to our God." The Hebrew term translated "hymn of praise" is תְּהִלָּה (t⁼hillāh), and it appears some twenty-eight times in the Psalms. It is understandable, therefore, why its plural form, t⁼hillîm — "songs of praise" came to be used in Jewish circles as the title of the book. In rabbinic literature the designation is often *sepher tehillim* (סֵפֶר תְּהִלִּים, sēpher t⁼hillîm), "Book of Praises." Not all of the psalms, by any means, fall under the category of praise hymns, and only one, Psalm 145, is designated *tehillah*. Therefore, *sepher tehillim* is inaccurate as a title for the whole, so far as content is concerned. But as a term that emphasizes one of the principle uses of many of the psalms, it deserves the veneration that it has acquired through the years.

Tephilloth — "Prayers"

Another biblical term that came to be applied to the Psalms is תְּפִלּוֹת (t⁼phillôth, "prayers"). This title is drawn from Ps 72:20, which states: "This concludes the prayers of David son of Jesse," This notation apparently marks the end of an early collection of psalms, and the designation may be the title that was given to this group earlier. It is true that only Psalm 17 among them is entitled "a prayer of David." Yet the element of petition occurs frequently. And in the broader significance of *tephillah* as communication of man with God (see 1 Sam 2:1), the title becomes more meaningful.

The Psalter — "Songs for Musical Accompaniment"

In Psalm 33, a congregational hymn, worshipers are exhorted to "praise the LORD with the harp; make music to him on the ten-stringed lyre" (v. 2). The word *psaltery*, from *psalterion* (ψαλτήριον) in the Greek translation of the Old Testament, indicates a stringed instrument plucked with the fingers. However, the term was also used to indicate the composition that was played or the song that was accompanied by such instrument. In this sense, Codex Alexandrinus used *psalterion* as the title for the Psalms. From the Greek into the Latin into English, the word came to be widely used to designate the book, and thus it became known as *The Psalter*.

Psalmoi — "Psalms"

In other Greek manuscripts the word *psalmoi* (ψαλμοί) became the title. From *psalmos*, denoting the music of a stringed instrument or a song sung to such accompaniment, *psalmoi* is thus similar to psalter in its significance. This is the term used in the New Testament. In Luke 24:44 Jesus speaks of "the Law of Moses, the Prophets and the Psalms." And in Acts 1:20 Peter says, "it is written in the book of Psalms." The Greek was a translation of the Hebrew מִזְמוֹר, (*mizmôr*), a word appearing in the titles of fifty-seven of the psalms and indicating singing and making music in praise of God. In view of the original nature of the hymns as praise sung to musical accompaniment, the designation *psalms* appears suitable also.[11]

Shir — "Song"

One other Hebrew term that is used to identify twenty-nine psalms is שִׁיר, (*šîr*), meaning "song." It is not used as a title for the book, yet it is significant in that it reflects the lyric nature of the Psalms. They were written to be sung. Referring to the musical provenance of the Psalter, J. B. Rotherham has said: "There is more evidence than has received adequate attention, that but for the *lyre* we might never have had *lyrics*; in other words, that but for the art of sweeping the strings which we call *psallein* ('psalming') we might never have had in our hands the poetic products which we call *psalmoi* ('psalms')."[11] Expressing the religious sentiments, aspirations, and changing moods of the human spirit, the Psalms reflect the music of the soul that has been stirred by God's self-disclosure in nature, in historic act, and in word. In the book of Proverbs there is poetry that is quite similar in style to that of the Psalms, but

---

[11]J.B. Rotherham, *Studies in the Psalms* (Joplin, MO: College Press, 1980 reprint of edition of about 1900), I:17.

there the nature is different. It is *didactic* rather than lyric.[12] Its purpose is to give instruction, to teach, whereas the Psalms are designed to give glory to God and expression to the deepest feelings of one who would live in fellowship with him.

We must not suppose that either the lyrics or the music of the ancient Hebrews approximated that which is now current. But the Psalms, from their lyric nature, were admirably fitted to the expression of one's spiritual longings and to the singing of praises to God.

The Hymn Book of the Second Temple

Beginning with Julius Wellhausen and other scholars of the nineteenth century, the Psalms came to be designated as the hymn book of the Second Temple. The prior existence of psalmic literature was not denied, but it was held that any earlier compositions had been adapted or rewritten for use in the temple services, while the majority were produced by temple personnel to be thus used by priests and people. It was in the Hellenistic period, Wellhausen concluded, that such editorial and literary activity produced the book of Psalms. Carl Cornill, among others, concurred, stating that "the Psalter, as a whole, in the form in which it now lies before us, cannot be older than the fourth century [BC]."[13]

Long before the Greek period, Psalms had undoubtedly been a source of comfort to the Jews in the exile — even though they were less than enthusiastic about singing them for their captors (Ps 137:3,4). But the emphasis of the nineteenth century scholars was upon the use of the Psalms in the worship of the repatriated Hebrews, subsequent to the building of the Second Temple. It is a mistake, however, to conclude that they necessarily owe their origin primarily to this period and circumstance. As a matter of fact, the participation of the populace in the temple ritual seems to have been slight. Furthermore, at least some of the Psalms are such as likely would *not* be recited at a sacerdotal service: "Sacrifice and offering you did not desire, . . . burnt offerings and sin offerings

---

[12]There are some psalms of a didactic nature also; Psalms 1 and 37, for example. It may be questioned, however, that they were designed as lyrics.

[13]Carl Cornill, *Introduction to the Canonical Books of the Old Testament*, trans. G.H. Box (New York: G.P. Putnam's Sons, 1907, p. 405.

you did not require" (Ps 40:6; see also Ps 50:13,14). These Psalms, apparently, were not composed for the temple liturgy.

Additionally, the Psalms of a didactic nature, as Emil G. Hirsch has observed, were more likely *recited* in a learning experience and *not sung*,[14] while others also are better suited to private rather than to public use. It would seem, therefore, that the designation "Hymn Book of the Second Temple" is a misnomer. More scholars today are finding themselves in agreement with Carroll Stuhlmueller, who observed that the temple "exercised less direction to the formation of the psalter" than has commonly been thought.[15]

ORIGIN OF THE PSALMS

Unfortunately, we do not have detailed information regarding how the Psalms came to be written.[16] But as one reads them, he or she gains the impression that they had their origin in the crucible of human experience. Apparently they are the work of devout Israelites who had experienced widely and felt deeply — both the agony of despair and the ecstasy of joy, the burden of guilt and the sweetness of forgiveness. And the individual wrote (or sang) to give expression to his own spiritual response to the divine righteousness and grace that had been manifest to him.

VIEW 1: DISTINCTIVELY INDIVIDUAL PRODUCTIONS

This has been the traditional view of how the majority of the Psalms came to be written. The book is a collection of separate, unrelated lyrics, written by many different people over a period of

[14]Emil G. Hirsch, "Psalms," *The Jewish Encyclopedia*, ed. Isidore Singer (New York: Funk and Wagnalls, 1905), p. 245.

[15]Carroll Stuhlmueller, *Psalms 1: Old Testament Message*. A Biblical-Theological Commentary, 21 (Wilmington, DE: Michael Glazier, 1983), p. 47. See also B.D. Eerdmans's *The Hebrew Book of Psalms* (Leiden: E.J. Brill, 1947), pp. 2-6.

[16]See William L. Holladay, *The Psalms through Three Thousand Years (Prayerbook of a Cloud of Witnesses)* (Minneapolis: Fortress Press, 1996).

several centuries. Each psalm is unique, and any similarity in style or form to others is considered to be incidental. The psalmist wrote in order to give voice to the stirrings of his own soul within him.

Evidence for this appraisal is seen to exist in the headings or superscriptions that appear with many of the Psalms. Fourteen of these headings are historical in nature and have been traditionally considered to be reliable indications of the situations out of which the Psalms arose. For example, Psalm 51 has the heading: "For the director of music. A psalm of David. When the prophet Nathan came to him after David had committed adultery with Bathsheba." This is taken to mean that David wrote this great penitential psalm after suffering remorse and being condemned by Nathan for his double sin of adultery and murder. Others understand the superscription to mean a psalm written "in relationship to" David's sin. This is a possible interpretation,[17] but one that seems scarcely plausible.

One must remember that these headings, while being ancient, are probably not a part of the original text.[18] They may have been supplied in the days of Hezekiah (around 700 B.C.). We are told that this king employed men to copy the proverbs of Solomon (Prov 25:1). That he was interested in the Psalms is also stated (2 Chr 29:30). However, Hezekiah lived some 300 years after the time

---

[17]Artur Weiser would punctuate the superscription with an extra (permissible) period: "A Psalm. Of David, when Nathan . . . etc." This could be interpreted to mean, "about David, when Nathan . . . etc." *The Psalms* (Philadelphia: The Westminster Press, 1962), p. 399.

[18]A brief but clear explanation of the "superscriptions" or "headings" of the Psalms is found in William L. Holladay's *The Psalms through Three Thousand Years*, pp. 70-76. He suggests that "the activity of adding the notations . . . . must have taken place during the fourth and third centuries B.C.E., that is, in the last part of the Persian period and in the Ptolemaic period, two centuries for which we have very little historical information" (p. 75). While the above may be true, the superscriptions are very old, indeed, and should not be overlooked as without value. There is no reason for us to dismiss the superscriptions as totally "unhistorical" whenever they make sense to the historical context given. Perhaps we would do best to use them when they illustrate the particular psalm well and simply question them when they seem not to fit the context of the psalm. The fault lies in our lack of understanding and not in the text. [Note: Prof. Tesh will use the superscriptions when they illustrate the psalm well and neglect them when they don't!)

of David. And by whomever provided, the superscriptions have been variously appraised. Of those of an historical nature, Julius Bewer says, quite bluntly: "These guesses are without value, there is not one of them that can be accepted as correct."[19] On the other hand, the German rationalist, Friederich Bleek, was far more inclined to treat the headings with respect: "If a consideration of the contents and character of the psalm does not discover anything which is in contradiction to the superscriptions, we have no reason to be so skeptical as to their statements as many expositors have been."[20] We would conclude that, even though the superscriptions are not a part of Holy Scripture, they may well have a valid tradition behind them and are not to be summarily dismissed.

The very nature of some of the Psalms would seem to indicate their personal, private origin — Psalm 23, for example: "The LORD is my shepherd, I shall not be in want." Though some scholars view this verse otherwise, it would seem to be an expression of the most personal and intimate relationship imaginable. But there are some who believe that even such a psalm as this personal affirmation of trust was really composed for corporate use. Others speak of a later adaptation to that purpose. And the fact that there are numerous Psalms that were unquestionably composed at the outset for use by the worshiping community has led scholars to reevaluate the concept of the Psalms as merely a collection of randomly produced lyrics and to seek new clues as to their origin.

VIEW 2: LATE COMPOSITIONS
ACCOMPANYING ADVANCED JUDAISM

The last half of the nineteenth century witnessed the rise of the study of literary analysis as applied to the Bible. The result, as related to the Psalms, was the complete renunciation of the traditional view that had prevailed. On the premise that any advanced concept of religion must necessarily be late, it was held that the

---

[19]Julius Bewer, *The Literature of the Old Testament*, rev. ed. (New York: Columbia University Press, 1922, 1963), p. 342.

[20]Friederich Bleek, *An Introduction to the Old Testament*, trans. G.H. Venables (London: George Bell and Sons, 1882), 2:233.

elaborate priestly element found in the Old Testament must date from the close of the Old Testament period. Furthermore, the same priestly circle that was responsible for the codification of the law was also the custodian of ritual and worship. Consequently, it was under the priestly direction that the Psalms were written (or that old ones were rewritten) for liturgical use in the worship of the temple — late compositions to accompany advanced Judaism.

The theology of the Psalms, exalted as it is, was said to be dependent upon the prophets, reflecting especially the influence of Jeremiah and of Isaiah (Isaiah 40–66). And these concepts were held to be wholly incompatible with the "primitive" era of David.[21] The superscriptions of the Psalms, therefore, were viewed much in the critical vein of Bewer, quoted above. The only value they might have would be such light as they could shed on the application and use made of the Psalms and on the editorial activity that accompanied their preservation. As later additions they provided no real evidence as to the actual circumstances surrounding the origin of the Psalms.

The conclusions of the school of literary critics, based primarily on internal evidence as *evaluated in the light of certain presuppositions* (basically Hegelian), were summarized by Briggs: "The final editorship of the Psalter could not have been earlier than the Maccabean period, and David wrote few, if any, of the Psalms, the most of them being postexilic."[22] These general conclusions were widely accepted in scholarly circles — "the assured results of Higher Criticism."

It was not denied that earlier Psalms existed. It was contended only that the book of Psalms, as we know it, is so much a product of the second century B.C. that it may be said to have been written then. Many critics denied that any of the Psalms were from David, or even that any could be dated before the exile (587 B.C.). T.K. Cheyne wrote: "That David may have written psalms is of course not denied; only that such psalms as he wrote can have been like our psalms."[23]

---

[21]Robert H. Pfeiffer, *Introduction to the Old Testament* (New York: Harper and Bros., 1941), p. 627.

[22]Briggs, *Commentary*, p. lvii.

[23]T.K. Cheyne, *Aids to the Devout Study of Criticism* (New York: Thomas Whittaker, 1892), p. 133.

Briggs was more moderate than those who would date all of the Psalms late. He assigned twenty-seven, "in their original form," to the period of the Hebrew monarchy, thus dating them in the preexilic period. Thirteen he assigned to the time of the exile, sixty to the following Persian era, and the remainder to the Greek period. Five of these latter, with parts of three others, were dated in the Maccabean age (after 168 B.C.). According to this view, the final book of Psalms is to be dated about 150 B.C., the accomplishment of the temple personnel of that period. Robert H. Pfeiffer (as late as 1941, amazingly!) proposed an even later date for the book, 100 B.C., as the culmination of a process that had begun shortly before 400 B.C.[24]

A number of circumstances led to a modification of this view in some respects and a repudiation in at least one other, namely, the dating of the Psalms. First of all, there was difficulty in harmonizing the contents of the Psalms to a late setting. For example, since there were no Jewish kings at any time during this period,[25] why were royal Psalms and others with references to the king included? Proposals were that the references in the Psalms were to an idealized king or to the Maccabean leaders. Pfeiffer suggested Persian rulers or Alexander the Great.[26] But in addition, if the priestly circle controlled the composition of the Psalms, how would disclaimers against sacrifice, such as we find in Ps 51:16, be included? And why are there so few specific references in the Psalms to liturgical ceremony?

Secondly, there were archaeological discoveries that would necessitate a reevaluation of the basic assumptions under which the higher critics labored. Of particular significance to the study of the Psalms is the vast quantity of Ugaritic literature mentioned earlier. These literary materials, in a Semitic dialect closely akin to biblical Hebrew, demonstrate that the supposedly late phraseology and style of the Psalms are not late at all. They were common currency in Palestine more than three hundred years *before* the time of David and six hundred years *before* the literary prophets.

---

[24]Pfeiffer, *Introduction*, p. 629.

[25]In 104 B.C. Aristobulus, son of John Hyrcanus, claimed the title of king, but his reign lasted only a year.

[26]Pfeiffer, *Introduction*, p. 630.

The Qumran discoveries have been equally valuable for the light they have shed upon the Psalms. The Qumran community wrote thanksgiving hymns or psalms of their own, but with a form and content unlike that of the Psalms of the Old Testament. In addition, it is apparent that the community possessed the collection of biblical Psalms known to us. This is evidence that the collection had been made before the time of the Maccabees, perhaps as much as two centuries before. These and other considerations justify the Ugaritic scholar Mitchell Dahood in his statement that: "it is impossible to accept a Maccabean date for any of the Psalms . . . Nor is a Hellenistic date more plausible."[27]

The evidence that demands an earlier date for many of the Psalms includes: (1) the contrast in style, structure, theme, and theology of the later hymns of Qumran as compared to the Psalms,[28] (2) the absence of any reference to historical events of a late period, except the ones mentioned in Psalms 126 and 137 (the Babylonian captivity, (4) the lack of concern with eschatology that seems to have been characteristic of later Judaism, (3) the evidence in prophetic literature of the prophets' acquaintance with Psalms (or of mutual acquaintance), and (4) the discovery in other ancient literature of psalms of an individualistic and personal nature, indicating that this type is not a later development as had been supposed.[29] On the other hand, one must reckon with the obvious prayer and eschatological concern of Psalm 89, strategically placed

---

[27]Mitchell Dahood, *Psalms 1: 1–50*, The Anchor Bible (Garden City, NY: Doubleday, 1966), p. xxxii. If one is interested in surveying the arguments for the existence of Maccabean psalms in the Psalter, he may see Cornill, *Introduction*, pp. 407-409. For most, the study today would be only academic. Even Cornill acknowledged that in the time of the Maccabees there was already a Psalter recognized as Holy Scripture. For a refutation of Maccabean psalms, see W.O.E. Oesterley, "The Question of Maccabean Psalms," *The Psalms* (London: SPCK, 1962), pp. 67-73.

[28]Johannes Hempel states: "The stylistic difference between the canonical Psalms and the hymns discovered in Qumran leaves no doubt that there are surely no Maccabean songs in our Psalter." See "Book of Psalms," *IDB*, 3:943.

[29]The factors indicating an earlier dating for the Psalms are covered quite thoroughly by Nahum M. Sarna, "Book of Psalms," *Encyclopaedia Judaica* (New York: Macmillan, 1972), p. 1311f.

at the end of Book 3, voicing the concern that God has rejected his anointed one, the king. The cry is: "O Lord, where is your former great love, which in your faithfulness you swore to David?" (Ps 89:49). It is clear that the Torah psalms (1, 19, 119) and others have been placed together with selected royal psalms to communicate the concerns of the postexilic community. (These concerns about the dating and shaping of the psalms in their final form will be discussed in volume two of this commentary.)

A further significant bit of evidence for the antiquity of the Psalms is found in an article by David N. Freedman, "The Spelling of the Name 'David' in the Hebrew Bible."[30] There are two spellings of the name in Hebrew, דִּוד and דָּוִיד, represented in (consonants only) transliteration as *dwd* and *dwyd*. Apparently, they were pronounced the same (*dāwîd*). The name appears 1,073 times in the Old Testament, 988 times as *dwd* and 285 as *dwyd*. Of the occurrences of *dwyd*, practically all (271) are to be found in Chronicles, Ezra, and Nehemiah, the latest books of the Old Testament. This is also the spelling at Qumran. The shorter spelling appears in the earlier books, and it is *only this* form that is found in the Psalms. The "correlation between the older spelling and the earlier books of the Bible," Freedman says, is "not just in content but in composition, compilation, and publication."[31] He observes, further, that "while most scholarship, supports a late date for the compilation of the Psalter . . . an earlier date for earlier editions of the Psalms would be quite plausible."[32] On the basis of his study he states this conclusion: "We would therefore assign the Psalter, with its conservative spelling in MT, in its essential content and orientation to the First Temple period."[33]

From the above, it is evident that the view that the Psalms were late productions of Judaism had become untenable. The "late" direction in the study of the origins of the book had been provided by Hermann Gunkel (1862-1932) in his Form-critical approach to the subject.

[30]Noel M. Freedman, "The Spelling of the Name 'David' in the Hebrew Bible," *HAR #7* (1983): 89-104.
[31]Ibid., p. 95.
[32]Ibid.
[33]Ibid., p. 101.

VIEW 3: FORMS OF LITURGY
IN RITUALISTIC WORSHIP

Gunkel reasoned that an examination of the character of the Psalms should provide clues to their purpose and thus to the situation in life that called them into being. In his study he noted that many of the Psalms fell each into one of a few recognizable types (genres). Through the study of songs of a similar type, the distinguishing characteristics of this particular literary form could be delineated. Acquaintance with these characteristics — structure, theme, components, formalized vocabulary, mood — would in turn help in the identification of other literature of a similar genre when it is encountered. (For example, in our era: "Be it known . . . party of the first part . . . party of the second part . . ." would immediately be recognized as a legal document of some kind. And the occasion would be quite different from that of a funeral oration or a Fourth of July address.)

One of Gunkel's early conclusions was that a psalm should not be considered first and foremost as purely a literary production of a poet. A long history lay behind the Psalms. The types by which they may be identified had their origin in antiquity, in a time when much material of this nature was spoken rather than written. Stereotyped forms developed, partly by design as an aid to memory. In any case, a psalm was to be interpreted in the light of its genre and history and not entirely on the basis of the subject matter it contained.

Gunkel concluded that the Psalms were cultic, associated with religious rites. He did not claim that all of them, as we know them, were designed for public worship, but in the earliest practice of religion this had been so. They were *forms of liturgical literature designed to accompany ritual.* Later, the concept of private devotion would develop, and a poet might compose a psalm for his own use; earlier, the life situation centered in the cult.[34] Gunkel admitted

---

[34]The term "cult" in this discussion is not used in its current connotation of some religious aberration. Rather, it refers to any system of religious worship, including Judaism, with particular reference to rites and ceremonies.

that "not many such Cult Songs have been handed down to us."[35]
Still, in broad perspective, the Psalms were seen as liturgy to be
recited — in primitive times, as incantations (?) — in connection
with specified religious rites. Word and act were combined, the
word, on the one hand, being the necessary complement of the
ritual, on the other.

An example of ritual and recitation is said to be indicated in
Deut 21:1-9. The occasion is a death by violence in the open
country, from an unknown assailant. A ritual is prescribed, to be
performed by the elders of the nearest village. They are to choose a
heifer, break its neck, and wash their hands over the slain animal.
The accompanying liturgy is also given. The elders shall say, in the
presence of the priests: "Our hands did not shed this blood . . . ."
In this fashion the village is to be spared from blood-guiltiness in
the sight of the Lord.[36]

That liturgy and ritual did exist in Israel is thus indicated. But
that they were always inextricably combined appears questionable,
since the priestly legislation relative to daily and festival rituals provides no accompanying liturgy nor even any reference to such. Nor
do the Psalms, as liturgy, provide any explicit information regarding the cultic ceremony they were designed to accompany. This
deficiency is explained as due either to a gradual separation of the
Psalm from its original purpose, or to the Psalm's being a later
composition, conforming to the ritual style or pattern but apart
from the cultic context. The picture is complicated further,
however, by the fact that in some of the Psalms there is recognized
a mixing of types. Gunkel considered this to indicate a later stage
in the development of Old Testament poetry, a position that has
been questioned by others.[37]

Much attention was directed by Gunkel toward an analytical and
comparative study of ancient Near Eastern literature. As a result,
certain distinguishable types were recognized as more or less

---

[35]Hermann Gunkel, *The Psalms, a Form-Critical Introduction*, trans.
Thomas M. Harner, with an introduction by James Muilenburg (Philadelphia: Fortress Press, 1967), p. 7.

[36]See also Deut 26:1-8 for the liturgy that was to accompany the religious
act of presenting the offering of the firstfruits to the Lord.

[37]See Weiser, *The Psalms*, p. 23f.

common throughout the area. There were hymns in praise of a god or gods, thanksgivings, petitions and prayers, and numerous incantations. These types, with the exception of incantations, Gunkel found exhibited in the Psalms. No claim was made that Israel necessarily borrowed directly from the literature of others, only that hers was a common heritage. And the uniqueness of the Psalms was recognized. In comparing them with Babylonian literature, for example, Gunkel noted two major differences. First, whereas the songs of the Babylonians reflect the polytheism of the worshipers, the Psalms indicate that, to the biblical writer, Yahweh alone is God. Secondly, in the Babylonian literature there is a pronounced magical content that Gunkel found to be altogether absent from the Psalms.

Convinced that form analysis and generic classification of the Psalms was a sound approach, Sigmund Mowinckel (1884-1965) gave the study new dimensions. In his view, all of the Psalms (with a few possible exceptions) were related to the cult, and were to be interpreted in terms of the ritual performed regularly at the sanctuary (or sanctuaries). The Psalms were, in short, originally cultic poems composed especially for repeated use in cultic ritual. Even Psalms of an individual nature, such as Psalm 3, were said to be cultic formularies, prepared for communal use.

By far the most important cultic celebration, according to Mowinckel, was an annual New Year's Festival, kept in the autumn in the temple. Some forty Psalms — hymns, psalms about the king, and even some complaint songs — were recognized as having their life situation within the framework of this comprehensive celebration. The basic theme of the festival was acted out in a ceremony of enthronement of Yahweh as universal king. It is admitted that the details of such an enthronement festival are not to be found in the Old Testament. Donald Anders-Richards gives an extensive presentation of the religious pageant, or ritual drama, as it may have occurred, in *The Drama of the Psalms*. For this he uses selected passages from the Psalms. Yet he admits that the reconstruction of events is based, not on biblical data, but on the analogy of "activities which scholars know took place in the worship of surrounding nations at this period in history."[38]

---

[38]Donald Anders-Richards, *The Drama of the Psalms* (London: Darton, Longman and Todd, 1968), pp. 29-47. An extended treatment of the

As a matter of fact, within the Old Testament there is no unequivocal evidence of any Enthronement Festival, and many scholars consider the argument from analogy to be insufficient to establish the case. That many Psalms are related to worship, reflecting a cultic origin, seems obvious. But even Mowinckel recognized that some, just as obviously, seemed not composed for that purpose. The didactic Psalms, specifically, are viewed by many scholars as not only outside the cult but actually anticultic in outlook. The truth is that the history and the scope of the Psalms are too extensive for one to restrict them in their origin to the cultic situation alone.

The contribution to the study of Psalms made by Gunkel and Mowinckel should not be minimized. The former, with deep insight, perceived the Psalms as literary documents arising from specific life situations and pursued his research in that direction. Mowinckel directed his attention to the cultic setting, which he believed to lie at the heart of their origin. One development, largely as a result of his work, was the recognition that the golden age of the Psalms was in the time of the Hebrew monarchy and not in the Maccabean period. Furthermore, as a result of his emphasis, insights have been gained into the nature of Israelite worship and the uses made of the Psalms. Several scholars, however, believe that Mowinckel depended too greatly upon comparative religion for many of his conclusions. R.K. Harrison, for example, suggests "one grave deficiency" relative to some of Mowinckel's speculations: "They cannot be supported by any objective evidence."[39] The fact is firmly established that the origin of many of the Psalms is to be sought in acts of worship in Israel. But to say that all of the Psalms arose as forms of liturgy to accompany ritual is to overstate the case. That they were used in worship seems obvious. That they were a necessary complement to ritual is not so clear.

---

concept of an enthronement festival in Israel and a statement of the grounds on which it is accepted by many scholars as an essential element in the early religion of Israel is found in the work by A.R. Johnson, *Sacral Kingship in Ancient Israel* (Cardiff, Wales: University Press, 1967). For Mowinckel's own treatment, see *The Psalms in Israel's Worship*, trans. D.R. Ap-Thomas (Nashville: Abingdon Press, 1967), I:106-192.

[39]R.K. Harrison, *Introduction*, p. 993. See Eerdmans's "The Classes of Psalms," *The Hebrew Book of Psalms*, pp. 6-11, for a well reasoned critique of Gunkel's thesis of the cultic origin of the Psalms.

Obviously, where one adopts Mowinckel's view of the origin of a particular Psalm in a specific cultic setting, his interpretation must be influenced by the cultic theme. Form analysis has value, but it is only an initial step in exegesis. The understanding of the various forms does shed light on the institutional life of ancient Israel, yet the quest for the precise setting in individual Psalms is an ongoing process. Scholars are not ready to abandon the form-critical study of Psalms. But, as Erhard Gerstenberger has noted, the methodology has changed because "ideological presuppositions and outlooks have changed."[40] The adoption of a particular form by a psalmist is one thing; the specific living reality that he is confronting is something else. James Muilenburg, in his presidential address to the Society of Biblical Literature, observed that "form criticism by its very nature is bound to generalize because it is concerned with what is common to all the representatives of a genre. . . . Exclusive attention to the *Gattung* [forms] may actually obscure the thought and intention of the writer or speaker."[41]

In pursuing the life situation, Gerstenberger recommends that one continue to seek clues from form analysis. Yet he recognizes the flexibility that exists in the use that may be made of forms. *They* may be standardized (theoretically), but life situations are not. Furthermore, the language that sprang from one life situation may be utilized in quite different situations by other persons, so the form of expression does not of necessity indicate identical situations.

In the continued quest for the setting and significance of the Psalms, Gerstenberger would augment the consideration of form by (1) a concern with philology and lexicography, (2) statistical counts of vocabulary to reveal specific typical usages, (3) research in the field of comparative literature, (4) form-critical study of Near Eastern cuneiform materials and utilization of archaeological discoveries, and (5) attention to the insights to be gained from the study of present day anthropology, specifically with reference to rites, feasts, and ritual activities. (Just how much is to be learned

---

[40]Erhard Gerstenberger, "Psalms," *Old Testament Form Criticism*, ed. John H. Hayes (San Antonio: Trinity University Press, 1974), p. 221.

[41]James Muilenburg, "Form Criticism and Beyond," *JBL* 88 (March, 1969): 1-18.

about the rites and practices of ancient Israel by analogy with the cultic practices of the twentieth century might be questioned.)

VIEW 4: SONGS FOR ALL SEASONS

Before the advent of form-criticism C.A. Briggs wrote: "Many of the Psalms in their original form were composed as an expression of private devotion. . . . Many others were composed for use in public worship."[42] This is the impression that the reader of the Psalms would likely experience for himself. Were there Psalms for special religious celebrations? Apparently so. Psalm 67, for example, could well have been written for use at the harvest festival, since it speaks of the earth "yielding her increase" as evidence of God's blessing. And are there Psalms of an intensely personal nature and application? Again, yes. Gunkel, Mowinckel, and others have shown that in form, development, and vocabulary the Psalms exhibit similarities to ancient cultic literature, literature produced for purely cultic use. But this does not preclude the possibility that the psalmist might utilize such forms to express his own individual thoughts and feelings. In so doing he would express himself in a style and idiom that were universally used in the offering of praise to deity and do so without respect to any liturgical use the language might have served in other situations. Gunkel recognized this. He saw in most of the Psalms their correspondence to the various cultic types but granted that many were composed independently of actual cultic association. There is really minimal information in the Scriptures about the use of the Psalms in liturgy. Stuhlmueller proposed: "It is possible that fewer psalms were composed directly for the temple liturgy than we often suppose to have been the case."[43] Others share this view.

Whether for liturgy or for private devotion, the Psalms have enhanced the worship of humankind for three millennia. Written over a period of several hundred years, here, by the providence of God, we have a collection of songs for all seasons. Actually, the

---

[42]Briggs, *Commentary*, p. xcv.
[43]Stuhlmueller, *Psalms I*, p. 47.

Psalms had their origin in hearts awakened to the grace and benefi-cence of God, inspired by the divine righteousness, mercy, and power. Under these circumstances the thoughts and emotions of the psalmist could not be contained but must issue forth in songs and hymns of praise, petition, and thanksgiving. The result is a hymn book, or book of devotions, that is timeless in its relevance. The experience of every person could well be that of the Eskimo who, reading it for the first time and in his own language, cried out: "This is my book; it speaks to my heart."

VIEW 5: A COLLECTION OF COLLECTIONS

Just how the collection of the Psalms came about, and by whom, we cannot determine with certainty.[44] Songs of praise and thanks-giving among the people of Israel date from their earliest history. In Exod 15:1-18 is recorded the song that was sung to celebrate God's deliverance of his people from the Egyptians. Since Moses kept a diary of the progress of the people (Num 33:2), we may well believe that he also preserved the song. By the time of David we find a group composed of Asaph and his brothers, who were spe-cially appointed to sing a song of thanksgiving to God (1 Chr 16:7). The song that they were to sing (16:8-16) is composed of Ps 105:5-15, plus a variant of Psalm 90, and an added doxology. In 2 Samuel 22 we have Psalm 18. Thus from Exodus, from Chronicles, and from Samuel we have evidence that some Psalms were preserved, with variations, independently of any formal collection.

But what about the book of Psalms? Here, without question, is a collection that includes the songs of various poets, written over a period of many years (much as a modern hymn book). More pre-cisely, it is several collections combined into one. In our biblical text this book is really five books of varying lengths. Book 1 is com-posed of Psalms 1-41; Book 2 of 42-72; Book 3 of 73-89; Book 4 of 90-106; and Book 5 of 107-150. That these existed formerly as

---

[44]See Holladay's *Three Thousand Years*, etc. See especially Gerald Henry Wilson's *The Editing of the Hebrew Psalter*, SBLDS (Chico, CA: Scholars Press, 1985).

separate collections is evident.[45] First of all, there is duplication of some Psalms. Psalm 53 in Book 2 is a duplicate of Psalm 14 in Book 1. A part of another Psalm in Book 1 (40:13-17) constitutes the whole of Psalm 70 in Book 2. Parts of two Psalms in Book 2 (57:7-11 and 60:5-12) make up Psalm 108 in Book 5. Apparently, the books did exist separately; and when they were combined, the duplicates were not eliminated.

There is evidence that previously there existed smaller collections that were combined to make up the five books of the finished work. This is indicated, in part, by the headings. There is a group of Psalms of David, another of Asaph, and still another of the sons of Korah. Furthermore, the conclusion of Book 2 seems to mark the close of a collection: "The prayers of David the son of Jesse are ended" (Ps 72:20). Yet other prayers of David appear in Books 3 and 5 (Psalms 86 and 142). We conclude that a group of prayers of David had been preserved as a nucleus of Books 1 and 2, but others had been preserved apart from this collection and found a place in the other books.

It is quite possible that King Hezekiah had a part in the history of the book of Psalms. The literary heritage of Judah seems to have been of particular concern to him. Hezekiah employed scribes to copy the proverbs of Solomon (Prov 25:1). And we may assume that he had an equal interest in Psalms also, since it is reported that he appointed musicians and singers "to praise the LORD with the words of David and of Asaph the seer" (2 Chr 29:30).

In the preceding three hundred years, between the time of David and Hezekiah, the responsibility for the collecting and preservation of the Psalms — and for the composing of many of them, some would hold — would have rested largely upon the personnel of Solomon's temple. It should be remembered that there were no printing presses at that time, or any books. The process of gathering pages and sewing them into book form did not become a

---

[45]Many scholars consider Books 4 and 5 originally to have been a single unit, since the name Yahweh is dominant throughout and they have other characteristics in common. The separation into two books, it is suggested, was to make the total of five correspond to the five books of the Torah. See N.M. Sarna, *Book of Psalms*, 14:1308.

common practice until after the first century A.D. But accurate memorization of extensive materials was commonplace, and without doubt the Psalms were often shared orally. Of course there were scrolls, and the scribes of Hezekiah, mentioned above, would have had their part in the preservation of Psalms by this medium.

After the fall of Jerusalem in 587/86 B.C., the Jewish exiles in Babylon would certainly have treasured and preserved such Psalms as they had, adding at least an additional one — Psalm 137. Scattered in different areas of Babylonia, various groups may have assembled their own collections. Upon the return of many to Jerusalem, after the rebuilding of the temple and the renewal of worship, the occasion would have arisen to complete the collection of the Psalms. The book, therefore, not in its origin but as a final collection, is in this sense said to be the hymn book of the Second Temple. And Weiser may be correct when he says: "It was the staff in charge of the worship of the second temple who were mainly concerned to collect, preserve and give fresh life to the early stock of liturgical songs; and indeed it seems to have been above all the guilds of temple singers who . . . had the duty of arranging the Psalms."[46]

CONCLUSION

Just when the final compilation of the Psalms was made cannot be determined definitely, but it was surely before the translation into the Greek of the Hebrew Psaltery (sometime after 250 B.C., possibly as late as 200 or 150 B.C.) The Pentateuch (Torah) was translated c. 250 B.C. Scholars have not agreed on when the rest of the books (the Prophets and Writings) were translated, but surely soon afterwards. True, there are Syrian manuscripts that contain five additional psalms, one of which is also appended to the Greek as Psalm 151 — but with the notation that it is "beyond the number." A Psalm scroll found in Qumran cave 11, 11QPs[a], contains all or part of thirty-nine of the biblical Psalms, although not in the biblical order. It also includes three of the Syrian hymns thus testifying to their existence in a Hebrew original. On the basis of this evidence, some scholars have suggested that as late as the close of the first century B.C. there was no uniformity either in content or in internal arrangement of the book of Psalms. However, others recognize that 11QPs[a] was not intended as a *copy* of Psalms but rather as a liturgical arrangement of materials for religious use. Such a work could include nonbiblical material, and the order of arrangement of individual Psalms would be determined by the use made of them.

It would appear, on the basis of what little evidence we have, that the final compilation of the five books into the one book of Psalms occurred, therefore, by the latter half of the third century B.C. at the latest. So when Jesus said: "Everything must be fulfilled that is written about me in the Law of Moses, the Prophets and the Psalms" (Luke 24:44), he was referring to the book of Psalms as we know it, plus the rest of "The Writings" (*K⁰thûbîm*).

In retrospect we would observe that the origin of the Psalms was a process rather than an event, in view of the extended time and personnel involved. The singing of songs in the praise of God was part of the life of Israel during the entire span of her history. And the book of Psalms reflects, in itself, the history of at least seven centuries. Attempts to determine the precise situations out of which the Psalms arose have been only partly successful, yet we realize that the larger background encompassed the whole ancient Near East. Yet nothing comparable to the biblical Psalms came out of the ancient world. Nor has there arisen since a collection of religious poems of such significance and influence.

CHARACTERISTICS OF THE FIVE BOOKS

The five divisions or books that make up the 150 Psalms exhibit specific characteristics in each division. This was one of the reasons for recognizing each as a separate collection preceding its inclusion in the whole. Each section closes with a doxology. So far as types of psalms are identified, each book contains examples of each of the most commonly recognized genres. In other ways, however, there are distinctions that characterize the individual groups. (Note: The

---

[46]Artur Weiser, *The Old Testament: Its Formation and Development*, trans. Dorothea Barton (New York: Association Press, 1961), p. 283.

Introduction to volume two of the Psalms commentary will discuss the final shaping and relationships of the five book divisions.)

Titles are prefixed to some of the Psalms attributing them to certain authors or to certain collections. In addition, the separate books are distinguished by the preference that is shown in the choice of the term that is used to indicate God, whether Yahweh or Elohim. The following chart indicates both characteristics of the various groups of Psalms.

BOOK	PSALMS	ASCRIBED TO	PSALMS	OCCURRENCES OF YAHWEH / ELOHIM	
1	1–2	Not ascribed			
	3–41	David	1–41	272 times	19 times
	(10, 33)	(Not ascribed)*			
2	42–49	Sons of Korah			
	50	Asaph	42–72	30	164
	51–71	David			
	72	Solomon			
3	73–83	Asaph	73–83	13	36
	84, 85, 87, 88	Sons of Korah			
	86	David	84–89	31	7
	89	Ethan			
4	90	Moses			
	101, 103	David	90–106	103	Never
		14 Orphan Psalms			
5	107–150	15 David			
		1 Solomon	107–150	236	7 times[47]
		28 Orphan Psalms			

*Psalms 9 and 10 show signs of being a single acrostic psalm at one time and Psalms 33–34 belong together as "forgiveness" and "rejoicing" belong together.

It is possible that the Psalms of David in Books 1 and 2 were originally one book. If Psalms 42–50 were placed after Psalm 72, then the Psalms of David would be grouped together, followed by the entire number of Asaph Psalms as one group.

---

[47]*Elohim* appears in only two psalms of Book 5, once in Ps 144:9, and six times in Psalm 108. This latter Psalm is a composite of 57:7-11 and 60:5-12, Book 2, the "Elohistic Psalter."

TERMS DESIGNATING DEITY,
AND THE DIVINE NAME *YHWH*

The people of Israel used a number of names to designate deity. These included: (1) *El* (אֵל, *ēl*), meaning *God* or *god* in the general sense. The term is thought to be derived from a root meaning "to be strong," although another possibility is "to lead." This term for God was widely used in the Semitic world. In the Bible it appears almost exclusively in poetic passages. *El* occurs 72 times in the Psalter. (2) *Elohim* (אֱלֹהִים, *ĕlōhîm*), a plural noun in Hebrew, may indicate, in the plural, heathen gods. Yet the same plural form, singular in meaning, is used over 2,000 times in the Scriptures to refer to the one God. Thus used, it is said to be "the plural of majesty," indicating deity in the fulness of his power. Notice, in the chart, that this term is dominant in Book 2, 164 to 30 times for *Yahweh*, and in Psalms 73–83 of Book 3. Elsewhere in Psalms the use of *Elohim* is *greatly restricted* or absent altogether. (3) *Eloah* (אֱלֹהַ, *ĕlōah*/אֱלוֹהַ, *ĕlôah*), an alternate form of *Elohim*, is used mostly in poetic literature, though only a few times in Psalms (see Ps 18:31). (4) *Elyon* (עֶלְיוֹן, *'elyôn*), an adjective meaning "higher" or "highest," was a name used by the Canaanites to indicate one of many gods, the one whom they recognized as the lord of the gods. "Not so," said Israel, "it is *Yahweh*, the only God, who is *El Elyon*, "God Most High." The term appears with Yahweh in Ps 7:17, and some 29 times elsewhere in the Psalms. (5) *Adon* (אָדוֹן, *'ādôn*), meaning "lord," is a title of respect or of honor, such as might be used in addressing anyone deemed worthy of respect. Thus Rachel would say to her father, "Don't be angry, my lord" (Gen 31:35). And David would address King Saul as "my lord the king" (1 Sam 24:8). The same term is used of God and is then transcribed with a capital letter, "Lord," or, with a suffix, as "my Lord." In the latter case, the form in Hebrew becomes אֲדֹנָי (*'ădōnāy*), *Adonai*. This word is used 31 times in Book 2, occasionally elsewhere in the Psalms. In Ps 97:5 it is used to designate God as "the Lord of all the earth." (6) *Shaddai* (שַׁדַּי, *šadday*), frequently translated as "Almighty," seems to have been used chiefly in the earlier period of Israel's history. It appears in Ps 68:14 and again in 91:1.

Of the above, *El*, *Eloah*, and *Elohim* may be considered as simple nouns, meaning God, gods, or god. *Elyon*, *Adon*, and *Shaddai*, strictly speaking, may have been proper names, but in biblical usage they are adjectival nouns, usually appearing in combination with *Yahweh*, *El*, or *Elohim*; thus, "Most High God," "Lord God." or "God Almighty." So, although all of the terms we have considered were used to designate deity, the one true God in particular, none of them could be said to be the name of God. That distinction remained for one specific and unique designation of God —YHWH.

(7) In keeping with the Hebrew practice of using only consonants in writing, the term יהוה appears without vowels, the latter being supplied by the reader using the consonantal text. Before the fall of Jerusalem the name was regularly used by the Hebrews and, of course, was properly pronounced. What that pronunciation was is not known certainly, but most probably it was *Yahweh*.[48] A short form of the name, *Yah*, appears in Ps 68:4 and 94:7. This is also a part of the word *Hallelujah*, "Praise Yah," and appears in numerous theophoric names, such as Isaiah, Hezekiah, Jeremiah, and others. However, by the third century B.C., and perhaps earlier, YHWH had become the "Ineffable Name," too sacred to be uttered, for fear that it might be taken "in vain" (Exod 20:7), and its pronunciation was religiously avoided.[49]

In Bible manuscripts the consonants YHWH (referred to as the *Tetragrammaton*—"the four letters") were carefully preserved, but in the reading of the text the devout would say *Adonai*, "the Lord," or perhaps more accurately "my Lord," rather than to utter the sacred name. The translators of the Old Testament into Greek, c. 250 B.C., knew this, and so they used the Greek word κύριος (*kyrios*), "Lord," for YHWH. In Hebrew circles, the reader continued to say *Adonai*.

In the early centuries after the beginning of the Christian era, the Jews were widely scattered from their homeland. Their spoken

---

[48]See B.W. Anderson, "Names of God," *IDB* (Nashville: Abingdon Press, 1962), 4:409f. The present writer [Edward Tesh] treats the topic in an unpublished thesis, "The Emergence and the Nature of the Tetragrammaton" (Indianapolis: Christian Theological Seminary, 1948).

[49]One should consult the study of Yahweh's Name in the *TDOT*. Freedman offers this opinion: "The correct pronunciation of the name was lost from Jewish tradition some time during the Middle Ages; late in the period of the Second Temple the name had come to be regarded as unspeakably holy and therefore unsuitable for use in public reading, although it continued to be used privately" (p. 500).

language became that of the countries in which they dwelled, and there was danger that the vocalization of biblical Hebrew would be lost. To prevent such a disaster, scholars known as the Massoretes supplied a system of vowel points to indicate the correct traditional reading. For the *Tetragrammaton* they chose to use the vowel points for *Adonai* (͐ ͤ, with a slight phonetic adjustment of the first vowel — ͐ ͤ). After all, *Adonai* is what the Hebrew reader would say when he came to this word, and the vowel points would remind him not to say *Yahweh*.

This odd combination of the vowels of *Adonai* (*'ădōnāy*) with the consonants YHWH produced the [impossible!] word YeHoWaH (יְהוָֹה, *yᵉhōwāh*). Not understanding how this form came about, Christian scholars of Europe in the 15th century, recently inducted into the study of Hebrew, introduced the **hybrid** term "Jehovah" as the pronunciation of the divine name. Of course it was altogether in error because one symbol was used for both a vowel "long o sound" and a consonant "v or w sound," something Hebrew does not allow, but the form persisted.

In any event, one should remember that YHWH, as the personal name of God, still occurs 685 times in the Psalms and 6,823 times in the entire Old Testament. The uninformed reader would not know this because the term LORD, all in small capital letters, appears in almost all modern translations as the rendering of the *Tetragrammaton*. However, the other two pronunciations can be found. The American Standard Version of 1901 consistently uses *Jehovah*, following the Hebrew text faithfully but continuing the mispronunciation. The *Jerusalem Bible* (and its revised form) uses *Yahweh*. The reader of the Psalms should know that while he or she is confronted by the word LORD in the text, it was the *name* of God that was in the heart and mind of the psalmist, and on his lips, as he sang the praises of God. Is it not a loss to us if we cannot address God personally by name, also?[50]

---

[50]Professor Tesh is gracious enough to say that "the reader of the Psalms may choose to say either *Jehovah* or *Yahweh*, or neither." He went on to say, "Is it not a loss to us if we cannot address God personally by name, also? To this writer, there is a certain feeling of intimacy experienced when we can sing: 'Guide me, O Thou great Jehovah, pilgrim through this barren land.'" My preference is to avoid "Jehovah" precisely because it is a "mistaken pro-

BOOK 1

It is commonly accepted that Book 1 is the earliest collection of Psalms and that it is to be associated with Solomon's temple. All of the Psalms of this group have titles and are identified as Psalms of David, with the exception of Psalms 1, 2, 10, and 33. Of these, Psalm 10, part of an acrostic, is clearly a continuation of Psalm 9; and Psalm 33, in the Greek text, is ascribed to David. Understandably, therefore, this collection has been often referred to as the early Davidic psalter. Altogether there are 73 Psalms identified by the title "a Psalm of David" (more in the Greek text of Psalms). The phrase "of David," in the English as well as in the Hebrew, may have several meanings, the basic idea being *related to* David, in some way. The phrase is commonly understood to indicate authorship, as it well may, but solely on the basis of the Hebrew preposition this could not be established. There are other reasons, however, for attributing psalms to David.

The discussion of Davidic authorship has taken some interesting turns. A number of scholars share the view of Richard G. Moulton that, through the years, the Psalms have passed through so many hands as to preclude any possibility of establishing either the original form of any given Psalm or its authorship. Moulton writes: "I would . . . say that we are separated from the literature in question by an interval so wide as to raise a doubt whether the term 'authorship' in application to the lyric poetry of the Bible be not altogether an anachronism."[51] For decades there were scholars who denied that David was related in any way to the Psalms but by tradition, that he could not have written any of them. This conclusion was based, in part, on their assumption that the literary skill and religious content reflected in the Psalms were too advanced to have been a part of David's primitive milieu. But this view underwent change, and Eugene Merrill could say:

---

nunciation," and to encourage the pronunciation of "Yahweh" for the NIV "LORD" because Christians need not be superstitious concerning God's personal name. Of course, we should be sensitive when we may be in an orthodox Jewish context and perhaps use "Adonai" or "LORD" [Walt Zorn].

[51]Richard G. Moulton, *The Literary Study of the Bible* (Boston: D.C. Heath, 1894), p. 97.

With the discovery of Canaanite poetry of a similar nature and equally advanced from a literary standpoint dating from four centuries before David, all arguments that David could not have written the Psalms have been quietly laid to rest. Now it is averred that David did not write them, except maybe a few, and not that he could not.[52]

Others, however, as J.W. Rogerson and J.W. McKay, went further, stating that "it is reasonable to assume that David was the author of some of the psalms."[53] And H.K. Hester noted, relative to Davidic Psalms: "The exact number of these may never be agreed upon, but for the average reader this is not important. There are good reasons for believing that David was the author of enough to make him the leader of Psalmody and to place him among the front ranks of the poets of the world."[54]

BOOK 2

The most distinctive characteristic of Book 2, as contrasted with the rest of the Psalms, is the rarity of the use of YHWH and the frequent use of Elohim in its place. Consequently, this group of Psalms, plus the Psalms of Asaph (73–83), have been designated "The Elohistic Psalter." That Elohim was substituted for YHWH is apparent in the two Psalms of Book 2 that appeared earlier in Book 1. Ps 14:2,4,7 has YHWH, which becomes Elohim in 53:2,4,6. The same change is evident in Ps 70:1a,4, as compared with 40:13a,16. Ps 50:7 has: "I am God, your God" for the familiar expression "I

---

[52]Eugene Merrill, *An Historical Survey of the Old Testament* (Grand Rapids: Baker, 1966), p. 235.

[53]J.W. Rogerson and J.W. McKay, *Psalms 1–150* (Cambridge: Cambridge University Press, 1977), p. 4.

[54]H.K. Hester, *The Heart of Hebrew History* (Liberty, MO: The William Jewell Press, 1949), p. 202. On the subject of Davidic authorship of Psalms, see Gleason L. Archer, *A Survey of Old Testament Introduction* (Chicago: Moody Press, 1944), pp. 425-428; Edward J. Young, *An Introduction to the Old Testament* (Grand Rapids: Eerdmans, 1949), pp. 313-321; Peter C. Craigie, *Psalms 1–50*, Word Biblical Commentary (Waco: Word, 1983), pp. 33-35; and Anthony L. Ash and Clyde M. Miller, *Psalms* (Austin: Sweet, 1980), pp. 13-19.

am YHWH your God" (Exod 20:2). And the words of Moses, "Rise up, *YHWH*, and let your enemies be scattered" (Num 10:35, my translation), becomes "Let *Elohim* arise, and let his enemies be scattered" in Ps 68:1 (my translation).

Just why this change was made is not fully understood. A proposal of A.F. Kirkpatrick which he admits is a guess, is that the Elohistic Psalter was adapted for the use of the exiles in Babylon, who would thus avoid uttering the divine name among heathen.[55] In the view of Artur Weiser, the change "can be most readily explained on the ground of (the Psalms') being read aloud at the divine service in later Judaism, which refrained with reverent awe from pronouncing the divine name and at the same time chose the more general Elohim as the designation of the one true God of its monotheistic religion."[56] Neither of these proposals explains why YHWH is retained in those cases where the name still stands in this group of Psalms. (See specifically Ps 70:1, where the change was made from YHWH to Elohim in the first part of the verse but not in the second, and compare this with Ps 40:13.) These name changes remain a mystery to the biblical scholars, especially when there are examples of the reverse, where Elohim is changed to Yahweh within the Elohistic Psalter.

BOOK 3

Book 3 contains all of the Asaph Psalms except one (Ps 50), four of the sons of Korah, one of David, and one of Ethan. Since the use of Elohim is prominent in the Psalms of Asaph, it is believed by some that Book 3 was joined to Book 2, where Elohim is dominant, before these combined psalms were added to Book 1, the earliest collection of Psalms. Books 1 and 2 contain a number of titles supplying a historical note on the occasion for the psalm. None of these is to be found in Books 3 and 4, and only one such reference is in Book 5 (Ps 142).

---

[55]A.F. Kirkpatrick, *The Book of Psalms*, Cambridge Bible Series (Cambridge: Cambridge University Press, 1902), p. xi.

[56]Weiser, *The Psalms*, p. 99.

Asaph, under David's appointment, was one of three founders of guilds of temple musicians, the other two being Heman and Jeduthan (1 Chr 25:1). In 2 Chr 29:30 he is identified as "Asaph the seer." Among those who returned to Jerusalem from Babylonian captivity were "the singers; the descendants of Asaph, one hundred and twenty-eight" (Ezra 2:41). The Psalms of Asaph bear an emphasis that is typical of the prophets. They condemn the hypocrisy of a religion that is only profession — lip service (Ps 50:16). They emphasize the life of trust (73:27,28). They recognize God as the judge of all the earth (75:2-8; 76:7-12). And to express the relationship of the Lord to Israel they use the figure of a shepherd and his flock (74:1; 77:20; 78:52; 79:13; 80:1), a comparison favored also by Micah, Jeremiah, and Ezekiel. Since the name Asaph means "Collector," it is quite possible that he should be considered the compiler of a group of Psalms rather than the author.

Reference to the sons of Korah also quite likely indicates the role of compiler rather than author. In the KJV the headings are rendered: "A Psalm for the sons of Korah." The RSV and NIV have "A psalm of the Sons of Korah." This is understood to mean one in their possession. Psalm 88, of the Korah group, is also identified in the superscription as "A maskil of Heman the Ezrahite," apparently indicating Heman as the author of this Korahite Psalm. The sons of Korah were descendants of the priestly family of Kohath (1 Chr 6:22) and thus were closely associated with the temple worship. It is natural, therefore, that they would have a close association with the Psalms.

BOOKS 4 AND 5

Books 4 and 5 of the Psalms may be considered together. As mentioned earlier in a footnote, it is believed by some that they were a single book originally. Of the thirty-four Psalms that appear without any kind of superscription or heading, twenty-nine are found here. Thus the greater number of "orphan" Psalms, Psalms for which no author is given, are found in these books.

Whatever use was made of other Psalms, whether for public worship or private devotions, it would seem that many of these were intended for use in the temple services, specifically Psalms

95–100 and 145–150. Another small collection included in this group
are the "Psalms of Ascent" (120–134). Also designated "Pilgrim
Songs," these are presumed to have been used by pilgrims on their
way to Jerusalem to observe the principal religious festivals.
Prominent also in Books 4 and 5, among the worship Psalms, are
the "Hallels," Psalms that begin and (or) end with the cry of praise,
"Hallelujah" — "Praise Yah" (Yahweh), commonly translated,
"Praise the LORD." Psalm 150, with its oft repeated call of praise,
has been noted as a fitting doxology with which to close the Psalter.

SUPERSCRIPTIONS TO THE PSALMS

All except 35 of the Psalms (or 34, when considering 9 and 10
as a unit); have titles or superscriptions of one kind or another. As
noted earlier, these titles are ancient but are recognized as later
additions to the text. Some have dismissed them as being no more
than the speculations of Jewish scholars of the exile. Others accept
them as a reflection of ancient tradition, but admit the difficulty of
establishing the accuracy of the tradition.[57] Brevard Childs believes
the superscriptions with historical references to the life of David
are based, not on tradition, but on the exegetical (midrashic) treatment of the text, in conjunction with the Books of Samuel, after
the period of Chronicles, by "a pietistic circle of Jews whose interest was particularly focused on the nurture of the spiritual life."[58]
In any case, the titles existed 250 years or more before the
Christian era, with an earlier date more likely.

The Hebrew Bible, and early translations thereof, numbered the
superscriptions as a part of the text, designating them as "verse
one" of the Psalm, or in some cases as "verses one and two" (as in
Ps 60, for example). In modern translations they appear simply as
headings before verse one. In the *New English Bible* they are
omitted altogether.

These superscriptions are of five general types. (1) *References to
persons* are found in the majority. Among these, the name of David

---

[57]See Ash, *Psalms*, p. 13.
[58]Brevard S. Childs, "Psalm Titles and Midrashic Exegesis," *JSS* 16 (1971):
143, 148f.

is most prominent, appearing in 73 of the Psalms, primarily in Books 1-2, and 5, but once in Book 3 and twice in Book 4. Psalms 72 and 127 refer to Solomon. Eleven have reference to the sons of Korah, twelve to Asaph, and one each to Moses, Heman, and Ethan. As stated earlier, "of David," "of Solomon," etc., may have a variety of meanings. The preposition may indicate "by" (authorship). This is almost certainly the case in the third chapter of Habakkuk. Or it may indicate possession, "belonging to," as belonging to a particular collection or group of Psalms, the Psalms "of the sons of Korah," for example. The preposition may indicate relationship, "about" or "pertaining to." Or it may have the meaning of "for" someone, or on his behalf.

(2) *References to historical occasions* appear in 14 Psalms, all of which are ascribed to David, except Psalm 102, and all of which are found in Books 1 and 2, except 102 and 142. That it was not unusual, even from early times, to provide titles indicating the occasion of a song, is indicated by the examples found in 2 Sam 22:1 and in Isa 38:9.

(3) *References to the type of poem* are found for many of the Psalms. The most common term is "Psalm," (מִזְמוֹר, *mizmôr*), appearing 57 times, chiefly in relationship to David. "Song," (שִׁיר, *šîr*) appears 30 times, often in combination with *mizmôr*, as in Psalm 30: "A Psalm of David, a song." Thirteen of the Psalms have the designation *maskil* (מַשְׂכִּיל, *măśkîl*), a term whose root meaning is "to be wise" or "to have insight." Sometimes the reference is to skill in the performance of some task. Does this mean that the Psalm is designed to inform, to make one wise? Or is it of such erudite nature as to require deep meditation? Some propose that the musical setting is such that a skillful musician is needed for its presentation. There is no consensus among scholars in this regard, and for this reason the term is left *untranslated* in many English versions.[59]

---

[59]The KJV, ASV, NASB, RSV, and NIV do not translate the term, but use either *maschil* or *maskil*. The NASB includes a marginal note: "Possibly, *Contemplative*, or *Didactic*, or *Skillful Psalm*." Other versions treat it as follows: Douay-Rheims, "Understanding"; Emphasized Bible, "An Instructive Psalm"; The Berkeley Version, "For instruction"; The New Jerusalem Bible, "Poem"; and An American Translation, "To be played skillfully" (with a footnote: "Conjecture, perhaps a Wisdom Song.")

Michtam (מִכְתָּם, *miktām*) appears in the title of six of the Psalms of David. The root of this word appears to be כתם, *ktm*, meaning "golden." Or the word could be related to כתב, *ktb*, "to inscribe," in keeping with the LXX εἰς στηλογραφίαν (*eis stēlographian*). Briggs accepted the former meaning, considering the term appropriate, since these Psalms "are artistic in form and choice in their contents."[60] Others prefer the rendering "inscription," recognizing the Psalms so designated as dealing with matters of such significance as to justify preservation in an inscription.[61] Another suggested meaning is "to cover," on the basis of analogy with the Akkadian *katamu*, incorporating the idea of atonement. But again, in view of the uncertainty, many versions leave the term untranslated.[62]

Psalm 7 is designated a *Shiggaion* (שִׁגָּיוֹן, *šiggāyôn*) of David. The apparent root (שגה) signifies "to go astray," "to wander." The term may be descriptive either of the poem or of the musical accompaniment, but its significance is not clear. Five Psalms bear the title, "A Prayer," and one is designated "Praise."

(4) Titles with a musical reference are quite numerous. These may refer to persons: "To the Chief Musician," occurring fifty-five times, *Alamoth* (sopranos?), and *Sheminith* (Basses?). Or there may be musical directions, indicating a familiar melody to be used with the Psalm indicated. These terms include: *Gittith, Muthlabben, Jeduthun, Aijeleth Shahar, Shoshannim, Yoneth elem rechokim, Mahalath, Mahalath Leannoth, Shushan-eduth,* and *Al-tashchith.* Other terms indicate musical instruments: *Nehiloth* (flutes), and *Neginoth* (stringed instruments).

(5) *References to the use of the Psalms* in worship appear in some titles: "For the Sabbath day" (Ps 92, NIV), "A Petition" (Ps 38, NIV),

---

[60]Briggs, *Psalms*, p. lx.
[61]Craigie, *Psalms 1-50*, p. 154.
[62]So in the KJV, ASV, RSV, NIV, NASB, and the Berkeley Version. The NIV has a note: "Probably a literary or musical term." And a marginal reading in NASB has: "Possibly, *Epigrammatic Poem,* or *Atonement Psalm.*" A footnote in the Berkeley edition states: "Miktam means 'covering,' hence, perhaps, a psalm of refuge." Other versions render the term in the title as follows: Douay-Rheims, "Inscription"; Emphasized Bible, "A precious psalm"; The New Jerusalem Bible, "In a quiet voice"; and An American Translation, "An inscription."

"For the memorial offering" (Ps 38, RSV), "For giving thanks" (Ps 100, NIV), "A Psalm for the thank offerings" (Ps 100, RSV), "For the dedication of the temple" (Ps 30, NIV), and the aforementioned, "A song of ascents" (Ps 120–134, NIV).

It may be appropriate here to discuss one further term, namely, *Selah* (סֶלָה, *selāh*), although it does not appear in the titles. The word is inserted seventy-one times in the Psalms, almost exclusively in Books 1, 2, and 3 (only twice in Book 5). It is also found three times in Habakkuk, chapter 3. Because of the numerous musical references in the headings of the Psalms in which *Selah* appears, it would seem that the term has musical significance. Believed to be derived from a Hebrew root (סלל) meaning "lift up," it has been proposed that: (1) a pause is indicated, (2) there is to be a lifting up of voices (in volume?), or (3) there is to be an instrumental interlude. Almost a hundred years ago Kirkpatrick observed that the precise meaning of this term is "quite uncertain."[63] More recently (1983), Craigie states that even today "the uncertainty of its meaning cannot be removed."[64]

TYPES OF PSALMS

Many classifications of the Psalms have been made, but none has met with universal acceptance. Great variety is characteristic of the book, and some individual psalms include elements of more than one "type" within a single unit. In view of such variety, it is little wonder that many categories have been suggested and that, through various, sometimes arbitrary and subtle distinctions that number has, from time to time, been extended. One who would attempt to fit the Psalms into a neat system of types is confronted with problems. Nevertheless, it is advantageous to see the relationships that do exist, and to consider the situation in life, or *Sitz im Leben*, that would be suggested by the employment, by the psalmist, of a particular type. With this in mind, and with attention given to

---

[63]Kirkpatrick, *Psalms*, p. xx.
[64]Craigie, *Psalms 1–150*, p. 154. (The assertion of one student that *Selah* is what David said when he broke a harp string has little to commend it!)

the literary form, content, formalized vocabulary, as well as to the life situation, Bellinger has given the Psalms reader helpful genre classifications so that one may read a particular genre as a group.[65]

We have noted earlier that Gunkel looked upon the Psalms as formalized liturgical literature designed to accompany ritual. This approach must, of necessity, subordinate the personal role of the individual composer, assuming that the psalm is composed for general use. Gunkel did recognize the majority of the Psalms to be privately composed, but by individuals who would fashion their work according to preexistent types. The premise is valid to a degree, but it could lead to a generalization of types where differentiation should be noted (and accepted). Even so, Gunkel's work has set the pattern utilized by many subsequent scholars and should be noted.[66]

---

[65]W.H. Bellinger, Jr., *Psalms: Reading and Studying the Book of Praises* (Peabody, MA: Hendrickson, 1990), p. 23. The four main genres that Bellinger identifies are Praise, Lament, Royal Psalms and Wisdom Psalms. Included in the last two categories are: Wisdom, 1, 32, 37, 49, 73, 78, 112, 119, 127, 128, 133; Royal, 2, 18, 20, 21, 45, 72, 89, 101, 110, 132, 144. He further divides the Laments into 2 subcategories: Individual (3, 4, 5, 6, 7, 9-10, 11, 13, 16, 17, 22, 25, 26, 27, 28, 31, 35, 36, 38, 39, 40, 42-43, 51, 52, 54, 55, 56, 57, 59, 61, 62, 63, 64, 69, 70, 71, 77, 86, 88, 94, 102, 109, 120, 130, 140, 141, 142, 143) and Community (12, 14, 44, 53, 58, 60, 74, 79, 80, 83, 85, 90, 106, 108, 123, 126, 137). The primary genre of Praise Psalms is subdivided even further: General Hymns (29, 33, 68, 100, 103, 105, 111, 113, 114, 115, 117, 134, 135, 139, 145, 146, 147, 149, 150); Creation Psalms (8, 19, 65, 104, 148); Enthronement Psalms (47, 93, and 95 through 99); Zion Psalms (46, 48, 76, 84, 87, 122); Entrance Liturgies (15, 24); Hymns with Prophetic Warnings (50, 81, 82); Trust Psalms (23, 91, 121, 125, 131); and Thanksgiving Psalms, both Individual (30, 34, 41, 66, 92, 116, 118, 138) and Community (67, 75, 107, 124, 129, 136).

[66]Hans-Joachim Kraus takes note of the contribution of Gunkel to Psalms study, at the same time expressing reservations as to the adequacy of his categorical designations. Kraus proposes starting with the designations of the Psalter itself — *shir, Zion, tephilah, tehillah*, etc, and gives the following classifications: *Songs of Praise, Songs of Prayer, Royal Psalms* ("verses for the king," Ps 45:1, NIV), *Songs of Zion*, plus *Didactic Poetry, Festival Psalms*, and *Liturgies*. See: Kraus, *Psalms 1–59*, trans. Hilton C. Oswald (Minneapolis: Augsburg, 1988), pp. 40-54.

GUNKEL'S CLASSIFICATION[67]

Gunkel's classification focused upon the literary forms of the Psalms, especially as the form was related to function. Of these, he identified five basic types, or genres (*Gattungen*), as follows:

1. *Hymns of Praise* (with subtypes: Enthronement Psalms, honoring God as King, and Songs of Zion)
2. *Laments of the Community*
3. *Royal Psalms* (pertaining to an earthly monarch)
4. *Laments of the Individual*
5. *Individual Songs of Thanksgiving*

In addition, Gunkel recognized seven categories of a minor nature:

6. *Psalms pronouncing Blessings and Cursings*
7. *Pilgrim Songs*
8. *National Songs of Thanksgiving*
9. *Historical Recital*
10. *Psalms of the Law*
11. *Prophetical Psalms*
12. *Wisdom Psalms*

Hymns of Praise were songs of devotion directed toward Yahweh in recognition of his majesty, his power, and his goodness, songs that would glorify God as God. The form generally reflects a three-fold pattern of development. The Psalm begins with a call to worship: "Worship the LORD in the splendor of his holiness" (Ps 29:2), or with a simple utterance of praise: "O LORD, our Lord, how majestic is your name in all the earth!" (Ps 8:1). This is followed by the body of the hymn, devoted generally to *specific reasons* why God should be praised or to an expression of amazement at his wonders. Often the theme centers in the redemptive acts of God on behalf of his people — the promise to Abraham, the exodus, the enduring covenant with Israel, God's care in the wilderness, and so forth. At

---

[67]Since Prof. Tesh's arguments and discussions are with the older commentaries and scholars of the Psalms, it is appropriate that he discuss Gunkel's classifications in spite of the fact that more modern classifications can be found in Craigie (1983) or Gerstenberger (*FOTL*, 1988).

other times the focus is upon God as creator and sustainer of the universe, extolling his majestic power and benevolence. The Psalm may then close with a further impassioned call to worship such a God and may also include a petition for some present blessing.

The nations around Israel had hymns to their gods also, hymns that show some similarity of style and phraseology to some of the Psalms.[68] Yet the songs of Israel in praise of the Lord were significantly and distinctly different. The pagan sought, through his hymns in praise of his gods, to soothe the deities or to cajole them. Nothing of this is to be found in the songs of Israel. These Psalms were not directed to the purpose of flattering God in order to secure some advantage; they were rather the outpouring of hearts overflowing with wonder and awe at the power and goodness of the one true and living God. As Artur Weiser has observed, the hymns of Israel were the "Amen" of the congregation, a response as a testimony to God, and at the same time a proclamation to the world by the congregation.[69] The hymns of Israel, therefore, were not so much an attempt to enhance the image of God, and certainly not an attempt to add anything to his glory. They were, rather, joyful manifestations of wonder and awe in response to what God had done and continued to do for his people. They were, at the same time, expressions of commitment to the God who had called Israel into covenant with himself. Examples of the hymns are Psalms 8, 19, 29, 33, 48, 65, 95, 96, 100, 103–105, and others.

Enthronement Psalms, as a subtype of Hymns of Praise, were recognized by Gunkel and Mowinckel. The latter, as mentioned earlier, related these Psalms to an annual New Year's festival celebrating the enthronement of Yahweh as divine King. The Ark of the Covenant, it is said, was carried in sacred procession to the temple, and Yahweh reascended his throne, thus insuring blessing

---

[68]See J.B. Pritchard, ed., *Ancient Near Eastern Texts Relating to the Old Testament* (Princeton: Princeton University Press, 1955). This volume cites some 100 similarities between the Psalms and other literature of the ancient Near East. A companion volume, *Supplementary Texts and Pictures Relating to the Old Testament*, from the same editor and publisher, 1969, has others. Also see D. Winton-Thomas, ed., *Documents from Old Testament Times* (New York: Harper and Row, 1958).

[69]Weiser, *The Psalms*, p. 53.

to the community for another year. Central to Mowinckel's view of
these Psalms was his understanding of the significance of the
expression "Yahweh reigns" or "Yahweh is king" that is found in
some of them (e.g., Ps 93:1; 97:1; 99:1). He interpreted it to mean:
"Yahweh has become king," an expression indicative of the liturgical purpose served by these psalms in the enthronement ritual.
(Hans Kraus, however, has demonstrated rather conclusively that
yahweh melek should be translated "Yahweh is king"— enthroned
forever, not needing to be reenthroned annually in the Babylonian
pattern.)[70] In the view of Mowinckel the ritual was believed to serve
a coercive or magical function. If the rites were performed faithfully, with due care being given to the proper words of the liturgy,
power would be released that would ensure the desired result.
Actually, wizardry was forbidden in Israel (Deut 18:11). Yet the pro-
hibition, it is said, is certain proof that it was practiced. In any case,
it is altogether possible that some did consider ritual and liturgy to
possess magical properties. (Are there none among us today who
would use holy Scripture as a fetish?) But to say that the Enthronement Psalms were designed for this purpose is to go beyond the
evidence.

The concept of an annual New Year (autumnal) festival of
renewal in Israel was assumed because this was apparently the practice of Israel's neighbors. In the *akitu* festival in Babylon, for
example, a drama was reenacted depicting the struggle of the god
Marduk with primeval chaos, the climax coming with the cry,
"Marduk is king." But that such a festival was ever observed in
Israel is questioned. In fact, it is flatly denied by various scholars.
One such is Roland deVaux who, in addition to citing the lack of
evidence, gives a theological reason that renders the proposal
unlikely. Since all power is possessed by the Lord, Creator of all,
there is no one who can enthrone him.[71] Even regarding the
Babylonian ritual, deVaux does not recognize any *reenthronement* of
Marduk, but rather a *celebration* of his power as acclaimed by the
Babylonians. It should be noted further that the Babylonian festival
was held in the spring, not in the fall.

---

[70]Kraus, *Psalms 1–59*, pp. 86-89.
[71]Roland deVaux, *Ancient Israel, Its Life and Institutions*, trans. John
McHugh, (New York: McGraw-Hill, 1961), pp. 504, 505.

Nevertheless, as reconstructed, the enthronement celebration is said to have incorporated three basic elements: a) A victory of Yahweh, as leader of the forces of light, over the forces of darkness, as represented by the primeval watery chaos. b) A struggle, in the course of history, between good forces and evil, ending in a glorious "Day of the Lord." (Here, an eschatological motif is recognized by many scholars.) c) A victory procession, culminating in the enthronement of the Israelite king in the temple, signifying the reenthronement of the Lord over his people. Each phase was dramatized, the priests and the king being the chief participants with the people providing appropriate responses. A mock battle was staged, to be followed by a celebration of victory.

It is evident that religious processions were not unknown in Israel. The bringing of the Ark into Jerusalem by David is an example of such (2 Sam 6:1-19). Psalm 68 speaks of God's "solemn processions . . . into the sanctuary" (68:24, RSV). Such processions were accompanied by singers and minstrels and maidens playing timbrels [tambourines, NIV] (68:25). (If such a celebration was, indeed, a part of an inauguration ceremony, as well it may have been, then the significance of the triumphal entry of Jesus into Jerusalem would not have been lost on those who witnessed it.) But the question is whether or not an annual enthronement of Yahweh was the occasion for which these psalms were composed. Scholars remain divided over the matter. Some do hold that an annual New Year's festival was observed in Israel but differ as to its purpose. Artur Weiser, for example, believed its purpose to be that of covenant renewal rather than reenthronement.[72] Such enthronement Psalms as do exist could well have been designed for the inauguration of the king in Jerusalem (Psalms 2, 110, for example). The Psalms involved do extol the sovereignty of God, but scarcely through the process of reenthronement. That they were used in worship seems obvious, but that they were the necessary complement to an enthronement festival remains to be demonstrated. We may do well, therefore, to leave the Enthronement Psalms, if such they are, as a subtype of the Hymns of Praise, as Gunkel recognized them.

---

[72]Weiser, *The Psalms*, pp. 35-52.

Songs of Zion, the other subtype of Hymns of Praise, are so called because of their reference to the glory of Zion, the city especially chosen and favored of God. "[T]he city of God . . . . God is within her, she will not fall" (Ps 46:4,5). It is "beautiful in its loftiness, the joy of the whole earth" (48:2). God's "dwelling place" is there (76:2), and there one may meet God (84:7). Yahweh "loves the gates of Zion more than all . . ." (87:2). Elsewhere reference is made to the "holy hill" (15:1), or to the "hill of the LORD" (24:3). These Psalms do not conform altogether to the hymn style as generally recognized but are of a mixed pattern. And the list of Psalms in this category varies according to individuals, some being inclined to include any Psalm that has any kind of reference to Zion. Basic to this genre, however, are Psalms 46, 48, 76, 84, 87, and 122.

Laments of the Community find their setting in some great disaster threatening the *entire nation*, a disaster such as war, famine, or plague. In the face of such terror, it would be natural for the people to approach God with prayer and fasting, entreating his help.[73] When the first temple was built, Solomon made reference to such occasions in his dedicatory prayer. "When your people Israel have been defeated by an enemy . . . . When the heavens are shut up and there is no rain . . . . When famine or plague comes to the land . . . . then hear from heaven, your dwelling place. Forgive . . ." (1 Kgs 8:33-39).

The lament is not always strictly uniform in structure, but it usually begins with a simple invocation: "Why have you rejected us forever, O God?" (Ps 74:1); "O God, the nations have invaded your inheritance" (79:1); "Hear us, O Shepherd of Israel, you who lead Joseph like a flock" (80:1). Following this, there may come a statement of the nature of the distress: "Your foes roared in the place where you met with us" (74:4); "O God, the nations . . . have reduced Jerusalem to rubble" (79:1c). (This feature is not clearly discernible in every case.) Usually there is a cry for help, a prayer for deliverance: "Pour out your wrath on the nations . . . for they have devoured Jacob . . . . Help us, O God our Savior" (Ps 79:6,7,9). A *reason* why God's help is appropriate may be included: "Help us, O God our Savior, for the glory of your name" (79:9a).

[73]In Joel, on the occasion of a terrible plague of locusts (Joel 1:4), the people are summoned to a time of lamentation and fasting (2:15-17).

Some of the laments include *a curse* upon the enemy: "May they ever be ashamed and dismayed; may they perish in disgrace" (83:17). Others may contain *a promise* to praise God when deliverance has come: "Then we your people, the sheep of your pasture, will praise you forever; from generation to generation we will recount your praise" (79:13).

In addition to the Psalms quoted above, Psalms 12, 44, 60, 83, 85, 90, 123, 125, and 126 are included in this group, although this list, also, differs according to individual identifications.

Royal Psalms are so designated because of their *content*, not because they constitute an independent literary genre. The latter may vary, according to the occasion of the Psalm. It may reflect the nature of the hymn of praise (Ps 18), or of the song of thanksgiving (Ps 21). It may be an individual lament (Ps 28).[74] Psalm 72 is a prayer on behalf of the king. Psalm 45 is designated a love song in its title. More particularly, it appears to be a royal wedding song.

From the above it will be seen that in the classification of the Psalm as "royal," the determining factor is the prominence of the king as the central figure. The king was also known as the Lord's anointed. And since, in Hebrew, the word for anointed is מָשִׁיחַ (*māšîaḥ* "messiah"), it is understandable that the royal Psalms may also be viewed as having messianic significance. There will be more about this later.

To the Psalms cited above should be added the following as belonging to this class: Psalms 2, 20, 101, 110, 132. Mowinckel would also include Psalms 63, 89, and perhaps others.

Laments of the Individual share basically the nature of the communal lament. There is a distinction, of course, due to the different circumstances out of which the Psalms grew and to the purpose for which they were intended. The *Laments of the Community* were occasioned, as we have observed, by some great threat of disaster to the nation. These Psalms would have been used in public assembly, sung by the congregation, perhaps on special days of prayer and fasting. The individual lament, on the other hand, is the outcry of a *single person*, a soul overwhelmed by trouble and misfortune, laying

---

[74]Mowinckel classed this psalm "Royal." Others question such a classification. The same may be said of Psalm 61, similar in nature.

bare his heart before the Lord, who alone is able to deliver him. Together, fully one-third of all of the Psalms fall into the class of laments, some thirty-four of these being individual in nature.

Characteristic of this type is Psalm 3: "O LORD, how many are my foes! How many rise up against me!" (3:1), and Psalm 7: "O LORD my God, I take refuge in you; save and deliver me from all who pursue me" (7:1). Frequently the occasion of the lament was the oppressive behavior of *enemies* or *adversaries* of the psalmist: "Keep me . . . from the wicked who assail me, from my mortal enemies who surround me" (17:8,9). Or, it might be that he was suffering some severe *illness*: "Be merciful to me, LORD, for I am faint; O LORD, heal me, for my bones are in agony" (6:2). This theme is also reflected in Psalm 25: "Look upon my affliction and my distress and take away all my sins" (25:18). (See also Ps 22:15; 39:13; 41:8; 71:9; 99:3,15; 102:3,4; and 109:23,24. All of these deal with physical sickness or weakness.) Other individual laments are found in Psalms 5, 13, 26, 28, 35, 38, 42, 43, 51, 54, 55, 57, 59, 61, 64, 69, 86, 88, 120, 130, and 140–143.

Individual Songs of Thanksgiving have much in common with the hymns of praise since both are designed to glorify God. The hymn speaks of the glory of God because he *is* God — creator, sovereign, sustainer of all. The song of thanksgiving directs praise to God for some *particular act* of his grace on behalf of his people. Many of these Psalms, therefore, could be classified also as hymns. The thanksgiving psalm may also share characteristics of the lament. For example, Psalm 28 obviously contains this element: "To you I call, O LORD my Rock" (28:1). But it closes with a note of thanksgiving: "Praise be to the LORD, for he has heard my cry for mercy. . . . and I will give thanks to him in song" (28:6,7). In the song of thanksgiving, it is God's present beneficence or mercy that is the occasion for the praise. Hymns may sing of the divine faithfulness as shown in the *past*: "By the word of the LORD were the heavens made" (Ps 33:6). But in the thanksgiving psalm, God is *presently active*: "Come and listen, all you who fear God; let me tell you what he has done for me. I cried out to him with my mouth . . . . God has surely listened and heard my voice in prayer" (Ps 66:16-19). The group of thanksgiving Psalms includes also: Psalms 30, 32, 34 (acrostic), 40, 41 (a lament?), 66 (hymn), 92, 116, and 138.

Blessings and Cursings are found in various Psalms and do not constitute an independent genre. They occur primarily in laments. An example of the blessing may be found in Psalm 67: "May God be gracious to us and bless us and make his face shine upon us" (Ps 67:1). Both the curse and the blessing are in Psalm 5, an individual lament. In regard to wicked enemies we read: "Declare them guilty, O God! Let their intrigues be their downfall" (Ps 5:10). In contrast: "But let all who take refuge in you be glad; . . . For surely, O LORD, you bless the righteous" (Ps 5:11,12). Other verses in a similar vein may be found in Psalms 35:1,4f,26; 59:5,13,16; 69:6,22f; 70:2,4; 83:9-17; 109:6-20,28,29; 137:8,9; 140:9-11.

In some of these, God is asked to do dreadful things to the enemies of the psalmist. "May they be like chaff before the wind . . . may their path be dark and slippery" (35:5,6). "[C]onsume them in wrath, consume them till they are no more" (59:13). "May their eyes be darkened so they cannot see, and their backs be bent forever" (69:23). In Psalm 109 the imprecation or curse includes the children of the enemy: "May his children be fatherless and his wife a widow. May his children be wandering beggars; may they be driven from their ruined homes" (Ps 109:9,10). And an even more horrendous fate is wished upon Babylon: "[H]appy is he who . . . seizes your infants and dashes them against the rocks" (Ps 137:8,9).

The imprecations found in the Psalms are quite disturbing to one who is familiar with the teachings of Jesus. "Love your enemies," Jesus said, "and pray for those who persecute you" (Matt 5:44). And our Lord manifested this spirit, for when he was on the cross he said: "Father, forgive them, for they do not know what they are doing" (Luke 23:34). Of course, the psalmists did not live to hear the words of Jesus. But even in the Old Testament Scriptures kindness to one's enemies is enjoined: "If your enemy is hungry, give him food to eat; if he is thirsty, give him water to drink" (Prov 25:21).

As stated by some, the problem is how to harmonize cries for vengeance, such as we find in the Psalms, with the Bible's teaching of love. But if this is the problem, it is wholly insoluble, for the two are totally incompatible. To establish harmony between them is impossible. The problem is, rather: How did these imprecations find their way into Holy Scripture? In view of the psalmist's being inspired of God, this question becomes as significant as the other. Obviously their inclusion was not proscribed by the Spirit. But does that mean that the Spirit approved? I would answer that, yes, the Spirit approved of their inclusion, permitting the psalmist to utter the sentiments of his own heart. (In Eccl 2:1 we read, explicitly: "I thought in my heart.") Craigie considers these words to be "Israel's response to God's revelation emerging from the painful realities of life." [75] We must look to these "painful realities" in the life of the psalmist and to the means at his disposal for meeting them, if we would begin to understand why he used imprecatory language.

Frequent reference is made to vicious enemies. Some have proposed that these included demoniacal forces of the unseen world, but the suggestion has little to commend it. They are referred to as "the wicked who assail me" (Ps 17:9), "ruthless witnesses come forward; they question me on things I know nothing about" (Ps 35:11), "bloodthirsty men" (Ps 59:2), "those who hate me without reason" (Ps 69:4), who "have spoken against me with lying tongues" (Ps 109:2). Suffering gross injustice, insults, and perhaps even bodily harm, the psalmist sought the redress of his grievances.

Mowinckel,[76] and some others, proposed that the imprecatory Psalms were of the nature of incantations for the warding off of evil. The pronouncement of the curse would cast a spell over the enemy that would neutralize his wicked designs. Yet, admittedly, the words of such incantations are difficult to identify. The psalmist was not using some magical formula, not casting spells. He was asking God to deal with the enemy – his enemy and God's enemy. He knew that vengeance belongs to God (Ps 94:1). He knew that God had promised blessing for the righteous and punishment for those who persist in evil. Yet he honored God and he was suffering at the hands of godless men; therefore his cry was, "Lord, why do you not deal with them?"

We may have difficulty with the extravagant language in which the imprecations are expressed: "Break the teeth in their mouths, O God" (Ps 58:6); "Pour out your wrath on them; let your fierce anger overtake them" (69:24); "The righteous will be glad when

---

[75]Craigie, *Psalms 1-50*, p. 39.
[76]Mowinckel, *The Psalms In Worship*, 1:202, 203.

they are avenged, when they bathe their feet in the blood of the wicked" (58:10)! But these expressions stem from the enthusiasm of the zealot. The prevalence of evil dishonors God. Many today are altogether complacent about injustice and discrimination. Others among us might be zealous to eradicate evil. The ancient Hebrew did not think in such abstract terms. For him, to destroy evil involved also the destruction of the evildoer. The utterance of these imprecations gave him an outlet for the anger he felt against those who opposed God, and it forestalled the development of a neurosis on his part. Furthermore, his willingness to leave the matter in the hands of God would forestall any violent or irrational behavior at his own hand. In addition to Psalms cited, others containing imprecations are: 7, 9, 10, 13, 16, 21, 23, 31, 36, 40, 41, 44, 52, 54, 55, 63, 71, 73, 94, 104, and 139.

How the Christian should understand and "pray" the *cursing* psalms has been a debate for the ages. One thing is clear: the Hebrew psalmist took right and wrong, good and evil more seriously than most and saw these things as an affront to God himself. Those who oppose God's people oppose God. Thus, it is right for God's people to "curse" such people, especially their actions. C.S. Lewis has given us insight into this discussion:

> If the Divine call does not make us better, it will make us very much worse. Of all created beings the wickedest is one who originally stood in the immediate presence of God. There seems to be no way out of this. It gives a new application to Our Lord's words about "counting the cost."[77]

In other words, we should be careful that our "righteous indignations" (cursings) do not shift into a deeper sin for us!

As *Pilgrim Songs* Gunkel recognized two that he believed had their origin in the pilgrimage to the temple by devout Hebrews. The first of these begins: "How lovely is your dwelling place, O LORD Almighty! My soul yearns, even faints, for the courts of the LORD" (Ps 84:1,2). The second opens with the familiar words: "I rejoiced with those who said to me, 'Let us go to the house of the

---

[77]C.S. Lewis, *Reflections on the Psalms* (New York: Harcourt, Brace & World, 1958), p. 32. See the chapter on "The Cursings," pp. 20-33.

LORD'" (122:1). Each of these Psalms may also be identified as a song of Zion. In addition to these, Psalms 120–134 have also been called pilgrim Psalms, not that a pilgrimage was the occasion for their writing (except for Ps 122), but that they were used by pilgrims to Jerusalem. This is problematic. Each of the Psalms of the pilgrim category bears some other classification, also, such as lament, praise, thanksgiving, or wisdom Psalm.

National Songs of Thanksgiving, again two in number in Gunkel's classification, were Psalms 76 and 124. (It will be noted that Gunkel also considered Psalm 76 to be a song of Zion.) In this Psalm there is celebrated a victory that God has given over some powerful enemy of the *nation*. The occasion of Psalm 124 (a pilgrim song?) was undoubtedly the deliverance of Israel from the fierce onslaughts of a ruthless enemy. Thanks are expressed in the opening words: "If the LORD had not been on our side," and in the closing words of the psalm: "Our help is in the name of the LORD, the Maker of heaven and earth." Other Psalms that some have also considered to be in the category of national thanksgiving include: Psalms 65 (a hymn), 67, 107:1-32, and 118.

The Psalms that were designated *Historical Recital* by Gunkel include Psalms 78, 105, and 106. Psalm 78 is an epic poem relating the glorious deeds of the Lord in his relationship with Israel through ages past. Its purpose, apparently, is didactic: "O my people, hear my teaching; listen to the words of my mouth" (v. 1) is the language of Proverbs, used by a father in the teaching of his son. Psalm 105 also speaks of God's faithfulness in his dealings with his covenant people, but here the material is treated as the theme of a great hymn of praise. Psalm 106 is similar, except that it deals with the mercy God had shown when his people had sinned, recounting the history of their repeated offenses and of God's grace. Bernhard W. Anderson identifies these three Psalms as *Salvation History*.[78] Because of their content, some would also consider Psalms 135 and 136 to be historical recital. Otherwise the first is a praise hymn while the second is either a hymn or a song of national thanksgiving.

---

[78]Bernhard W. Anderson, *Out of the Depths: The Psalms Speak for Us Today* (Philadelphia: The Westminster Press, 1974), pp. 175, 176.

The Psalms of the Law, although only two in number, are of great significance to the Psalter. In Israel, the law (*torah*) was respected as instruction in the ways of God, the way of blessedness. Consequently, it was held in high esteem. This esteem is evident as indicated in the very first Psalm (a didactic poem), where it is said of the godly man: "But his delight is in the law of the LORD" (v. 2). But it is Ps 19:7-14 and 119 that really extol the law. The opening verses of Psalm 19 speak of the glory of God as seen in the heavens. The remainder of the Psalm glories in the precious benefits that are afforded through the law. In Psalm 119, the great acrostic, there is a reference to the law, either as *torah* or by a synonym, in every one of the one hundred seventy-six verses except seven. Although there are only the two Psalms of this nature in the Psalms, throughout the book one's blessed relationship with God and one's delight in life are predicated on following the instruction found in the *torah*. (Gunkel's classification of *Torah liturgies,* Psalms 15, 24, and perhaps 134, was based, not on their content as Psalms of the law but on their alleged function.)

Prophetic Psalms, one might suppose, would be those in which the future is envisioned. But in Gunkel's classification the term indicates, rather, Psalms that contain oracles such as a prophet might utter, without specific reference to the predictive element, such utterances having become a part of the liturgy of worship. It is assumed that, in addition to priests, there would be prophets attached to a shrine. On appropriate occasions, especially on occasions of lamentation, the prophets would utter their oracles, words from God, in response to the need. An example of such is Ps 12:5,6: "'Because of the oppression of the weak and the groaning of the needy, I will now arise,' says the LORD. 'I will protect them from those who malign them.' And the words of the LORD are flawless." Ps 60:6 records that "God has spoken from his sanctuary," and the oracle follows: "In triumph I will parcel out Shechem." And Ps 110:1 opens with a phrase that is common on the lips of the literary prophets: יְהוָה נְאֻם (*nᵉʾum YHWH,* "says the LORD"). Gunkel concluded that the form of the lament regularly included a plea on the part of the afflicted person, to be answered by the oracle. Yet, as Weiser observes: "The remarkable fact that the great majority of the laments do not refer to such an oracle refutes Gunkel's postulate that in these cases, too, we are presented with a stylistic form, cast into a rigid mold, which at an earlier stage presupposes such an oracle."[79] What may be prophetic oracle in the Psalms, coming from a prophet attached to a shrine, and what is to be attributed to the psalmist alone is impossible to distinguish with certainty.

In addition to prophetic oracle, prophecy in the sense of a forward look does exist also in the Psalms. This theme will be considered in our treatment of the messianic motif in Psalms.

Wisdom Psalms, in the style of other Old Testament wisdom literature, are not uncommon. That style is manifested in two general forms, the gnomic statement or proverb, expressing in short form a universal truth, and the short essay. An example of the latter is Psalm 1, which draws a bold contrast between the blessedness of godliness and the despair of the ungodly. How to realize true success in life — this is the thrust of Psalm 1, just as it is of other wisdom writings in the Scriptures. Psalm 37, aphoristic in style, does take note of the seeming prosperity of the wicked, but then advises patience, asserting that such prosperity will be of short duration: "Do not fret because of evil men . . . for like the grass they will soon wither" (37:1,2). Ps 33 is a praise hymn, yet it contains pithy sayings that would fit nicely in the book of Proverbs. For example: "No king is saved by the size of his army; no warrior escapes by his great strength" (33:16). Compare this to Prov 11:4: "Wealth is worthless in the day of wrath, but righteousness delivers from death." The sentiment differs, but the style is the same. Other wisdom psalms or psalms with expressions in the form of aphorisms are: 34, 36 (a lament), 49, 73, 112, 127, 128, and 133.

Gunkel included some other minor types of Psalms in his classification. In some cases there is difficulty in identifying a "type" since the *criteria* for determining such are not always present and identifiable. The criteria are: (1) a common life situation that would call for psalms of a particular type, (2) a common theme and distinctive mood, and (3) a common literary development or form. Even among the recognized types of Psalms the criteria are not always fully evident. Where these are absent, the task of classification may become quite subjective. In any case, among Gunkel's minor types were: *Psalms of Confidence* (or *of Victory*) such as: Psalms

---

[79]Weiser, *The Psalms*, p. 79f.

4, 11, 16, 23, 62, 91, 121 (Gunkel did not list all of these), *Liturgies*: Psalms 8 (a hymn), 15, 42–43 (a lament), 50, 82, and *Mixed Poems*: Psalms 9, 10, 40, and 78.

THE VALUE OF GUNKEL'S WORK

Gunkel's classification of the Psalms has proved helpful, especially in two areas: (1) its focus upon the characteristics of the various types of Psalms, and (2) its concern with the life situation underlying the use of a particular type. If a Psalm is to become meaningful, it must do so in reference to the situation that called it into being and to the function it had in that situation. Basic to Gunkel's approach, as we have noted, was the belief that it was the needs of formal (cultic) worship in Israel that must account for the origin of the Psalms, and that they must be studied in that light. (The concept of private devotions of a meditative nature was said to be a later development.) This approach would give less attention to a specific historical setting for a Psalm, more to the liturgical (and universal) need it was designed to serve, less to the Psalm as the expression of the heart of an individual, more to its conscious attempt to meet the need of the congregation. It should be noted, however, that Gunkel did recognize most of the Psalms as basically the private compositions of pious Israelites. Even so, it was believed that they were composed to be used in the religious ceremony of the sanctuary, or else that they were adapted to that purpose. As a matter of fact, for the most part the cultic motif in the Psalms is conspicuous by its absence, so its great significance has been questioned. Some believe it to have been lost with the passing of time. This Norman Gottwald indicates when he says that there was a move from "live cultic performance" of the Psalms to the stage of their being collected as literature, and that their cultic function, in large part, consequently became "lost or obscured."[80]

In some cases, the move could have been in the other direction; that is, from private compositions to corporate worship. This could be true even when the Psalm is of a clearly recognizable type such

---

[80]Norman Gottwald, *The Hebrew Bible, a Socio-Literary Introduction* (Philadelphia: Fortress Press, 1985), p. 525.

as a lament. No matter what may have been the cultic association of a given type, it could be employed by a psalmist without cultic implications. Indeed, he would subconsciously seek to express his thoughts in the recognized style, since it would be appropriate to such expression. That the Psalms *were* used, from earliest times, to accompany ritual, is indicated in the reference to "rejoicing" and "singing" that, by order of David, should accompany the offering of sacrifices (2 Chr 23:18). We recognize that many of the Psalms were undoubtedly composed for such use. Yet there are others, such as Psalm 23, that appear to be most personal, the individual expression of trust and confidence of the psalmist, speaking for himself and not especially for the congregation. This was the position of Julius Morgenstern regarding Psalm 23.[81]

Others, however, view even this Psalm as having been prepared for liturgical use in a ritual of thanksgiving — Drijvers, for example.[82] A.A. Anderson considers this a possibility, regarding the reference to "the house of the Lord" in verse 6 as an indication of a cultic setting and the "table" in the presence of enemies as possibly implying a thanksgiving meal.[83] Yet many share the view that some of the Psalms were originally private compositions later incorporated into the worship of temple or synagogue. This likelihood was suggested by Briggs, some years before the work of Gunkel and Mowinckel: "Many of the Psalms in their original form were composed as an expression of private devotion. These features remained after they were adapted by editorial revision for use in the synagogues."[84] And H.H. Rowley observed:

> Some (of the Psalms) are calculated to express the corporate thought and feeling of men in united worship, or on national occasions, while others are more calculated to express the individual spirit's feelings in some solitary experience of joy or sorrow. How they came to be used in worship can never be known with any assurance.[85]

---

[81]J. Morgenstern, "Psalm 23," *JBL*, 1946, pp. 13-24.
[82]Drijvers, *The Psalms*, p. 84.
[83]A.A. Anderson, *Psalms 1-72*, p. 195.
[84]Briggs, *Psalms*, p. xcv.
[85]H.H. Rowley, *The Re-Discovery of the Old Testament* (London: James Clarke and Co., 1945), p. 174f.

Paul Auvray considers it an exaggeration to see a liturgical origin for all of the Psalms, certain that many were "the pure products of individual devotion."[86] Oesterley and Robinson concur in this: "There can be little doubt that a large number of the psalms . . . were not used in the public worship of the temple, nor were they ever intended to be."[87]

It would appear that Gunkel may have overemphasized the cultic influence underlying the Psalms. Nevertheless, his contribution to their study is unmistakable and of great value in the areas that we have indicated. We would agree that many of the Psalms obviously served the needs of corporate worship. Yet there were others serving the needs of private devotions. This, we may well believe, was God's intention in their writing and in their preservation. They arose from definite situations in life and they found their expression in forms with which the psalmists and their contemporaries were familiar. Yet there is a timelessness about them that has made them of value to every age and a diversity that enables them to speak to the human heart, or for the heart, in almost any circumstance. Consequently, whatever their history, however they came to be written, utilized, and preserved, the Psalms, as they are, are admirably suited to the needs of man, as he is. For this we may thank God.

Some Psalms have been placed in categories other than the above. Thus Psalms 77, 80, and 81 have been designated *North Israel Psalms* by some, because of place references or mention of Israel in contradistinction to Judah. Psalms 29, 38, 65, 104, and 107 (hymns), because of their content, have been called *Nature Psalms*. Another proposed classification is *Penitential Psalms*, those in which one acknowledges guilt before God and/or seeks his mercy. Psalms of this type are: 6, 32, 38, 51, 102, 130, and 143. Psalms 111, 112, 113, 115, 116, 117, and 146–150 each begins with *Halleluia* ("Praise the Lord"), and for this reason have been called the *Halleluia Psalms*. In rabbinic literature Psalms 113–118 were designated the

---

[86]Paul Auvray, "The Psalms," in *Introduction to the Old Testament*, A. Robert and A. Feuller, eds., trans. P.W. Skehan, et al. (New York: Desclee Co., 1968), p. 393.

[87]Oesterley and Robinson, *Introduction*, p. 194.

Egyptian Hallel. They were read or sung during the observance of Passover. (See Mark 14:26.)

MESSIANIC PSALMS

Among other categories of Psalms that could be suggested, there is one that should receive particular attention; namely, those Psalms that have messianic content or implications. In a broad sense, the term "messianic" has come to be used to signify a time of blessing that would accompany the establishment of God's kingdom in Israel and in the world. Throughout the Old Testament there is a note of expectancy, a forward look. The people of Israel endured more than their share of suffering, much of it in consequence of their sins. In 587 B.C. Jerusalem was destroyed and its inhabitants transported to Babylon (modern Iraq). There was every reason for a gloomy outlook, yet hope persisted. In the face of disaster and defeat, Israel clung tenaciously to the certainty of future glory. The people could see the hand of God's discipline upon their nation because of their sins, but they believed that the God who was faithful in judgment would be equally faithful in mercy. This hope rested upon the promise God had made with Abraham their father. "I will make you into a great nation," God had said, "and all peoples on earth will be blessed through you" (Gen 12:2,3).

Confidence in the future did not stem from what the people of Israel saw in the world around them. They did not place their hope in what man might accomplish. And they would have been the last people on earth to hold that the world would automatically get better. On the contrary, their hope was rooted and grounded in God. The hope of the world lay, in their eyes, not in the issues of man's connivings but in the certainty of God's purposes and of his promises. God's promised kingdom would come and the Messiah would be the instrument by whom it would be established. In the broad sense, therefore, everything in the Old Testament referring to the coming kingdom may be said to be messianic.

But are there Psalms that are messianic in the particular sense of reference to the messiah who was to come? It must be understood that the word "messiah" in the Old Testament is a common noun, not a proper name or title. From the verb meaning "to anoint," it signifies one who has been anointed to a particular task. The term was a common designation for the king, and so David, sparing the life of King Saul, would not lift up his hand against "the LORD's anointed"; that is, against the Lord's messiah (1 Sam 26:11). As a synonym for king, messiah identified the monarch particularly as God's agent. In 1 Kgs 19:15 Elijah is instructed to anoint Hazael to be king over Syria. And Isa 45:1 designates Cyrus, king of Persia, as the Lord's anointed ("my messiah").

In the Psalms, the use of the verb "to anoint" and of the noun "anointed one" parallels the above examples. In the twelve passages in which the term, in any form, is found,[88] the reference appears to be to the king, except in Ps 105:15. There we find the plural, "my anointed ones" ("my messiahs" in the Hebrew), a reference to the patriarchs, including Abraham, Isaac, and Jacob. No reference is to be found in the Old Testament Scriptures where the article is used, designating "the messiah."[89] However, the prophets indicated clearly that God would raise up a righteous descendant of David, who would establish an everlasting kingdom of righteousness and justice. In Jer 33:14,15, the prophet announces: "'The days are coming,' declares the LORD, 'when I will fulfill the gracious promise I made to the house of Israel and to the house of Judah. In those days and at that time I will make a righteous Branch sprout from David's line; he will do what is just and right in the land.'" And Isaiah says: "Of the increase of his government and peace there will be no end. He will reign on David's throne and over his kingdom, establishing and upholding it with justice and righteousness from that time on and forever. The zeal of the LORD Almighty will accomplish this" (9:7).

A reign of righteousness was to be introduced by a Davidic king. This assurance would naturally inspire new hope every time a new monarch came to the throne. "Will this be the promised one?" the

---

[88]Ps 45:7 has "God . . . anointing you with . . . oil"; 89:20, "with my sacred oil I have anointed him"; 2:2, 18:50, 20:6, 28:8, "his anointed one"; 84:9, 89:38,51, 132:10, "your anointed one"; 105:15, "my anointed ones"; and 132:17, "my anointed one" (David).

[89]In Dan 9:25,26, reference is made to a future "anointed one" (literally, to "a messiah, a prince") and this is surely messianic. Yet even here, in the Hebrew, the definite article is omitted.

people would wonder. King Josiah, of David's line, even named one of his sons Zedekiah, "Yah(weh) is my righteousness." But far from fulfilling messianic expectations, Zedekiah's reign ended with the destruction of Jerusalem by Nebuchadrezzar, and the last king of Judah ended his career as a prisoner in Babylon (Jer 52:4-11). Yet hope did not die. Various anointed kings had come and gone; the kingdom had come to an end. Nevertheless, God would raise up One who would yet establish the reign of righteousness, and this One would be *The* anointed One, *The* Messiah.

The promise is stated in Psalm 89: "I have found David my servant; with my sacred oil I have anointed him. . . . I will establish his line forever, his throne as long as the heavens endure" (Ps 89:20,29). The promise is given while God is casting off the reigning king, the current anointed one (89:38). Elsewhere, much that would transpire in the life of the coming Messiah is reflected in the Psalms. Jesus indicated this when he said: "Everything must be fulfilled that is written about me in the Law of Moses, the Prophets and the Psalms" (Luke 24:44). However, much of the material we see as messianic may not have been so understood by the psalmist nor by his contemporaries. Elsewhere in the Old Testament prophecies may open with the words: "Behold, the days are coming, says the LORD, when . . . ." The prophetic content of the Psalms is basically of a different type. It is of the nature of a mosaic.

Visualize a great tapestry portraying a series of historic events, clearly delineated. But this tapestry has more, as revealed by close examination. Here is a red thread or two, there another, and another. Presently it becomes apparent that there is a design in these random threads, clearly discernible, and distinct from the general picture. So pronounced are they that one must recognize that the artist (the Spirit of God) designed it so from the beginning. For example, when Matthew records that Joseph and Mary fled with the young Jesus into Egypt, he recognizes one of these threads in Hosea, when he writes: "And so was fulfilled what the Lord had said through the prophet: 'Out of Egypt I called my son'" (Matt 2:15). A prophecy of Jesus? The picture in Hosea is of Israel and the Exodus, as the prophet himself tells us: "When Israel was a child, I loved him, and out of Egypt I called my son" (Hos 11:1). In what way could this reference to a past historical event be considered a prophecy?

In isolation, the reference is clearly to the Exodus. But it is one
of those threads in the tapestry that appears in a different light
when the whole is viewed. And there are many of these in the
Psalms. For example: "He said to me, 'You are my Son; today I
have become your Father'" (Ps 2:7). "Even my close friend, whom I
trusted, he who shared my bread, has lifted up his heel against me"
(41:9). "They have pierced my hands and my feet" (22:16). "They
. . . gave me vinegar for my thirst" (69:21). "They divide my garments among them and cast lots for my clothing" (22:18). "He pro-
tects all his bones, not one of them will be broken" (34:20). "You
will not abandon me to the grave, nor will you let your Holy One
see decay" (16:10). "The stone the builders rejected has become the
capstone" (118:22). "May his name endure forever; may it continue
as long as the sun. All nations will be blessed through him, and they
will call him blessed" (72:17). A single one of the above, in isolation, might be judged a coincidence in its description of a circumstance in the life of Jesus. But taken altogether (and there are
others), the likeness is too detailed and too exact to be coincidence.
The records of the events, in the words of Kirkpatrick, "were so
moulded by the Spirit of God as to prefigure . . . Christ even in cir-
cumstantial details."[90] This messianic significance in the Psalms
may not have been understood by the psalmists, nor those who
heard them, but it was in the mind of the Spirit who inspired them.

If one denies that divine inspiration wove the tapestry that has so
many intimations of Jesus, then he must account for the phenomenon in some other way. This being true, it is not surprising that the
theory has been advanced that Jesus, knowing the Psalms and the
prophets, mistakenly considered himself to be the Messiah and consciously or subconsciously fulfilled the role as best he could. Just
how he contrived to be born in Bethlehem (in accordance with
Micah 5:2) the theory does not take into account, or how he was
able to keep a bone of his body from being broken (John 19:31-36),
or how he managed to be buried in a rich man's tomb (Isa 53:9,
Matt 27:57-60). And for a deluded visionary to arrange his own resurrection from the dead is more remarkable still — a fact verified by
eleven jurors who would die rather than to deny it, and by five
hundred other witnesses as well (1 Cor 15:6). And as to the

[90]Kirkpatrick, *The Book of Psalms*, 3:lxxix.

psalmist's statement, "May his name endure forever" (72:17), two thousand years is certainly not forever, but it is a good start!

Auvray observes: "Messianism is a phenomenon of such importance in the history of Israel that the absence of psalms representing this religious attitude would be incomprehensible."[91] However, the value of the Psalms to us is not restricted to their messianic content. That is but one of the treasures they offer. As literature, they are unexcelled and timeless, having lost none of their charm and appeal during three millennia. Wonderfully, they provide an exact mirror for every soul. Here are reflected the religious aspirations of humankind — in despair and in trust, in the sorrow of sin and in the assurance of forgiveness, in the agony of defeat and in the joy of victory. The Psalms are on the living edge of the encounter of God and man in a variety of circumstances. H.C. Leupold bears witness to this when he says: "There does not seem to be any situation in life for which the Psalter does not provide light and guidance."[92] Jesus quoted from the Psalms often to support key ideas in his teaching (Ps 118:22-23 in Mark 12:10-11; Ps 110:1 in Mark 12:36, 14:62; Ps 22:2 in Mark 15:34; Ps 37:11 in Matt 5:15; Ps 48:3 in Matt 5:35; Ps 6:9 in Matt 7:23; Ps 8:3 in Matt 21:16; Ps 118:26 in Matt 23:39; and Ps 31:6 in Luke 23:46). The first gospel sermon ever preached, on the occasion of the birthday of the church, included quotations from Psalms (16:8-11 in Acts 2:25-28, and 110:1 in Acts 2:34-35). Facing persecution, the apostles made the Psalms a part of their prayer (Acts 4:24-26 quoting Ps 2:1-2). When Paul and Silas were imprisoned at Philippi, their singing surely included portions of the Psalms (Acts 16:25). Other Christians sang them while on the way to the arena to face wild animals and certain death. From the time they were given until the present — a period of thirty centuries! — people have found in the Psalms lyrics helping to lift their own spirits in praise and prayers giving wing to their own thoughts before God. The Psalms are a living fountain of refreshment, a source of blessing, for any who would desire a daily encounter with God. Their messianic content but serves to enhance the blessings they afford to the devout reader.

---

[91]Auvray, *Psalms*, p. 390.

[92]H.C. Leupold, *Exposition of the Psalms* (Grand Rapids: Baker, 1959), p. 28.

OUTLINE OF PSALMS 1–72

BOOK ONE
PSALMS 1–41

PART ONE: THE BELIEVER'S LIFE — PSALMS 1–15

I. INTRODUCTORY PSALMS — 1:1–2:12
   A. Wisdom and Folly — 1:1-6
   B. Hopelessness or Happiness — 2:2-12
II. LIVING CONFIDENTLY — 3:1–7:17
   A. Troubled but Unafraid — 3:1-8
   B. Confidence at Evening — 4:1-8
   C. An Appeal to a Righteous Lord — 5:1-12
   D. A Cry for Mercy under Judgment — 6:1-10
   E. An Innocent Man's Appeal to the Righteous Judge — 7:1-17
III. LIVING EXPECTANTLY — 8:1–10:18
   A. The Glory of God and the Dignity of Man — 8:1-9
   B. An Appeal to God for Deliverance — 9:1–10:18
IV. LIVING VICTORIOUSLY — 11:1–15:5
   A. In God We Trust — 11:1-7
   B. Wicked Words and the Word of God — 12:1-8
   C. From Despair to Hope — 13:1-6
   D. As a Man Thinks, So Is He — 14:1-7
   E. Togetherness with God — 15:1-5

PART TWO: THE BELIEVER'S SALVATION — PSALMS 16–29

I. THE GOD OF LIFE — 16:1-11
   A. Joy in the Lord — 16:1-11
II. THE GOD OF DELIVERANCE — 17:1–18:50

BOOK TWO
PSALMS 42-72

PART ONE: DELIVERANCE
FOR THE ESTRANGED — PSALMS 42-51

PART TWO: THE FAITHFUL AND THE FAITHLESS —
PSALMS 52-60

PART THREE: DAVID AND THE GREAT KING —
PSALMS 61–72

BIBLIOGRAPHY

I. COMMENTARIES

Alexander, J.A. *The Psalms Translated and Explained.* New York: Charles Scribner, 1963.

Allen, Leslie C. *Psalms 101–150.* Word Biblical Commentary. Waco, TX: Word Books, 1983.

Anderson, A.A. *The Book of Psalms.* 2 vols. New Century Bible Commentaries. Grand Rapids: Eerdmans, 1972.

Ash, Anthony L. and Clyde M. Miller. Psalms. Austin, TX: Sweet, 1980.

Barnes, Albert. *Notes on the Old Testament: Psalms.* Grand Rapids: Baker, 1950 (reprint).

Briggs, Charles A. and E.G. Briggs. *A Critical and Exegetical Commentary on the Book of Psalms.* 2 vols. The International Critical Commentary. Edinburgh: T & T Clark, 1906-1907.

Brueggemann, Walter. *The Message of the Psalms: A Theological Commentary.* Minneapolis: Augsburg, 1984.

Buttenwieser, Moses. *The Psalms Chronologically Treated, with a New Translation.* New York: KTAV, 1969.

Cohen, A. *The Psalms.* Soncino Books of the Bible. Ed. by A. Cohen. London: The Soncino Press, 1964.

Craigie, Peter C. *Psalms 1–50.* Word Biblical Commentary. Waco, TX: Word Books, 1983.

Dahood, Mitchell. *Psalms I, Psalms II, Psalms III,* The Anchor Bible. Garden City, NY: Doubleday, 1966.

Delitzsch, Franz. *Biblical Commentary on the Psalms.* 3 vols. Trans. by Francis Bolton. Edinburgh: T & T Clark, 1884.

Drijvers, Pius. *The Psalms: Their Structure and Meaning.* New York: Herder and Herder, 1965.

Eerdmans, B.D. *The Hebrew Book of Psalms.* Leiden: E.J. Brill, 1987.

Gerstenberger, Erhard S. *Psalms, Part I.* Grand Rapids: Eerdmans, 1987.

Guthrie, Harvey H., Jr. *Israel's Sacred Songs.* New York: The Seabury Press, 1966.

Holladay, William L. *The Psalms through Three Thousand Years (Prayerbook of a Cloud of Witnesses).* Minneapolis: Fortress Press, 1993.

Kidner, Derek. *Psalms 1–72: An Introduction and Commentary.* Tyndale Old Testament Commentaries. Downers Grove, IL: InterVarsity, 1973.

_____. *Psalms 73–150: A Commentary.* Tyndale Old Testament Commentaries. Downers Grove, IL: InterVarsity, 1975.

Kirkpatrick, A.F. *The Book of Psalms.* Cambridge Bible Series. Cambridge: Cambridge University Press, 1902, 1910.

Kraus, Hans Joachim. *Psalms 1–59.* Trans. by Wm. C. Oswald. Minneapolis: Augsburg, 1988.

_____. *Psalms 60–150: A Commentary.* Minneapolis: Augsburg, 1989.

_____. *Theology of the Psalms.* Minneapolis: Augsburg, 1986.

Leslie, Elmer. *The Psalms, translated and interpreted in the Light of Hebrew Life and Worship.* Abingdon: Abingdon-Cokesbury, 1949.

Leupold, H.C. *Exposition of the Psalms*. Grand Rapids: Baker, 1959.

Mays, James L. *Psalms*. Interpretation. Louisville, KY: John Knox Press, 1989.

_____. *The Lord Reigns: A Theological Handbook to the Psalms*. Philadelphia: Westminster, 1994.

McLaren, Alexander. *Psalms*. Exposition of the Bible. Vol. 3. Hartford: S.S. Scranton Co., 1914.

McCullough, W. Stewart. *The Book of Psalms* (exegesis). The Interpreter's Bible. Vol. 4. Nashville: Broadman Press, 1955.

Miller, Patrick D., Jr. *Interpreting the Psalms*. Philadelphia: Fortress Press, 1986.

Morgan, G. Campbell. *Searchlights from the Word*. Westwood, NJ: Fleming H. Revell, 1952, (reprint) 1986.

Mowinkel, Sigmund. *The Psalms in Israel's Worship*. 2 vols. Nashville: Abingdon, 1963.

Oesterley, W.O.E. *The Psalms: Translated with Text-Critical and Exegetical Notes*. London: SPCK, 1939.

Perowne, J.S. *The Book of Psalms*. Third London Edition. 2 vols. Andover: Warren F. Draper, 1901. Reprint, Grand Rapids: Zondervan, 1976.

Poteat, Edwin McNeil. *The Book of Psalms* (exposition). The Interpreter's Bible. Vol. 4. Nashville: Broadman Press, 1955.

Rhodes, Arnold B. *The Book of Psalms*. The Layman's Bible Commentary. Vol. 9. Richmond, VA: John Knox Press, 1960.

Rodd, Cyril S. *Psalms 1–72*. London: The Epworth Press, 1963.

Rogerson, J.W. and J.W. McKay. *Psalms 1–50, Psalms 51–100, Psalms 101–150*. Cambridge: Cambridge University Press, 1977.

Rotherham, J.B. *Studies in the Psalms*. 2 vols. Joplin: College Press, 1980 (reprint).

Sclater, J.R.P. *The Book of Psalms* (exposition). The Interpreter's Bible. Vol. 4. Nashville: Broadman Press, 1955.

Stuhlmueller, Carroll. *Psalms I, Psalms II*. 2 vols. Wilmington: Michael Glazier, 1983.

Tate, Marvin E. *Psalms 51–100*, Word Biblical Commentary. Dallas: Word Books, 1990.

Taylor, William R. *The Book of Psalms* (exegesis). The Interpreter's Bible. Vol. 4. Nashville: Broadman Press, 1955.

Trapp, John. *A Commentary of Exposition upon the Books of Ezra, Nehemiah, Esther, Job, and Psalms*. London: Thomas Newberry, 1657 (facsimile).

vanDyke, Henry. *The Story of the Psalms*. New York: Charles Scribner's Sons, 1892.

Weiser, Artur. *The Psalms*. The Old Testament Library. Philadelphia: Westminster Press, 1962.

_____. *The Psalms: Structure, Content, and Message*. Minneapolis: Augsburg, 1990.

Westermann, Claus. *The Psalms: Structure, Content, and Message*. Minneapolis: Augsburg, 1980.

Williams, Donald M. *Psalms 1–72*. The Communicator's Commentary. Waco, TX: Word Books, 1986.

II. SPECIAL STUDIES

Anderson, B.W. *Out of the Depths: The Psalms Speak for us Today*. Philadelphia: Westminster Press, 1974.

Anders-Richards, Donald. *The Drama of the Psalms*. London: Darton, Longman, and Todd, 1968.

Bellinger, W.H., Jr. *Psalms: Reading and Studying the Book of Praises*. Peabody, MA: Hendrickson Publishers, 1990.

Bonhoeffer, Dietrick. *Psalms: The Prayer Book of the Bible.* Minneapolis: Augsburg, 1970.

Brueggemann, Walter. *The Psalms & the Life of Faith.* Minneapolis: Fortress, 1995.

Cross, Frank Moore, Jr., and David Noel Freedman. *Studies in Ancient Yahwistic Poetry.* Missoula: Scholars Press, 1975.

Eaton, J.H. *Kingship and the Psalms.* Naperville, IL: Alec R. Allenson, 1975.

Gevirtz, Stanley. *Patterns in the Early Poetry of Israel.* Chicago: University of Chicago, 1963.

Gray, George Buchanan. *The Forms of Hebrew Poetry.* New York: KTAV, (a reprint) 1972.

Gunkel, Hermann. *The Psalms: A Form-Critical Introduction.* Trans. by Thomas M. Horner. Introduction by James Muilenburg. Philadelphia: Fortress, 1967.

Hester, H.K. *The Heart of Hebrew History.* Liberty, MO: The William Jewell Press, 1949.

Johnson, A.R. *Sacral Kingship in Ancient Israel.* Cardiff, Wales: University Press, 1967.

Keel, Othmar. *The Symbolism of the Biblical World: Ancient Near Eastern Iconography and the Book of Psalms.* New York: Seabury Press, 1978.

Kugel, James. *The Idea of Biblical Poetry: Parallelism and Its History.* New Haven: Yale University Press, 1981.

Lewis, C.S. *Reflections on the Psalms.* New York: Harcourt, Brace & World, 1958.

Longmann, Tremper, III. *How to Read the Psalms.* Downers Grove, IL: InterVarsity, 1988.

McCann, J. Clinton, Jr. *A Theological Introduction to the Book of Psalms*. Nashville: Abingdon, 1993.

_____, ed. *The Shape and Shaping of the Psalter*. Journal for the Study of the Old Testmaent Supplement Series 159. Sheffield: JSOT, 1993.

Milton, John P. *The Psalms*. Rock Island, IL: Augustana Book Concern, 1954.

Prothero, Rowland E. *The Psalms in Human Life*. London: John Murray, 1905.

Ringgren, Helmer. *The Faith of the Psalmists*. London: SPCK, 1963.

_____. *The Messiah in the Old Testament*. Chicago: Alec R. Allenson, 1956.

Ryken, Leland; James C. Wilhoit; Tremper Longman III, Gen. Eds. *Dictionary of Biblical Imagery*. Downers Grove, IL: InterVarsity, 1998.

Sakenfeld, Katherine Doob. *Faithfulness in Action – Loyalty in Biblical Perspective*. Philadelphia: Fortress Press, 1985.

_____. *The Meaning of Hesed in the Hebrew Bible, a New Inquiry*. Missoula: Scholars Press, 1978.

Spurgeon, Charles H. *The Treasury of David*. 3 vols. McLean, VA: MacDonald, n.d. (reprint).

Westermann, Claus. *Praise and Lament in the Psalms*. Atlanta: John Knox Press, 1981.

_____. *The Living Psalms*. Trans. by J.R. Porter. Grand Rapids: Eerdmans, 1984.

Zenger, Erich. *A God of Vengeance? Understanding the Psalms of Divine Wrath*. Trans. by Linda M. Maloney. Louisville, KY: Westminster John Knox Press, 1996.

BOOK ONE: PSALMS 1–41

PART ONE: THE BELIEVER'S LIFE (PSALMS 1–15)

I. INTRODUCTORY PSALMS (1:1–2:12)

A. WISDOM AND FOLLY (1:1-6)

The first Psalm, a suitable introduction to the book, might properly be designated *The Two Ways*. It contrasts two opposite directions that one's life may take, the one leading to blessing, the other to despair and ruin. The phraseology and style of this psalm resemble that of Proverbs. (See, for example, Prov 2:20-22; 3:12-17.) Thus, it is of the nature of the wisdom literature of the OT. It is didactic rather than lyric, designed for giving instruction rather than for singing.[1]

It is in view of this nature that we choose for its title Wisdom and Folly, desiring thus to indicate the sharp distinction between the two ways that are contrasted. Such distinction was surely in the mind of the psalmist, and although he does not use the words *wise*

---

[1]It is difficult to hold that these were composed for ritualistic use, a fact that confronted Mowinckel with a problem relative to his view of the cultic origin of Psalms. Erhard Gerstenberger has observed: "The influence of the 'sages' on some of the extant psalms cannot possibly be overlooked . . . and since 'wisdom' in Old Testament scholarly terminology is tantamount to acultic or even anticultic attitudes, form critics really are in trouble" ("Psalms," in *Old Testament Form Criticism*, ed. John H. Hayes [San Antonio: Trinity University Press, 1974], p. 218). L.G. Perdue maintains that the wisdom writers of the OT were *not* anticultic (*Wisdom and Cult, A Critical Analysis of the Views of Cult in the Wisdom Literature of Israel and the Ancient Near East* [Missoula: Scholars' Press, 1977]). Mowinckel treats the problem in "Psalms and Wisdom," *VT Supplement III* (Leiden: E.J. Brill, 1955): 204-224.

or *wisdom*, it would appear that, without being stated, his purpose was to show the reader the wisdom of walking in the ways of God and the folly of ungodliness. The psalm is brief, consisting of only some 65 words in Hebrew, and to the point. The challenge it gives is unexpressed, yet alarmingly simple — "Why be a fool!" So this short introduction to the book would impress the reader of the Psalms with the seriousness of his undertaking. More than this, it would press him for a decision relative to the way of life he would choose to pursue.

The meter of Psalm 1 has been recognized by some scholars as "uncertain." Consequently, attempts have been made to recast it on the basis of certain emendations of the text. But let us be reminded of the observation made earlier that the line between poetry and prose in Hebrew is not always sharply delineated. In regard to Psalm 1, Sebastian Burrough makes a strong case for its recognition as prosaic rather than poetic. He states: "Most writers agree that Psalm 1 is a kind of introduction . . . prefixed to the Psalter, instead of what I am convinced it is, namely a half page of prose providing an edifying preface to the ensuing collection."[2] The need for emendation in the direction of a more balanced meter would appear to be, consequently, unnecessary.

1. The Wise Man (1:1-3)

Righteous or wicked, godly or ungodly, wise or foolish — whichever terms are used, the contrast in the psalm is well defined. In the OT Scriptures if one is not godly, he is not wise, for there wisdom and godliness are inseparable. This wisdom directs one in the ways of God and is to be distinguished from mere knowledge, such as an encyclopedic accumulation of facts. In the Hebrew, the term wise has the meaning of "skillful" or even "practical." And nothing is more practical or more wise than to live in accordance with God's directives for life. Consequently, "The fear of the LORD is the beginning of wisdom" (Prov 9:10). One who does not have a

---

[2]Sebastian Burrough, "The Question of Metre in Psalm 1," *VT* XVII (Leiden: E.J. Brill, 1967): 46.

reverence for God that leads him to pursue righteousness, a way free from wrong, is not wise, no matter how much knowledge he may possess. Many otherwise intelligent persons do not have the sense to be decent. The very word "righteous" in our language, is from the Middle English *rightwyss* (right + wise), which means "wise way, manner."[3] True wisdom leads one to do what is *right* in the *sight of God* and to refrain from evil. The psalmist commends this kind of life indicating what it avoids, what it delights in, and what it is like.

1:1 The commendation is expressed in the opening words, **blessed is the man**. The term "blessed" does not imply that God has bestowed some particular favor; a different Hebrew term is used to indicate that. Rather, it means that the person has so conducted himself that a condition of blessedness has resulted. "Oh, the happiness *that man* experiences," the psalmist is saying. And it is a happiness that is very definitely related to conduct. The good life is attractive and brings real, not superficial, happiness.

The source of this happiness is twofold. First, it lies in the avoidance of all of the ways of the wicked. There are some things that a righteous man, a wise man, will not do. (He) **does not walk in the counsel of the wicked**, refusing to adopt their hedonistic philosophy or to be taken in by their devious casuistry.

The wicked are the godless. Isaiah says that they "are like the tossing sea, which cannot rest, whose waves cast up mire and mud," adding, "'there is no peace,' says my God, 'for the wicked'" (Isa 57:20-21). **Or stand in the way of sinners.** Note the progression — "walks, stands, sits." That is the nature of involvement in sin. One begins by tuning in on evil counsel. He next ventures an occasional indulgence, in the presence of bad company, even if it means a violation of his conscience. Then, before he realizes it, his life is cast in the new mold; and the change has been so complete that he has become one of that circle who take delight in sneering at goodness and ridiculing religion. The righteous man habitually shunned all of this. The verbs, in the Hebrew, are *perfect* (completed action), indicating with the negatives what, all the while, he has never done, i.e., "who has never walked."

---

[3] *The Oxford English Dictionary* (Oxford: Clarendon Press, 1933).

1:2 The state of blessedness or happiness in life finds its source more in what a person does than in what he refrains from doing. The wise man refuses to walk in the way of evil, not because he is bound by an oversensitive conscience but because he has chosen to walk a better way. When it is a matter of choice between the counsel of the wicked and the way of the Lord, for him it is no contest. He chooses the latter. To him **the law of the LORD** is not a burden to be borne, nor even an obligation to be met, but a **delight** to be enjoyed.[4] It is a gift from the Creator of life providing instruction on how best to live in such a way as to find fullness of life and, consequently, happiness. In a word, happiness is not found by searching for it, not an achievement of the will; happiness is doing what is right. And God has revealed what right is. Any of us who ignores God's direction does so at great peril, for the law of the Lord alone gives meaning and direction to human existence. To abandon the Scriptures is to be left adrift on the sea of life without chart or compass.

On his law he meditates. The purpose of such concern for God's law is indicated in Josh 1:8 – "that you may be careful to do everything written in it." The delight lies in doing the will of God, not just in knowing it. Thus Jesus would say: "Blessed rather are [Oh, the happiness to them!] those who hear the word of God and obey it" (Luke 11:28).

1:3 To indicate what it is like to walk in the way of God, the psalmist uses the figure of a luxurious tree **planted by streams of water**.[5] The tree, thus situated, is enabled to do what is natural to it; **which yields its fruit in season**. Just so, vitality and fruitfulness are characteristics of the life of righteousness, not as a reward or enticement, but as a natural consequence of such a life. In bearing fruit, the tree is fulfilling the purpose for which it was created. The

---

[4]Words describing God's law, its beauty and desirability, may be found in Psalms 19:7-11 and 119:1-176.

[5]The similarity of verse 3 to Jer 17:5-8 is readily seen. Some say that the psalmist was dependent upon Jeremiah, but it is just as possible that Jeremiah was quoting from the psalm. Indeed, the figure of a tree by a stream of water as indicative of prosperity was so common in the semiarid lands of the Middle East that it is gratuitous to say that either was borrowing the idea from the other.

man of wisdom is doing the same, finding his purpose in life and life's fulfillment in doing the will of God.

Whatever he does prospers. This statement appears to be a categorical assertion to the effect that the righteous man will never experience any reverses. However, human experience says the contrary (consider Job, for example), and elsewhere the Psalms deal with the suffering of the righteous. Dahood proposes an alternate translation: "Whatever it (the tree) produces is good."[6] On the basis of the Hebrew text, this is possible. Charles A. Briggs and others translate: "So all that he doeth, he carries through successfully"[7] — or to a successful outcome — meaning that whatever he does will result in good. A righteous man, like a good tree, will bear good fruit. God's law of the harvest is immutable.

2. The Foolish Man (1:4-5)

1:4 The opposite is true of the ungodly man. Verse 4, in the Hebrew, opens with a negative, expressing a strong antithesis to what has gone before: **Not, so, the wicked!**

What the righteous man is *not*, the wicked is. The latter does walk in ungodly ways; he does stand with sinners, and he takes his place among scoffers. And what the righteous man is, the other is not. He is not blessed with that happiness that comes from God; he has not discovered the *delight* of walking in God's way, and he is not firmly *planted*, not flourishing, not fruitful. Instead, he is like **chaff** which is without appreciable substance and useless, destined to be swept away by any passing breeze. Man's life, apart from God, is without significance or genuine worth, and is utterly futile.

1:5 The psalmist was not unaware that at times the wicked may prosper (Ps 73:3-12); yet even so, they occupy "slippery ground" (73:18). **The wicked will not stand in the judgment.** The translation would appear to indicate a particular judgment, such as the final great judgment day when "each of us will give an account of himself to God" (Rom 14:12). But the definite article in our text

---

[6]Dahood, *Psalms 1–50*, p. 4.
[7]Briggs, *Commentary*, p. 6.

was supplied by the Massoretes and the consonantal text could equally be read "judgment," without the article. It would appear certain, on the basis of verse 6, that a judgment of God is indicated, not that of a human tribunal. Yet A.F. Kirkpatrick is probably right when he states that it is not "merely in the last judgment . . . but in every act of judgment by which Jehovah [Yahweh] separates between the righteous and the wicked."[8] Anthony L. Ash concurs in this general view when he says: "It is best to take the words here in the overall sense of a life which cannot stand God's inspection."[9]

So, those who take their stand with **sinners** will not stand in the judgment; those who sit with mockers will have no place **in the assembly** of the people of God. These words of the psalmist are not the pronouncement of a bigot but of an evangelist. He is appealing for a verdict, pressing for a decision, challenging to commitment.

3. The Crucial Difference (1:6)

1:6 Why does the righteous man experience a special blessedness? **For the LORD watches over the way of the righteous.** This means, not merely that God is acquainted with that way, but that he is involved in it, watching over it and caring for it. It is the way designed by a loving God whereby humankind might experience what life is all about. It is the way of fruitfulness, for a righteous life is never barren. It is in this way alone that one may find fullness and completeness. Surely all who walk in it are wise.

And why is it folly to reject God's way? Because **the way of the wicked will perish**. This is not a hostile pronouncement of judgment. It is an anguished cry. Only too well the psalmist recognizes that "there is a way that seems right to a man, but in the end it leads to death" (Prov 14:12).

The first word of Psalm 1 is "blessed," describing the condition of one who walks in God's way. The last word is "perish" and refers to the end of those who reject the way of God. These two words, the first and the last, encompass all that is in between. Thus the psalm

---

[8]Kirkpatrick, *The Book of Psalms*, 1:4.
[9]Ash and Miller, *Psalms*, p. 35.

is ended. The righteous will lay it to heart. Regrettably, the foolish, unless they turn from their folly, will go on with their mocking.

B. HOPELESSNESS OR HAPPINESS (2:1-12)

The contrast between wisdom and folly introduced in the first Psalm is reflected also in the second, with this difference. There the distinction was between the ungodly man and the godly. Here, although the same distinction could be made, the contrast is between those who "rage against God" and those who "put their trust in him." Again, the contrast is sharply drawn, depicting the hopelessness of the "ragers" and the blessedness of the "trusters." There is the further difference between the two Psalms: in the first the focus is upon one's attitude to God's *torah* (God's instruction). Here the crucial test is one's attitude towards God's Messiah.

Psalm 2 is classified as a royal psalm, with its setting in Jerusalem. A king is being crowned, and subject nations in rebellion seize the moment as an opportunity to revolt. Buttenwieser does not consider the psalm to be a portrayal of a real situation. Instead, he believes it to be a visionary scene of revolt against God and his anointed one. This position is necessitated by his view that the psalm is postexilic, written at a time when there were no kings in Israel, and therefore indicating a future idealized ruler *whom God would* raise up.[10] Gunkel, on the other hand, with many others, holds that Psalm 2 does indeed belong to the royal period of Israel's history.[11] Kirkpatrick suggests that the king is Solomon.[12] David had extended his kingdom from the borders of Egypt and the Gulf of Aqabah to the Euphrates river in Mesopotamia. While David was yet living, Solomon was anointed king at the spring Gihon, from which he ascended the hill of Zion to occupy the throne (1 Kgs 1:38-48). However, the setting of the psalm cannot be definitely determined.

---

[10]Moses Buttenwieser, *The Psalms Chronologically Treated, with a New Translation* (New York: KTAV, 1969), p. 792.

[11]Gunkel, *The Psalms*, p. 23.

[12]Kirkpatrick, *The Book of Psalms*, 1:5.

From earliest Christian times the messianic implications of Psalm 2 have been recognized. Some would say that it was intentionally or directly messianic, with no reference to any revolt or to any king of the time when it was written. It seems more likely, however, that a situation within the experience of the psalmist is depicted. Nevertheless, five times this psalm is quoted in the NT with reference to Christ, and the application fits so perfectly that we may see in the psalm a foreshadowing — a prophecy, if you will — of Messiah Jesus. The psalm may be set at a definite point of time in history, yet with content anticipatory of Jesus. More than this, we may see its focus yet in the future, beyond history, upon the time of the ultimate and final triumph of the Messiah. In a very real sense, the psalm is applicable to any occasion of *rebellion* against the Lord.

1. The Nations Are Rebellious (2:1-3)

2:1 The psalm begins with a question — **why?** Why, indeed, should any **conspire** against God? Consider the folly of it. The kings of the earth would utterly destroy Israel, if they could. But God had made a promise to this people (Gen 12:2-3). In his plan, there was a destiny they must fulfill. With whatever fury men mount their rebellion against the Lord, within a few decades, at most, they pass out of the picture, and the purposes of God go on toward their realization! What folly it is for a people to set themselves in opposition to God's design. "Nations are in uproar, kingdoms fall; he lifts his voice, the earth melts" (Ps 46:6). The futility of rebellion against God should be obvious.

The rebellious are the *goyim*, a term usually signifying non-Israelite peoples, hence the translation "heathen," otherwise "nations." They *rage* (KJV), they *conspire* (RSV), they *make a tumult* (Berkeley Version). Jude describes such persons as "wild waves of the sea, foaming up their shame" (Jude 13a). In Psalm 1 the godly man *meditated* on the will of God. Here the same verb (translated **plot**) describes the activity of the rebellious nations. However, they *meditate* evil. It is important that beings with intelligence should think. But what we think about is also important, whether it be the things of God or the alternative, *vain things* (the ultimate futility), whether we meditate upon good or evil. Here a word from the

Apostle Paul is appropriate: "[W]hatever is true, whatever is noble, whatever is right, whatever is pure, whatever is lovely, whatever is admirable, — if anything is excellent, or praiseworthy, — think about such things" (Phil 4:8).

2:2 The kings . . . take their stand . . . against the LORD. To reject the Lord's anointed king was to reject God himself. The Psalmist (David, according to Acts 4:25) would understand the expression **his Anointed One** (as in 1 Sam 26:11) to refer to the human king whom God had chosen to maintain justice in the land. Yet here is also a foreshadowing of the Messiah who was to come; that is, Jesus. To reject him is to reject the God who sent him (cf. Matt 10:40; John 12:48).

2:3 God asks of his king a reign of righteousness and he calls all peoples to be loyal to such a reign. Yet how quick some are to cast off any restraint put upon them by God. **Let us break their chains, . . . and throw off their fetters.** The verbs are cohortative, indicating, in this case, "a more or less emphatic statement of a fixed determination . . . . *Come! let us break asunder.*"[13] The paraphrase of J.A. Alexander is illuminating: "Let us fling away from us with scorn these feeble bands by which we have been hitherto confined."[14] There are many who would thus casually free themselves from any restraints God would impose, not realizing that the cords with which he would bind us are cords of love (see Hos 11:4). To free ourselves from God's restraints is to subject ourselves to a bondage from which there is no escape!

The revolt depicted in Psalm 2 finds application in Acts 4:24-28 to Herod, Pilate, the Gentiles, and the people of Israel in their conspiracy against God and his Messiah, Jesus. The rulers supposed that by crucifying Jesus and by persecuting the witnesses of the resurrection even to death, they would overthrow the kingdom of God. But of course those who engaged in such unbridled acts of rage did so in vain. So it is always with those who rage against the Lord.

---

[13]William Gesenius, *Hebrew Grammar*, 28th ed., trans. A.E. Cowley, ed. E. Kautzsch (Oxford: Clarendon Press, 1910-1966), p. 320.

[14]J.A. Alexander, *The Psalms Translated and Explained* (New York: Charles Scribner, 1863), 1:10.

2. The Lord Is Undisturbed (2:4-6)

2:4 We may be thankful that God has a sense of humor. Martin Luther wrote: "If I were as our Lord God, and had committed the government to my son, as He to His Son, and these vile people were as disobedient as now they be, I would knock the world in pieces."[15] But what does God do? **The One enthroned in heaven laughs!** G. Campbell Morgan emphasizes that this laughter of God is "derision . . . contempt for those who in foolish pride of heart oppose themselves to him."[16] Perhaps a note of contempt is involved, but it would seem, also to be the laughter of amusement.

The laughter of God would have seemed ironic to the great empires of the ancient world. The rulers of Assyria, Egypt, and later of Babylonia, would have laughed at little Israel. But Israel, though a small people, had the promise of God, existed as the covenant people of God, and would become the instrument of God, through whom Messiah would come. There was a divine purpose invested in this people, and any attempt by even the most powerful of the earth to thwart that purpose could only give rise to divine amusement and, towards the unrepentant, to divine wrath.

2:5 God abounds in love and is slow to anger (Exod 34:6), yet the time comes when he will call the rebellious to account. There is a limit to his patience. **Then he rebukes them in his anger and terrifies them in his wrath**. H.C. Leupold notes the general vagueness of the term "then," and its ominous import — "you can never tell when His anger will flash forth."[17] But let us be assured that in the fullness of time the wrath of God will be poured out upon evil. Jonathan Edwards (1703–1758) is known for his famous sermon, "Sinners in the Hands of an Angry God." Perhaps we hear little such preaching today, yet the theme is neglected at our peril. God is "not wanting anyone to perish, but everyone to come to repentance" (2 Pet 3:9b). Yet we are duly warned that only divine anger

---

[15]Quoted by Rowland E. Prothero in *The Psalms in Human Life* (London: John Murray, 1905), p. 123.

[16]G. Campbell Morgan, *Searchlights from the Word* (Westwood, NJ: Revell, reprint of 1952), p. 153.

[17]Leupold, *Exposition*, p. 48.

and judgment remain for "those who do not know God and do not obey the gospel of our Lord Jesus" (2 Thess 1:8).

2:6 Nations and people plot in vain against God. "You are at liberty to do so," God would say, "but I . . ." — and the **I** is emphatic (v. 6). He sets his king on his throne on the **hill of Zion** (Jerusalem). If this psalm is part of a coronation ceremony in its original context, the king may have been Solomon, as Kirkpatrick suggested. In terms of the Psalm's messianic use in the NT we see Jesus who, in spite of the opposition of humankind, has been enthroned over the everlasting kingdom of God and sits at the Father's right hand (Col 3:1).

3. The Son Is Enthroned (2:7-9)

2:7 In this verse the chosen one quotes **the decree of** Yahweh — perhaps a reference to 2 Sam 7:11-16, which records God's promise to David. **You are my Son; today I have become your Father.** In the ancient code of Hammurabi words such as these were part of an adoption ceremony. They are relevant to the relationship between Solomon and the Lord, for God had said to David: "I will be his father [Solomon's], and he will be my son" (2 Sam 7:14).[18] If these words are part of a coronation liturgy, then it is said that their recital indicates God's adoption and acknowledgment of the new king as the legitimate ruler of his people. This day would indicate the day of the inauguration. Other elements of the ceremony are said to be the anointing, the promise of victory over enemies, the promise of the continuance of the kingdom of David forever (Ps 89:29), and a plea that God endow the king with righteousness (Ps 72:1). In the NT, the words of verse 7 are recognized in their application to Jesus (Acts 13:33), "today" being a reference to his resurrection as the day of his inauguration (Acts 13:32).

2:8 Great expectations arose whenever a new king came to the throne of David, such as expressed in **I will make the nations your**

---

[18]Elsewhere God calls Israel "my son" (Exod 4:22; Hos 11:1). And in Ps 89:27, it is said of David (with messianic implications): "I will also appoint him my firstborn, the most exalted of the kings of the earth."

inheritance (the *goyim*, the *ethnoi*) and **the ends of the earth your possession.** These expectations were never realized by any king in Jerusalem. Their fulfillment had to await the coming of the only begotten Son of God, whose kingdom would indeed become world-wide in its scope. In the ancient inaugural, however it was not unnatural to use hyperbolic language, just as Daniel might say to Darius, "O king, live forever" (Dan 6:21).

2:9 You will rule them with an iron scepter. In the inaugural ceremony, it is said, these words would be uttered as the scepter was presented to the king. At the same time, foreign kings would offer acts of homage. The verb "rule," in the Hebrew, may also mean "shepherd" (them) [i.e., a king's rule was like that of a shepherd over his sheep, to rule was to shepherd], as it is translated in the LXX (ποιμανεῖς, *poimaneis*) and quoted in Rev 2:27; 12:5; and 19:15 (NIV translates it "rule"). And the rod may signify the shepherd's rod, as in Lev 27:32. The parallelism of verse 9 would then be antithetic: "[Some] you will rule/shepherd . . . ; [others] you will dash . . . to pieces." However, until verse 12 this psalm is dealing exclusively with rebellious nations and kings. The KJV rendering for the word "rule" is "break" (them) [representing a different vocalization of the Hebrew word תרעם]. "Break them" is a better parallel with **dash them** in verse 9. Therefore, the KJV translation "break them" is preferred here.[19]

4. The Ones Who Trust Are Blessed (2:10-12)

2:10-11a The theme of wisdom, evident in Psalm 1, is definitely expressed in Psalm 2, with a reference to that wisdom that will lead

---

[19]The quotations in Revelation are, as noted, from the LXX of about 200 B.C. and have "rule" instead of "break." The Greek version would be the one with which John's readers would be familiar. And although it differs from the original Hebrew text, it is equally true as a description of the activity of the Messiah and John would have no hesitancy in using it. [editor: On the other hand, the Hebrew may have been accurately translated as "rule/shepherd" by the LXX and maintained in the Revelation paraphrases. Only the vocalization would change between "break" (תְּרֹעֵם from רעע) and "rule" (תִּרְעֵם from רעה) as translations.] See also a masterful exposition on Psalm 2 by James L. Mays, *The Lord Reigns: A Theological Handbook to the Psalms* (Louisville: Westminster John Knox Press, 1994),

its possessor to serve God; this, in sharp contrast to the folly of rebellion against him. **[B]e wise; be warned**. No matter how intellectual one may be, if he refuses warning (as instruction), if he is no longer teachable, he is no longer wise. **Serve the LORD [Yahweh] with fear**, since it is he who holds the ultimate fate of kings and nations in his hands.

2:11b-12 Rejoice with trembling. This seems an odd combination of terms, although it is conceivable that one might rejoice before the Lord even while trembling in reverential awe. From ancient times, translators have wrestled with how best to render the text of verses 11 and 12. Crucial to the understanding of the passage is the true significance of the term rendered "Son" in the NIV and some other versions, that term being בַּר (*bar*). In Aramaic it does mean "son" and when so translated yields **Kiss the Son**. But in Hebrew the term means "pure" (Ps 19:8; 24:4; 73:1) or "an open field," "a plain" (Job 39:3, RSV). On the basis of these meanings for the Hebrew, instead of "Kiss the Son," the following have been proposed.

"Worship purely" (Jerome), "kiss sincerely" (Briggs, with reference to kissing the hand in honor of a deity, as in Job 31:17), "do homage truly" (Moffatt), "do homage (in) purity" (Soncino, with reference to the king), and "kiss the ground" (Ringgren). Adherence to the Hebrew text, as it is, would require some such reading. Still retaining the Hebrew, but separating the letters into different words, Dahood proposes: "O men of the grave" or "mortal men," attaching the words to the preceding verse: "Live in trembling, O mortal men!"[20] William L. Holladay follows Dahood, except that he recognizes a participle, "forgetting," instead of the construct noun,

---

pp. 108-116. With reference to verse 9 Mays wrote: "Read literally, those two lines seem cruel and pointless. They smack of an insane tyranny that possesses only to destroy. But in its original sphere of use, these words were not meant in that way at all. Behind them is a ritual, known particularly from the ceremonies of Egypt as part of the procedures of installing a king. The names of the nations over which he claimed sovereignty would be written on clay tablets, and in a symbolic ritual the king would smash these tablets with his scepter. Translated, this dramatic ritual language simply means, 'You shall claim and rule them with a power they cannot resist'" (p. 111).

[20]Dahood, *Psalms 1-50*, pp. 13f.

"men" (the terms are similar in Hebrew) with the result: "Ones forgetting the grave,"[21] that is, forgetting their mortal nature. A slight change of the Hebrew *bar* would allow the root meaning "choose" with "Kiss the chosen one" (Goodspeed) as a possibility. Beyond this, definite emendation of the text, involving a relocation of terms, is necessary to secure the reading, "Serve the Lord with fear, with trembling kiss his feet" as in the Revised Standard Version and others.

Those who declare, *ipso facto*, that the Aramaic *bar* (son) must be rejected, of necessity must rely on such proposals as the above. In view of the fact that the Hebrew word for son (*ben*) appears in verse 7, the question naturally arises, why would the writer substitute the Aramaic word in verse 12? Why indeed? Two reasons have been suggested. One, it is for the sake of euphony; the following Hebrew term is *pen* "lest," and so *bar pen* is substituted for *ben pen*. Again, and with more feasibility, it is suggested that since the admonition of verses 10-13 is addressed to foreign kings, the foreign term is appropriate. A Phoenician inscription with such usage of the Aramaic *bar* lends credence to the argument. It is even possible that *bar* came to have significance as a title, equivalent to a name. The New English Bible reflects such a possibility in its translation, "Kiss the mighty one." In the ancient world, homage was shown to rulers by kissing their feet.

Reviewing the proposed translations, it will be noted that, in some, verse 12 is interpreted as relating to God: "Serve the Lord with fear . . . kiss his feet," "worship purely," etc. The phrase **lest he be angry** points in this direction, judging that elsewhere in the OT where the expression occurs, the reference is always to God. (Even so, God could be angry if one refused to kiss the Son.) So the verse is also interpreted as having reference to the Son: "Kiss the chosen one," "Kiss the mighty one." Since the earlier verses of the psalm include both the Lord and his anointed, it would seem that the Lord (v. 11) and the Son (v. 12) would be an appropriate parallel here, the Lord being equally angry whether the nations rejected

---

[21]William L. Holladay, "A New Proposal for the Crux in Psalm 2:12," *VT* 28 (1978): 110-112. Holladay states flatly that "'Kiss the son' is clearly impossible."

him or his anointed. It would be the part of wisdom to honor the divinely appointed king lest God is the one who becomes angry, or the Son, or both.

The psalm closes on a positive note. Although some may engage in the attempt to thwart the purposes of God, others find life and happiness in what is to them the privilege of serving him. The rebellious are urged to pursue the course of wisdom. Their rebellion can only lead to ruin, but **blessed are all who take refuge in him.**

II. LIVING CONFIDENTLY (3:1–7:17)

A. TROUBLED BUT UNAFRAID (3:1-8)

Psalm 3 has been classified as an individual lament. Many have considered it to be a morning prayer. The title, "A Psalm" (*Mizmor*) provided by the ancients, together with three appearances of the term *selah*, indicates that it was designed to be recited, or sung, to musical accompaniment. On the part of numerous scholars, the psalm is believed to have been written for, or adapted to, liturgical use by a congregation of worshipers. Buttenwieser considers the "I" of the psalm to be a personification of general distress in the land, without reference to the personal suffering of the writer.[22] This, if true, would put the psalm in the class of communal lament. However, the content seems to reflect rather a personal experience.

The historical reference to David in the superscription is dismissed by many as without validity. As we have observed, the superscriptions do represent later additions to the text. In the present instance, the following comparisons have been suggested as indicative of a relationship to the event in the life of David that is indicated. His enemies are many (v. 1); compare "The hearts of the men of Israel are with Absalom" (2 Sam 15:13). His enemies said, "God will not deliver him" (v. 2) — "The LORD has handed the kingdom over to your son Absalom" (2 Sam 16:8). David ascended the Mount of Olives with his head covered (2 Sam 15:30) — "But you . . . O LORD . . . lift up my head" (v. 3). Absalom had a multitude of

---

[22]Buttenwieser, *The Psalms*, p. 397.

followers (2 Sam 17:11) — "I will not fear the tens of thousands drawn up against me on every side" (v. 6).

Those who question the validity of the superscription see no parallel between the situation depicted in the psalm and that in which David found himself when Absalom rebelled. It is observed that David had subjugated one foe after another, until, by the time of Absalom, his enemies had been practically eliminated. Further, the David depicted in the Books of Samuel, although confident of God's leading, relied upon military power and strategems for victory. Again, it is objected that the religious tone of the psalm reflects the attitude prevailing years after the time of David, even after the preexilic prophets. In the preexilic period, it is said, there would have been more concern for turning the people back to God as a condition for receiving his forgiveness and deliverance. Buttenwieser, following this line of reasoning, would date the psalm in the late postexilic period.[23] Many, however, without reference to the superscription, believe the psalm to be preexilic. In actuality, the religious and historical data are of such limited extent as to preclude an exact determination of the setting on this basis alone.

Whether it was David, or some other, the author of Psalm 3 was undoubtedly a man of great faith. At a time when enemies were multiplying against him (v. 1) and ridiculing his reliance upon God (v. 2), he would reaffirm his faith (v. 3) and recall the times God had responded to his prayers (v. 4). He would sleep peacefully (v. 5) and put away fear (v. 6). He would call on the Lord for deliverance (v. 7), from whom alone salvation would come (v. 8). He was troubled but not dismayed.

The focus of the Psalm is upon the help that one may receive from God in times of distress. The Hebrew concept of *salvation, deliverance, victory* (from the Hebrew יָשַׁע *yāša‘*) is dominant in this short poem. One form of the word appears in verse 2: "God will not *deliver* him." Again, in verse 7: "*Deliver* me, O my God!" And in verse 8: "From the LORD comes *deliverance*." In these cases, as primarily throughout the OT, "salvation" is not a theological term. The reference is to deliverance from dangers, from enemies, sometimes from sickness, famine, or even from death. Various forms of

---

[23]Ibid., p. 400f.

the root word appear 353 times in the OT. The one who brings deliverance is called "deliverer" or "savior." This may be a person — Moses, for example (Exod 2:17) — but often the deliverer is God. That is the case in Psalm 3.

1. The Distressing Situation (3:1-2)

3:1-2 Characteristic of psalms of lament is the voicing of a complaint, a statement of the cause of distress. Here, such words open the Psalm. **O LORD, how many are my foes!** In verse 7 these foes are identified as enemies of God, also the wicked. They **rise up against me**. The words suggest the possibility of revolt, or rebellion. The number of the enemies is overwhelming — "the tens of thousands" (v. 6). Is it not said that troubles often come in droves? **Many are saying of me** — "me," in Hebrew is "my *nefesh*, here meaning *the person*."[24] The KJV renders it literally "my soul." *Nonexistent is any help for him from God.* This is the order of the Hebrew words. Not content with revolt, the enemies would make this verbal attack, decrying the faith of the psalmist. It would be a great victory for them if they could instill in him the fear that God had abandoned him. Even Jesus was thus confronted when he cried out: "My God, my God, why have you forsaken me?" (Matt 27:46). (But he was not forsaken. The trying hour was not taken away, but through faithfulness he was able to face it and through the resurrection to triumph over it. Nevertheless, we note that times of distress do come, even to those who walk by faith in God.)

Selah (v. 2b). This term has been discussed in the introduction. However, a comment from Charles H. Spurgeon adds interest:

> This is a musical pause, the precise meaning of which is not known. . . . At least, we may learn that wherever we see "Selah," we should look upon it as a note of observation. Let us read the passage which precedes and succeeds it with greater earnestness, for surely there is always something excellent where we are required to rest and pause and meditate, or

---

[24]For a consideration of the Hebrew term נֶפֶשׁ (*nepheš*), see the discussion of Ps 6:3,4.

when we are required to lift up our hearts in grateful song. "Selah." [25]

2. Confidence in God (3:3-4)

3:3 "God has forsaken you," the enemies charged. "I know otherwise," the psalmist replies. And he addresses his words to God in a strong affirmation of faith. **But you are a shield around me, O LORD.** This is his answer to his accusers. They might deny the reality of help from God, but he had experienced it. They might address him with contempt, but God was his **glory.** To know such a God is true glory or boasting, lasting honor, not to be compared to any honor the world might offer. And although the world might call him wretched, even the least child of God has a glory and an immeasurable honor that cannot be taken from him.

You . . . lift up my head. "Shield" and "glory" are nouns. The participle is used here, "the (one) lifting up." It may indicate imminent action, anticipated as just about to begin. Just what that action would be we cannot determine, but the metaphor of lifting up the head likely points to the defense of his honor.

3:4 To the LORD I cry aloud. The verbs in verse 4 should not be translated in the past tense, unless it be, "As often as I cried, he heard." It is better to translate with Buttenwieser: "When I cry . . . he will answer."[26] Or with Dahood: "If with full voice I call . . . he answers."[27] "I cry aloud." Naturally so! Hebrew has few adverbs and so here uses the noun "with my voice" (see KJV) adverbially, meaning "loudly." This is no silent meditation! **And he answers me from his holy hill.** This would be Zion, where David had erected a tabernacle and enshrined the ark of the Lord (2 Sam 6:17). As the "dwelling place" of God with his people, it was especially holy. Verses 3 and 4 constitute the psalmist's answer to the jibes of his

[25]Charles H. Spurgeon, *The Treasury of David* (McLean, VA: MacDonald, reprint n.d.), 1:23.

[26]Buttenwieser, *The Psalms*, p. 396.

[27]Dahood, *Psalms 1-50*, p. 15. For a discussion of the tenses appearing in Hebrew poetry, see Craigie, *Psalms 1-50*, pp. 110-113.

enemies. He had not been untouched by trouble in the past, but always he had found help from God.

3. Peace amid Turmoil (3:5-6)

3:5-6 It is on the basis of verse 5 that the psalm has been called a morning prayer. It is suggested that **I lie down and sleep**, etc., describes the night just past. However, it may be better to consider the verb perfect to indicate established practice. The *I* is emphatic. "*You* may set yourself against me, but *as for me*, I will sleep peacefully, knowing that I can trust God to watch over me." He was not unaware of the problems that confronted him, but he had a greater awareness of the watchful care of God: **the LORD sustains me**. The verb is durative; he "goes on sustaining me." His was a courage, not based upon any exaggerated opinion of his own powers but on God. Consequently, he could say, **I will not fear**. Such a statement of confidence is characteristic of the psalms of lament. And always there will be a petition to the Lord for his help.

4. Prayer for Deliverance (3:7-8)

3:7 Such a petition is found in verses 7 and 8. The translation of verse 7 has occasioned difficulty for expositors. **Deliver me, O my God! Strike all my enemies on the jaw**, is a bit incongruous from the lips of David in flight from Absalom. Some have suggested that David added these words after his victory. J.B. Rotherham, on the other hand, proposed that the original Davidic psalm may have been used by King Hezekiah, who adapted it, with these words, after God had smitten the hosts of Sennacherib in 701 B.C. (2 Kgs 19:35).[28] This is an interesting proposal, because of its aptness and also because it suggests that what God had inspired on the part of David could be supplemented by words from a second inspired writer (as in 1 Sam 9:9). All of this, of course, remains in the realm of conjecture.

---

[28]Rotherham, *Studies*, 1:74f.

Crucial to the understanding of verse 7 is the significance of the Hebrew term כִּי (*kî*), followed by verbs in the perfect tense ("strike," "break!"). As a conjunction, *kî* means "for," or "because." As we have noted, however, to say, "Deliver me, *because* you have struck all my enemies" is a bit strange. Dahood sees *kî* as an emphatic particle, "O that," and the verbs as *precative perfect*, not stating a fact but expressing a wish or entreaty.[29] This is quite likely, since the perfect verbs are conditioned by the first verb, "Deliver me," which is imperative. Thus we have, "O that you would smite, etc." The NIV simply translates these verbs as imperatives (*Strike* and *break!*) without indicating the Hebrew word *kî*.

Strike . . . on the jaw; break the teeth, so that they may no longer speak vicious things about me nor tear me to pieces — treat them like the vicious animals they are. The language obviously is metaphorical (as in Job 29:16,17). Note that the psalmist is committing the judgment of his enemies into the hand of God.

3:8 This verse is shortened, deliberately it would seem, for emphasis and dramatic effect. And here the mood changes from that of petition to one of thanksgiving: Deliverance (victory, salvation) belongs to the LORD [Yahweh]. The Hebrew is definite: to Yahweh alone is "salvation." Thus the psalm would end on a note of confidence, but not without a benediction: **May your blessing be on your people.** In the first seven verses, the psalm is very personal. Here the broader concern for the whole people is said to be an indication that it was also used in the congregational worship. The personal experience of the psalmist has become a source of encouragement to all.

B. CONFIDENCE AT EVENING (4:1-8)

Traditionally, Psalm 4 has been recognized as an evening prayer, a companion to the morning prayer of Psalm 3. Similarities to Psalm 3, in language, structure, and spirit, have been indicated

---

[29]Dahood, *Psalms 1–50*, p. 19. For an excellent discussion of the precative perfect, see Buttenwieser, *The Psalms*, pp. 21-25. Gesenius did not acknowledge a precative perfect in Hebrew (*Grammar*, p. 312).

COLLEGE PRESS NIV COMMENTARY

by Kirkpatrick, who observes that the two are "clearly the work of
the same author."[30] Kirkpatrick also considers this psalm to be
related to Absalom's rebellion, a sequel to Psalm 3, but its relationship to that event is not readily discernible. Rotherham questions
whether David would address the rebels as great men — "men of
rank" (Dahood, v. 2), or advise them to meditate upon their beds.[31]
The author is, apparently, a man of some station in life (or of some
boldness) since he does not hesitate to speak to the men of rank
with a note of authority.

Some consider Psalm 4 to be a lament of one who has been
falsely accused by his enemies, a cry of distress. However, the identity of the sufferer and the nature of his suffering are not readily
discernible. Buttenwieser, as with Psalm 3, sees Psalm 4 as a communal lament, the prayer of a nation in distress.[32] The use of the
plural "us" in verse 6 and the plural verbs of verses 4 and 5 are said
to be evidence in this direction. That the psalm was used in public
worship seems evident, from the musical notation in the heading,
"with stringed instruments" ("on *Neginoth*" — בִּנְגִינוֹת, *bin°gînôth*),
and the two appearances of *selah*. Rotherham proposed that the
psalm was written by David for a Levite, to be used in evening
worship.[33]

An altogether different setting is advanced by Dahood, who sees
this psalm as a prayer for rain. Carroll Stuhlmueller observes that
the occasion is, perhaps, a time of drought, but does not pursue
the matter.[34] On the other hand, Dahood's entire exegesis is a
development of this theme.[35] Crucial to his understanding is the
identification of the good, in verse 6, with rain, a possibility, in view
of the fact that elsewhere such identification seems to be indicated
(as in Jer 5:25; Ps 85:12). The distress of the psalmist, in this time of
drought, is increased because the national leaders have turned to
idols for help (to "delusions" and "false gods," v. 2). They have
expressed skepticism of receiving any help from the LORD (Yahweh,

---

[30]Kirkpatrick, *The Book of Psalms*, p. 13.
[31]Rotherham, *Studies*, 1:80.
[32]Buttenwieser, *The Psalms*, p. 403.
[33]Rotherham, *Studies*, 1:79f.
[34]Stuhlmueller, *Psalms 1*, p. 62.
[35]Dahood, *Psalms 1–50*, p. 23f.

v. 6). The psalmist, however, is unshaken in his confidence in God. He will utter his prayer and then enjoy peaceful sleep.

Dahood makes a very strong case for his interpretation, although it has not been widely accepted.[36] In any case, it would seem that the time has not yet come when we can say that we have no need for further study of the Hebrew text. Evening prayer? Communal lament? Petition of one falsely accused? David's experience during Absalom's rebellion? A prayer for rain? These various proposals make one conclusion rather obvious — the psalm can fill the need of many souls under many circumstances. But isn't that, after all, the nature of Scripture?

Without attempting further to identify the occasion, we may yet see Psalm 4 as a petition for help from God, by one who is confident, in spite of the skepticism of others, that God will respond.

1. A Cry for Help (4:1)

4:1 The psalm opens with a threefold petition: **Answer (me), be merciful to (me), hear (my prayer)**. The three verbs are imperatives. **Give (me) relief** (i.e., "expand the boundaries that encompass me") may be added as a further request, recognizing the fourth verb as a precative perfect (a completed action of request or entreaty), a distinct possibility. Others, on the basis of a simple perfect, see here a reference to God's past helpfulness — "you have given me relief" — and reason enough to inspire confidence in the present circumstance. "The God of my righteousness," (literally in Hebrew) has rightly been understood in the NIV as "my God of righteousness," and thus translated **my righteous God**. We may trust such a one to deal fairly with the innocent, vindicating him when he is unjustly attacked.

---

[36]W.O.E. Oesterley (*The Psalms*, p. 129), as early as 1939, did set forth an explanation of Psalm 4, somewhat like that of Dahood.

2. A Warning to the Ungodly (4:2-5)

4:2 O men (Hebrew literally, אִישׁ בְּנֵי, *bᵉnê 'îš*, "sons of man-
[kind]"). The term designates men of rank or position. Elsewhere
we find אָדָם בְּנֵי (*bᵉnê 'ādām*, "sons of man[kind]"), indicating the
commoner. (In Ps 49:2 both terms appear, translated as "low and
high.") Who were these men? Absalom's lieutenants, opposed to
David? Israel's leaders, turning from Yahweh to idols in a time of
drought? Foreign kings taunting oppressed Israel? Or personal
enemies of the psalmist, villifying him? Whoever, specifically, were
involved, it was another circumstance in which the ungodly set
themselves against those who sought the way of the Lord.

How long, O men, will you turn my glory into shame? Had these
persons been guilty of slanderous attacks upon the honor and
integrity of the writer? The Revised Standard Version follows this
interpretation: "How long shall my honor suffer shame?" Dahood,
however, here recognizes national leaders with little faith in the
Lord, *insulting God* (not the psalmist) by the pursuit of idolatry.[37]
This view calls for the translation of the Hebrew: "My Glorious One"
instead of "my glory." This rendering was proposed by Cheyne years
ago[38] and is cited as a possibility in a footnote to this verse in the
New International Version.

How long will you love delusions and seek false gods? This
translation is better than the RSV's "vain words" and "lies," referring to verbal attacks upon the integrity of the psalmist. Elsewhere
the terms, "vanity" and "falsehood" (KJV translation) are used as
synonyms for idols and may be translated "delusions," "false gods,"
as the NIV has done. In addition, the verbs "love" (אָהַב, *'āhāb*) and
"seek" (בָּקַשׁ, *bāqāš*) are often used with God (or gods) as the
object.[39] The reprimand seems to be directed against idol worship
and its folly — "How long will you worship vanities or consult
idols?" (Dahood). A similar reproof is found in Jeremiah, directed
against the idolaters of his day, in words that show how utterly irra-

---

[37]Dahood, *Psalms 1–50*, p. 23.
[38]T.K. Cheyne, *The Book of Psalms* (New York: Thomas Whittaker, 1904),
1:11.
[39]See O.R. Sellers, "Seeking God in the Old Testament," *JBR* 21 (Oct.
1953), pp. 234-237.

tional such behavior is: "My people have committed two sins: They have forsaken me, the spring of living water, and have dug their own cisterns, broken cisterns that cannot hold water" (Jer 2:13).

4:3 Know that the LORD has set apart the godly for himself. The psalmist is speaking of himself, as the remainder of the verse indicates. This is no arrogant boast. It is not a claim to sinless perfection. The godly (*ḥasîd*) signifies one who responds to God's lovingkindness (חֶסֶד, *ḥesed*, "covenant love"/"loyalty") with steadfast love on his own part, one who is devoted to God in word and in deed. In Ps 86:2 the *ḥasîd* describes himself as a servant of God. It is such a one as this that God *sets apart* for himself.

4:4 In your anger (do not sin). "Stand in awe," (KJV), "Be angry" (RSV); literally, "tremble" or "shake violently" (רִגְזוּ, *rigzû*). These words are addressed to the men who "love delusions" (v. 2). Actually one word in Hebrew, it is not the usual term to indicate reverence toward God, though it may mean to shake in fear in his presence. It is a physical reaction to deep emotion or distress of any kind. Was this trembling occasioned by drought, and must they guard against the sin of seeking the help of false gods? Are they trembling in their anger against the psalmist, in danger of sinning against him? Or, is theirs a fear of nations hostile to Israel? "Do not sin." The verb is from a root that means to miss the mark or the way, to fail to reach a goal.

4:5 Offer right sacrifices. These would be the sacrifices that had been prescribed for the worship of the Lord in distinction from sacrifices to idols. In Ps 27:6 it is noted that these sacrifices to the Lord are accompanied with joy. Naturally, since they are directed to the *living* God, they would also be accompanied by **trust in the LORD** (Yahweh). The words of the psalmist, up to this point, have been directed to the idols and to idol worshipers.

3. Joy in the LORD (4:6-8)

4:6 Many are asking. Are these many the idol worshipers? If so, they are expressing their skepticism toward Yahweh, when they ask, **Who can show us any good?** The following words would then be those of the psalmist, a prayer for the "light" of God's presence with his people. But it could be the ordinary people asking for the good, and the translation could be: "O that someone would show us good." The good then being sought could be rain, as Dahood suggests, or it could be prosperity in general. The plea for God's blessing that follows would then be suitable on the lips of the multitude.

4:7 Many clamor for the good, but where is it to be found? And who will recognize it when he has found it? Is it to be experienced in an abundant harvest? Perhaps. But "a man's life does not consist in the abundance of his possessions" (Luke 12:15). For the psalmist there was a greater good, an inner joy, a gladness of the heart, that did not depend upon the harvest. **You have filled my heart**, he could say, **with greater joy than when their grain and new wine abound.**

4:8 I will lie down and sleep, because of confidence in the Lord. Professor Arthur Holmes used to say that sleep, for the Christian putting himself absolutely in God's care, is an act of pure worship! The psalmist, whatever the occasion of his anxiety, could yet sleep **in peace.** With a prayer on his lips and heavenly joy in his heart, he was sustained by his God. His was an experience of genuine security that comes from faith in one who is reliable. We are not told that the cause of his distress was taken away. Who knows? But in any event, it could not negate his security in the Lord.

C. AN APPEAL TO A RIGHTEOUS LORD (5:1-12)

Psalm 5 consists of the words of one who is opposed by wicked and bloodthirsty men, attacking him with false accusations and lies. As such, it has been classed as a lament. However, the psalmist does not articulate a precise complaint, nor does he make a formal statement of confidence such as is characteristic of many psalms of lament. Some classify this work as *a psalm of innocence.* Such psalms assert the psalmist's innocence as a basis for God's vindication. (See Psalm 26, for example.) But this is not the clearly defined nature of Psalm 5. Buttenwieser, as with Psalms 3 and 4, sees Psalm 5 as a lament of the community, citing the plurals of verses 11 and 12 as evidence.[40] It is better to retain the view that it is a prayer of one

---

[40]Buttenwieser, *The Psalms*, p. 406.

falsely accused, yet a psalm that yielded itself readily to congregational use. That it was so used is indicated by the reference in the heading to the *chief* Musician (לַמְנַצֵּחַ, *lamᵃnaṣēaḥ*) and to *Nehiloth* (flutes – אֶל־הַנְּחִילוֹת, *'el-hanᵃḥîlôth*). It has been commonly held that the psalm was recited in connection with the offering of the morning sacrifices (at the temple). This may be assumed, but it is not a conclusion established with certainty since the text does not specifically mention sacrifice.

The psalm opens with a threefold appeal to the Lord by one who, in the morning, would approach God (vv. 1-3). He states reasons why he can draw near with confidence (vv. 4-7), asks for guidance and that God will deal with the wicked, his enemies (vv. 8-10). The psalm then closes with a petition that joy and protection may be granted to the righteous who put their trust in the Lord (vv. 11-12).

Verses 8 and 9 supply the key to our understanding the psalm as the prayer of one falsely accused. He is confronted by enemies who speak lies and seek his destruction. That the psalm would be a fitting prayer from the lips of David is readily apparent when we consider his plight when at the court of Saul, or rather when he was fleeing from Saul.

1. Hear My Case, O God! (5:1-3)

5:1-2 By the use of verbs that are emphatic imperatives, the psalmist indicates the urgency of his plea — **Give ear, consider, listen to**. His situation was one of deep distress, and the earnestness of his entreaty indicates how fully he would rely upon the Lord for a just solution. He is not directing mere words to the Lord, but a **sighing** or "groaning" (RSV), a "meditation," "the murmur of my soul" (Moffatt), an agonized cry. This is no casual prayer! It is an impassioned appeal for justice, and as such it is addressed to God as King; that is, as the all-wise and righteous ruler to whom judgment belongs.

5:3 You hear my voice. The verb in the imperfect may express customary or habitual behavior, hence the translation: "Morning by morning . . . you hear my voice." However, since in verses 1 and 2 we have a *request* that the Lord hear, it is better to recognize the present verb as a request also: "(You) hear my voice!"

Apparently the psalmist is approaching God in the morning, but any special significance of this fact, as related to his situation, is a matter of conjecture. Whatever his need — whatever our need! What better way to start the day than to direct one's thoughts, one's praise, one's prayers to God, and look up? Is it not better to face every day, whatever the circumstances, with God than without him? However, in the OT world, as Drijvers has noted,[41] early morning was the preferred time for hearing cases of law (cf. 2 Sam 15:2). If one had spent the previous days and nights in anticipation of a day in court, we may well imagine how fervent in prayer he would be on the morning when he would face slanderers and false accusers.

I lay my requests before you. "I prepare a sacrifice" (RSV), "I draw up my case" (Dahood). The various translations are occasioned by the fact that the Hebrew text supplies no object for the verb. It states, simply, "I set in order." In 1 Sam 17:2 Israel and the Philistines "set in order" army against army. In Ps 23:5 God "sets in order" a table before me. In Lev 1:8 the priests "set in order" the parts of the sacrifice on the altar. And in Ps 50:21 God "sets in order" the particulars of his case against the wicked. A similar use of the term appears in Job 37:19 (RSV) and would be appropriate here. "In the morning I will present my case."[42] The psalmist is ready to appear before the Lord and before the human tribunal that would render a verdict in the case.

2. You Are a Righteous Judge (5:4-6)

5:4 Among the societies of humankind injustice is not uncommon, but in the Lord the psalmist could have full confidence: "Shall not the Judge of all the earth do right?" (Gen 18:25). He is not a God **who takes pleasure in evil**. Among the ancients (and among some moderns?) gods were worshiped that delighted in deceit, in evil, in debauchery. But not the Lord! He is distinguished

---

[41]Drijvers, *The Psalms*, p. 114.

[42]If one views the Psalm as liturgy accompanying morning worship, then the translation, "I prepare a sacrifice," would seem appropriate.

by at least three characteristics. He is the *living* God — not a lifeless idol, not a mere abstract "uncaused cause," not a postulate of the intellect. He is *righteous*. And he is *faithful*, always to be depended upon. It is the righteousness of God that is here emphasized — **with you the wicked cannot dwell,** ("cannot be thy guest," Briggs). The righteousness of God is not a whim; it is his very nature. Evil cannot exist in the presence of God any more than darkness could exist where there is light. In each case the two are wholly incompatible. (It is for this very reason that one desiring God's fellowship must turn away from evil and accept God's deliverance from it.) Wickedness always alienates one from God, creating a chasm of separation that can only be bridged by repentance on our part and by God's merciful forgiveness.

5:5 The arrogant ["the boastful," RSV; "the foolish" KJV] **cannot stand in your presence.** Menahem Mansoor, from a study of the *Thanksgiving Hymns Of Qumran*, understands the term rendered "arrogant" to mean "deceivers, dealers in falsehood." This would be suitable if we are dealing with false accusers (see v. 6). **You hate all who do wrong.** Is not the God of the OT a God of love? He is. God's love for all people is not explicitly expressed in the OT, yet it is foreshadowed — in his concern for Nineveh, for example (Jonah 4:11). Love is a part of God's nature. But so also is his wrath against evil and against evildoers. These he hates, much as one might say, "I hate spinach." They are abhorrent. But his hatred is not malevolent. Even toward these he would show his love in redeeming activity, if they should be willing to receive it. A righteous God, by his very nature, must hate wickedness wherever and in whomever found, both because of what it is and of what it does, especially the latter. Even Jesus could experience anger toward men who would show concern for a sheep that had fallen in a ditch but not for a suffering fellow-being needing help (Mark 3:5; Luke 6:6-11).

5:6 On the basis of analogy with ancient Near Eastern patterns, it has been suggested that the liars and deceitful men, the bloodthirsty men of the psalm, may be demonic forces,[43] but this does

---

[43]See Helmer Ringgren, *The Faith of the Psalmists* (London: SCM Press, 1963), pp. 5, 45; and Johannes Pedersen, *Israel, Its Life and Culture* (London: Oxford University Press, 1973), p. 453f.

not seem likely given the general setting of the psalm. Dahood makes a much stronger case for his view that it is "the man of idols and of figurines" whom **the LORD abhors**.[44] The Hebrew has been traditionally translated: "a man of blood and of deceit," (**bloodthirsty and deceitful men,** NIV). But the word rendered "blood" may be from the root meaning "likeness," that is, "image, idol." And "deceit" may be the equivalent of "deceitful *thing*," a term descriptive of an idol, so "figurine." Dahood suggests that the psalmist has been accused of idolatry by false witnesses. If true, he would be denied entrance to the house of the Lord. But he replies that he is fully aware of the fact that God abhors idolaters. Then he pledges himself to the worship of God, expressing the desire to be led in his righteous ways.

3. I Seek Your Will and Your Way (5:7-8)

5:7 But I. The Hebrew is emphatic. This commitment is not conditioned by what others may do. I **will come into your house**, and not be guilty of worshiping idols. How could the psalmist speak so confidently about entering the Lord's house? Had he not said that evil cannot be a guest of God? Is he claiming that he has attained a degree of righteousness that assures his admittance to the presence of God? Not at all! He does come with confidence, but it is a confidence founded upon (God's) **great mercy**, the "abundance of (his) steadfast love" (RSV).[45] Some persons seem to believe they are doing God a favor when they go to church and that they should receive praise for the effort. The true worshiper knows that it is only by the mercy of a righteous God that he can approach the throne of his grace. And so he comes in a spirit of thanksgiving.

5:8 Lead me, O LORD, in your righteousness. The principal concern of the psalmist is to be led in the way of the Lord, because that way is right. The Hebrew word צְדָקָה (ṣᵉdāqāh, "righteousness") is not primarily an ethical term. It could be applied to

---

[44]Dahood, *Psalms 1-50*, pp. 31f.

[45]For the significance of the Hebrew *chesed* (ḥesed, "mercy," "steadfast love") see the discussion of Ps 6:4.

weights and measures, indicating those that conform to the norm, or the standard (Lev 19:36). The Scriptures indicate that God has provided a standard for life, or a norm, to guide humankind. To direct one's life in accord with this standard is to walk in righteousness; that is, in the way that is right. Since one has a choice, it does become an ethical matter — and a moral one. In the confrontation of the psalmist with his enemies (literally, the ones "eyeing him," "the insidious watchers") he knew that there was a right and a wrong way that he himself might take. He wanted to be shown that right way. **Make straight your way before me.** Only when he was willing to follow God's way could he call upon the Lord to deal with his enemies.

4. Deal with the Wicked According to Their Wickedness (5:9-10)

5:9 Verses 9 and 10 indicate the wickedness of the enemies to be an evil and malicious use of the tongue. **Not a word from their mouth can be trusted. Destruction** (also, RSV), is the very nature of their **heart.** And **their throat is an open grave** left uncovered, itself full of corruption and an invitation or summons to death. In Romans 3:13 the Apostle Paul quotes this verse and adds, "The poison of vipers is on their lips" (See Ps 140:3.). **They speak deceit** literally means they speak "smooth things" with the intention of distorting the facts.

5:10 Banish them . . . for they have rebelled against you. To be guilty of a wrong against a fellow human being is to be guilty of sin against God. This we should remember before we bring harm to any. The Hebrew term, נָדַח (nādaḥ), translated "banish" has the element of guilt in its meaning; thus, "Make them bear their guilt" (RSV). The term includes the full spectrum of the sinful act, the sinful condition of the heart, the responsibility for the act, and the inevitable judgment that must follow. There is no question what the final outcome of sin will be. The psalmist wanted to see justice administered immediately — **Declare them guilty, O God!**

This prayer does not seem to reflect the spirit of the NT. Jesus said: "Love your enemies and pray for those who persecute you" (Matt 5:44). And on the cross his prayer was: "Father, forgive them; for they do not know what they are doing" (Luke 23:34a). Even in the OT we are told: "If your enemy is hungry, give him food to eat;

and if he is thirsty, give him water to drink" (Prov 25:21). The prayer of Ps 5:10 is not, obviously, such as a Christian should pray today, unless it be in the spirit of Dietrick Bonhoeffer, who said: "I leave the vengeance to God and ask him to execute his righteousness to all his enemies."[46] In a measure, this is what the psalmist said: "Act, Lord, in such a way towards these persons as is consistent with your righteousness and justice, vindicate your name in the world."

5. God Blesses Those Who Trust Him (5:11-12)

5:11-12 But let all who take refuge in you be glad. In spite of the abuse inflicted by enemies, those who trust in God, "take refuge in him" (as in Ps 2:12), find cause for rejoicing. The crisis may not be passed, but the final outcome is in the hands of God, and this knowledge in itself is cause for hope, inner joy, and peace. **Let them ever sing for joy.** The child of God can sing — and should sing! — even in adverse circumstances, for nothing can separate him from the love of God (Rom 8:35-39). Such is the joy of those who **love [his] name.** The name stands for the individual, so that to love the name of God is to love him. **For surely, O LORD, you bless the righteous.** Jesus said, "Blessed are those who hunger and thirst for righteousness, for they will be filled" (Matt 5:6). The psalmist had not heard the words of Jesus, but he had experienced the blessing.

D. A CRY FOR MERCY UNDER JUDGMENT (6:1-10)

From early times Psalm 6 has been regarded as one of seven *Penitential Psalms*, that consist of confessions of sin, accompanied by prayers for forgiveness (and often for healing). The seven include 6, 32, 38, 51, 102, 130, and 143. All of them except 102 and 130 bear the heading: "A Psalm of David." That David needed to repent and that he needed forgiveness after his double sin of adultery and homicide is obvious (See 2 Sam 11:1-27.). He likely needed forgiveness on other occasions as well. In the matter of Bathsheba,

---

[46]Dietrick Bonhoeffer, *Psalms: The Prayer Book of the Bible* (Minneapolis: Augsburg, 1970), p. 59.

when he was confronted with his guilt by the prophet Nathan, he confessed his sin (2 Sam 12:13).

Some would consider psalms of this nature to be part of a liturgy of repentance, used in times of emergency, distress, or disaster, personal or national. That Psalm 6 was used in public worship is suggested by the musical notations in the heading. Actually, however, it does not contain an explicit confession of sin, and there is no plea for forgiveness. On the other hand, the psalmist does not plead innocence, and in the terminology he uses, an acknowledgment of guilt is implied. This would justify its inclusion in the group of Psalms of a penitential nature.

The title we have chosen is that proposed by Franz Delitzsch: *A Cry for Mercy under Judgment.*[47] This seems best to describe the occasion for its writing. The second verse begins with a cry for mercy, and that the psalmist considers himself to be suffering under the judgment of God, we shall see. He has had to endure anguish, threefold in nature: illness that has brought him to the confrontation with death (vv. 4-5), the villainy of enemies who in some way have intensified his suffering, perhaps by saying that he deserved it as a sinner (vv. 6-7), and the haunting fear that he has been forgotten by the Lord, abandoned to his misery (vv. 3-4). He is desperately ill, terrified by his physical and emotional condition, reduced to such straits that, in his distress, he can only address his petition to God — and wait.

1. O LORD, How Long? (6:1-3)

6:1 There is no labored or elaborate introduction to his prayer, such as, "Kind and most-loving God." The psalmist simply utters God's name, "Yahweh!" in a cry of desperation, using the covenant name by which God had revealed himself to Moses. **Do not rebuke me in your anger.** The order of the words in the Hebrew is: "Do not, in your anger, rebuke me." The implication is that a rebuke may well be deserved; the request is that it be administered not in anger, but tempered with mercy. It is thus that we understand the

---

[47]Franz Delitzsch, *Biblical Commentary on the Psalms*, trans. Francis Bolton (Edinburgh: T & T Clark, 1884), 1:129.

psalm to be penitential in nature. The verb rendered "rebuke" (from the Hebrew יכח, *yākaḥ*) is a juridical term that may be translated, "Render a judgment" (as in a court of law). This significance is reflected in the translation, "Do not condemn me" (NEB). That his illness might indeed be a judgment from God, the psalmist recognized. His suffering was viewed as discipline (to purify and strengthen him in character?). True, he does not make an explicit confession of sin, as in Ps 51:3, perhaps because he is unaware of the particular sin for which he may be suffering. At the same time, he makes no claims of innocence, as we have noted. His only plea is for God to be merciful. So the emphasis of verse 1 rests upon the words, "not . . . in your anger." We have no claim upon the mercy of the Lord. Neither did the psalmist. But as one whose desire is to be faithful and loyal to his God, he might dare hope for it. And he did.

6:2 Be merciful . . . for I am faint. Weakness of the body is indicated. "I am languishing" (RSV), "withering" (Achtemeier),[48] and the condition is accompanied by inner terror. The mind of the psalmist lingers on thoughts of death rapidly approaching (v. 5). And so his prayer: **Heal me, for my bones are in agony**: "troubled" (RSV), "disturbed" (Craigie). These alternate translations bear the concept of the Hebrew. "In agony" (NIV) and "racked" (Dahood) are less exact, since the term describes an emotion more than a physical condition — "in panic" we might say. And since "my bones" is a synecdoche indicating the whole body, the psalmist is saying: "I am terrified, body and soul!" Thus does he give expression to the extreme gravity of his condition. "Soul," in this context, indicates the inner being.

6:3 O LORD, how long? A cry of despair, yet also of hope. The call is to Yahweh, the God of Israel, who keeps "his covenant of love to a thousand generations of those who love him and keep his commands" (Deut 7:9), a God who has proven himself to be merciful in time past. As Walter Brueggemann has observed, "The speaker of the lament does not come *de novo* to God, but out of a context of faith and loyalty."[49]

---

[48]Elizabeth Achtemeier, "Overcoming the World — an Exposition of Psalm 6," *Int* 28 (1974): 91.

[49]Walter Brueggemann, "From Hurt to Joy, from Death to Life," *Int* 28 (1974): 7.

2. Spare My Life, for Mercy's Sake (6:4-5)

6:4 Turn, O LORD. The plea of the psalmist is that he might enjoy again that fellowship with God that he had previously known but had lost a while — "come back" (NEB). **Deliver me.** Here the meaning is, "Spare my life," since the Hebrew word translated *me* is literally "soul" (נֶפֶשׁ, *nepheš*), here meaning "person." **Your unfailing love.** "Love" is the translation of the Hebrew חֶסֶד (*ḥesed*). Other translations include: "mercy" (KJV), "steadfast love," (RSV), "faithful love" (NJB), "kindness" (Dahood), "goodness" (Buttenwieser), and "for thy love's sake" (Moffatt, NEB). These various renderings are similar in basic concept, each suggesting the general idea of *ḥesed* as an act of love. Nelson Glueck championed the view that the term indicates "covenant love/loyalty," in obligation, moral or otherwise, imposed upon one by reason of a covenant (contractual) relationship. In other words, *ḥesed* is faithfulness to covenantal obligations.[50] Ludwig Koehler reflects this view when he defines the term as having reference to "mutual liability."[51] However, "obligation" or "liability" is scarcely the proper word, since *ḥesed* may be shown where no prior obligation exists. (For example, consider the kindness of Rahab to the spies of Israel, to whom she was in no way obligated — Josh 2:12.) A better term, as suggested by Katherine Doob Sakenfeld, would be "responsibility" if we stress the concept of response where an opportunity for showing kindness exists. Mercy must not be eliminated from the understanding of *ḥesed*, since the one who grants the favor is perfectly free *not to act*, if he so chooses.

Sakenfeld has demonstrated beyond questioning that *ḥesed*, whether of men or of God, involves *loyalty*.[52] Indeed, she considers this to be the primary significance of the term. Thus she would

---

[50]Nelson Glueck, *Hesed in the Bible*, trans. A. Gottschalk (Cincinnati: Hebrew Union College Press, 1967).

[51]Ludwig Koehler and Walter Baumgartner, *Lexicon in Veteris Testamenti Libros* (Leiden: E.J. Brill, 1951). For a comprehensive summary of the data upon which the meaning of *ḥesed* may be determined, see *TWOT*, R. Laird Harris, ed. (Chicago: Moody Press, 1980), 1:305-307.

[52]Katherine Doob Sakenfeld, *The Meaning of Hesed in the Hebrew Bible, a New Inquiry* (Missoula, MT: Scholars Press, 1978). Also, by the same author,

translate Ps 6:4b, "Deliver me for the sake of thy loyalty." But no one word in English is adequate to carry the fullness of meaning of the Hebrew term (as Sakenfeld, of course, is aware). In whatever way the word is translated, whether as "mercy," "unfailing love," "loyalty," or "lovingkindness," *ḥesed* is absolutely essential where any meaningful relationship is to exist between parties, since it signifies active, responsive love. It is a giving of oneself in kindness, as opportunity affords. No wonder the psalmist relied upon this as the basis of his plea to God. He could depend upon the Lord's steadfastness in mercy towards the penitent (see Num 14:18), and for this reason he would call on him to deliver him from the death that threatened.

6:5 No one remembers you when he is dead. Who praises you from the grave [Sheol]? The implied answer to the question is, "No one." We do not see any of the dead praising God. The writer is speaking phenomenologically; that is, of events as seen through human eyes or experience. The psalmists had not heard the words of Jesus: "I am the resurrection, and the life. He who believes in me will live, even though he dies; and whoever lives and believes in me will never die" (John 11:25,26). Just how much was revealed in OT times about life beyond the grave is difficult to determine. However, Psalms in which Kirkpatrick, 100 years ago, saw the "germ and principle of the doctrine of eternal life"[53] have yielded precise statements to Dahood, who finds many references to the future life in the Psalter. Depending upon the validity of Dahood's etymology, his conclusions are valid. Certainly, in many cases, he has reasonable data upon which his decisions are based. Altogether, he finds references to resurrection or future life in some forty texts.[54]

Nevertheless, the picture of what lies beyond the grave is not fully disclosed in the OT. The focus of verse 5 is on the fact that

---

see *Faithfulness in Action: Loyalty in Biblical Perspective* (Philadelphia: Fortress Press, 1985).

[53]Kirkpatrick, *The Book of Psalms*, p. lxxvii.

[54]Dahood, *Psalms 1–50*, p. xxxvi, and *Psalms 101–150*, pp. xli. Dahood's texts of resurrection and future life include 11:7; 16:10,11; 17:15; 21:7; 23:6; 27:4,13; 36:8,9; 37:37,38; 41:12, and others. Some of these will be treated in the course of our study.

death brings an end to the activities of this life, and thus to the joy
the psalmist had known in praising God. That joy would be his no
longer. "No one remembers you when he is dead" (a corpse). The
psalmist desired to continue, in this life, his remembrances of
God, for these had brought inner joy. And so, his petition, "Spare
my life."

3. My Grief Is Unbearable (6:6-7)

6:6 An uncontrolled sobbing or outpouring of grief is depicted in
verses 6 and 7, a flood of tears. **I am worn out from groaning.** The
term translated "groaning" expresses deep grief and alludes to
weeping in any sorrow. (It is not the word usually associated in the
OT with the mourning at funerals.) That the psalmist suffered physically is clearly stated in verse 2. But would this alone have caused
such a continual outpouring of unbridled grief? It would seem,
rather, that mental anguish was the cause of his incessant tears.
Could this be from his consciousness of sin and for his alienation
from God that sin had caused? Leupold recognizes this possibility.
"The author is deeply pained because of his sins," he writes. "These
tears are wept in the sight of God . . . a part of the earnest prayer . . .
[of one who] believes that God hears men when they cry thus."[55]

6:7 My eyes grow weak with sorrow, or "waste away" because of
grief. Again, as in verse 2, we may have a figure of speech in which
the eye, a part of the body, stands for the whole; thus, "I grow
weak/waste away." Some scholars (Buttenwieser, for example[56])
hold that in the penitential psalms the "I" personifies the nation,
which was in dire straits from its enemies. The sickness, then, is
understood as metaphorical, and not real, and the language is that
of corporate worship of a people seeking their deliverance from
enemies who were about to destroy the nation. It is noted that, in
the conclusion of Psalm 6, it is the enemies who are dealt with, not
sickness. The psalm may have been used communally. Yet the
description of suffering pictures so vividly the distress of a real

---

[55]Leupold, *Exposition*, pp. 87, 88.
[56]Buttenwieser, *Psalms*, p. 560.

experience that it is difficult to deny its personal nature. The enemies are mentioned for the first time in verse 7 and are not identified. Obviously they have caused harassment in some way (by the permissive will of God, of course). In the next verse they are identified only as *you who do evil.*

4. God Hears! My Enemies Are Shamed (6:8-10)

6:8 Away from me, all you who do evil. "Begone!" (Butten-wieser). Verses 8-10 are a cry of victory and reflect a striking (and surprising) change of mood from the preceding verses. From deepest despair to blessed assurance — the change is so abrupt that some have considered the closing verses to have been added at a later time, after the author had recovered from his illness.[57] There is no obvious reason, however, to view the psalm otherwise than as a perfect whole, with the closing verses bearing testimony to the fact that God had heard the psalmist's cry and had accepted his prayer. This would account for the note of jubilation with which the psalm ends.

There is, however, speculation as to what brought about the change of spirit. Some would say that an inner consciousness of God's forgiveness flooded the writer's soul, as when one kneels to pray and arises with joy that he has been heard. Others believe that a priest had spoken words of assurance such as Eli had spoken to Hannah when she had prayed (1 Sam 1:17). (The use of the psalm in public worship, it is said, would naturally elicit the priestly response.) But, whatever, the cause, the experience of God's response was such a reality to the psalmist that his heaviness was turned to joy, and those who had taunted him were put to shame.

6:9-10 It is interesting that Jesus quoted from Psalm 6:8 — "Away from me, you evildoers!" (Matt 7:23). And verses 9 and 10 are just such words as he might have uttered on the cross — **The LORD has heard . . .** In the midst of his defeat, there was victory;

---

[57]This possibility is suggested by A. Cohen, *The Psalms* (London: The Soncino Press, 1964), p. 13; and W.O.E. Oesterley, *The Psalms, Translated with Text-Critical and Exegetical Notes* (London: SPCK, 1939), p. 136.

from the depths of a tomb, there was resurrection; out of death came life forevermore. Let **all [his] enemies . . . be ashamed!** And seek his forgiveness and his way.

E. AN INNOCENT MAN'S APPEAL
TO THE RIGHTEOUS JUDGE (7:1-17)

The key to our approach to Psalm 7 is to be found in verse 3 — "O LORD my God, if I have done this . . ." Such a disclaimer implies that the psalmist has been accused, without justification, of some heinous offense. The accusation made by his enemies could destroy him. But he is innocent of the charges and therefore does not hesitate to present his case before God. He is confident that he will be exonerated and that just retribution will fall upon those who seek his ruin. The psalm is, by type, an individual lament, more specifically, the lament of one falsely accused. As is true of similar psalms, some consider it to be a national lament. Buttenwieser, for example, says that "the very tone and language of the psalm leave room for no other conclusion." [58]

In the heading of the psalm the word *Shiggaion* (שִׁגָּיוֹן, *šiggāyôn*) appears, apparently from the root *šāgāh* (שָׁגָה) meaning "to go astray, to err" or "to wander aimlessly" (as a sheep). Some consider the word to be descriptive of the nature of the poem, deeply emotional; others, of the music, irregular; and still others, of the psalmist, deeply agitated, ecstatic. The precise significance of the term eludes us.

The reference to David in the heading is not without significance. That he was accused of traitorous conduct is indicated in 1 Sam 24:9. It has been commonly accepted that Cush was the ringleader among his enemies, but no reference to this man is found elsewhere in the Scriptures. As a matter of fact, the reference here to Cush, with more probability, is indicative of a musical orientation rather than of a villain. Thus, it is a psalm sung by David, to the tune of, or in the manner of, "the words of Cush," and not "concerning" Cush (as in NIV). This, as Brevard S. Childs has

---

[58]Buttenwieser, *The Psalms*, p. 412.

pointed out, is in keeping with the way similar headings are translated throughout the Psalter,[59] the preposition not elsewhere being
rendered "concerning," but "according to" (RSV) or "upon" (KJV).
(See the headings of Psalms 8, 9, 12, 22, 45, 46, 56, and others.)

The Davidic origin of the psalm seems most appropriate. That it
was later incorporated into the liturgy of Israel (notice the use of
Selah after verse 5) only indicates that it is highly suitable as the
expression of the soul's cry of any person who is falsely accused.
Some see verses 6-9 in the context of God's universal judgment and
consider them to be a later addition. (In verse 9 God is called upon
to judge "peoples" — plural.) Rotherham makes the interesting
observation that David himself may later have added to the psalm
words that "greatly strengthened it."[60]

Buttenwieser is certain that the occasion of the psalm was the
threat to God's people of imminent national destruction "in post-
Exilic times prior to the rise of the Maccabees."[61] The psalm would
undoubtedly have been cherished in a time of crisis such as that
depicted in the Book of Esther — Haman's plot to destroy the Jews.
It is understandable, therefore, why later Judaism associated the
psalm with the feast of Purim, the feast commemorating the time
of Esther. Nevertheless, it seems rather that the psalm had its origin
in the time of a personal crisis.

Solomon, in his prayer of dedication for the temple, asked that
the Lord judge his servants whenever one should come before him
seeking justice (1 Kgs 8:31,32). A number of scholars consider this
to supply the setting of the psalm, regarding it as cultic in nature, a
part of the ritual whereby one's guilt or innocence would be determined by priestly decision in the temple setting. However, this evaluation and the diversity of views stated above serve less to indicate
the origin of the psalm and more its applicability. We find no valid
reason for not crediting the psalm, in its origin, to David.

---

[59]Brevard S. Childs, "Psalm Titles and Midrashic Exegesis," *JSS* 16 (1971): 138.
[60]Rotherham, *Studies*, 1:97.
[61]Buttenwieser, *The Psalms*, p. 416.

1. A Plea for Deliverance (7:1-2)

7:1a Grave danger threatens the psalmist, leading him to turn to God for refuge. Note the intimacy of his address — *Yahweh* **my God**. This is the first time in the psalms that the two designations for deity appear side by side (again in v. 3). Their use suggests the basis of the confidence of the psalmist. The first, *Yahweh* (always translated LORD with SMALL CAPITAL lettters in the NIV) speaks of God in his covenant relationship with his people; the second, *Elohim*, of his infinite power and perfections. One who is within the covenant can with confidence draw near to God. Just to speak his name is to set in motion heaven's response.

7:1b-2 Save . . . deliver me. The verbs are synonyms. At times they have reference to salvation from sin and its consequences, but here the meaning is without theological overtones. The psalmist is asking that God deliver him from the assaults of his enemies. The latter are so vicious that he feels as helpless before them as he would in the clutches of a lion. The words of verse 1, "and deliver me" should be read as the opening words of verse 2, as Dahood states (citing D.N. Freedman).[62] **Or they will tear me**. The verb is singular, though many translations change to the plural (as NIV), as suggested by the many "pursuers" (v. 1). Kirkpatrick asserts that "his enemies are many, but one is conspicuous above all for merciless ferocity."[63] However, the "all" in verse 1 means "the whole lot" (singular). This could account for the singular verb in verse 2, and all of the enemies would be involved. Not one, therefore, but many, are pursuing him, and would tear him **to pieces** if he should fall into their hands. Not permitted this, they will seek his ruin through lies and slander.

2. A Declaration of Innocence (7:3-5)

7:3 O LORD my God, if I have done this. "This" is not defined (but see our following discussion of the pronoun). The specific

---

[62]Dahood, *Psalms 1-50*, p. 41.
[63]Kirkpatrick, *The Book of Psalms*, p. 30.

crime or crimes of which the psalmist has been accused are not clearly indicated. Elmer Leslie states categorically that he has been charged with theft (v. 3) and with the breaking of confidence with a fellow countryman (v. 4).[64] Stuhlmueller says the charge was possibly murder, and that the psalmist has sought sanctuary in the temple until his innocence can be proven.[65] Whatever the alleged crime, of great concern to the psalmist is the fact that his life is in jeopardy, his person has been degraded, and his good name villified, without just cause, since he is innocent of the charges. His statement of innocence is in the form of a solemn oath.[66] In it he lists three charges made against him, each introduced by "if," (Hebrew אִם, 'im, the NIV omits the second "if" at v. 3b for style only) and then, in the three lines of verse 5, states his willingness to suffer punishment – rather, he calls for punishment, if he indeed be guilty. The threefold indictment is thus balanced by the threefold self-imprecation.

If I have done this. The pronoun here (*this*) used without antecedent is awkward. It is commonly taken to mean, "if I have done any of the following things," but such usage in the Hebrew is unusual. Briggs takes it to mean "the specific things charged against him by his pursuer,"[67] but no charges of the pursuer have been mentioned. Craigie sees here reference "in general terms to the accusations laid against him."[68] But no accusations have been previously mentioned. Buttenwieser disposes of the problem by the simple expedient of placing verse 3 after verse 4, assuming that the verses became transposed in transmission. However, should this be the case, one would expect "these" – "if I have done these (things)"

---

[64]Elmer Leslie, *The Psalms* (Nashville: Abingdon-Cokesbury Press, 1949), p. 316.

[65]Stuhlmueller, *Psalms I*, p. 83.

[66]First Kings 8:31,32, cited earlier, indicates the place of the oath in the process of determining guilt: "When a man wrongs his neighbor and is required to take an oath and he comes and swears the oath before your altar in this temple, then hear from heaven and act. Judge between your servants, condemning the guilty and bringing down on his own head what he has done. Declare the innocent not guilty, and so establish his innocence."

[67]Briggs, *Psalms*, p. 43.

[68]Craigie, *Psalms 1–50*, p. 100.

— instead of "this." The solution should be sought in the direction proposed by Dahood; that is, in recognizing זֹאת (*zō'th*, this) as a substantive and not a pronoun.[69] Sensing the need for a noun, Rudolf Kittel, as editor of *Biblia Hebraica*, proposed some years ago changing *zō'th* to *gē'ûth* (the words appear similar in Hebrew; i.e., זֹאת with גֵּאוּת).[70] This would then give a meaning, "if I have done arrogance (acted arrogantly)." But Dahood sees no necessity for emendation of the text. Rather, he makes a strong case for recognizing in *zō'th* a noun meaning "insult," or "indignity," hence his translation, "if I have committed an indignity." Consequently, the three conditional statements are: "If I have insulted, **if there is guilt on my hands**, if I have done evil to an ally."

7:4 "Yea, I have delivered him that without cause is mine enemy." With the above understanding, these concluding words of verse 4 remain a declarative (not conditional) parenthetical statement, as in the King James Version. As such, the translation is not strained and emendation of the text is unnecessary. Many, however, continue the "if" clauses to include verse 4b; This is syntactically acceptable, unless *the clause is parenthetical.* Robert G. Batcher would simply make an "if" statement of the above: "if I have spared the man who for no reason was my enemy."[71] (This would have violated the law of "eye for an eye and tooth for a tooth.") Others read "his enemy" instead of "mine" — "If I rescued my ally's enemy [freeing him to pursue my ally], may an enemy pursue me."[72] But most, in addition to introducing the "if," seek a different meaning for the verb "delivered" or "rescued." For example, "if I have plundered" (RSV, NASB, NKJV, Delitzsch), **If I . . . have robbed** (NIV), "if I have made havoc" (Moffatt), "'if I have distressed" (Weiser). In spite of the above explanations of the text, the present writer rejects the conditional nature of verse 4b. The three *ifs* preceding

---

[69]Dahood, *Psalms 1–50*, p. 42.

[70]Rudolf Kittel, ed., *Biblia Hebraica* (Stuttgart: Wurttembergische Bibelanstalt Stuttgart, 1937).

[71]Robert G. Batcher, "A Translator's Note on Psalm 7:4b, 11," *BT* vol 23, no. 2 (April 1972): 241.

[72]Jeffrey H. Tigay, "Psalm 7:5 and Ancient Near Eastern Treaties," *JBL*, LXXXIX (June, 1970): 178-186. Craigie's translation parallels Tigay: "if I have rescued his adversary."

these words balance the three imprecations that follow. (The intervening words are parenthetical with a verb form in **the imperfect**).
The writer is saying that, in actuality, his conduct has continually
been the very opposite of that with which he was charged. The *ah*
ending of the Hebrew verb is emphatic — "I was determined to
deliver [or to rescue] my enemy." The psalmist is entering a plea of
"not guilty."

7:5 In concluding the oath of innocence, he gives voice to a
curse to be executed upon himself if he is guilty. **Let my enemy
pursue and overtake me; . . . trample my life to the ground, and
make me sleep in the dust.** (The words "soul," "life," and "honor"
in verse 5 are all synonyms meaning the *person "me."*

3. The Cry for God to Act (7:6-10)

7:6 The psalmist never entertains any doubt about the justice of
God, nor of the judgment of God, both are sure and certain. His
plea is for that judgment to come soon, for God to act speedily in
his case. **Arise, O LORD . . . rise up . . . Awake.** Does he believe that
God is asleep to the evil that he, the psalmist, is suffering? Not
really. He is but expressing that impatience that many experience
when they see "truth forever on the scaffold, wrong forever on the
throne." When evil continues unabated and unchecked, the victims
of that evil are distressed by God's apparent unconcern. It is sometimes difficult for even the most patient soul to suppress the cry for
God's immediate justice to fall upon his enemies.

7:7-10 Verses 7 and 8 speak of God as the judge of the peoples
of the earth (plural). It is before this universal judge that the
psalmist would present his case, knowing that justice would be
done. **Judge me, O LORD, according to my righteousness.** The reference to *my righteousness* is no display of egotism nor of self-righteousness. The writer is laying no claim to sinless perfection but is
only saying, "I have done none of the things of which I have been
accused." He is sure that God knows this. The Lord has no difficulty in distinguishing between innocence and guilt, since he *tries,*
or **searches** *out,* what is in the **minds and hearts** of men, knowing
their thoughts and motives as well as their deeds. And since God is
righteous, he will render a righteous judgment. "Will not the Judge

of all the earth do right?" (Gen 18:25). The psalmist, in faith, can commit his cause unreservedly to the Lord — **My shield is God Most High** (v. 10, reading עַל ['al] as a proper name ['Elyôn] and not as a preposition).

4. The Fate of Those Who Do Evil (7:11-16)

7:11-13 Justice will be done; the righteous will be vindicated; the wicked will fall under condemnation. Judgment may not fall immediately, but God does not wink at wickedness. Not a day passes when the workers of evil may escape the anger (or, "indignation," RSV) of God. If he turn not; that is, if the wicked does not repent, אֵל ('El, "God") will whet his sword. The time of accounting will come. It is possible to translate verse 11f. (v. 12 in Hebrew) thus: "God vindicates the righteous, but God denounces every day the unrepentant; he sharpens his sword, etc." A translation in this vein is proposed by A.A. McIntosh.[73] In any case, the thought is clear that the wicked will not go unpunished.

7:14-16 He who is pregnant with evil . . . gives birth to disillusionment. The Prophet Micah writes of those who lie upon their beds at night plotting evil (Micah 2:1). The psalmist, using a metaphor of pregnancy and childbirth, suggests the agony the sinner undergoes in his pursuit of sin, and to what purpose? Only to give birth to falsehood (KJV), or, better, to "disillusionment" (NIV). We would translate verse 14 as follows: "Behold, the wicked man is in labor pains with evil; he (masculine!) has conceived (LXX) mischief, but the resulting birth will disillusion him." Buttenwieser catches the significance of the verse in his translation: "His (the enemy's) dark design shall prove abortive."[74] This interpretation is thus parallel with verses 15 and 16 that follow. Taken together, all indicate that the result of the pursuit of evil will be altogether different from what was intended or anticipated. God would see to that. The schemes and deeds of the wicked would result in his own destruction.

---

[73]A.A. McIntosh, "A Consideration of Psalm vii,12f." *JTS* (Oct. 1982): xxxiii:2:481-490.
[74]Buttenwieser, *The Psalms,* p. 412.

5. Praise and Thanksgiving (7:17)

7:17 I will give thanks to the LORD because of his righteousness. It *is* fitting that one respond with thanksgiving to the goodness of God. Such goodness would be further acknowledged by singing praise to his name. Joyfully the psalmist would do this, and in doing so would rise above any constraints laid upon him by his adversaries.

III. LIVING EXPECTANTLY (8:1–10:18)

A. THE GLORY OF GOD AND THE DIGNITY OF MAN (8:1-9)

Psalm 8 very likely was used as a hymn of praise in the congregation of God's people. We gather this from the opening words, "O LORD, our Lord, how majestic is your name in all the earth!" as if numerous voices were joined together in adoration. The surpassing majesty of God is celebrated, both on earth and in heaven. Further cause for wonder beyond that of God's own glory is the place he has accorded man in his design. In view of the greatness of God and of his creation – this illimitable universe – how insignificant man appears. Yet God has created him in his own likeness, giving him dominion over all the earth and its creatures. The psalm closes, as it began, praising the majesty of the Lord.

1. God's Glory and Majesty (8:1-2)

The heavens and the earth are stamped with the glory of their Maker. The power, the wisdom, and the majesty of God, as reflected in nature, stagger human consciousness. We speak of the mysteries of creation, but they are an open book to God. The intricate wisdom evidenced in the natural world is but a dim reflection of his wisdom. The unbelievable power packed into a single atom scarcely hints of the power of him who placed it there when he called the universe into being. The psalmist, overawed by the greatness of God, could scarce refrain from responding with praise.

**8:1 O LORD, our Lord [Yahweh our Lord],[75] how majestic is
your name in all the earth!** It is no small god that is envisioned
here, no local deity such as those worshiped by Israel's neighbors.
The psalmist is singing the praises of the Lord of the universe, of
Yahweh, the eternal, self-existent One. In Hebrew thought, names
are indicative of the nature of the person. Consequently, the
majesty here praised attaches to God himself, not just to his name.
Consider the word "majesty." It refers to God as surpassing all that
is. His name is above all others. Emphasis is given to this "beyond-
ness" of God. Isaiah wrote of the "high and lofty One . . . he who
lives forever" (Isa 57:15). This reverent attitude of mind is essential
for all true worship. The very heart of the worshiper needs to be
filled with a sense of the glory of God.

8:2 Amazingly, even the speech of **children and infants** testifies
to the greatness of their Creator. The power of speech, in God's
earthly creation, is reserved to man alone. This demonstrates that
man is unique, a rational being, thinking, reasoning, and able to
express his thoughts. It is thus that he is made in the image of God.
The earliest speech of a child, therefore, testifies to the creative
power of God, and thus puts to shame any enemy of God who
would withhold praise from the Creator.

This makes Jesus' quotation of Ps 8:2 (Matt 21:16) as a rebuke
against the chief priests and the teachers of the law even more
poignant! Children were shouting in the temple area: "Hosanna to
the Son of David!" Even children recognized and welcomed his mes-
siahship, but not so the religious leaders. They were indignant. Jesus
confirmed the children's praise by responding to them: "Yes, have
you never read, 'From the lips of children and infants you have
ordained praise.'" Have they never read? They knew it by heart, but
they refused to praise the One whom God had sent, the Messiah!

2. The Insignificance of Man (8:3-4)

8:3-4 The psalmist, gazing into the expanse of the starry heavens
on a still night — how often this must have been the experience of

---

[75]For the discussion of *Yahweh*, see the Introduction, pp. 43-44.

David, the shepherd boy! — was overwhelmed by a sense of the majesty of God. The effect of such an experience is to impress one with a consciousness of his own insignificance. How can a human being, one among millions inhabiting a speck in God's universe, be significant? The question of the psalmist is one that has surely been asked, at some time, by every human being: What is man (אֱנוֹשׁ, *'enoš*)? This word refers to man as a mortal being. The thought is of his frailty, of humanity with all its weaknesses and limitations. How could God be **mindful**, or concerned at all, about such a one who is no more than a bit of chaff in all the universe? **That you care for him**. While the KJV translation here carries the literal meaning, i.e., "That thou visitest him," the Hebrew term means to visit for a purpose, in this case benevolent concern. This is the basis for the translation "care for him" found in some versions, including the NIV. That God would even take thought of such an insignificant creature is cause for wonder. How marvelous that he *cares*!

3. The Exalted Status Given Man (8:5-9)

Of all God's creatures on earth, only man is addressed as "You." Everything else is an "it." Compared to the immensity of the universe, man does appear to be of little consequence. Yet in his own heart he knows that he is more than animal, more than a bit of animated protoplasm. The awe that he feels when he looks outward upon the universe is matched by an equal wonder as he turns his gaze upon his own God-given nature. As the philosopher Kant observed, these two things fill the mind with admiration and reverence — "the starry heavens above and the moral law within."

8:5 God has made man **a little lower than the heavenly beings**; literally, "a little lower than *elohim*." The term usually designates God. "A little less than divine" would represent the meaning. While *elohim* is the general word for God, it also is used to refer to the angels (Ps 97:7; 138:1). Usually angels are referred to as "sons of God." The LXX rendered *elohim* as "angels," i.e., "heavenly beings" and the New Testament writer to the Hebrews used this version to argue the submission of Jesus to the role of a human being and thus his post-resurrection appearance as "glorified Man — Man as man was meant to be." Man, therefore, is of an entirely different nature from every other earthly creature. It is not a matter of degree, of his being a superior animal. It is a difference *in kind*. This fact poses one of the greatest weaknesses in the evolutionary theory. There is a discussion of the "missing link" in the evolutionary chain. But when we compare the highest of the animals and man, we find that it is not a link that is missing; the entire chain has disappeared, if it ever existed!

This does not mean that man cannot act like an animal. He can and often does. But even while doing so, he is fully conscious of the fact that he has made a perversion of what he was intended to be. He knows that he is a human being sunk to the animal level.

You . . . crowned him with glory and honor. This gives credit where credit is due. Let no man boast of his exalted position in creation. Let no one think that he has put the crown upon his own head. At the same time, every individual should be conscious of the dignity which is his by God's design, the dignity of being formed in the likeness and image of God. Every child of God, however humble his circumstances, can rejoice in the realization that God has crowned him with his likeness.

8:6 You made him ruler. God, as Creator, is the Sovereign of the Universe. But he has chosen to share his sovereignty on earth with man! What a privilege this is, but also what a responsibility. The right use of the privilege leads to marvelous achievement. Man is able to tap sources of energy that can bring blessing and freedom from drudgery. But these same powers may be directed by man toward evil and death.

8:7-9 Man's dominion extends over all other living things on earth, in spite of the fact that many are far more powerful than he. Man possesses the superior power of intelligence with which God has endowed him. Obviously, this power entails moral responsibility. Ruthless slaughter of wild creatures, some even to the point of extinction, is not the proper use but is abuse of the preeminence given to man.

Because of the uniqueness of man, he alone of all God's creatures can enter into the plan and purposes of God and with intelligence to fulfill them. Without man there would be no sufficient purpose for the existence of the earth, just as there would be no purpose for beautiful vistas if there were no appreciative eyes to behold them. "The heavens declare the glory of God," we are told (Ps 19:1). But neither the heavens nor the earth could declare God's glory unless there was one created in God's image both to comprehend and to appreciate what is revealed of his majesty and excellence.

In light of the above discussion it is interesting to note how the author to the Hebrews in the New Testament applies Psalm 8 to the Messiah Jesus. After quoting Ps 8:4-6 the author indicates that this psalm indeed was intended for all mankind, but the implication is that since all mankind are sinners "we do not see everything subject to him [sinful humanity], but we see Jesus [perfect humanity, man as man was meant to be!]" (Heb 2:8b-9a). Only in Jesus do we see the subjection of all things. Jesus is the beginning of a whole new race of mankind and he is in the business of "bringing many sons to glory" (Heb 2:10). He is not ashamed to call us "brothers [and sisters]," so writes the author to the Hebrews as he quotes yet another psalm (Ps 22:22). The Apostle Paul says the same thing essentially, only he presents Jesus as our "firstfruits," the first human to so live as to experience the subjection of all things under his feet (1 Cor 15:22-28). It is clear that Psalm 8 is used in the New Testament messianically and only secondarily "in Christ" do we fulfill the dominion mandate. One day we will be like Jesus!

B. AN APPEAL TO GOD FOR DELIVERANCE (9:1–10:18)

Psalms 9 and 10 are definitely related. Psalm 9 begins an alphabetic acrostic with the Hebrew letter א (*aleph*); an acrostic that is completed, although in broken form, in Psalm 10. The same current of thought is also found in both — the desire for God's deliverance from oppressive enemies. Yet scholars have held divided opinions as to whether the two psalms were originally one, as in the LXX, or whether they should be considered distinct compositions. The absence of a title for Psalm 10 supports the view that, even in the Hebrew original, it was a continuation of 9, that the two are in reality one psalm.

Nevertheless, numerous scholars have viewed them as separate compositions. Drijvers considers it "unfortunate" that the LXX ever combined the two.[76] Kirkpatrick regarded Psalm 10 as a companion to, but separate from, Psalm 9, and not a part of it, since he held that 9 is complete in itself.[77] Cohen quotes Professor Davison as regarding Psalm 10 to be "a later Psalm composed as an appendix, or a continuation of the earlier under different conditions."[78] Derek Kidner also considers the two to be "companion pieces."[79] Those who would thus maintain the division between 9 and 10 also classify them differently. The first is identified as a song of thanksgiving (Kirkpatrick, Delitzsch, Cohen, Eaton, et al.), whereas Psalm 10 is recognized as a lament. Even those who regard the two as a unit state that we are dealing here with a mixed type of psalm where thanksgiving for victory achieved gives way to lament — "praise and lament combined."[80] It is not unusual to have expressions of thanksgiving in a psalm of lament. But it is odd, as Anderson observed, that the lament follows the thanksgiving.[81]

The present writer agrees with Robert Gordis that in Psalms 9 and 10 we have "two halves of a single alphabetic psalm."[82] Furthermore, the unity exhibited in the whole is not superficial — we are not dealing here with a psalm of mixed type. From first to last, Psalm 9/10 is *an appeal to God for deliverance*, hence, a lament. The key to this understanding is the recognition of the verbs in 9:4-6 as *precative perfects*, i.e., beseeching God to act, not stating what he has already done. This approach to the interpretation of the psalm was proposed by Buttenwieser some 60 years ago.[83] More recently, the validity of Buttenwieser's proposal has been recognized by others, including Dahood and A.A. Anderson. It provides an understanding of the text that eliminates a number of difficulties. One should take heed of Craigie's warning that "not enough is yet known about

---

[76]Drijvers, *The Psalms*, p. 22.
[77]Kirkpatrick, *The Book of Psalms*, p. 42.
[78]Cohen, *The Psalms*, p. 18.
[79]Derek Kidner, *Psalms 1-72, An Introduction and Commentary* (London: The Tyndale Press, 1973), p. 68.
[80]Arnold B. Rhodes, *The Book of Psalms*, The Layman's Bible Commentary (Richmond: John Knox Press, 1960), p. 36.
[81]A.A. Anderson, *Psalms 1-72*, p. 104.
[82]Robert Gordis, "Psalms 9-10 — a Textual and Exegetical Study," *JQR* 48 (Oct. 1957), p. 108.
[83]Buttenwieser, *The Psalms*, p. 429.

the nature and development of the Hebrew verbal system to permit a sure translation of Hebrew's verbs *in poetic texts* on the basis of the form alone."[84] But in Psalm 9 the context is decisive.

Reference was made above to the broken nature of the acrostic pattern in Psalm 9/10. If the pattern were complete, we might expect to have 44 verses in the combined psalm, since the acrostic continues with every other verse and there are 22 letters in the Hebrew alphabet. However, there is a total of only 38 verses in the two psalms. From this we might conclude that 6 verses have been lost in transmission.[85] Psalm 9 completes its acrostic pattern with the first 11 letters (half) of the alphabet, except for the omission of any verse beginning with the fourth letter, ד (*daleth*). Psalm 10 has more omissions, since it apparently includes only 7 of the final 11 letters. Buttenwieser, by an ingenious rearrangement and transposition of words, phrases, and whole verses, produced a rather completely restored acrostic, consistent throughout. His proposals were based in part on logic and partly on linguistic analysis, although the impossibility of excluding a certain degree of subjectivity in making such a reconstruction should be obvious. Sarna, who recognized the great contribution of Buttenwieser to the study of the Hebrew precative perfect, admitted that "it is difficult today to accept his theory of the wholesale dislocation of verses as a proper procedure in the reconstruction of the text."[86]

The psalm is, *in toto*, an appeal to God for deliverance. It opens with a vow, to praise God when the psalmist's enemies have been "turned back" (vv. 1-3). This promise is followed by a plea that the Lord will bring these enemies to judgment (vv. 4-6, see discussion), since God does occupy his throne (vv. 7-10). Recognition of this latter truth elicits a call to worship God, since he is the guarantor of justice (vv. 11-12). Then comes a renewed plea for help (vv. 13-14),

---

[84]Craigie, *Psalms 1-50*, p. 112.

[85]Another possibility is that the psalm existed in its complete form at one time, but was altered when it was incorporated into its present role. Compare, e.g., the alteration of Ps 14:5 as it appears in 53:5.

[86]Nahum M. Sarna, in the prolegomenon of the 1969 edition of Buttenwieser's *The Psalms*, p. xxxiii. In 1898, G. Buchanan Gray, largely by "correctly" (his word) dividing and punctuating the Hebrew text, sought to reconstruct the acrostic. See "The Alphabetic Structure of Psalms IX and X," *The Expositor* (Sept. 1898), pp. 207-220.

followed by a call upon God to deal with the wicked (vv. 15-20). Psalm 10 continues the plea.

The heading of the psalm, with its musical reference, indicates that it was incorporated into the worship of Israel, a conclusion that is reinforced by the appearance of *Selah* at the end of verses 16 and 20. The significance of עַל־מוּת לַבֵּן (עלמות לבן, *'al-mûth labbēn*) cannot be determined with certainty. The *'al* means "upon," "concerning," or "according to." *Mûth labbēn* means "death (in relation) to the son." Apparently it is a note that the chief musician would understand, perhaps a reference to a familiar hymn tune to be used in the rendering of the psalm. However, some Hebrew texts combine the עלמות into one word (עֲלָמוֹת, *'ălāmôth*) meaning "maidens" (or, "sopranos," see Ps 46). Thus we may have sopranos among the young men, or a boy choir.

1. A Promise to Praise God (9:1-3)

The psalmist is in distress because of his enemies. Nevertheless, he begins his plea for help with a note of joy and confidence a confidence that makes him willing to commit his case into the hands of a God who is both powerful and just.

9:1 I will praise you, O LORD . . . . "My enemies turn back" (v. 3). Deliverance has not yet come. However, the remembrance of the Lord's *wonders* (works of past deliverances of his people, of judgment and redemption) inspires the present promise. This is no bargaining with God. It is not "I will praise you *if* my enemies are turned back," but *when*. The writer anticipates the deliverance that will come.

The nature of true praise is revealed in these verses. It is with the *whole **heart***. That is, the heart is the proper instrument of praise and not the lips only. To praise God also involves sharing with others — recounting publicly — the wonderful works of God. In addition, praise involves "rejoicing and singing" (v. 2). *Rejoicing* is an attitude of the heart that should accompany our worship. The *singing* is the natural overflow of a joyful heart. True worship involves both the feeling and the expression of adoration to God.

9:2-3 I will be glad and rejoice in you, although enemies may press about me. The Apostle Peter wrote of those who, even while enduring heavy trials, "are filled with an inexpressible and glorious joy" (1 Pet 1:8). Here is a joy that is from the Lord, and no one can take it away (John 16:22). **I will sing praise to your name.** God's name is worthy of praise. It was vouchsafed to Israel in an enduring covenant, and so Israel could call upon and praise that name.

2. A Plea for God's Intervention (9:4-6)

The verbs of verses 4-6 (*the suffixed verb* in Hebrew) have characteristically been translated as perfect tense in English, describing what God has already done to the enemies of the psalmist. However, if this were so, then how do we account for the plaintive cry of verse 13: "O LORD, see how my enemies persecute me! Have mercy and lift me up from the gates of death?" Kidner considers the verbs in verses 5 and 6 to be the *prophetic perfect*, describing action to take place in the future as though it had already happened, so certain is it of fulfilment.[87] This is a possibility (and the position of the NIV translation). However, it is better, with Buttenwieser and Dahood to recognize the verbs of verses 4-6 to be the *precative perfect*, expressing a request or entreaty.

9:4-6 "Oh that you would defend my right and my cause" (Dahood). The cry is of one who has confidence in God's righteous judgment. The psalmist asks only that God will convene his court, sit upon his throne of judgment, and see that right prevails. **You have rebuked the nations and destroyed the wicked.** (Again, the *prophetic perfect* interpretation probably should be the *precative perfect*, a plea or request here: "Rebuke the nations and destroy the wicked!") These *nations* and the *wicked* apparently are the *enemies* mentioned in verse 3. The threat, therefore, is not to the psalmist alone, but to his people. And so the psalm takes on the nature of a lament of the community, even as it is the expression of one agonizing soul. **[You have] blot[ted] out their name for ever and ever. Endless ruin [has] overtake[n] the enemy, [you have] uproot[ed] their cities; even the memory of them [has] perish[ed].** (Note that the brackets attempt to change the so-called *prophetic perfects* to the

---

[87]Kidner, *Psalms 1-72*, p. 69.

plea of the *precatives*.) Such expressions became the language of eschatology. Thus Isaiah wrote: "See, the LORD is going to lay waste the earth and devastate it . . . . The earth will be completely laid waste and totally plundered" (Isa 24:1-3). Both the psalmist and Isaiah were certain of God's ultimate exercise of his sovereignty in salvation and judgment. The former gives reasons for his confidence in the following verses.

3. A Basis for Confidence (9:7-10)

9:7-9 The LORD reigns forever. The eternal nature of God fills us with wonder. Kingdoms come and go. Despots arise upon the earth and pass away. Blasphemers rant and rave, shouting obscenities against God, but years hasten by, and soon they, too, are dead and buried. And God's **throne** is just as secure when they have passed as if they had never existed. Furthermore, God **judge[s] the world in righteousness**. He becomes **a refuge for the oppressed**, and he does not forsake those who seek him. It was this assurance that led David to call upon the Lord **in times of trouble.**

9:10 Those who know your name will trust in you. The name of God, in Hebrew thought, stands for the person of God and for his character. His name, and thus his nature, became known through revelation. That name stands for awesome power, for righteousness, and for goodness or goodwill. To *know* the name is to have walked in fellowship with him who bears it and to have learned that we can trust in him, whatever may come to us. Thus it is a glorious privilege to know his name.

4. A Call to Worship (9:11-12)

9:11-12 The knowledge of God, in the sense indicated above, was sufficient to elicit from the psalmist a call to worship. **Sing praises**. Even in the midst of affliction, when he was seeking deliverance, he could call for praises to be lifted to God. The verb "sing" is plural; this is a call for congregational praise. **To the LORD, enthroned in Zion** (in Jerusalem). It was recognized that God's throne is in heaven but that he is also present with his people on earth, "in his holy temple" (Ps 11:4). **Proclaim among the nations what he has done.** The news of God's deeds was never intended to be the property of some exclusive privileged class but is to be shared with all "peoples" (literally in Hebrew, plural) and in our text this includes particularly the humble or the afflicted (v. 12). **He who avenges blood** is one who exacts from the murderer the penalty for his deed. It might be the next of kin of the murder victim, but ultimately it is God himself who will require a reckoning from those who shed the blood of another human being — "Whoever sheds the blood of man, by man shall his blood be shed; for in the image of God has God made man" (Gen 9:6). God does not settle his accounts every Saturday night, but neither does he **ignore the cry of the afflicted.**

5. A Renewed Plea for Help (9:13-14)

9:13-14 Have mercy. The verb is imperative (חָנְנֵנִי, *ḥānᵊnēnî*), from a root (חָנַן, *ḥānan*) that means "to show compassion." The nature of the suffering that was endured is not declared. Was it the psalmist alone who was suffering, or all of his people with him? Reference to the "nations" (vv. 15-20) suggests that the entire community is distressed. In that case, "Behold what I suffer" (RSV) would be but an individual expression of the experience of the whole community. Again, as in verses 1-3, deliverance is sought in order that the psalmist might, once again, have special cause to rejoice and to sing praise (v. 14).

6. A Cry for Judgment (9:15-20)

9:15-16 Verses 13 and 14, as we have seen, are a plea for deliverance, and the psalm closes with a similar cry (vv. 19-20). Is it not strange, therefore, to consider verses 15 and 16 as indicating that the wicked have already been dealt with — **The nations have fallen into the pit?** Again, it is better to consider the verbs as either the *prophetic perfect* — "The nations will surely sink," or, better, the *precative* — "Let them sink." The retributive justice of God is invoked here. Elsewhere we read that the wicked "like beasts . . . too will perish" (2 Pet 2:12). These verses are continuing the plea for God's judgment to fall: **[Let] the wicked [be] are ensnared by the work of their hands.**

9:17-20 The wicked return to the grave (or, in the Hebrew, into *Sheol*, "the place of the dead"). The verb is active, not passive, as in the KJV, "shall be turned." The wicked have themselves chosen the path and made the turn that leads to the grave. They are hastening toward their own death. **Let the nations be judged.** The universality of God is implicit. Yahweh is no local deity, but the judge of all the earth (as in Gen 18:25). **Let the nations know they are but men.** Of the four Hebrew words usually translated "man," the one used here is אֱנוֹשׁ (*ʾnoš*), meaning "mortal," marked for death! Supermen? A super race? The most highly exalted will be brought low. Spurgeon has expressed it well:

> Crowns leave their wearers — *but men*, degrees of eminent learning make their owners not more than *men*, valor and conquest cannot elevate beyond the dead level of "*but men*"; and all the wealth of Croesus, the wisdom of Solon, the power of Alexander, the eloquence of Demosthenes, if added together, would leave the possessor but a man. May we ever remember this.[88]

With this lesson in humility the psalm closes.

We have stated that Psalm 9/10 constitutes a unit, of the type of a lament. The appeal to God for deliverance that was begun in Psalm 9 continues in 10. There is, however, this difference. In Psalm 9 the enemies are godless nations hostile to the people of God. In Psalm 10 they are the ungodly within Israel, who oppress the poor and the weak, although mention is made of the nations (the *goyim*) again in 10:16. The psalmist and his people are thus suffering double distress, from enemies without and within.

At this point it should be observed that some interpreters see many of the Psalms as descriptive of events of the Christian era, including reference to the time of the last days. Luther, for

---

[88]Spurgeon, *Treasury of David*, p. 101.

example, considered the enemies of Psalm 10 to be the ungodly who oppose the kingdom of God, specifically the *antichrist*. It seems far more probable that the psalmist had an immediate adversary in view. This fact does not, of course, prevent one's seeing in the psalm a reflection of the typically godless of any generation.

Psalm 10 opens with the question of the ages — why? It seems to the writer that God is standing aloof, while the wicked ignore him. Boastfully, they pursue their own lusts and attack the innocent who are crushed before them. The question *why?* cannot be stifled. Nevertheless, the psalmist is still certain that the Lord is sovereign and king. Consequently, he closes the psalm with a final appeal for God to act.

7. A Plaintive Cry — Why? (10:1-2)

10:1 Why, O LORD, do you stand far off? The wicked were prospering in their wickedness while the innocent were suffering. Why did God hesitate? Why did he not intervene? In Ps 9:9 it was acknowledged that the Lord is a refuge in times of trouble, and in 46:1 that he is "an ever present help in trouble." But now he seems to be "far off." The wicked continue to exploit the poor. **Why do you hide yourself in times of trouble?** Perhaps the trouble could be borne; it is the hiding of God's face from us that intensifies the anguish.

This question of theodicy has troubled the souls of many of the righteous and has been a point of attack by skeptics. Beginning with Pierre Bayle (1647–1706), many have held that there can be no rational explanation of the existence of evil in a world that is governed by a God who is good. They conclude either that God is not good or that he is not God. Bayle was a believer, but his advice was to abandon reason in favor of faith. He would not attempt a vindication of the goodness or justice of God in ordaining or permitting natural and moral evil. A contemporary, G.W. Leibnitz (1646–1716), asserted that God does not will moral evil in itself, but permits it because man is free and in order that a greater good might result. One will never know the exhilaration of standing on the mountaintop if he has not experienced the grueling climb to its summit. Leibnitz insisted that the world as it is is the best possible world and that the evil in it is necessary to the existence of the greatest moral good, as shadows in a picture. Such philosophizing is unhelpful and of minimum comfort, if at all, to the innocent person whose suffering continues unabated. Consider Job. He never received an explanation of the why of his suffering, not even when God addressed his case. He did receive the assurance that God was not in hiding, that God was concerned. And thus Job received a new vision of God and a new vision of himself (Job 42:5-6)..

10:2 The persecution by the wicked is not incidental; it is deliberate and premeditated. **In his arrogance the wicked man hunts down the weak.** Many versions follow with a call for divine judgment upon the wicked: "Let them be taken." However, it is better, with the LXX and the Latin, to view the two lines of verse 2 as synonymous parallelism. The cry for help comes later. Verse 2 would then read: "With pride the wicked hounds the poor. He takes him in the devices that he has conceived."[89]

8. The Attitude, the Prosperity, and the Deeds of the Wicked Man (10:3-11)

10:3 The plunderings of the wicked, his arrogance, together with his seeming impunity, are vividly depicted in verses 3-13. The precise and certain meaning of the Hebrew, especially of verses 3 and 4, is elusive. However, the first clause may be rendered, as in the KJV: "For the wicked boasteth of his heart's desire,"[90] or, "of his lust" (Gordis). Self-gratification and pride are at the heart of his evil. Fraudulent, rapacious, oppressive, and altogether without shame, he places himself at the center of the universe. He holds himself answerable to no one, not even to God.

The second half of verse 3 may yield the following: "The covetous one congratulates[91] himself; he renounces the LORD" (anti-

---

[89]This translation follows the Hebrew text, but with vocalization that differs somewhat from the Massoretic. See Oesterley, *The Psalms*, p. 143f.

[90]For "boasteth" Buttenwieser proposes a passive verb, suggesting that the wicked *is praised*, "in spite of his greedy soul" (*The Psalms*, p. 421).

[91]"Congratulates": the Hebrew has "blesses," (as in NIV). At times the term is used euphemistically, meaning "to curse," when the object is God (see Job 1:5; 2:9, Hebrew text). That does not seem to be the case here.

thetical parallelism). The verb "renounce" (translated **reviles** in the
NIV) connotes blasphemy, as in Ps 74:10, where the enemy blasphemes, or reviles, the name of God. It is possible that **reviles the
LORD** constitutes a part of verse 4. In that case, we may render it
thus: "The wicked blasphemes the Lord (saying) in his arrogance:
'God will not require a reckoning; God is nonexistent!' Such thoughts
underlie all of his treacherous schemes." This is not an avowal of
atheism. As Gordis has observed: "The sinner is voicing ancient dis-
belief in its most characteristic form, which did not negate the existence of Divine beings, but doubted their intervention in human
affairs."[92] Only in the recognition of God do we find the basis for
any moral law. Without this recognition, the wicked person considers himself immune to retribution. This truth is expressed succinctly in Prov 29:18 — "Where there is no revelation, the people
cast off restraint."

10:4-11 Many have sought a basis for moral conduct elsewhere,
but in the final analysis, there is none. Without a firm belief in
God, a person's conduct is either imposed by force from without,
or else every man does what is right "in his own eyes" (Judg 17:6).
The Scriptures indicate clearly that God is interested in human
behavior — not merely with the overt act, but with the condition of
the heart out of which the action springs. Get the heart right and
right deeds will follow. And the only way for the heart to be right is
to be brought into fellowship with the living God. Paul states categorically: "Those controlled by the sinful nature [flesh] cannot
please God" (Rom 8:8). Obviously for as long as they so live, they
will make no attempt to please God. They will go on ignoring God
and renouncing (reviling) God. Only thus can they find excuse for
their evil conduct, only thus can they present their claim that there
are no moral absolutes.

Many whose philosophy includes some concept of God live nevertheless as though God did not exist. This was the condition of the
evildoer in Psalm 10. Consequently, he continued plotting the evil
he would pursue. In spite of this, and in spite of the blasphemy, his
ways prosper at all times, and with apparent impunity, for God's
judgments "are on high, out of his sight" (RSV) or as in the NIV:

---

[92]Gordis, "Psalms 9–10," p. 113.

your laws are far from him. Theoretical judgment may be admitted, but it seems never to be executed. As for his enemies, he **sneers** at them. The Hebrew word is onomatopoeic, having a sound similar to "phooie," a further expression of a contemptuous attitude. His arrogance is again reflected in verse 6, when he boasts to himself: **Nothing will shake me.** In speech he is vile, deceitful, a liar, a trouble maker (v. 7). Like a beast he stalks his prey, the poor and the helpless, not stopping even at murder (vv. 8-10). And with no appreciation of God's patience with him, he concludes that **God has forgotten; he covers his face and never sees.**

9. A Final Plea to God for Help (10:12-18)

10:12-13 The psalmist had no question about the justice of God or about his power. Inevitably, judgment would come.[93] Hopefully, it would not be delayed any longer. So now the appeal that was voiced in Ps 9:19 is repeated: **Arise, LORD! Lift up your hand, O God. . . . Why does the wicked man revile God?** Why, indeed? As we have intimated, it is a psychological necessity. He knows that he is living out of harmony with the will of a righteous God. He does not intend to change his manner of living, so he must put all thought of God out of his mind. He gambles his life on the assumption that he will never be called to account, since God takes no note of his deeds.

10:14 The psalmist knows differently. In verse 14 he uses a verb indicating the past action of God that is also a present reality. The Lord never ceases to notice what goes on upon the earth. **But you, O God, do see [and you see today] trouble and grief; you consider**

---

[93]It is of interest to note that nothing is said here of judgment beyond the grave. In OT times God's revelation included comparatively little about future reward and punishment. That would come later. In the book of Job, not once do the friends suggest: "Job, you suffer now, but you know that one day the joys of heaven will be yours." God had not yet lifted the veil of the future to that extent. In Isa 26:19 we do read: "But your dead will live; their bodies will rise. You who dwell in the dust, wake up and shout for joy" (also LXX). But this word from God came after the time of the author of Psalm 10. See also Dan 12:2.

it to take it in hand. **The victim commits himself to you; you are the helper of the fatherless.** Knowledge of God's care in the past is reason enough for believing that he is concerned now.

10:15 Break the arm of the wicked and evil man. To the ears of a Christian, this may seem to be an appeal for cruel and inhuman treatment. The language is not necessarily to be taken literally. The clear call is for God to break the power of the wicked to such an extent that he is unable to cause trouble any more. Seek out his wickedness (and deal with him) until you find no more; that is, let no act of injustice remain unresolved or unpunished, i.e., **that would not be found out.**

10:16-18 The LORD is King for ever and ever. With this triumphant cry of faith the psalmist is ready to leave the matter in God's hands. Whether deliverance would come or not, he would continue his earthly pilgrimage secure in the knowledge that God was present in his life. He did not walk alone. And the time would come, he knew, when the **nations** (that set themselves against God) **will perish** (prophetic perfect, certain to occur). God had heard the petition of the afflicted; he would encourage their heart; his ear would be attentive (v. 17). He would see that justice was done, so that the **man, who is of the earth** (earthling) would **terrify no more.**

IV. LIVING VICTORIOUSLY (11:1–15:5)

A. IN GOD WE TRUST (11:1-7)

Psalm 11 is no lament, although it clearly reflects a situation dominated by evil and in which imminent danger threatened. The very foundations of society were crumbling. Villains without mercy, weapons ready, moved in the shadows, waiting but the opportunity to ambush and to strike down the unwary. The despairing, with eyes focused only upon the terror loosed on the land, could think only to run. "Flee to the mountains, escape!" they cried.

The psalmist was not unaware of the distressful conditions that alarmed his countrymen, nor immune from the danger. Perhaps he had been specifically marked for attack. But the focus of his

concern was upon God and not upon man.[94] Glory belongs to the
Lord, and he *would be glorified*. This he knew. Escape? Yes, surely.
But the only escape from the danger threatening the land was in
the Lord. And so, with resolute confidence, he responds to the situation, not with a lament addressed to God, but with words of
encouragement addressed to the fainthearted and unbelieving
around him. It is a psalm of trust, closing with a warning to the
wicked declaring the fate that would surely befall them from the
hand of a righteous God.

1. The Challenge (11:1-3)

11:1 The psalm opens with a simple affirmation of faith. With
just two words in Hebrew, בַּיהוָה חָסִיתִי (*bayahweh ḥasîthî*), the
psalmist speaks with eloquence: **In the LORD [Yahweh] I take
refuge**, or, "I trust in the Lord." His associates, filled with despair,
had proposed what they considered to be the sensible thing to do.
But he recognized in their advice to flee a challenge to his faith. It
is more likely that his faith had been ignored on their part, or dismissed as irrelevant. Persons who are themselves devoid of faith
find it difficult to accept the reality that it can be genuine in others.
For the psalmist, faith in God was the foundation of his life. Under
the circumstances he might not be able to forestall a time when he
would tremble upon that *Rock*, but he knew that the rock would
never tremble under him. Impatiently, therefore, and with mild
reproach, he would put his question to these who thought that
escape was the only alternative to despair.

**How then can you say to me: "Flee like a bird to your moun-
tain?"** How, indeed, can anyone suppose it to be good to forsake
the Lord, just at the time when life is most difficult? We may ask

---

[94]Some believe the psalmist had sought divine protection in the sanctuary, from whence he recited the words before us. For example, W.H.
Bellinger, Jr., in "The Interpretation of Psalm 11," *EvQ* 56 (April 1984): 95-
101, considers this a probability as to the origin of the Psalm. Yet he also
recognizes the validity of interpreting it (and other Psalms) in the light of
their application to other situations.

why the wicked are unrestrained, why their attack has been directed against us, but surely it is better to face any difficult situation in life with the Lord than without him.

11:2-3 But this did not enter into the thinking of the psalmist's associates. In verses 2 and 3 we have a continuation of their urgency to flight, verses that view the situation as hopeless. Each begins in Hebrew with the particle, כִּי (*kî*, "because"). "Flee, *because* wicked men are loosed in the land. Flee, because (not "if") the foundations are destroyed. What have the righteous been able to accomplish?" The implied answer to this question is: "Nothing that will make any difference." But they were asking the wrong question –"What can man do?"[96] The psalmist's thoughts were centered elsewhere upon what God could and would do. In verses 4-7 we have his response.

2. The Answer of Faith (11:4-7)

11:4 The LORD is in his holy temple. He is still present in the midst of his worshipers no matter how fiercely people or nations may rage. God has not abdicated, nor is he dead. His presence may not be demonstrated by a visible sign other than the change that it makes in individuals and in circumstances, but that is adequate. Associations influence lives, and when lives are influenced, strengthened, and motivated in association with God, we realize that he is present. This nearness of God, his imminence, is one of the cardinal teachings of the Scriptures, and it was this assurance that gave the psalmist confidence in time of trouble. Yet God also transcends this earth. He is not like some weak mortal; The LORD's throne is in heaven. And from this dual vantage point — on earth and in heaven

---

[95]Who the persons were who advised flight we are not told. Alexander MacLaren and others after him have suggested the possibility that the psalmist was deliberating with himself, that two voices within him were clamoring to be heard — "the voice of sense which spoke to his soul, and that of the soul, which spoke authoritatively to sense." However, it appears that flesh and blood questioners are involved, for in verse 1 they are addressed as "you" in the plural. See MacLaren, "Psalms," *An Exposition of the Bible* (Hartford, CT: S.S. Scranton, 1914), 3:34.

— he knows what transpires among humankind. **He observes the sons of men.** Not only so, but he discerns between the good and the evil. **His eyes examine them,** or "test" individuals. "He takes their measure at a glance" (NEB). God is aware!

11:5 The LORD examines the righteous. If it is true that God "causes his sun to rise on the evil and the good, and sends rain on the righteous and the unrighteous" (Matt. 5:45), it is equally true that times of trial and testing come upon the righteous. To some degree we can understand this. One would never know the mettle of which he is made if he were never tested. I cannot know that I am honest if there is never the opportunity to be dishonest; or truthful, if there is never the temptation to lie. Thus testing may serve to prove one's integrity. In addition, it can reveal flaws in our character and motivate us to correct them, just as the refining of precious metals in the fire removes the impurities. It is possible that times of testing may shatter one's soul and spirit. On the other hand, they can enrich the soul and cause the spirit to shine with greater radiance.

In verse 5 one should note the antithesis between the wicked and the righteous. One (**the wicked**) the Lord's **soul hates.** Do we not then expect to read that he *loves* the righteous? Instead, we read that he **examines** (tests) the righteous. But is it not the same thing? God does love, and *that is why* he tests the righteous. To grow and develop as God's children, one needs to face times of testing. A loving parent will encourage a little one to take his first steps, knowing that he may fall, but also believing that he will get up and try again. Such testing from God is directed both to our good and to his glory. And so James could write: "My brothers, whenever you have to face trials of many kinds, count yourselves supremely happy, in the knowledge that such testing of your faith breeds fortitude, and if you give fortitude full play you will go on to complete a balanced character that will fall short in nothing" (Jas 1:2, NEB).

The wicked do not require such testing as may come to the righteous, for they have already shown their depravity. They are *hated* by the Lord. This may seem to be harsh language, but what other attitude toward evil would be consistent with the nature of a righteous God? The wicked **love violence** and their violence is directed toward the innocent. They fail to recognize and to respect human life as divinely given and sacred. Such violence must always bring God's condemnation.

11:6-7 The promised destruction of **the wicked** is not to be taken lightly (v. 6). The theme is repeated throughout the Bible. Ezek 18:4 states clearly: "The soul who sins is the one who will die." The writer of Psalm 11 was willing to rest his case at that point, to let **fiery coals and burning sulfur** and a horrible, **scorching wind** be the cup from which the wicked must drink. He knew that "the wages of sin is death" (Rom 6:23). He did not know that in years to come, God's own Son would drink from that cup and experience that death for sinners, in order that we might live. And yet the psalmist did know that confidence that comes from one's contemplation of the nature of God. Foundations may crumble. Enemies may threaten. But God remains. Furthermore, he is **righteous** and he continues to love **justice.** Consequently, one who lives accordingly will know that he does not walk alone. Even through the shadow cast by times of crisis he knows that God is present, for the **upright . . . will see his face.**

B. WICKED WORDS AND THE WORD OF GOD (12:1-8)

Language, in the sense of the spoken word that communicates thoughts and feelings, may be said to be the chief distinctive mark of humanity. This wonderful gift of God may be, and often is, used perversely. This Psalm deals with the wicked words of evil men over against the word of God. Psalm 11 made reference to crumbling foundations that were evidenced by deeds of violence of wicked men. Psalm 12 reflects a threatening situation also, but here the danger is defined differently. Men with no thought of devotion to God and equally lacking in integrity are achieving their evil designs by word of mouth. With perverted speech they flatter, lie, deceive, manipulate.

Such use of speech, or misuse, brought oppression and ruin to the humble and to those whose low estate made them defenseless. (Who, among average citizens, could afford a costly lawsuit maliciously brought?) Yet perverse speech was not limited to the public arena. Everyone might be found to be speaking lies, even to those closest to him. Certainly the situation was alarming enough to justify a lament such as the one before us. Under the circumstances, the psalmist sought help from the Lord and received from God the assurance of that help. Consequently, he could close the Psalm with an expression of confidence, for he knew that the word of the Lord is sure. And God will deal with the wicked.

1. The Pernicious Words of Ungodly Men (12:1-4)

12:1 The opening verses of the Psalm are a cry for help, citing the cause of the distressful conditions that prevailed in the land. **Help, LORD, for the godly are no more.** For the term translated "godly" (חָסִיד, *ḥasîd*) no one word in English is adequate. Various translations reflect different aspects of the term.[96] We may summarize these as follows: "Persons devoted to God, loyal and faithful, manifesting kindness and uprightness of character, and thus confirming their relation as indeed children of God and brethren one of another **have vanished from among men.**" The psalmist must have felt very much as Elijah after his flight from the wicked Queen Jezebel, when he cried out to God: "The Israelites have rejected your covenant . . . . I am the only one left" (1 Kgs 19:10). How threatening is the state of affairs when the people of a land have forsaken God and his righteousness. Wickedness increases. Sin feeds upon itself, and when God is forgotten or ignored, it spreads

---

[96]Note the variety of translations. (1) *As an attribute:* "loyalty" (NEB), "love" (Oesterley), "faithfulness" (Leupold), "piety" (Leslie), "kindness" (Briggs), "mercy" (Basic English Bible), "goodness" (Moffatt). (2) *As one possessing the attribute:* "the godly man" (KJV), "good man" (Buttenwieser), "faithful one" (Craigie), "the devoted man" (Dahood), "principled and godly" (Amplified Bible), "saint" (Douay-Rheims), "the upright" (New Catholic Edition), "men of lovingkindness" (Emphasized Bible), "one loyal" (New Jerusalem Bible), "the faithful" (NKJV), "a good man" (Good News Bible). Properly understood, the term חָסִיד embodies the concept of "covenant love/loyalty" and various contexts may require more refinement as the translations above seek to do (some inadequately). Any word must be understood in a given context and not isolated from such. One word definitions are primarily given for convenience's sake in language study and are not meant to be exhaustive for that word in various contexts.

like a cancer, from the highest echelons of a nation to the lowest levels.

12:2 As a consequence, people can no longer be trusting of one another, and one must always be on guard. When honor for God is gone, when the divine imperative has been denied, honesty suffers. **Everyone lies to his neighbor.** When the foundations of moral living have been destroyed, what else could one expect? With **flattering lips** and **with deception** they speak, or with "flattering lips and . . . boastful tongue."* Verse 5 reveals the use to which these deceitful words were directed; namely, to despoil, or to plunder, the poor. Possibly the problem involved corrupt leaders, as Anthony Ash has suggested.[97] Verse 8 refers to the exalting of vile men. Since these occupied positions of power, their twisted words were devastating, and they became guilty of prostituting God's gift of language to evil purposes.

12:3-4 This perversion of speech is reason enough to call for God's intervention, for it is a sin against God as well as against man. And since the Psalm opens with a plea for the Lord's help, the verb in verse 3 may be understood as voluntative [desire for God to act] (not as a statement of fact as in the King James Version). **May the LORD cut off all flattering lips and every boastful tongue.** Although some ancient monarchs were fiendish enough to cut out the tongue of an offending subject, that is not proposed here. Instead, we have a figure of speech in which the tongue stands for the person. The meaning is: "May such persons be cut down," as in Ps 37:9: "For evil men will be cut off" – [The person] **that says, "We will triumph with our tongues."**[98] The LXX has, "We will magnify our tongue; our lips are our own." The question that follows, **Who is our master?** implies a negative response. "We answer to no one, not even to God." Rather than to practice moderation or restraint in their use of free speech, they threaten even greater boldness and irresponsibility, defying God, as it were, to do anything about it. They would practice freedom of speech with a vengeance! This defiance is dealt with in verse 5.

---

[97]Ash, *Psalms*, p. 64.
[98]A prefixed ל (*lᵉ*) in the Hebrew text suggests that "tongue" is accusative and not instrumental; i.e., not "with our tongues" as in NIV, RSV, KJV and other translations.

2. God's Promise and the Psalmist's Response (12:5-6)

12:5 This verse, in the nature of a prophetic oracle (see Isa 33:10), is a promise of God's help. The objects of his concern are the **weak** and the **needy**. In the Hebrew, the terms are not exact synonyms, the former indicating more specifically those who are suffering some distressful condition (in this case the oppression of the wicked). The latter word indicates the condition of poverty.

I will now arise, says the LORD. This is God's promise to the psalmist in response to the plea expressed in verse 1. There the cry was, "Help" or, literally, "Save" (הוֹשִׁיעָה, *hôšî'āh*, from the root יָשַׁע, *yāša'*). Using the same root word, God responds that he will protect them. **I will protect them from those who malign them.** The verb translated "malign" is apparently from a root that means "to blow, breathe, pant, puff." The meaning seems suitable here, not "puffeth at him" (KJV). However, the translation is not without difficulty.[99] In any case, God will respond favorably to the plight of the afflicted.

12:6 Whatever lying and deceitful words men may speak (and they are many), **the words of the LORD are flawless**, unadulterated by any falsehood or deception, fully reliable. This is the testimony of the psalmist, his response to God's promise of help.

---

[99]On the basis of the Greek and Syriac versions, the text has been emended to read: "I will set in safety; I will shine forth for him." But a direct object is needed for "I will set in safety" ("I will protect . . ."), and so the NIV translation given above. Patrick F. Miller, Jr., in "*YAPIAH* in Psalm 12:6," *VT* (Oct. 1979): 495-500), reviews evidence indicating that the word translated "pants for" or "yearns" may be recognized as a noun. By analogy with Ugaritic examples, the meaning would be "witness" and this would provide an object for the preceding verb, thus: "I will set in safety the witness that is his." This is an interesting possibility, assuming that the psalmist is facing false accusers. Its validity might be enhanced if we knew more about the life situation that was involved. Aside from the above discussion, the NIV considers the word "malign" to express the idea of "one who puffs, blows, pants" against an opponent. Also, the singular suffix, לוֹ, has been changed to a plural in accordance with the context, i.e., "them."

3. Confidence in the Face of Continuing Danger (12:7-8)

12:7-8 Whether it is translated as a petition, "O LORD, keep us
safe," or as a statement of fact, **O LORD, you will keep us safe**
(LXX), verse 7 is an expression of confidence, based upon the certainty of God's word. The foundation of God is sure and will never
be moved by the machinations of humankind. The psalmist had no
illusions. He knew that so long as vileness is exalted in a land, the
wicked will continue to multiply, and evil will increase. This is an
alarming reality of life. But he also knew that neither the boastful
words and deceptions of men nor their deeds could negate the
word of God. This, too, is a reality. **The wicked** may continue to
freely strut about, but God's Word endures. It was so in David's
time, and for 3,000 years it has continued to be so, having withstood every assault made against it. That Word has met successfully
the test of time.

C. FROM DESPAIR TO HOPE (13:1-6)

Psalm 13 begins with a sigh and ends with a song. It moves from
despair, through prayer, to confident hope. The despair is heightened by the feeling that God has forgotten the plight of his servant.
Yet trust in the ultimate beneficence of God brings a renewal of joy
and confidence to the psalmist, a joy that is made even more precious because of the previous despondency. The sunshine seems
always brighter after the storm. It is understandable, therefore, that
the psalm should close with a burst of singing, the outpouring of a
heart that has experienced goodness from the hand of God.

The heading, **For the director of music**, would indicate that
Psalm 13 was used in congregational worship. However, the psalm
is intensely personal in its origin, an individual lament of a soul
wholly devoted to God. The precise setting cannot be determined,
but there were a number of experiences in the life of David out of
which the psalm could have arisen. The time of his flight from Saul
would have been such an occasion. (See 1 Kgs 27:1.)

Reference in verse 3 to the immediate threat of death has led
some to infer that the writer was suffering from a severe, lingering
illness. This is a possibility, but if so, the suffering was aggravated by

the fact that enemies were hounding him and gloating over him. Oesterley, noting the absence of any mention of sickness, considers the suffering to have been purely mental.[100] However, the possibility of sickness should not be excluded. A model of brevity, the psalm moves quickly from an expression of anxiety to an impassioned plea for the Lord's help, to a song of triumphant thanksgiving.

1. The Anxiety (13:1-2)

13:1-2 Life is filled with questions, some of which are beyond our capacity to answer. It is just such a question that troubled the psalmist. He was in anguish of soul, experiencing deep sorrow, whether from an extended illness, or whatever. In addition, his anxiety was greatly increased by a sinking feeling that maybe God had forsaken him and that his suffering could only end in death. And so his cry, **How long, O LORD? Will you forget me forever?** It is to be noted that in his distress his first concern is for his relationship with God. For any troubled soul, this is a good place to begin. Otherwise, the night of despair is interminable. In his heart, the psalmist knows that God is still there.

But does God indeed forget his own? Does he hide his face from them? There are undoubtedly times in the lives of many when they feel that this must be the case. Even Jesus, on the cross, would cry out, "My God, my God, why have you forsaken me?" (Matt 27:46). Yet this same Jesus, who knew the agony of the cross, knew also the glory of the resurrection. In Heb 13:5 we find God's promise, "Never will I leave you; never will I forsake you."

2. The Prayer (13:3-4)

13:3-4 The approach to God was through a prayer of supplication. How else? Through the ages, God has responded to earnest prayers directed to him. Realizing this truth, the psalmist's complaint changes to petition. **Look on me and answer, O LORD my**

---

[100]Oesterley, *The Psalms*, p. 151.

God. Days of anxiety had prompted his questions, yet in his heart he knew still that he was God's child, an object of his concern. He could still say, "O LORD *my God*" **Give light to my eyes.** The eyes are darkened by illness and grief and are restored to brightness again upon the recovery of one's spirits and health. **Or I will sleep in death; my enemy [death] will say, "I have overcome him," and my foes will rejoice when I fall.** The writer is not merely concerned that his fall will result in his opponent's gloating over him, humiliating as that would be. He has a genuine concern that, since he has identified himself with the Lord, his downfall would cause God's name to be dishonored.

3. The Confidence (13:5-6)

13:5-6 Having concluded his prayer, the psalmist once again experiences the confidence of one in fellowship with God. He cannot yet say, "I have been delivered." But he can acknowledge: **But I trust in your unfailing love; my heart rejoices in your salvation.** Here is combined a confession of faith with a joyous cry of assurance that results in an overflow of praise: **I will sing to the LORD.** Thus the sigh of verse 1 has given place to the song of faith.

Throughout the OT it is reiterated again and again that the Lord is the *living God.* This distinguishes him from all others that are called god. Little wonder, then, that the psalmist was moved to direct his petition to him. Nor is it any wonder that he was blessed in so doing. We may rejoice that God still lives and that we also may address our prayers to him. John R. Finney and H. Newton Malony, discussing prayer and its place in the present age, consider the contemplative aspect, which they see as "a patient waiting on God to deepen one's confidence in God's power and love."[101] This was the experience of the psalmist. We do not presume that he had ever taken courses in contemplative thinking, but his confidence in God was deepened.

---

[101]John R. Finney and H. Newton Malony, "Contemplative Prayer and Its Use in Psychotherapy: A Theoretical Model," *Journal of Psychology and Theology* (1985): 171.

D. AS A MAN THINKS, SO IS HE (14:1-7)

God loves righteousness. But who cares? Amos the prophet cries out: "But let justice roll on like a river, righteousness like a never-failing stream!" (5:24). But who gives heed? Not the ungodly! Those whose lives are totally devoid of any thought of God are not concerned about doing his will. They march to a different drummer. Their hearts are filled with thoughts other than of God, and as a man thinks in his heart, so is he.

Psalm 14 speaks of those who say in their heart that there is no God. The evil consequences of such denial are then noted, including corruption and wicked deeds, with attacks upon the godly poor. Even so, it is noted that the latter do have refuge in God. The writer then closes with a prayer for God's deliverance or salvation.

As to type, the psalm does not fit well into any one of the usually recognized categories. It has commonly been identified as an *individual lament*, decrying oppression by the godless. Yet verses 1-3 are quite like the wisdom literature of the OT, such as is found in the book of Proverbs. And verses 4-6 remind one of the words of the prophets (as in Jer 5:1, for example). Arnold B. Rhodes regards the psalm as a prophetic liturgy,[102] but it may, with equal propriety, be called a wisdom psalm.

The repetition of Psalm 14 as Psalm 53 gives rise to at least three questions. First, why does it appear twice? The answer — evidently it was a part of two separate collections of Psalms, Books 1 and 2, that were later combined, without the elimination of the psalm from either collection. The psalms are practically identical, except for the portion found in 14:5-6. This differs almost entirely from Psalm 53. How do we account for this? One suggestion is that in one collection the text suffered in transmission and was restored as best it could be by a later hand. Or, it is possible that the original psalm was later altered for use under a different set of circumstances.[103] If this is the case, we have the interesting possibility that

---

[102]Rhodes, *The Book of Psalms*, p. 89.
[103]Leupold, in *Exposition*, p. 415, discusses a possible setting in which Psalm 53 could have been used. His proposal will be considered in our treatment of that psalm.

the material of one inspired writer could be utilized and altered by another. A further difference between the two psalms is the use of the divine name. Whereas Psalm 14 employs both *Yahweh* (LORD) and *Elohim* (God), Psalm 53 uses *Elohim* only, consistent with the preference in Book 2 for that designation for God.

Of the scholars who see a poorly preserved text as the cause of the diversity in the two psalms, there is no unanimity as to which text is to be preferred. William R. Taylor affirms that "the text is better preserved in Psalm 53."[104] Buttenwieser, however, considers Psalm 14 to be "the superior text."[105] Perhaps the view that sees the one psalm adapted to a different situation best accounts for the differences in them.

In the interpretation of the psalm there are three general approaches. The *historical*, which would identify the one who rejects God as one of Israel's enemies, ridiculing their faith, or else as an Israelite of the exile who despairs of any hope of deliverance; the *ethical*, which views the psalm as designed to indicate the wickedness that results from a denial of God; and the *philosophical*, as a polemic against atheism.[106] It seems best to consider the psalm a combination of the latter two, although in the reference to the corrupt among the "sons of men" it is difficult to escape the conclusion that the psalmist is referring to persons, or a class of persons, that have come under his personal observation.

The contrast that appeared in Psalm 1 between the wise and the foolish, between the godly and the ungodly, is found also in Psalm 14. Here the distinction is between those who deny God and those whom the Lord calls "my people," or between "evildoers" (v. 4) and the "righteous" (v. 5). The evil of the former has its roots in the rejection of God.

---

[104]William R. Taylor, "Exegesis, Psalms 17:1," *The Interpreter's Bible* (Nashville: Abingdon Press, 1955), p. 75.

[105]Buttenwieser, *The Psalms*, p. 476.

[106]See Sh. Weissblueth, "Psalm 14 and Its Parallel — Psalm 53, *Beth Mikra* 29 (1983–1984): 133-138.

1. The Denial of God and Its Consequences (14:1-3)

If Psalm 14 is a lament, it lacks the opening cry for help that one expects in psalms of this type. Instead, it begins with a condemnation of the one who denies God, indicating the consequences such denial has for the community. Johann Goethe wisely observed that the battle between belief and unbelief is the only significant warfare in the history of the world. All else depends upon the outcome of this battle! To believe that God lives, and that he sets standards of moral and ethical behavior for humankind, and to believe further that we are ultimately responsible to him, provides meaning, purpose, and direction to life. Without this belief, one may delude himself into thinking that he has freedom to live without restrictions, that he is the master of his fate, the captain of his soul. But if this be true, then it is also true that all others are equally unrestricted, and too soon it becomes obvious that people so liberated are free primarily to destroy both themselves and others. We can begin to understand why the psalmist designates such persons as *fools*. Some may look upon freedom from God and freedom from religion as progress. But if there is no sure direction for humankind, who knows what progress is? Could not that which some call progress be regression instead?

14:1 The fool says in his heart, "There is no God." Psalm 14 is not dealing with the blatant atheist. In the days of the psalmist it would have been difficult to find one so arrogant. It takes a rather heightened ego to say, "There is no God." Man is finite. God is infinite. Man's powers of observation are restricted to a relatively small area of all reality. Has the atheist been everywhere in the universe? Examined every nook and corner? If not, who knows what or Who might be there? Actually, the assertion, "There is no God," today as then, may be more a cry of defiance than a reflection of intelligence. Edwin McNeill Poteat aptly describes it as "a major prejudice, not a major premise."[107]

---

[107]Edwin McNeill Poteat, "The Book of Psalms" (Exposition), *The Interpreter's Bible*, George Arthur Buttrick, ed. (Nashville: Broadman Press, 1955), p. 278.

The psalmist's fool only speaks in his inner consciousness. Even so, the denial is sufficient to determine the misguided direction of his life. It is this result of his denial that gains for him the epithet of fool. (How ironical is the dehumanizing influence of humanism!) Let us add that there are some people who ought to know better who live *as though God does not exist.* They do believe there is a God but are willing to shut him completely out of their lives. Would you say that theirs is even greater folly?

They are corrupt. The use of "they" indicates that the writer is referring to all those who ignore God in making their moral decisions. **Their deeds are vile,** or their works are vile in the sight of God, since they are unrestrained by any consciousness of the divine imperative. **There is no one who does good.** We would understand this as Paul applied it, to mean that "all have sinned and fall short of the glory of God" (Rom 3:23). Others would see here a reference to the total depravity of the human race. But the psalmist, we believe, was not so much concerned with doctrinal statements and religious formulas, as in describing the moral cancer that develops along with unbelief.

14:2-3 The LORD looks down from heaven. How patient God is and how persistent! Even now he looks in our direction; his silent gaze rests upon us. And for what does he seek? **To see if there are any who understand, any who seek God.** Continually we are challenged to choose between wisdom and folly. And do we need to be reminded that reverence for God is "the beginning of wisdom" (Prov 9:10)? As Alexander MacLaren has observed: "One who is religiously and morally wrong cannot be intellectually right."[108] It is possible that one may have a fine intellect and yet not have sense enough to be decent. But more than indecency results when humankind forgets God. That is only the beginning. Just as genes out of control produce biological monstrosities, so, as men turn aside from the Lord, there are no bounds to the corruption that follows, no limit to the depravity. This is what verse 3 is telling us.

If the final curtain were drawn at this point, the picture would be dark indeed. But the following verses indicate that there are still those who are in fellowship with God and that they are the objects of his concern and care.

---

[108]MacLaren, *Psalms,* p. 40.

2. God, the Refuge of the Just (14:4-6)

14:4 Will evildoers never learn — those who devour my people.
The general description "sons of men" of the preceding verses
gives way to a specific reference to persons who are oppressing the
people of God. Whether these are foreign overlords or wicked
countrymen is not stated — probably the latter. The prophet Micah
speaks of those in Israel who "eat my people's flesh" (3:3). The
implication is that the ungodly not only harass and attack the godly
but that they take a particular delight in doing so. This is further
evidence of their mental aberration, and so the question: Will they
never learn? Do they not understand what has happened since they
parted company with God? In spite of their braggadocio, in their
heart there is a gnawing fear, occasioned by the fact that the people
of God experience a peace that is beyond their comprehension. A
Bonhoeffer or a Niemöller in a Nazi prison could know a freedom
that could not be denied them by locks and bars.

14:5-6 On the other hand, those who boast that they are free of
any fear of God will have other fears to plague them, especially
when they come to the realization that **God is present in the
company of the righteous**, or "in the brotherhood of the godly"
(NEB), and totally absent from their own lives. When all of the
philosophical arguments against belief in God have been exhausted,
there remains the evidence of the presence of God in the lives of
individuals, sustaining them in trials and giving new dimensions to
those lives. One who shuts God out of his or her life will someday
awaken to the fact that he or she has turned into a dead-end street.
Is that not, in itself, sufficient to cause him or her great fear (NIV:
overwhelmed with dread)?

3. Prayer for Deliverance (14:7)

The fact remains that belief and unbelief continue to exist side
by side. On the one hand, there are the determined attacks of those
who would, if they could, stamp out every vestige of religion. On
the other, there is the faith that "God's solid foundation stands
firm" (2 Tim 2:19). As the confrontation continues, the believer
does experience the sustaining presence of God in his life. The

Lord is his refuge. And he anticipates more. As the struggle continues on earth, the believer can see, in certain events, the execution
of God's judgment. The psalmist, too, was certain of God's
concern. In view of this, it is not surprising that he should close the
psalm with a prayer that God would intervene immediately.

14:7 Oh, that salvation for Israel would come out of Zion! In
context, this would seem to be a plea for deliverance from the
foolish who say there is no God. However, this is a plea for national
deliverance or salvation, for an improvement in the fortunes of the
people of God who are trusting in him. It is thought by some that
this verse was a later addition, at a time when national disaster
threatened. Ferdinand Hitzig proposed that it may have been an
utterance of Jeremiah when the Scythians were overrunning the
land — an interesting possibility, but only a conjecture.[109] In any
case, if this is an addition, it would have been made some time
before Psalms 14 and 53 had a separate existence, for it is present
in both.

Zion designated Jerusalem, in general, and particularly the
temple area. God's abode is in heaven (v. 2), but he promised to
honor the temple with his presence (1 Kgs 9:3). It would be natural,
therefore, to anticipate deliverance/salvation as coming out of
Zion: **When the LORD restores the fortunes of his people.** Not if,
but when, an affirmation of faith, anticipating a deliverance that
would bring great rejoicing. The reference has messianic overtones,
as it constitutes another thread in the prophetic tapestry we have
mentioned earlier. There is the longing for deliverance. Christians
see the realization of this hope through the Christ, whose message
of deliverance (the gospel) was first proclaimed in Zion on the day
of Pentecost after the resurrection and ascension (Acts 2:1-41).
Subsequently, this "salvation . . . out of Zion," has gone into all the
world. The prayer of the psalmist has been answered in a greater
way than he could have imagined.

---

[109]Delitzsch, *The Psalms*, 1:209.

E. TOGETHERNESS WITH GOD (15:1-5)

The prophet Amos asks: "Do two walk together unless they have agreed to do so?" (Amos 3:3). The inquiry involves more than proximity. It speaks of togetherness, of meaningful companionship. That one could have companionship with God seems too much to be hoped for, but that is what the Bible is all about. In Psalm 1 we saw a wise man meditating upon God's law, an indication of his desire for guidance. But more than meditation is required. If one would have fellowship with God, a welcome into his presence, he must attune his life to God's wavelength and seek fulfillment in following the divine pattern. In doing so, he will also find a firm foundation upon which to build his life. This is the message of Psalm 15.

A masterpiece of brevity, the psalm raises the question as to who may be a guest in the house of the Lord, and then states those virtues that should be manifest in the life of one who would approach God. The closing words then give the assurance that he who walks in this way shall "never be shaken." The psalm thus gives us a cameo view of the godly man, in sharp contrast with Psalm 14, which spoke of the ungodly fool.

For those with unholy hands to deal with holy things was a matter of deep concern in ancient Israel. Consider the fate of Uzzah, who died for putting unclean hands upon the ark of God (2 Sam 6:6,7). In Num 4:15 is recorded a warning to the sons of Kohath that they "not touch the holy things or they will die." This concern was for ritual purity. In Psalm 15 the concern is for the moral and spiritual purity that is fitting to any who would come into God's presence.

1. The Question Presented (15:1)

15:1 Some have considered the psalm to be liturgical in nature. A worshiper, a band of pilgrims, or perhaps a person seeking asylum comes to the entrance of the sanctuary, desiring to be admitted. The priest, invoking the Lord, asks: **Who may dwell in your sanctuary? Who may live on your holy hill?** The worshipers respond by reciting that which is required of those who would enter. The implication is that they have understood and have met the requirements. They are then assured that "he who does these things will never be shaken" and are admitted.

That the psalm was so used is possible. There is evidence that among Israel's neighbors those who frequented the temples were informed of any cultic prerequisites to admittance. But no cultic acts are involved in the psalm, and it is better to consider the questions to be the soul-searching of an individual who desires to draw near to God in true devotion, rather than part of a ritual. The psalmist knows that worship is more than formality, that nearness to God is more than ritual. He might fashion the psalm in the style of an entrance liturgy without intending it for that purpose. This seems to be the case.

The question, then, as phrased in the psalm, is what kind of person does one need to be, not just to enter God's sanctuary, but to abide (continue to abide) in his presence, to make his holy mountain one's habitat? What are the conditions for such an experience? That is the question. Or, more specifically, what is to be expected on the part of one who would continue in God's fellowship?

2. The Answer to the Question (15:2-5b)

It is interesting that the answer to the question lists no spiritual or religious prerequisites. God is not in search of one who might classify as the religious type (whatever that may be). Here the requirements of those who would walk with him are ethical in nature. The emphasis is upon right conduct toward others. It is not fluency in prayer nor a tongue gifted in praises that will commend one to God, but a life that is in harmony with his righteous will. And harmony with God is to be demonstrated in one's treatment of his fellow man. Many may suppose that nearness to God is to be achieved *in worship*. The psalmist would not minimize one's need to worship God, as other psalms indicate. But he knew that unless one's worship issues in right conduct toward others, it is in vain and unacceptable to God. To such worshipers God says: "Away with the noise of your songs! I will not listen to the music of your harps. But let justice roll on like a river, righteousness like a never-failing stream!" (Amos 5:23,24).

15:2 Verse 2 consists, in the Hebrew, of only seven words. Three are participles — walking, doing, speaking — used to indicate continuing practice. The answer to "Who may dwell?" then, is clearly stated: the one who is walking blamelessly, doing right, and speaking truth from his heart. To walk blamelessly is to maintain one's integrity as a child of God. To do right is to conform one's life to moral and ethical standards above reproach, to shun every corrupt practice. To speak truth is to be free from any deceit or falsehood, and when this speaking is from the heart, it will have proper motivation, as Jesus taught in the Sermon on the Mount. One who has truth in his heart will speak the truth. These principles are to guide the one who walks with God.

15:3 Verse 3 provides an application of the principles to flesh-and-blood situations. It may be translated, quite literally: "He does not stumble over his tongue;[110] he does not do evil to his fellow-man, nor does he take up a reproach against his neighbor." The three parts of this verse are parallel with verse 2, thus:

Verse 2	Verse 3
Walking blamelessly	— not "stumbling" (*slander*)
Doing right	— not doing evil (*does no wrong*)
Speaking truth	— not casting reproach (*no slur*)

The three positive statements of verse 2 are balanced by the three negatives of the other. It is possible, however, to arrange the lines of the two verses as three successive doublets, as follows:

(2a) Walking blamelessly (2b) doing right
(2c) Speaking truth   (3a) Not stumbling over tongue
(3b) Not doing evil   (3c) not reproaching neighbor

This is the pattern followed in the Stuttgart edition of the Hebrew text and demonstrates an equally valid parallelism.[111] In view of this ambiguity, some would ask which arrangement of the lines is correct. Yet one may dismiss the question and agree with Patrick D.

---

[110]Not to stumble over the tongue is to be free from double-talk (and double-dealing).

[111]See *BHS* (Stuttgart: Deutsche Bibelstiftung, 1967/77).

Miller, Jr., who notes that *genuine ambiguity* (intentional, we would say) is involved. The two ways of reading the lines are equally correct, thus "different nuances or force" are given to the psalm.[112] In this way the psalmist gives added dimension to his writing.

15:4 The opening lines of verse 4 state a principle that will guide one in his relationships with others. Stated negatively: He will not accord honor to a scoundrel, no matter how greatly such a one may be acclaimed by others. No matter how wealthy or influential, he will not align himself with those who do wrong. Nor will he despise or consider of little account, a godly person, no matter how humble, how poor, how seemingly insignificant. On the contrary, in his eyes it is the vile person who is to be *despised*, who is worthy of contempt, and the godly one who is to be *honored*, who is worthy of respect. (Yet how often in modern society have we seen the wicked glamorized, and the righteous ridiculed!)

The concluding line of verse 4 is the first of three additional negative statements parallel, in style at least, with verse 3. In various versions the translation of this line has followed the thought of the King James: "He that sweareth to his own hurt, and changeth not." But the translation is not without difficulty. The Hebrew does not have the pronoun *his*, though it may be implied. The LXX (with Jerome's *Gallican Psalter*) reads, from an alternate meaning of the Hebrew: "He swears to his neighbor and does not disappoint." (Compare this with v. 2.) A literal translation could be: "He swears (in relationship) to evil, and does not change." The meaning would be that he swears to do no evil and keeps his pledge. This thought follows naturally the preceding statement that he would not condone evil in others.

Even so, when viewed in the context of the following two negatives, the traditional translation has much to commend it, for both of the following are related to financial matters. In this light the godly man might pledge his oath to a contract that would turn out to be to his disadvantage, but would keep the bargain nevertheless. He would not go back on his word.

---

[112]Patrick D. Miller, Jr., "Poetic Ambiguity and Balance in Psalm XV," *VT* 29 (1979): 419.

15:5a-b In addition, he would not take advantage of another's misfortune for his own enrichment. He **lends his money without usury**; instead, he views the dire need of others as an opportunity to help rather than one for increasing his own store of wealth. In the OT no reference is made to the practice of borrowing for investment, but there was borrowing to meet human need. The godly man would respond to such need, not with avarice but with generosity. Furthermore, he **does not accept a bribe against the innocent.** He cannot be bribed to pervert justice. Deuteronomy 16:19 states: "You shall not pervert the course of justice or show favour, nor shall you accept a bribe; for bribery makes the wise man blind and the just man give a crooked answer" (NEB). The assessment of the sin of bribery made by Hugh Latimer (1485-1555) is still valid: "I am sure this is *scala inferni*, the right way to hell, to be covetous, to take bribes, and to pervert justice." [113] One who would walk with God will spurn every temptation in this direction.

The answer to the question of verse 1 is not intended to be all-inclusive in its particulars. Yet it is comprehensive in scope, describing in broad outline the character and conduct of the one who would experience the presence of God in his life. These requirements, positive and negative, may be seen as ten in number, as many have noted — ten commandments, as it were. In summary, they are:

1. You shall walk blamelessly.
2. You shall do what is right.
3. You shall speak truth from the heart.
4. You shall not use your tongue in duplicity.
5. You shall not do evil to your fellow man.
6. You shall not gossip.
7. You shall scorn the evildoer and respect the godly.
8. You shall not go back upon a promise.
9. You shall not exact interest for a loan.
10. You shall not take a bribe against the innocent.

---

[113]See Spurgeon, *Treasury of David*, 1:212.

3. The Consequence and the Reward (15:5c)

15:5c The assurance of dwelling in God's presence, the quest of verse 1, is granted in the promise with which the psalm closes: **He who does these things will never be shaken.** What a promise! What a blessing! It is the one who goes on doing these things who shall not be shaken. This is not to say that the person who chooses the way of godliness will always prosper or always experience tranquility. It does mean that he will have the strength and integrity to withstand trials and testings when they come. He will have experienced God's acceptance and that will sustain him.

He will also have discovered that the pursuit of godliness has brought him to that point where he can accept himself. As he has endeavored to walk with God according to the divine ethic, he has learned not only how to live with others but also how to live honorably with himself. Indeed, when his life is so oriented, so in tune with the will of God, he shall never be *shaken*.

PART TWO: THE BELIEVER'S SALVATION (16–29)

I. THE GOD OF LIFE (16:1-11)

A. JOY IN THE LORD (16:1-11)

The significance of the term *miktam* (מִכְתָּם, *miktām*) in the title of Psalm 16 (and in Psalms 56–60) is not known with certainty. Believing it to be related to the Hebrew כֶּתֶם (*kethem*, poetic term for gold), Martin Luther, following rabbinic tradition, understood it to mean "golden," and designated the psalm "a golden jewel." This conclusion seems unlikely, however, since other psalms could just as aptly be so identified. Some of the rabbis considered the term descriptive of David –"meek" (מָךְ, *māk*) and "undefiled" (תָּם, *tom*). Others would relate it to the Arabic *maktum* ("hidden"), considering the psalm to have an element of mystery, or else to have remained secret (or hidden) for some time. This likewise is to be questioned. The LXX has στηλογραφία ("inscription") and the Old Latin *tituli inscriptio*, with a similar meaning. Since כתם (*ktm*) could be an alternate form of the Hebrew כתב, (*ktb*, "to engrave," "to inscribe"), this would seem to be the preferred understanding of the term, indicating that the psalm had appeared as an inscription.[1]

The keynote of the psalm is joy. "Therefore my heart is glad and my tongue rejoices" (v. 9). The occasion of the joy is the experience of fullness of life that the psalmist has found in God, a completeness experienced by the creature in harmonious relationship with the creator. The Greek philosophers might think of God as the highest in a series of what is good; the psalmist recognized in God the all-inclusive good, realizing that in possessing God he possessed

---

[1]For a discussion of these and other proposals relative to the term, see: Delitzsch, *Psalms*, 1:218, and Craigie, *Psalms 1–50*, p. 154.

all: "I have no good apart from thee" (16:2, RSV). It is because of this note of joy that we do not consider the psalm to have been written at a time when death threatened, as some propose. From beginning to end, the psalm breathes confidence. After an opening word asking God's protection, the writer confesses him as Lord and wholly commits his life to God's care and fellowship. He disavows any inclination toward any other god, finding his delight in God alone. The Lord is his refuge, his portion, his counselor, and his life. And that is enough.

1. Introductory Prayer and Commitment (16:1)

16:1 Keep me safe, O God! This is the petition of one who would daily seek God's watchcare. Brief (only two words in Hebrew), it nevertheless reflects confident expectation. **For in you I take refuge**, as one who would come in out of the storm. This recognition of God as refuge is foundational to the joy in life that the psalmist experiences. His is an inner peace unknown by those without such trust and confidence.

2. The Lord Is My Refuge (16:2-4)

16:2 The concept of God as his refuge was fundamental to the psalmist, the foundational principle of his life, the immovable rock upon which he would stand. It involved a disavowal of allegiance to any other deity. **I said to the LORD, "You are my Lord; apart from you I have no good thing."**[2] This unreserved commitment to the Lord is the secret of his happiness and it entertains no desire to turn to any other.

16:3-4 In the opinion of J. Leveen, the Hebrew text of verse 3, "as it stands . . . defies explanation." However, it seems to be set in

---

[2]The text of verses 2-4 has been described as difficult, obscure, or hopelessly corrupt. Even so, the general thrust of the psalm is discernible; that is, the declaration of the psalmist of his trust in God alone. See the New English Bible; Dahood, *Psalms 1-50*; and Craigie, *Psalms 1-50* for widely divergent translations.

contrast with verse 4, which describes those who worship gods other than the Lord. Leveen would render it thus: "All the saints that are in the earth shall be exalted; all those who take delight in thee shall glorify thee."[3] Such a rendering necessitates some emendation of the Hebrew and cannot be taken as final, but it may reflect the tenor of the passage. In contrast, sorrows will overwhelm those who would follow other gods (v. 4). There is no refuge in that direction.

3. The Lord Is My Portion (16:5-6)

16:5-6 In committing his life to God, the psalmist made a great discovery. He found a joy in living that did not depend upon fortune or circumstances. **LORD, you have assigned me my portion and my cup.** Others might believe that life is to be measured by the nature and extent of one's possessions. He knew that life does not consist of an abundance of things but in a constant relationship with God that transcends the mundane. "Ruthless men gain only wealth" (Prov 11:16). The psalmist rejoiced that he could say, **You have made my lot [destiny] secure.** The life that is open to the Lord will be filled with blessings without number. That life has a **delightful inheritance.**

4. The Lord Is My Counselor (16:7-8)

16:7-8 Furthermore, such a one enjoys the counsel of the Lord, and for this he is grateful. **I will praise the LORD, who counsels me.** I will praise God for directing me, thankful that he does not coerce. We are free to respond as we will. Only thus do we attain maturity. But like a wise parent, God does counsel us. No information is provided here to indicate how the counsel is given, but elsewhere the psalmist writes: "Your word is a lamp to my feet and a light for my path" (119:105). And, "I have hidden your word in my heart that I

---

[3]J. Leveen, "Textual Problems in the Psalms," *VT* 21 (1971): 52,53.

might not sin against you" (119:11). Conscience also may be considered as counsel from God, when it is informed and directed by his Word. "I will praise Yahweh," the psalmist says, **even at night [when] my heart⁴ instructs me.** One who has a love for God's Word may welcome the urgings of conscience, even if they rob him of sleep, if they prompt him to be a doer of the word and not a hearer only. For it is not the one who hears the word of the Lord, but he who does it, who is blessed. It is only in this very practical way, in daily living the word, that one may say with the psalmist: **I have set the LORD always before me, . . . I will not be shaken.** Only thus is the counsel of God made effective.

5. The Lord Is My Life (16:9-11)

16:9 Helmer Ringgren has noted that it was not a mystical identification with God that the psalmist enjoyed.⁵ There was no fusion of the human with the divine in some numinous ecstasy. Rather, his was the every day experience of life in fellowship with God. He was not overly concerned with the transcendental or metaphysical. It was the reality of God's nearness in his daily life that provided the reason for his joy. **Therefore my heart is glad and my tongue⁶ rejoices; my body also will rest secure.** The "heart" signifies the intellect — notice, "As (a man) thinketh in his heart" (Prov 23:7, KJV). The psalmist is saying that his mind entertains joyful thoughts, not the least of which is the consciousness of God's presence. Who

---

⁴The Hebrew has "my kidneys," the KJV "my reins" (in the archaic sense of the region of the kidneys), and the NEB "inward parts," for which many translators including the NIV substitute "heart" in keeping with modern terminology. Compare our use of such terms as "gall" (meaning "brazen impudence") and "spleen" (as "bad temper").

⁵Ringgren, *The Faith*, p. 60.

⁶So the LXX. The Hebrew text has "my glory" (see KJV). Peter, in his use of the psalm in the Pentecost sermon, quoted "tongue" instead of "glory." In doing so he followed the LXX. This would have been the text of the Psalms with which his hearers would have been familiar. Obviously, the inspired apostle did not consider it amiss to use a version that differed from the Hebrew text. Modern translations consider the LXX a "superior" reading which makes more sense in the context.

would dare think that he might have God at his right hand? It is enough to bring joy. "My glory/tongue" signifies the inner man, or the spirit. The joy is deeply felt. "My body" is literally in Hebrew "my flesh." So the writer is saying that his relationship to God involves the entire person, body, mind, and spirit.

There is a definite look to the future in verse 9 — "My body also will rest secure." Here is an expression of confidence for tomorrow, and for the next day. But for how many tomorrows? And would the companionship with God one day be terminated by death? For such a question, if it arose, the psalmist has an answer. He does not formulate some kind of doctrine of future life. He is not philosophizing about the "immortality of the soul" (a Greek idea!). He only knows that God is the giver and sustainer of life, and that he has power over death and the grave. Furthermore, he can believe that God, so near to him in life, will be near in death and even beyond death. Where God is, there is life.

16:10-11 Kirkpatrick, with insight, observed that: "The truth may be that the antithesis is not between life here and life hereafter, but between life with and life without God; and . . . death fades entirely from the psalmist's view.[7] The path of life that God walks knows no death. Consequently, there is rejoicing, and even the body has hope: **Because you will not abandon me to the grave, nor will you let your Holy One see decay.** The translation, "Thou dost not give me up to Sheol" (RSV) or "will not abandon me to the grave" (NIV, cf. NEB), may mean simply, "You will, for the time being, spare me from death." However, this is to ignore the basic meaning of the verb עָזַב ('āzab), namely "to leave behind, to depart from."[8] And since it is precisely the presence of God with him that sustains the psalmist in life, he can hope for a continuance of that presence, and thus of life, even beyond the grave. His hope is not predicated on the idea that there is some element of the human

---

[7]Kirkpatrick, *The Book of Psalms*, p. 28.

[8]Koehler and Baumgartner define the term in four ways: (1) *verlassen* ("leave, abandon"), (2) *zurücklassen* ("leave behind"), (3) *übrig lassen* ("leave over"), and (4) *gehen lassen* ("let go, leave") (*Lexicon*, p. 693). Lisowsky also includes *hinter lassen* ("leave behind"), and *loslossen* ("let loose"): Gerhard Lisowsky, *Konkordanz zum Hebraishen Alten Testament* (Stuttgart: Deutsche Bibelgesellschaft, 1981), p. 1425.

psyche that lives forever. Rather, he believes that God who has given life can sustain it — and enhance it! — beyond the grave. "You will go on showing me the path of life," he says, "fullness of joy for evermore." All of his tomorrows he will entrust to God, for the Lord is his life. That is enough.

That the one who spoke these words was David is clearly stated in Acts 2:29-31. That he spoke prophetically is there indicated. Peter reminded his hearers that "David died and was buried, and his tomb is here to this day" (v. 29). Yet God had promised David that his kingdom would not end, that from his descendants one would be raised up to sit on his throne. "Seeing what was ahead," Peter said, "he [David] spoke of the resurrection of the Christ, that he was not abandoned to the grave, nor did his body see decay" (v. 31). The words of David, however understood at the time, found their literal fulfillment in Christ. David anticipated life with God beyond death, he knew not how. Christ, through his victory over death and the grave, provided the way, bringing "life and immortality to light through the gospel" (2 Tim 1:10). To those who would follow him Jesus said, "Because I live, you also will live" (John 14:19). And again it is written that "whoever believes in him shall not perish but have eternal life" (John 3:16). To all who have not accepted Christ and the life he offers, God's word is: "Turn! Turn from your evil ways! Why will you die . . . ?" (Ezek 33:11). And to all who have ears to hear, he says: "Whosoever will may come." The deliverance from the grave that David anticipated has become a reality in Christ. We have even greater cause for rejoicing than did David!

II. THE GOD OF DELIVERANCE (17:1–18:50)

A. A PLEA FOR DELIVERANCE (17:1-15)

Psalm 17, according to some, is the prayer of a king for his distressed people, a prayer for national deliverance. For example, it is noted that the psalmist says in his prayer to God, "Show the wonder of your great love, you who save by your right hand those who take refuge in you from their foes" (v. 7). But this difficult verse, (only six words in Hebrew) may be but the *introduction* to the psalmist's petition. As such, it may be translated: "Show the wonder of your steadfast love, you who save . . . those seeking refuge." This, then, is followed by the prayer: "Keep me .. . hide me" (v. 8).

With this latter understanding, the psalm is seen as the prayer of a devout soul experiencing hostility from the ungodly among his countrymen. Such an experience is not uncommon. In every age those who refuse to yield to corrupt or immoral behavior may be subject to the unjustified ridicule, hostility, and abuse of the ungodly.[9] This seems to have been the situation of the psalmist, and so he comes, as one falsely accused, to plead his case before God and to be delivered from his enemies. He comes in the evening to the sanctuary, some say (referring to v. 3), where he spends the night. In the morning he awakes reassured, having received his answer from the Lord (v. 15). Whether or not there was this night in the sanctuary, it does seem better to understand the psalm as individual in nature rather than national. The distress reflected throughout appears to be that of an individual, not of the nation.[10]

The opening words of the psalm are a request for God's help. The appeal is based, at the outset, on common justice – the petitioner is innocent of evildoing, of evilspeaking, and of violence. He has consistently followed the paths of God (vv. 3-5). In addition, he dares ask for deliverance from his enemies and help from the Lord on the basis of God's steadfast love. He dares to believe that God will show mercy to him – not just because he is innocent, but because it is God's nature to be merciful (vv. 6-9). Further, he would show the urgency of his plea by a description of the savagery of his enemies (vv. 10-12), and he prays for their destruction (vv. 13-14). The psalmist then ends with a note of confidence that he will yet experience the joy of God's presence (v. 15). And so the prayer that began with an anguished cry closes on a note of hope and peace.

---

[9]Note the strong anti-Christian bias evident in television programing. Apparently with malice aforethought, characters identified as Christian are stereotyped almost without exception as scoundrels or bigots, or both.

[10]Briggs says: "The Ps. was originally the prayer of an individual. It has been generalized and made into a congregational prayer," *Commentary*, 1:128.

1. For Justice's Sake (17:1-5)

17:1 The psalm opens with a petition for God to help one who is suffering injustice. **Hear, O LORD, my righteous plea, listen to my cry. Give ear to my prayer.** The nature of the injustice is not disclosed, but it may have been occasioned by the psalmist's refusal to go along with the ungodly (the violent ones) in their wickedness (v. 4). In any case, his enemies seek to destroy him (v. 9). Yet, without hesitation, he will plead the righteousness of his cause before a God who discerns all things. "Probe my heart . . . examine me . . . test me," he says to God, "you will find nothing." Such a statement may be offensive to our ears, but this is not proud boasting. True, the speaker may not qualify as the epitome of humility. But sometimes the one who confesses to being "a poor, humble sinner" may seek by such confession to excuse his sin and to justify himself in doing nothing about it. He pleads, "O Lord, I'm just a miserable sinner." And God says, "You are? Have you not received my forgiveness and my salvation? Are you not now my child? Indeed! So now go out and live as a child of God ought to live. No more of this talk of being *just* a poor sinner. Go, and sin no more!"

17:2-5 The psalmist was not guilty of such reverse hypocrisy. He was simply saying, "I have, in life, chosen the way of God and have committed myself to walking in that way." Therefore, he could accept the judgment of a righteous God. Admittedly, it is a bold request: **May my vindication come from you.** If the psalmist had not, himself, been at peace with God, he could not have made such a supplication. There is importance in doing the will of God! When one's cause is just, he may take comfort and find hope in knowing that "the Judge of all the earth [will] do right" (Gen 18:25, KJV). He may plead God's help on the basis of justice.

2. For Love's Sake (17:6-9)

17:6-7 In addition, the psalmist knew that he could anticipate help from the Lord because it is his nature to be merciful. He would appeal to God's love. **I call on you, O God, ... Show the wonder of your great love.** No one word in English is the equivalent of the Hebrew term חֶסֶד (*ḥesed*). "Lovingkindness," as in the

KJV, conveys the basic concept; that is, love that manifests itself in kindness, love that is active on behalf of the beloved. It is a virtue akin to grace. The RSV translates the term as "steadfast love," sometimes as "loyalty." These translations, as well as the NIV's "love," are apt, if they are understood to indicate love that is dependable. But they are also used to convey the thought that *ḥesed* is "covenant love," a view widely held, especially since publication of the work of Nelson Glueck, *Hesed in the Bible*. In this vein, *ḥesed* is defined by Koehler-Baumgartner as "the mutual liability of those who are relatives, friends, master and servant, (etc.) . . . joint liability."[11] The emphasis is upon liability, somewhat contractual in nature, the fulfillment of obligation. Certainly faithfulness is characteristic of *ḥesed*. This love is dependable. But it is a mistake to consider responsibility to be the basic motivation, for there are references in the OT to indicate that *ḥesed* is a love freely given — mercy, if you please, and not just an obligation. For example, Ben-Hadad, king of Syria, was shown kindness (*ḥesed*) by Ahab of Israel before any covenant obligation existed (1 Kgs 20:31). And in Gen 19:19 *ḥesed* appears as parallel with חֵן (*ḥēn*, "grace"), indicating a love that is not merely covenant responsibility. The awareness that this kind of love (or loving-kindness) was God's nature gave added encouragement to the psalmist in distress. He would not hesitate to pray to such a God for help.

17:8-9 Keep me as the apple of your eye; literally, as "the little man" of the eye, indicating the image one may see of himself reflected in the eye of another. The reference is to the pupil of the eye, which, being quite sensitive, needs careful protection. And it is protected. God has provided eyelids that may be closed over it, eyelashes to keep out foreign objects, and eyebrows that exclude the sweat of one's toil. In addition, the forehead above and the cheekbones below give added security. It is not too much to suppose that the God who has so provided for the care of the eye will be concerned for the whole man and respond to his call for help.

Hide me in the shadow of your wings. The appeal for God's care continues, although the figure is changed to that of a mother bird caring for her young. (Or, we might think of the care of a hen

---

[11]Koehler-Baumgartner, *Lexicon*, 1:318.

for her chicks, a figure that Jesus used.) What a great promise we
are given: "Come near to God and he will come near to you" (Jas
4:8). The psalmist had not heard James, but he was aware of God's
love and he would not hesitate to call on him for help.

3. The Savagery of the Enemy (17:10-12)

17:10 The urgency of his petition was heightened by his awareness of the unbridled savagery of his enemies. Like wild beasts they
surrounded him, stalking him, glaring at him, biding the time when
they could tear him to pieces. **They close up their callous hearts.** It
is literally in Hebrew: "They are enclosed in their own fat," (recognizing the verb as a simple Passive [Qal passive]). They are "wrapped
up in themselves." The meaning is that they have become arrogant
(Dahood). They are rebellious. In Deut 32:15 we read that "Jeshurun
(Israel) grew fat and kicked; . . . He abandoned the God who made
him." The figure is that of a well-fed animal that had grown fat and
cantankerous. Thus it was with these enemies — with their mouth
they **speak with arrogance.** They are entirely without any restraint
by thoughts of accountability to God.

**17:11-12 They have tracked me down . . . to throw me to the
ground.** Relentlessly the psalmist has been pursued by enemies
who will be content with nothing less than his destruction. One
could question whether these were really human beings. Of course
they were, but they behaved like beasts, ready to tear and to devour
a helpless victim. On the face of it, the righteous person is at a very
great disadvantage because he will not stoop to the evil practices of
the enemy. In the words of Martin Luther, the people of God can
say: "Were not the right Man on our side, our striving would be
losing." Luther found in God a "mighty fortress." This was also the
experience of the psalmist.

4. "Bring Them Down" (17:13-14)

17:13-14 The thought of verse 13 is reasonably clear, an appeal
to God to deliver the psalmist by overthrowing the enemy. Literally, we may read: "Rise up, LORD, meet him face to face, bring him

to his knees. Deliver my life from the wicked by your sword."[12] However, verse 14 is difficult and has been translated in widely divergent ways. The King James Version, even with its addition of numerous words (in italics) makes little sense. Common translations recognize no verbs in the sentence until the reference to "filling" on the part of God. But this makes for very awkward Hebrew. The NIV "adds" verbal ideas that are not in the MT in order to make sense of it. However, it is better to recognize the word מְמְתִים (mim°thîm) twice translated **from (such) men** as a verb (מְמְתִים, m°mithîm, from מוּת, mûth; see Jer 26:15) instead (as in the LXX, ἀπολύω [apolyō, "destroy"] and διαμερίζω [diamerizō, "cut in pieces"]). Thus we would read, in accord with Dahood, "Slay them by your hand, O LORD, slay them from the earth; make them perish from among the living."[13]

Those who read these words in the light of Jesus' teaching to "love your enemies" (Matt 5:44) may suppose that the psalmist was of a very vengeful spirit. Buttenwieser, who views the psalm as a national lament and sees the nation "hemmed in by deadly enemies," considers it only human that the psalmist should desire their overthrow.[14] But, viewing the psalm as an individual lament, one should note that the concern is for justice and vindication, not for revenge. The psalmist will trust God to deal with his enemies, not taking matters into his own hands. Significantly, he recognizes the evil of his enemies as an affront to God himself, a challenge to God's government of the world. And so when he says, "Slay them" (as Dahood reads this; the NIV reads differently), it is not so much a

---

[12]Dahood considers the last word to be a participle, not a noun (sword), thus: "Rescue my life from the wicked who war on you." However, we may well retain the Masoretic pointing and recognize the noun as adverbial (there are comparatively few adverbs in Hebrew). We may then translate: "Deliver my life from the wicked *swordfully*;" that is, by the skillful use of the sword. (See Gesenius, *Hebrew Grammar*, 144:1,m, p. 461.)

[13]Craigie, Leslie, and Oesterley, in addition to Dahood, also treat the words as verbs. A.A. Anderson, Eaton, and Rodd see this as a possibility. The NEB so translates, and so did Briggs (1906). Buttenwieser, on the other hand, leaves the first phrase of verse 14 untranslated, declaring the text to be "hopelessly corrupt" (*The Psalms*, p. 484).

[14]Buttenwieser, *The Psalms*, p. 480.

call for personal vengeance as it is an appeal that God will vindicate himself by triumphing over the wicked. In the days of the psalmist, if unrelieved disaster were suffered by the righteous at the hands of the wicked, it was considered an indication of weakness on the part of the God of the righteous. "Say it isn't so," the suffering one says to God, "deal with them, bring them down, destroy them, and vindicate your name." Elsewhere, as we have noted, the OT teaches: "If your enemy is hungry, give him food to eat; if he is thirsty, give him water to drink" (Prov 25:21). And David, on more than one occasion, showed mercy. Here the concern is for justice and deliverance.[15]

The key to understanding the latter part of verse 14 is the Hebrew word וּצְפִינְךָ with which it opens. The root of the term, צָפַן (ṣāphan), means "to hide, treasure up" (BDB). It could be rendered, literally, as "your hidden one," or "your hidden thing." The following translations have been given: "And they store up wealth," (NIV), "thy hid treasures" (KJV), "what thou hast stored up" (RSV), "thy good things" (NEB), "thy stored up penalty" (Briggs), and "your treasured ones" (Dahood). It is better to understand the meaning in this latter vein; specifically as "the ones whom you hide" (from trouble, as being precious), as in Ps 27:5, and translate as follows: "But the ones whom you cherish, let their belly be filled (that is, provide their daily food), may they have an abundance of children, and may they store up wealth for their little ones." [Note the slight difference between this translation and the NIV.] This is seen, then, as a prayer for the blessing of the righteous in antithesis to the call for judgment upon the wicked.

5. Affirmation of Trust (17:15)

17:15 The contrast has been drawn between the wicked and the righteous, a contrast that is inevitable when one recognizes the existence of a righteous God. The psalmist, fully conscious of the contrast, continues: **And I —** (significant words!) . . . "I have made my

---

[15]But see Psalm 18:47, and the discussion of imprecatory psalms on pages 61-63.

choice, and I know that" — **in righteousness I will see your face.** Whether he is anticipating a spiritual consciousness of God's presence, "as seeing him who is invisible" (Heb 11:27, KJV), and deliverance from the present crisis, or is looking to a time beyond death when he shall see God, is difficult to determine. The clue to our understanding are the words **when I awake.** Is this awakening from a night of sleep in the sanctuary? (See v. 3.) Or is the awakening from the sleep of death? Dahood considers the latter to be "the plain sense," and translates, "At the resurrection."[16] Kirkpatrick was convinced that the concern of the psalmist was, for "the blessedness of fellowship with God" here and now. Nevertheless, he observed that: "It is inconceivable that communion with God thus begun and daily renewed should be abruptly terminated by death."[17] Since the Lord is recognized as the *living* God, the concept of a continuing future in his presence is only natural.

The psalmist began with a plea for justice, for vindication (v. 1). He closes with a note of confidence. Vindication will come, and with it a continuation of his fellowship with God. The contrast here, as in Psalm 1, is between the way of the righteous and the way of the ungodly. He had chosen the former way, believing that "in righteousness" he would see God. His assurance does not rest solely on a judicial basis, as Kidner has noted, but on the axiom that "only like can communicate with like."[18] Jesus said, "Blessed are the pure in heart, for they will see God" (Matt. 5:8), because, we might add, they have something to see God with.

B. THANKSGIVING FOR DELIVERANCE (18:1-50)

From the reading of Psalm 18 one may conclude that the writer is a king who has achieved victory over many enemies. He has become the head of the nations (v. 43), but only after a period of severe encounters in which he despaired even of life (vv. 3-4). Without reservation, he attributes his deliverance to the Lord, who

---

[16]Dahood, *Psalms 1-50*, p. 99.
[17]Kirkpatrick, *The Book of Psalms*, p. 84.
[18]Kidner, *Psalms 1-72*, p. 89.

has rewarded his faithfulness with victory (vv. 20-21). His lips burst forth with praise and thanksgiving of such fervor as to indicate that his experience of God's help must have been wonderful indeed.

Because of the strong personal element of the psalm we do not believe that it was written originally as a liturgy for an annual religious festival, as some have proposed. Rather, we have here words of an individual directed in praise and devotion to God for deliverance from enemies. Apparently, the thanks do not stem from any one particular episode but from continued God-given victories that have culminated in a time of peace and security. And since these experiences are indicative of the help God affords the righteous, the psalm became a part of the worship of others who would celebrate similar blessings, with more emphasis, however, on *Heilsgeschichte* ("salvation history") than upon the historical events that gave rise to the psalm in the first place.[19]

The same psalm, with slight variations, appears also in 2 Sam 22. Apparently, each was preserved and transmitted independently of the other. There is evidence that the text in Samuel was preserved in the northern kingdom (Israel). Differences in orthography reflect the local dialect.[20] The superscription to the psalm, included in the opening words of the passage in Samuel, identifies David as the author. The antiquity of the psalm is widely acknowledged, with comparatively few scholars who would assign it, in its origin, to a late date. Weiser, among others, makes a strong case for its provenance in the era of David.[21]

---

[19]Buttenwieser takes an entirely different view of the psalm, seeing it, not as a celebration of victory, but as a plea for deliverance from impending tragedy. The verbs in the imperfect in verses 6,16,17, "admit of no other interpretation than that the writer is entreating God now" (*The Psalms*, p. 457). Buttenwieser's claim is not without rationale. However, others, with good reason, consider these verbs as indicating past tense. See Craigie, "The Translation of Tenses in Hebrew Poetry," *Psalms 1–50* (pp. 110-113, 167).

[20]For a discussion, see Frank Moore Cross, Jr. and David Noel Freedman, *Studies in Ancient Yahwistic Poetry* (Missoula, MO: Scholars Press, 1975), p. 125.

[21]Weiser, *The Psalms*, p. 185f.

1. A God Worthy of Praise (18:1-3)

18:1-3 The psalm opens fittingly with an affirmation of devotion to Yahweh. **I love you, O LORD.** (The verb should not be translated as future [as in KJV] but as present, continuing action.) However, the term here used is not the usual one for *love* (אָהַב, *'āhab*, as in Ps 116:1, Deut 6:5; nor is it חֶסֶד, *ḥesed*, as in Ps 17:7). It is from a root, רָחַם (*rāḥam*), the basic meaning of which is to show compassion or mercy, such as one in exalted position might show to one of lesser estate. The term is frequently used elsewhere to indicate God's loving-kindness to his people. But nowhere else is it used with God as its object. (The verse is missing from 2 Samuel 22.)

It should be noted that the Hebrew text opens with, "And he said," (The NIV translators have relegated these words to the superscription.) But if they open the verse, as in the Hebrew, then we must ask, "Who said?" From the superscription, the answer could be Yahweh (who delivered David). Thus: "My Lord, my strength said: 'I have compassion for you.'" Stuhlmüeller suggests that it is either the Lord or else "the presiding liturgical officer" speaking to Israel and saying, "I have pity on you."[22]

A further possibility would be to consider the opening verse to be an exuberant expression of praise: "I will exalt you, O LORD" (as in Ps 30:1).[23] For it is immediately followed by such an overflow of praise as is seldom encountered. One metaphor is heaped upon another in the desire of the psalmist to show the fullness of meaning of the grace and power of God that he has experienced. God is his rock, his (craggy) **fortress.** David, when being hunted down, had spent much time in the craggy fastnesses around En Gedi and could readily have thought of the Lord as a refuge totally inaccessible to his enemies. **The horn of my salvation.** "Horn" was a metaphor for strength or power in ancient times. Thus, God is the power by which his deliverance is accomplished, one who imparts strength to those who walk with him.

---

[22]Stuhlmueller, *Psalms I*, p. 129.
[23]The verb in 30:1 (אֲרוֹמִמְךָ) and that in 18:1 (אֶרְחָמְךָ) are quite similar in appearance and a copyist could have confused one with the other.

2. The Testimony of the Psalmist (18:4-6)

18:4-6 The psalmist had been delivered from certain death, as the following verses indicate. **The cords of death entangled me.** The text in 2 Sam 22:5 is to be preferred. It reads: "The waves of death swirled about me." The figure is of one caught in a mighty flood of waters that would sweep him to certain death were it not for the Lord's help. David had experienced the assault of powerful enemies, like "torrents of perdition" (v. 4, RSV). Nevertheless, he had experienced also the deliverance that only God could have provided. This is his testimony. **In my distress I called to the LORD, [and] . . . . From his temple he heard my voice.** To hear, in the Hebrew idiom, means to respond. Since no temple existed in Jerusalem until after the time of David, the reference here is seen by some as an anachronism. (In fact, the tabernacle, while in Shiloh, is referred to as the "temple" in 1 Sam 1:9, 3:3.) However, it is altogether possible that the psalmist is not referring to Jerusalem but to God's temple in heaven, from whence God had heard his plea. God "reached down from on high," he tells us (v. 16), in order to deliver his servant from his enemies. Another possibility is that the "temple" is not figurative for "heaven," but real and that the Psalm was written "about" David instead of "by/belonging to David." The former interpretation is preferred, i.e., God is speaking from his "heavenly temple."

3. The Lord's Response (18:7-19)

18:7-19 The response of the Lord was mighty in its execution because he was angry (v. 7). The wrath of God against injustice and all wickedness is a solemn reality with which evil men must ultimately reckon. The outpouring of that wrath is portrayed in highly symbolic language, indicating the unleashing of terrible power, such as that of a volcanic eruption (vv. 7-8) or of a tremendous storm (vv. 9-15). God is pictured as coming in the storm, riding upon a cherub, unleashing a fury so great that none can stand before it (vv. 16-19). "In such mighty fashion," the psalmist is saying, "He delivered me . . . from them which hated me." Apparently, there had been various deliverances from many

184

enemies over an extended period of time. The psalm is a song of thanksgiving at the end of such period.

4. The Reward of the Righteous (18:20-30)

In a moral universe it is to be expected that there will be both a reward for righteousness and punishment for evil, and such execution of justice is stated in the Scriptures as inevitable. This is not to deny grace and mercy, nor the long-suffering patience of God. But it is basic, a principle summarized in the well-known words of Paul: "A man reaps what he sows" (Gal 6:7). From his confidence that this is so, the writer of Psalm 18 was emboldened to persevere in the ways of God. And he was not disappointed.

18:20-21 The LORD has dealt with me according to my righteousness. If we interpret this to mean, "What a good boy am I!" then we would dismiss the statement as the words of a pious fraud. But the psalmist is not laying claim to absolute righteousness or sinless perfection, only that in his lifetime he has sought to walk in the ways of God![24] Elsewhere he says: "Taste and see that the LORD is good" (Ps 34:8). The Lord's covenant with his people provided blessings for those who would keep it (see Deut 28:1-14), and it is the keeping of that covenant that is here involved (vv. 21-23). David was not without sin, but he sought God's forgiveness and sought also once again to walk in the ways of God.

18:22-30 All his laws are before me. In context, the "laws" (מִשְׁפָּטִים, mishpāṭîm) are specific ordinances, though in a broader sense the term indicates the entirety of God's just claims. **I have not turned away from his decrees.** The designation "decrees" was usually indicative of written or engraved decrees (חֻקּוֹת, ḥuqqôth). To say, "I did not put them away" (literal Hebrew which the NIV has "I have not turned away") is a figure of speech meaning, "I kept them diligently." Even so, David did not lose sight of the fact that

---

[24]That David could have spoken of his righteousness and cleanness of heart after his sin of adultery and murder (2 Sam 11:1-17) is questioned by some. Cohen affirms that David wrote these words much earlier, just after his deliverance from Saul (*The Psalms*, p. 48).

he had been the recipient of God's mercy (see v. 50). The tenor of his life had been to honor God, and God had dealt more than honorably with him. The psalmist realized that this principle of response underlies the Lord's dealings with all (vv. 25-26), a principle summarized by Jesus in the words: "With the measure you use, it will be measured to you" (Mark 4:24). But Jesus added: "And even more!" David had experienced this latter result, too (vv. 28-30).

5. God, the Source of Strength (18:31-45)

18:31-45 When the young David stood before King Saul as a volunteer to do battle with the giant Goliath, the king had remonstrated that he was too young and inexperienced for such an encounter. But David had assured Saul: "The LORD . . . will deliver me from the hand of this Philistine" (1 Sam 17:37). Now, much later, and after many victories, he says: **It is God who arms me with strength.** Whatever the contingencies of life, he recognized that God had equipped him to meet them (vv. 33-36). God had given him the victory over (literally) those that rose up against him (v. 39). These enemies had been the aggressors, having attacked him out of hatred (v. 40), not for any just cause. But God had provided his servant with strength to face them.

6. A Concluding Doxology (18:46-50)

18:46 Because his cause was just, the psalmist saw the victory as a vindication of God himself, since God would not permit the attacks of evil men to go unpunished. In the words of Longfellow, "God is not dead, nor does he sleep." **The LORD lives!** The victories experienced were a demonstration of the fact. Not that David ever questioned the existence of God but he now sings praises because it has become abundantly clear to him that the existence of God is greatly relevant: "Yahweh lives, and it makes a difference in my life."

18:47-50 With the beginning of verse 47 we seem to have words addressed directly to the Lord. Instead of "it is God" (KJV), "the God who" (RSV), or "He is the God" (NIV), it seems preferable to recognize the vocative, "O, God, the one giving me vengeance

(avenging me) and subduing nations under me, the one saving me."
This moves smoothly then into the direct address of verse 48: **You
exalted me.** God's majesty and awesome power had been shown as
in a mighty upheaval of nature, a raging torrent, a thunderous
storm. But rather than to stand shuddering in the presence of such
a God, his servant would address him, one on one, in grateful
praise. **From violent men you rescued me.** The power of God had
been directed to his benefit! **Therefore I will praise you among the
nations, O LORD.** And with this note of praise the psalm ends.

III. THE GOD OF REVELATION (19:1-14)

A. GOD'S GLORY – IN HIS WORKS AND IN HIS WORD (19:1-14)

C.S. Lewis describes Psalm 19 as "the greatest poem in the
Psalter and one of the greatest lyrics in the world."[25] Such high
praise is fully justified. What a pity that many college and university
students and professors are not familiar with it! Not only is the
psalm superb poetry. Its theme is of the utmost significance: the
revelation of God through the heavens and the revelation of God
through his *torah* (the law).

Some scholars are of the opinion that the psalm was originally
two independent poems. It opens with reference to the heavens
and to the glory of God. But in verse 7 there is an abrupt change to
a discussion of the law of the Lord, with no transitional element.
Deity is addressed as *El* (God) in the earlier verses but as Yahweh
(LORD) in verses 7-14. Besides the use of two different themes and
of two different designations for God, there is a decided change of
style, of rhythm and of meter. The first part is in the nature of a
hymn of praise, the second a didactic poem extolling the excellence of the *torah*. And the two parts, it is alleged, "differ from
each so much that they cannot be composed by the same author."[26]

---

[25]Lewis, *Reflections*, p. 63.
[26]Weiser, *The Psalms*, (p. 197). Others who consider the work to be
composite are: Anderson, by implication; Buttenwieser, who considers
the second part of the psalm to be "commonplace and artificial," and

Consequently, it is said that the psalm, as it now stands, is the work of a compiler who took two psalms and combined them into one (after the fashion of Psalm 108, a combination of 57:7-11 and 60:5-12).

However, we do not have any evidence of the independent existence of any part of Psalm 19 elsewhere, and if a compiler felt free to combine such disparate elements, why not the original author? In reality, there is close affinity between the two parts, such as was felt by Kant when he marveled at "the starry heavens above and the moral law within." And in both parts the glory of God is extolled. In reference to the heavens it would be appropriate to refer to God as *El*, since this term focuses upon God's great creative power. *Yahweh*, on the other hand, is the covenant name of God, made known to Israel in the giving of the law through Moses. The change in style, beginning at verse 7, could be deliberate because of the change in subject matter. Yet the close relation between the two themes was so much a part of the consciousness of the psalmist that it did not enter his thought that he needed to give an explanation or to introduce a transitional phrase. As Moulton has observed: "No literary device could make the equality of the two (themes) so forcible as the simple placing of them side by side without a word of explanation."[27] Considering all of the above, the present writer concludes that Psalm 19 is not composite, but the work of a single author.

The opening verses of the psalm proclaim the glory of God as manifested in his creation, with a descriptive reference to the movement of the sun and to its effect upon all the earth and its inhabitants (vv. 1-6). From this reference to the general revelation of God

---

"commonly overrated," *The Psalms* (p. 170 and 853); Briggs, Delitzsch, Leslie, Oesterley, Rhodes, and Wm. R. Taylor. Ringgren states that the second part may "well be later," *The Faith* (p. 111). Some who recognize the unity of Psalm 19 are: Dahood, provisionally — "If the use of the double-duty suffixes (in the Hebrew) is a safe criterion, the author of both parts of the psalm was the same poet," *Psalms 1–50* (p. 121); Eaton, and Leupold. Ash, Kidner, and Stuhlmueller are noncommittal. Craigie states only that "it is reasonably certain that the psalm in its present form is a unity," *Psalms 1–50* (p. 179).

[27]Moulton, *Literary Study*, p. 95. Moulton's position is that the psalm possesses a literary unity, "the unity of contrast," whether or not there is diversity of authorship (p. 93).

through nature the psalm moves to the special revelation of God through his law (vv. 7-10). The poem then concludes with the psalmist's response, a prayer that he be delivered from the guilt and power of sin and that he be accepted by the Lord (vv. 11-14).

1. The Glory of God in the Heavens (19:1-6)

19:1 The heavens declare the glory of God, or, "go on declaring" (a participle in the Hebrew). David, as a shepherd, had experienced many nights under the open sky, in a land where a myriad of stars are visible and especially brilliant. It would never have entered his thinking that such could have existed by chance, but that all of nature bears testimony to the divine. The psalmist was not concerned with philosophy. He knew nothing of Aristotle's inherent purposiveness of nature nor of the neo-Darwinian's "efficient causation." Foreign to him also would be Alfred Whitehead's view of the "urge of organisms" to "acquire an increase of satisfaction."[28] Whatever forces might be at work in the cosmos, above all and controlling all, was אֵל, (*El*, "God," "powerful one"), and the love of the psalmist was directed, not in some abstract sort of way to nature itself, but to God. All of creation is viewed as his handiwork, testifying to his greatness, showing forth his glory, inspiring his creature to sing his praise.

19:2 Day after day they pour forth speech – not speech in an abstract sense but some significant pronouncement, a message indeed for all who would hear. This translation is to be preferred. It is not day speaking to day, as in some versions – how could that be, with a night intervening? But continually, day by day and night by night, all creation pours out its testimony to the power and wisdom of God. In a similar vein the Apostle Paul could write:

---

[28]The debate relative to cause in nature, whether it be "efficient causation," the "urge of organisms," or some "Lifeforce" that is unknown today, we may leave to the process philosophers, physicists, and neobiologists, asking only the age old question: What caused the cause? That purposiveness is intrinsic to nature is coming to be accepted more and more. And he is no fool who recognizes that the ultimate source of purpose is to be found in divine intelligence rather than in blind chance.

"Since the creation of the world God's invisible qualities – his eternal power and divine nature – have been clearly seen, being understood from what has been made, so that men are without excuse" (Rom 1:20).

19:3-6 There is no speech or language, where their voice is not heard – meaning that, whatever the language or dialect of a people, they can still hear and comprehend the message of God as told by creation, told in a language that all can understand.[29] From this general reference to the testimony of the heavens, the focus is changed to the particular role of the sun. **In the heavens he has pitched a tent for the sun.** In the ancient world the sun was worshiped as a god, a practice not unknown in Israel (Deut 4:19; 2 Kgs 23:5; Ezek 8:16). By a slight emendation of the text, some would make of verses 4c-6 a hymn in praise of the sun. To the contrary, the words appear to be a strong refutation of sun worship. It is God who gives the sun a place in the heavens and determines its orbit. The sun is indeed glorious, **like a bridegroom coming forth from his pavilion.** It pursues its course jubilantly, **like a champion.** It is a glorious ball of fire whose light and warmth continue to amaze us. But the psalmist is not praising the sun. In Egypt, Akhenaton might revere the solar disk as the power behind all powers, but the praise of the psalmist is for God alone, the maker of heaven and earth with all their hosts. It is not his purpose to exalt the sun, but to demonstrate and marvel at the wisdom and power of God as revealed in his creation.

2. The Excellence of the Law (19:7-10)

Having considered the glory of God as revealed in nature, the psalmist would now fix heart and mind upon the excellence of God's law. As the former revealed God's wisdom and power, this shows his wisdom and concern in providing guidance for his people. As God gave the sun to illumine the earth, he has given the law to enlighten the mind and soul and to illumine man's path upon the earth. The glory of God revealed in creation is paralleled by the glory revealed in the law.

---

[29]See Weiser, *The Psalms*, p. 198f. and Leupold, *Exposition*, p. 179.

Because of the connotation of the word *law* it is unfortunate
that we use this term to translate the Hebrew *torah*. The latter is far
too broad in its scope to be limited simply to a code of legal injunc-
tions. The basic concept of torah is instruction or direction. It may
include commandments, positive or negative, but even these are
designed to teach, to give instruction in living. The psalmist found
joy in discovering that God had not only created a marvelous world
and provided us with life. He has also included the instructions on
how to put it all together.

19:7a Admittedly, rival directions for living are being constantly
advocated and tried — "alternate lifestyles" they are called ("pagan-
ism" is the earlier designation). But the alternatives apart from God
are really only two: either anarchy, in which "every man does what
is right in his own eyes" ("My will be done!"), or repression, by a
dictator or by an elitist group ("Our will be done!"). Pressed to its
ultimate conclusions, neither way can prove to be satisfactory. But
there remains the alternative. There is the will of God, not dictator-
ial but benevolent! Not compulsory (He has given us a will also!)
but persuasive, asking of us what is good, because it is good. His
way is the way of fullness of life. The psalmist found it to be so and
marveled at its excellence. **The law of the LORD is perfect reviving
the soul.** What nourishment does for the body, God's word does
for the soul, the life of the person. The psalmist found delight in
the way of the Lord. For him, the law (God's revelation) was a
means of grace.

**19:7b-10 The statutes of the LORD are trustworthy, making
wise the simple.** Instead of "simple," Dahood proposes, with
reason, that we read "mind." Thus God's directives revive the *soul*,
give wisdom to the *mind*, rejoice the *heart*, and enlighten the *eyes*.
One who has this appreciation for God's word, who can say from
his heart, "O, how I love your law!" (Ps 119:97), will experience awe
and reverence for God ("the fear of the LORD") that will endure, in
spite of every circumstance (v. 9). He will have discovered something more valuable than material wealth — **pure gold**, more
delightful than gourmet dainties — **sweeter than honey**. Psalm 19,
like Ps 1:2, recognizes that the law of the Lord is no burden to be
borne, but a delight to bring joy to life.

3. The Psalmist's Response (19:11-14)

19:11-13 The psalmist was filled with wonder from his contemplation of the glory of God as declared by the heavens. No less was his awe and jubilation when he contemplated the excellence of God's *torah*. His reaction to the latter was both natural and rational, for here he found help that he needed. **By them is your servant warned** (illumined). The illumination is necessary, for "there is a way that seems right to a man, but in the end it leads to death" (Prov 14:2). But here are directions for life. In keeping them there is great reward. They "revive," "make wise," it "gives joy to the heart," "gives light to the eyes." Moreover, they "endure forever," and they are "sure and altogether righteous." The result is peace, peace with oneself and peace with God. (Note that the psalmist, in these verses, is talking directly to the Lord.) Did he feel apprehensive as he contemplated God's perfect way? Perhaps, but he had confidence that he could call on the Lord to help him. **Forgive my hidden** (hidden even from myself!) **faults.** Some actions or attitudes are so much a part of our lives that we never once entertain the idea that they may be wrong. But such may be the case. Also in the limbo of forgetfulness are those good things that we ought to have done but did them not. (Recognition of these facts should, if nothing else, keep us from any feelings of self-righteousness.) **Willful sins** are deliberate and open defiance of God. If we trifle with these, they are certain to have dominion over us. However, with God's word to guide and with his help to enable us, we can walk in his way. **Then will I be blameless,** not sinless, but forgiven for the unwitting fault and restrained from presumptuous sins.

19:14 The prayer with which the psalm closes has been used by many. As we, in our study, have shared the thoughts of the psalmist about God's glory and the glory of his way, may we also join in sharing the prayer? **May the words of my mouth and the meditation of my heart be pleasing in your sight, O LORD, my Rock and my Redeemer.**

IV. THE GOD OF BATTLE (20:1–21:13)

A. CONFIDENCE IN PRAYER (20:1-9)

In our seeking the orientation of Psalm 20, a few observations are in order. First, the Psalm opens with a prayer by a group of persons ("we," v. 5), calling for blessing for someone (v. 1), who has brought offerings and sacrifices to the sanctuary (vv. 2-3). The petition, in particular, is for some kind of victory or deliverance (v. 5). After this opening prayer, an individual ("I," v. 6) responds with a word of assurance that Yahweh will help "his anointed." After this, "we" speak again, affirming trust and confidence in God, and declaring the fate of those who put their trust in horses and chariots (vv. 7-8). The psalm then ends with a short closing prayer, asking the Lord's blessing upon both the king and the people (v. 9).

Apparently, the occasion of the psalm was some kind of threatening situation, possibly an impending battle, if the reference to horses and chariots is sufficient evidence. With this understanding, Spurgeon stated: "We have before us a National Anthem, fitted to be sung at the outbreak of war, when the monarch was girding on his sword for the fight."[30] Mowinckel designated the psalm as "national . . . intercession for the King before he goes to war."[31] And Gunkel, in similar vein, says that "Psalm 20 was performed by the royal choir when the king went forth to battle."[32] T.K. Cheyne, years earlier, had proposed and rejected a setting for the psalm in the time of Josiah, before this king lost his life in the battle of Megiddo.[33] Weiser, also did not consider the evidence for the above to be convincing. For one thing, he considers the tone of the psalm too calm to be a reflection of a state of war. He favors the view that the psalm is a part of the ritual of the (alleged) annual New Year's festival when God is acclaimed as King.[34] J.H. Eaton agrees that the position of Weiser is "more probable" than the

---

[30]Spurgeon, *Treasury*, 1:300.
[31]Mowinckel, *The Psalms*, 1:225.
[32]Gunkel, *The Psalms*, p. 24.
[33]Cheyne, *Origin*, p. 198.
[34]Weiser, *The Psalms*, p. 205f.

other, saying that "the mood and style of Psalm 20 are indeed in great contrast to the pieces I have connected with prayers before battle."[35] But since the existence of an annual enthronement festival in Jerusalem is problematic at best, we must conclude that this interpretation, also, is less than convincing.[36] Even so, the assignment of the psalm in the superscription to the "chief Musician" would indicate that it was used in public worship. And it appears to have been composed at a time when danger of some kind threatened, even if the particular historical event cannot be determined. The psalm does present an example of those who put their trust in the Lord and were not disappointed. For this reason, it is of value to us as a source of encouragement.

1. The Petition for Victory (20:1-5)

20:1 May the LORD answer you. Evidently, the one for whom this prayer was uttered had also been praying. **When you are in distress.** Dahood has "in time of siege," because of the "military language" elsewhere in the psalm. The assumption may be correct, but the Hebrew term is such as to cover various situations that might cause distress. The group uttering these words is not identified. Some suppose it to be the congregation or a choir. Others suggest the warriors whom the king would be leading into battle.

May the name of the God of Jacob protect you. Why not say, simply, "May God protect you" instead of "the name of the God of Jacob"? It has been said that this is the language of a later Judaism that would not be so bold as to think in terms of the material presence of God, but would sublimate the thought. The name of God, then, would indicate the power of God at work without any implications of immediacy. Yet from earliest times in Israel, names were significant as revelatory of the nature of those who bore them. We used to say a person has achieved a name for honesty or for kindness. It is in this sense that the psalmist speaks, voicing his petition to God in all the essence of his being.

---

[35]J.H. Eaton, *Kingship and the Psalms* (Naperville, IL: Alec R. Allenson, 1975), p. 117.

[36]See the reference to Enthronement Psalms on pp. 55-57.

Reference is made to "the name" again in verses 5 and 7. Ps 91:14 states a promise of God: "I will protect him, for he acknowledges my name." The word "protect" is literally in Hebrew "set on high," that is, by providing a place that is out of reach of the enemy.

20:2-5 From the sanctuary . . . from Zion (in Jerusalem) was placed the ark of the covenant, a reminder of God's presence with his people. Thus Zion became the earthly counterpart of heaven, from whence also God's deliverance is said to come (v. 6). It was at the sanctuary that offerings and sacrifices were presented. The prayer was that God would **remember** these (that is, that they might bring to God's attention the plight of the offerer) and **accept** them. **We will shout for joy!** Or better, "May we rejoice" (the prayer continues). The petition is that they may witness the salvation, the deliverance, the victory, of the one for whom they have been making intercession.

2. The Assurance of Triumph through God's Help (20:6)

20:6 The prayer has ended. At this point it is assumed by many that something happens to bring the assurance of victory. It may be only that the offering of the sacrifice is complete. God has accepted it and will surely respond favorably. Some believe that a prophet or a priest is here speaking, having received insight from God relative to a victory that will be forthcoming. Whatever the circumstance, verse 6 is climactic, the opening word "now" being emphatic. **Now I know that the LORD saves his anointed.** The anointed would be the king (1 Sam 26:9). Whether it is the king who speaks the words of verse 6, or another about him, is impossible to determine. Leupold believes that it is the nation speaking as an individual, but this interpretation seems a bit strained. It would appear, rather, to be an individual who was, in some way, a leader in the worship. By whomever expressed, the words of verse 6 reflect the assurance that comes to those who know that their prayers have been answered.

3. Confidence in the Lord Justified (20:7-8)

20:7 In verses 7 and 8 the people speak again. The sharp contrast, in the Hebrew, between those who trust in fleshly power and those who trust in the Lord is, to an extent, lost in the translation, but it is emphatic. Actually, the verb is not "trust" but "remember" (זכר, *zākar*). These, on the one hand, remember **horses** and **chariots** (and that is all that they have to remember — perishable flesh). But we remember **the name**. The name! There it is again. God has revealed himself to his people by name. He is not the great Unknown. And that name represents what he has been through the ages — the living God, the God of Abraham, Isaac, and Jacob. Yes, and much, much more — the God who kept his covenant with Israel, the God and Father of the Lord Jesus Christ, the God of our fathers and mothers. When "we remember the name," we too have confidence in victory. We have an assurance for the future predicated upon our remembrance of the faithfulness of God in the past — blessed memories.

20:8 They are brought to their knees and fall, but we rise up and stand firm. We are only so strong as that to which we commit ourselves, that which we *remember* as basic to life. They who are committed to the flesh will fall with the failure of the flesh. But those whose way is with God will stand so long as God stands, and that is forever. This is a confidence whose foundation is not in the "unconquerable soul" of which one may boast, but in God the creator, the giver and sustainer of life.

4. A Closing Prayer (20:9)

20:9 O LORD, save the king! Answer us when we call. This translation, following the LXX, seems better to fit the context than the KJV: "Save, LORD: let the king hear us when we call." The psalm opened expressing concern for the welfare of (it would appear to be) the king. It closes, expressing a similar concern. Significantly, also, the psalm began with a reference to some kind of "distress" (literally, "the day of trouble"). It closes with the thought focused upon "the day of our calling" (Hebrew); that is, the day of our calling upon God for help. The day of trouble has been transformed by becoming the day of prayer. Paul recognizes this need when he tells Timothy to pray especially for leaders (1 Tim 2:1-2).

B. A SONG OF PRAISE FOR ROYAL BLESSING (21:1-13)

In 1906 C.A. Briggs designated Psalm 20 as "a Litany before a battle," and Psalm 21 as "a *Te Deum* for the victory won."[37] Through the years this view has been shared by many. In the former psalm petition was made that the Lord would grant the king "the desire of [his] heart" (v. 4). In Ps 21:2 it is stated: "You have granted him the desire of his heart." The latter psalm was then said to be a hymn of praise and thanksgiving for a great victory that God had made possible. In the reading of the hymn, the element of praise is prominent in the opening verses, but any note of thanksgiving is only by inference. In verse 1 God is acclaimed for his "strength" and his "victories." This may refer to a recent military victory, but if so, it is not otherwise identified and the reference appears alongside numerous other blessings that the Lord had given.

In verse 3 mention is made of the crowning of the king. This, together with the reference to the king's trust in the Lord (v. 7), strongly suggests that the occasion of the psalm was a coronation, whether of David or of some other.[38] Again, we would notice the superscription, which would indicate that, with the passing of the years, this psalm, like others, was used in the worship of Israel on many occasions. Its use would be appropriate in any case in which a nation and their leader had been greatly blessed or were greatly threatened by enemies.

---

[37]Briggs, *The Psalms*, 1:175, 173.

[38]Buttenwieser agrees that Psalm 21 is a coronation hymn. He says, however, that it is a misinterpretation to consider it a song of victory. In his view it is, rather, a *prayer* for victory by a people in dire straits. The verbs in verse 2 — "you have granted" and "have not withheld" — he recognizes as precative perfect and thus as indicative of a request: "Give" and "Do not withhold." The people are pleading that their new king may be made glad through victory (*The Psalms*, p. 97f.). The position of Buttenwieser is worthy of consideration.

The opening words of the psalm are clearly directed to the Lord (vv. 1-7). Many scholars believe that the words in verses 8-12, however, are spoken to the king, encouraging him by assuring him that he will overpower all enemies, while others believe those verses are directed to the Lord. Scholars are divided on the issue, though the majority favor the first view.[39] Anderson acknowledges the possibility that the second part is addressed to God, but he does not commit himself. And Weiser says, "it cannot be stated for certain to whom vv. 8-12 are addressed. If these words were meant to refer to the king, they would have to be regarded as boundless exaggeration."[40] However, B.D. Eerdmans declares unequivocally that it is the Lord who is addressed throughout the psalm.[41] The present writer agrees.

The psalm opens with a song of praise to the Lord for the joy and blessings he has given the king, and this section closes appropriately with an affirmation of the king's trust in God. This is followed by a declaration of how God will deal in the future with his enemies (who are also the enemies of his people). The people then join in a final note of praise to the Lord.

1. The King's Joy and His Trust in the Lord (21:1-7)

21:1-3 O Lord, the king rejoices in your strength, or "The king is even now rejoicing." **In the victories you give.** Joy in God's help (RSV) may infer victory (NEB) in battle, though the Hebrew term is not explicit. In any case, the king has been praying, and God has answered his prayer (v. 2). **You welcomed him with rich blessings.** The Hebrew term for "rich" carries the idea of being beneficial, contributing to one's well-being, literally "good" blessings. Such is the nature of God's blessings.

---

[39]This includes the following: Delitzsch, Kirkpatrick, Briggs, Mowinckel, Gunkel, Leslie, Cohen, W.R. Taylor, Kidner, Leupold, Ash, Eaton, Stuhlmueller, and Craigie.

[40]Weiser, *The Psalms*, p. 215.

[41]B.D. Eerdmans, *The Hebrew Book*, p. 171.

[You] placed a crown of pure gold on his head. The king reigns
by the grace of God and not by some inherent right of his own. In
Israel the modern distinction between *secular* and *religious* was
unknown. Even the terms are absent from the Scriptures.[42] There is
no secular, because all of life on God's earth is by God's grace; there
is no escaping the "religious" dimension. Every act of mankind,
whether personal, in the family, in business, in politics, whatever
might be called secular, has a bearing on his or her relationship to
God and cannot therefore be distinguished from what might be
called religious. In Israel, the Lord himself was King. The one upon
whom he placed the crown was his servant, established on the
throne only that he might execute God's righteous will for all.[43]

21:4-6 In verse 4 it is indicated that the specific prayer of the
king had been for **life**. Was this his "heart's desire" rather than
victory in battle? Or was it in the anticipation of battle that he
prayed for victory and asked that his life be spared? Whatever the
case, God had answered his prayer and had given him life — **length
of days, for ever and ever**. Buttenwieser considers it most strange
that this is stated as an accomplished fact (in the past tense). He
would translate: "He asks life of thee; grant it unto him, length of
days forever."[44] Dahood, however, understands here a clear reference to immortality: "Life eternal he asked of you, you gave it to
him."[45] Dahood sees the statement in relation to the belief that the
king, on the day of his coronation, was thought to have received
immortality. Such a belief was not unheard of in the ancient world,
but it is not expressed in the Scriptures.

---

[42]In the NT English translations the noun "religion" or the adjective
"religious" appears in Acts 26:5 and in Jas 1:26,27. Yet the idea embodied
in the term is that of religious conduct or practice, not *religion* as the word
is understood today. The KJV also has "religious" in Acts 13:43, (NIV,
"devout"), but the Greek is "God-fearing." And "the Jew's religion" appearing in Gal 1:13,14, is (in Greek) "Judaism," as indeed the NIV translates it.

[43]Secularism, as a way of life, may or may not deny the existence of God.
But it denies his presence in the world and also man's religious nature;
that is, that man is in any way related to deity. Of course, such a concept is
altogether foreign to the Scriptures.

[44]Buttenwieser, *The Psalms*, p. 97.

[45]Dahood, *Psalms 1-50*, p. 130.

Many have considered Psalm 21 to be, from beginning to end, Messianic, referring specifically to the "offshoot of David" who was to come. The language describing the king — his "length of days," his "eternal blessings," his "glory," "splendor," and "majesty" — is scarcely applicable to any ordinary mortal. For this reason, we can understand that the psalm finds its ultimate meaning in the Messiah.[46] It thus becomes a part of the overall OT tapestry or mosaic of which we have spoken. Yet in its origin the psalm seems to have been written for an earthly king. Its extravagant language is hyperbolic, not uncommon in royal circles. God, indeed, had promised David that his throne would be established forever (2 Sam 7:16).

21:7 Throughout the psalm the relationship between God and king is dynamic in its effect. On the king's part, trust is emphasized — **for the king trusts in the LORD.** And on the Lord's part there is *hesed* — steadfast love, loyalty, mercy. As a result there was joy, victory, blessing. Moreover, there was confidence for the future. So long as the king continues to trust, he shall not be moved.

2. Anticipation of the Lord's Future Triumph (21:8-12)

21:8-9 We have accepted the view that, throughout the psalm, the words of the worshipers are addressed to the Lord, including verse 7. Verses 8 and following are spoken in anticipation of the future triumph of God over all his enemies. **Your hand will lay hold on all your enemies.** There are no exceptions. Isaiah warns: "Woe to those who go to great depths to hide their plans from the LORD, who do their work in darkness and think, 'Who sees us? Who will know?'" (Isa 29:15). God knows. He knows who they are that hate him as well as he "knows those who are his" (2 Tim 2:19). **You will make them like a fiery furnace . . . and his fire will consume them.** Thus we should read the verse and put in parentheses or brackets, **In his wrath the LORD will swallow them up.**[47] In Deut

---

[46]The Targum (Aramaic Scripture) interprets the psalm as referring to "the Messiah King."

[47]Since the metrical pattern is basically 3+3 throughout the psalm, the change to 5+5 in verse 9 strongly suggests that the second line is parenthetical. It also recognizes that it is the Lord who is dealing with his enemies, not the king.

4:24 it is stated that "God is a consuming fire." And this is restated in the NT (Heb 12:29). We delight in the love of God. Yet nothing is stated with more clarity in the Scriptures than that unrepentant wickedness brings punishment. The focus here is upon those who do evil in open defiance of the Lord — they intended evil against him (v. 11). Such persons may boast of their self-sufficiency. They may be ever so secure, safe from everything but the wrath of God and so not safe at all!

21:10-12 The desire expressed that God destroy even the **descendants . . . posterity** (the children) of his adversaries seems to be, and is, a far cry from the teachings of Jesus relative to one's attitude and treatment of enemies. Some would say, cynically, that little rattlesnakes grow up to become big ones. But this is recognized at once as being purely a rationalization. Furthermore, a child is not a rattlesnake. We cannot fully comprehend the mind of the psalmist, but basically he is desiring that God deal decisively and thoroughly with the workers of evil, completely destroying root, trunk, and branch. And some day, when the day of grace is past, he will do just this. The love of God is real. "He is patient with you, not wanting anyone to perish" (2 Pet 3:9). Yet to those who would choose the way of wickedness, the way of ungodliness, the warning is given: "It is a dreadful thing to fall into the hands of the living God" (Heb 10:31). The psalmist desired that God execute the sentence of judgment speedily upon his foes because they intended evil against him.[48]

3. Praise of the Lord (21:13)

21:13 In this concluding verse the psalmist returns to his opening theme. From beginning to end it is the power of God as demonstrated on the human plane that elicits the praise of his people. That in which the king rejoiced ("your strength," v. 1) is once again in view. **Be exalted, O LORD, in your strength.** The psalmist anticipated the continuing active participation of God in

---

[48]For further treatment of this theme see the discussion of imprecatory psalms on pp. 61-63.

human events. And God would be exalted whenever he manifested his strength as he had done before.

So **we will sing**, recognizing his **might** and his goodness, acknowledging the glory due him, and praising his name for the victory that he makes possible. How jubilant this song will be when the ultimate victory is realized. It awaits only the coming of him who "hands over the kingdom to God the Father after he has destroyed all dominion, authority and power. For he must reign until he has put all his enemies under his feet." (1 Cor 15:24,25).

V. GOD AS SAVIOR, SHEPHERD, AND SOVEREIGN (22:1–24:10)

A. FROM DESPAIR TO JUBILATION (22:1-31)

The opening words of Psalm 22 should leave little doubt that here is the impassioned lament of an individual: "My God, my God, why have you forsaken me?" The speaker is surely one who has experienced the nearness of God in his life, for only one who has known the love and companionship of another can feel forsaken, as he does in his present condition. He feels that God has abandoned him and he does not know why. He has prayed for relief but seemingly to no avail. He stands a solitary figure, alone and overwhelmed by his misery. He is suffering the physical agony of a tortured and emaciated body, plus jeers and taunts from those around him. Surely these words of anguish come from the lips of one who actually experienced the woes depicted in the psalm.

Some, however, have suggested that the poem was written to portray the condition of *the ideal righteous sufferer.* He may, indeed, have to undergo great distress, but God will restore him, to the glory of God and to the vindication of his cause. The psalm may well be viewed in this light, as an encouragement for all of God's people who suffer. But to say that it was written for this purpose, that it was composed as a polemic on theodicy, would be to minimize – or to trivialize – unduly the real agony suffered by a real person. The same objection must be made when considering an alternate view that the psalm is a personification of the suffering of Israel during the exile, after her seeming rejection by the Lord.[49] The one who suffered is not the nation, but an individual, calling on his brethren, the "sons of Jacob," to join him in praising God (vv. 22-23). Of course, the nature of the psalm is such that it could, and would, be used to bring comfort to all the people in times of national distress. Yet in its origin it is a reflection of individual suffering. (The writer refers to his tongue, his jaws, heart, clothing, etc.).

Even so, those who see the psalms primarily as related to the ritual of public worship, view Psalm 22 as liturgical. It is, they say, the liturgy for one who has come to offer sacrifice and to pay his vows as he presents his petition to the Lord. The psalm, though originally an individual lament, could have been adapted and used for this purpose, as no doubt it was.

Whatever the significance of this poem to the psalmist, to his contemporaries, and to those who came after, and whatever the agonizing experience that elicited its impassioned plea, for those who are Christian a greater significance is seen in its application to Jesus, giving expression, as it does, to his soul's agony, to his cry of distress, and to his ultimate confidence in the Lord as he suffered crucifixion.

The psalm expresses both agony and ecstasy, despair and jubilation. The change from the former to the latter comes abruptly at the end of verse 21. Verse 22 introduces words of praise and thanksgiving. The lament, "You do not answer," has given way to the shout of triumph, for God has heard. The suffering reflected in the opening verses is seen as but the prelude to the glory that would come after.

---

[49]Buttenwieser, espousing this view, states that "the psalmist does not speak of personal suffering but of the common misery" (*The Psalms*, p. 590). He gathers from the reference to the Lord's concern for "our fathers," in time past, that the concern in the present is for the nation, not for an individual. Our view is that the psalmist as an individual is distressed because his own experience is in stark contrast with that of the fathers in time past.

1. Despair (22:1-21b)

22:1 When prayers apparently go unanswered, when a soul
devoted to God unexpectedly suffers great misfortunes, the despair
that is experienced is often expressed in the one word, "Why?" or
"Why, Lord?" The irreligious person, facing the same circumstances, feels similar despair, but not with the same poignancy. For
him the why has little significance, other than to suggest the mecha-
nistic connection between cause and effect. The child of God recognizes the immediate causes, but still must ask, "Why?" because he
believes that God could have decreed otherwise, and it is because
he believes, that he cries out: **My God, my God, why have you forsaken me?** Far from being the cry of a skeptic, these words of the
psalmist are an affirmation of trust. In agony of body and soul,
taunted by evil men that God has abandoned him, even now he
would lay his burden upon God, so that even in his cry there is a
mingling of faith with the despair. It is a way of saying, "Lord, this
is indeed too much for me. You alone can handle it."

22:2 The psalmist could reason within himself that the testing of
faith develops patience and perseverance and maturity (see Jas
1:3,4). And he could understand that one who has suffered is better
able to sympathize with and comfort others. But why must the
righteous, at times, bear a much greater load of suffering than
others? Is this the will of God? It is not necessary to say that God
wills it. Yet he does permit it, and so the question remains.
Directed, as it is, to the Lord, there is the implication that with him
there must be an answer. Even so, for the psalmist no answer came,
in spite of his pleading day and night — **You do not answer.**

22:3-6 This was the supreme agony, the greater burden and
matter of concern. He could endure the insults of the vicious ones
around him, the ridicule. He could even learn to live with the sickness and the pain. But to believe that God had abandoned him!
This was too great a burden to bear. But see how, even in this dark
hour, faith shines through. If those who taunted him expected to
shake his faith in God, they failed. In verse 3 there is a crescendo
that is lost in the English translations: "But you! Holy! Enthroned!
The Praises of Israel!" (All of the intervening words in our versions
are supplied by the translator.) It is the surpassing greatness of God
that is here acknowledged and proclaimed, and former victories are

recalled. **In you our fathers put their trust . . . . and were not disappointed.** They were helped, but not I. I am **scorned by men,** no more than a **worm.**

22:7-11 Elsewhere the devout person is assured: "Commit your way to the LORD; trust in him and he will do this." (Ps 37:5). But there are those who sneer, ridicule such a promise, and say, **"Let the LORD rescue him."** The irony of the situation could not be ignored by the psalmist, but again he returns to what he is sure of – God has been faithful in the past. "I may not understand the reason for my present condition, Lord, but you are he that **brought me out of the womb,** and you have been my God ever since." Thereupon he renews his plea for God to be near once again, (v. 11). It is this continued communing with the Lord that sustains him in his darkest hour. The storms he endures are overwhelming, but so long as he can talk with God, his faith remains and his anchor holds. (Judging from the testimony he left, this was also the experience of Dietrich Bonhoeffer as he suffered in a Nazi prison.)

22:12-18 The wretchedness of the psalmist's position is shown here. Foes like wild animals surround him, waiting to attack him in his weakened condition. He is at the point of death, and his executioners will divide his clothing among them. The severity of his suffering is given in vivid detail – **poured out like water . . . bones are out of joint,** etc. The psalmist, assuredly, was not undergoing crucifixion, and yet the agonies of that cruel means of execution could not have been described with more stark realism. Understandably, Paul the apostle could say that "Christ died for our sins according to the Scriptures" (1 Cor 15:3). That is, the sufferings of Jesus are seen to be in accord with this predisclosed pattern.[50] Note the minute details, as Rotherham has observed them:

(The one suffering) is exposed to public view; for he refers to *all who see* him. He is fixed to one spot; for his enemies *gather round* him. He has been deprived of his clothing; for he can

---

[50]The motif of the suffering servant of the Lord is seen most vividly in Isaiah 53. However, it is reflected in certain of the psalms and in similar language. These psalms are 18, 22, 49, 69, 86, 88, 116, and 118. See Helmer Ringgren, "The So-called Servant Psalms," in *The Messiah in the Old Testament* (Chicago: Alec R. Allenson, 1956), pp. 54-64.

count his own *bones*, . . . and sees his *garments* distributed to others. . . . His body is so distended that his *bones* are *dislocated*; his mouth is parched with *thirst*, his strength floats away *like water*, his physical courage fails like *melting wax.*[51]

From NT times the translation of the latter part of verse 16 has been disputed. The Hebrew has, "Like a lion, my hands and feet." But since, in the context, this makes little sense, all of the ancient versions and most modern scholars propose a verb instead of the noun "lion." The Greek translation has a form of the verb ὀρύσσω (*orysso,* "to dig"), and from this Jerome (c. 400 A.D.) derived "pierced," and so the translation: **They have pierced my hands and my feet.** Undoubtedly Jerome was thinking of the crucifixion, but such a rendering of the Greek root or the Hebrew from which it came is not without difficulty.[52] Yet, however the verb is to be translated, in some way special attention is called to the hands and feet of the suffering victim, and that in itself is of significance when one considers the crucifixion.

22:19-21b Once again there is an impassioned plea for deliverance: **But you, O Lord, be not far off; O my Strength, come quickly to help me. Deliver my life from the sword.** Apparently the deliverance comes, for the remainder of the psalm consists of praise and thanksgiving.

2. Delivered! (22:21c)

22:21c If Psalm 22 is a unit, as we believe, then we should expect some kind of transition from part one, the lament, to part

---

[51]Rotherham, *Studies,* 1:200f.

[52]Other verbs have been proposed, yielding the following translations; "They have hacked off" (NEB), "They have bound" (Eaton, Leslie, Oesterley), "They mangle" (Buttenwieser), "They gnaw" (Jewish Targum). J.M. Roberts, without changing the root letters, would propose a meaning not attested in Hebrew but found in Syriac and Akkadian, "to be short" = "to shrink," "to shrivel"; thus: "My hands and my feet are shriveled up." Cf. "I can count all my bones." (See Roberts, "A New Root for an Old Crux," *VT,* 1973, pp. 247-253.) Craigie proposes: "My hands and my feet were exhausted," explains his reasoning for this, and gives a summary of other proposals (*Psalms 1-50,* p. 196).

two with its call to worship. This, naturally, would be expected in verse 21. A literal translation of the Hebrew of this verse would be: "Save me from the lion's mouth and from the horns of wild oxen you answered me." But since it appears a bit strange for an answer from God to come from between the horns of a wild ox, various alternative readings have been suggested.[53] The usual solution has been to substitute a noun in the place of "you answered." Typical of this treatment is the RSV: "Save . . . my *afflicted* soul from the horns of the wild oxen." Granted, this provides a parallelism for the first line of the verse. But is the emendation necessary? We prefer to adhere to the Hebrew, except to insert a full stop after wild oxen. Thus, we would translate:

> Save me from the lion's mouth
> And from the horns of the wild oxen.
> You have answered me.

Admittedly, this is a bit irregular syntax, but the abrupt change of mood evident in verse 22 must have had an abrupt cause — namely, the assurance that God had responded. How this assurance came is not stated. Some have suggested that the psalmist was praying in the sanctuary when a prophet or a priest, by revelation, brought God's response. For example, after King Hezekiah had prayed for recovery from illness, Isaiah brought God's answer: "I have heard your prayer . . . I will add fifteen years to your life." (Isa 38:3-5). In whatever way the revelation came, the psalmist also had received the assurance he longed for. Deliverance was his.

3. Jubilation (22:22-26)

22:22-24 It scarcely seems possible that the same person who had experienced the anguish expressed in the opening verses of

---

[53]Eerdmans does not consider it strange. He would associate the expression with the Egyptian symbol that depicts the sun rising between the horns of a bull. Since the sun was a god to the Egyptians, this would be a representation of deity. Further, it was said of the Pharaoh that the sun god would arise each day to hear his prayer. However, it is certain that the psalmist would not identify the solar disc as Yahweh, and questionable that he would employ the symbolism. See Eerdmans, *The Hebrew Book*, p. 175.

our psalm could know the jubilation that is reflected in verses 22ff. The lament is transformed into a hymn of praise. From proximity to the grave itself ("the dust of death"), the psalmist comes to call on his brothers to join him in the praise of the Lord — "Praise him! . . . glorify him, and stand in awe of him" (RSV). And why? Because God is concerned for the afflicted, he does *see*, and he *hears*. This is the testimony of one whose trust in God has been vindicated.

22:25-26 There are two reasons why one would acknowledge publicly the blessings God has given. The first is gratitude, the desire to express thanks. And the second is that others may come to share similar blessings. Both are to be found in the psalm. **My praise in the great assembly** (thanksgiving). Furthermore, others who will seek the Lord will find reason to praise him also. (This implies a sharing of the good news.)

4. Anticipation — God's Universal Dominion (22: 27-31)

22:27-28 Eerdmans states that the original psalm ended with verse 26, though he cites no evidence other than to say that the scope of the following verses is much wider.[54] True, they embrace **all the ends of the earth . . . all the families of the nations.** It should not be thought strange, however, that the psalmist should anticipate the universal reign of the Lord. He recognized that the God in whom he had trusted is the living God (in distinction from all others that are called god), and consequently the God of all creation. A corollary of monotheism is necessarily the universality of God. The psalmist could only hope that all peoples might come to know such deliverance as he had experienced and thus be encouraged to seek God also and to join in praising him.

22:29-31 The Hebrew of verses 29-30 is difficult, and various interpretations have been proposed. The usual understanding has been that all classes will bow before God, both the affluent, **the rich of the earth,** (Hebrew, literally, "fat" upon earth!) and the humble, **all who go down to the dust.** This, however, leaves verse 29c dangling in air: **those who cannot keep themselves alive.** How can this

---

[54]Eerdmans, *The Hebrew Book*, p. 177.

be related to the context? Numerous emendations of the text have been proposed, none without some difficulty. One manner of keeping the Hebrew text very much as it is would be to consider verses 29 and 30 to be antithetical, with 29c indicating the antithesis. The translation, paraphrased, would then be: "All of the rich ones of the earth may partake of the sacrificial meal in worship, all of the poor may bow before God, but not a one can keep his own soul alive. However, a seed will **serve him** (and not just bow before him), and this will be enumerated to the Lord as the generation that is pleasing in his sight." (See Psalms 14:5; 24:6.) **They will proclaim his righteousness to a people yet unborn — for he has done it.** The psalmist was certain that God had responded to his cry of distress, certain also that testimony to the righteousness of God would become the inheritance of generations to come. That legacy now is ours.

B. YAHWEH'S GRACIOUS CARE (23:1-6)

It is not without significance that Psalms 22 and 23 are placed in juxtaposition. In the former there is the agony and distress of one who feels abandoned by the Lord; in the latter the joy and confidence of one who lives daily in God's fellowship. The first, as we have seen, is an apt portrayal of the suffering servant of the Lord; the second, an expression of joy of one who has experienced God's grace. Spurgeon has noted that in Psalm 22 David "bewailed the woes of the Shepherd." while in the 23rd he "tunefully rehearses the joys of the flock." adding that "it is only after we have read, 'My God, my God, why have you forsaken me?' that we come to 'the Lord is my Shepherd.'"[55] Unless we have known of the sufferings of the shepherd, we cannot fully appreciate the shepherd's care of the flock. For the Christian, therefore, the 23rd Psalm, just as the 22nd, finds its ultimate meaning in Jesus.

The present writer deliberated at length before affixing a title to this most beloved of the Psalms. To be definitive of the contents, the title might well be *The Lord – Shepherd and Host*, recognizing

---

[55]Spurgeon, *Treasury*, 1:354.

that the metaphor of shepherd gives way to that of a guest seated before a well-prepared table. Kidner proposes *Shepherd and Friend,* an apt suggestion. However, the thought of the psalmist was not focused on figures, but on the fullness of God's goodness and mercy. It is doubtful that he was even conscious of the fact that he was mixing metaphors. Perhaps it is necessary for us to analyze the psalm according to its constituent parts, but it is with the desire that the overall theme be kept in focus that we use the title: *Yahweh's Gracious Care.*[56] This care, as many have noted, is to be seen in the psalm as that of a shepherd, a guide, and a host.

1. The Lord as Shepherd (23:1-2)

23:1a The LORD is my shepherd. In Hebrew, this simple statement consists of only two words. Two words! Yet their portent is almost too great to be grasped.

To begin, attention should be directed to the nature of the utterance. When David says, "The LORD is my shepherd," he is not dealing with philosophical speculation, he is not introducing a matter for debate, nor is he uttering a prayer for what might be. Instead, he is making a simple affirmation of a truth realized and experienced. He speaks with artless simplicity, without equivocation and with no inhibitions, making a statement that some might consider presumptuous. And yet his words are altogether devoid of any spirit of boasting. Rather, they are the spontaneous outcry of one who himself is overjoyed by the truth he utters. In order to appreciate the significance of that truth, let us repeat the statement again and again, emphasizing a different word each time.

First, the LORD is my shepherd — not some idol of wood and stone, dumb and impotent, not the almighty dollar, so deceptive of many, but Yahweh, Almighty God, Creator of heaven and earth.

---

[56]Charles Foster Kent proposes this title in *The Songs, Hymns and Prayers of the Old Testament* (London: Hodder and Stoughton, 1914), p. 194. [Editor's note: Kent, and thus, Prof. Tesh actually used the title *Jehovah* instead of *Yahweh*; my attempt is to be consistent with the name *Yahweh* throughout the book.]

He is my shepherd! Is one's mind capable of a thought greater than this!

But can it be true? Indeed yes, the psalmist responds, "The Lord *is* my shepherd" — not potentially, in some moment of crisis when I might call to him in desperation, but *now*, a present companion and guide who will continue to be with me when the crisis does come. He *is* my shepherd.

Again, the Lord is *my* shepherd — what a bold claim! "Other sheep I have," he says, and this I know. Yet the fact remains that I, too, am his, loved by him and the object of his concern. The Lord is *my* shepherd, and this gives me the confidence I need for life.

Finally, he is my *shepherd* – not in the sense of the western herdsman who drives his sheep, will-less and passive, before him, but in the oriental fashion, wherein the shepherd goes in front, leading the flock. He is not an abusive taskmaster, but indeed a caring shepherd, whom I can follow with confidence and joy.

But how can I know this to be true? Calling him shepherd does not make it so. The reality is experienced only as I hear his voice and respond to his leading.

23:1b-2 I shall not be in want, or suffer from a lack of what is needful. If I am in his care, then all anxiety may be dispelled. The provision afforded is summarized in the next verse — **green pastures . . . quiet waters**. The shepherd sees to it that the flock is provided sustenance, protection, and rest.

2. The Lord as Guide (23:3-4)

23:3 Almost imperceptibly, verse 3 introduces a transition of thought. **He restores my soul** may be taken to mean "he restores my vitality," and read in connection with the green pastures of verse 2. But here it is introducing a new verse and a new thought. Elsewhere the expression indicates the restoring of the soul that results from walking according to the "law of the LORD" (Ps 19:7), and that is its meaning here. The Lord is my guide for life. He restores my soul by **guid[ing] me in the paths of righteousness**; otherwise I will perish.

The sheepfold has been left behind. Even the green pastures fade from the scene. Now it is the journey of life that comes into view, and for that journey I have a dependable guide, the very same Lord who has been my shepherd. The paths of righteousness in which he leads are "right paths" in the sense that they are proven and lead to the desired destination. They are also the ways of moral rectitude, since they are God's ways. In no sense am I driven to walk in this way except as I take delight in my companion and guide and respond to his kindness by following him. The way of the Lord is not one of compulsion but of trust. **For his name's sake** I know he will lead rightly — his reputation is involved. And for his name's sake I want to follow his guidance, for I bring reproach upon that name when I fail him. Even so, he will never compromise his own righteous nature by leading me astray or by striking a bargain with evil. He is a true guide to all who will follow him in faithfulness.

23:4 To follow him does not mean that I shall be spared the vicissitudes of life nor the **walk through the valley of the shadow of death.** But I shall not walk alone. Notice that the psalmist now speaks directly with God — **for you are with me** (not, "he is"). It is the experience of fellowship with the Lord as companion and guide, one who is fully equipped with whatever is necessary to insure his safety, whether it be **rod** or **staff.** The former was a short, thick stick used as a weapon for protection and the latter a long stick used for help and comfort when climbing in hilly country. Whatever the circumstance and however trying, the presence of this divine guide would be adequate to dispel all fear — **I will fear no evil.**

3. The Lord as Host (23:5-6)

23:5 Once again, as before, the figure changes imperceptibly from that of companion on a journey to that of a guest in the house of a gracious benefactor and protector, where God is recognized as the host. **You prepare a table before me in the presence of my enemies.** Among Bedouin peoples it was a point of honor and a sacred obligation for one to ensure the security of a guest, and he had received such protection from the hand of God. The threats of enemies have been turned into triumph. Those who would ridicule or attack him can now only look on in envy as they see evidence that he is indeed blessed of God, seated at God's abundant table. In Ps 34:8 there is the challenge: "Taste and see that the LORD is good; blessed is the man who takes refuge in him." The table that God spreads, we may be sure, is a feast suited to the needs of one who is created in God's image. With this provision, why should any desire to "fill his stomach with the pods that the pigs [eat]" (Luke 15:16).

But more than security and sustenance are provided. **You anoint my head with oil.** This speaks of gladness. Such treatment afforded a guest was recognized as a special courtesy on the part of the host, and it had been his! **My cup overflows.** The blessings were more than abundant. How full his life had become through his relationship with the Lord! One is reminded of the similar exaltation of the apostle Paul, in his words to the brethren at Philippi: "And my God will meet all your needs according to his glorious riches in Christ Jesus" (Phil. 4:19).

23:6 With all of the above, even greater joy was experienced by David from the realization that his was a continuing relationship with the Lord, not a fleeting interlude. **Surely goodness and love will follow me all the days of my life.** The verb, literally, is "pursue." Where before there had been the threat of being hounded by enemies, now there is the awareness that nothing life can bring can separate him from the "goodness" that comes from God nor from his loving mercy, his steadfast love (*ḥesed*). These personified heavenly attendants are always with him. (See Rom 8:35-39.)

The implication that this was a covenant relationship with the Lord is indicated by the text. Goodness is a covenant term, as found in ancient Near Eastern usage, indicating the amity established by treaty. And in Israel, the mercy of God (*ḥesed*) could also be defined as covenant love. Since it is impossible for God to lie (Heb 6:18), his covenant is sure. His goodness and mercy, blessing and love, are a promise to be enjoyed with the utmost confidence. (Since this was true of the old covenant, how much greater cause for joy and confidence in the new, seeing that it was sealed by the blood of God's own Son! See Heb 8:6-13.)

And I will dwell in the house of the LORD forever. The reference to the house of the Lord has been taken by some to mean the temple. Leslie considers it thus, citing the example found in Luke

2:37 of Anna, who "never left the temple."[57] It is better, however, to consider that here we have a metaphor for living daily in companionship with God, not a literal dwelling in the temple. But is the writer affirming his anticipation of life with God for eternity? The expression "forever" in the text is, literally, "for length of days," and in Ps 91:16 it is translated "long life." However, we must not underestimate the magnitude of the experience that had been his in the fellowship of Yahweh, the living God. That is what the psalm is all about. Is it reasonable to suppose that this would be terminated by death? Would his experience not rather inspire confidence that God's care for him would continue for all time to come, even beyond the grave? We believe so. In this vein, Dahood asserts: "After a peaceful life under the guidance and protection of Yahweh, the psalmist looks forward to eternal happiness in God's celestial abode."[58] The companionship with God that he experienced in this life would become a more glorious reality in the life to come. The sheep would be safely in the master's fold; the journey of the pilgrim would be ended; the child of God would be at peace in the father's house.

C. THE KING OF GLORY (24:1-10)

For years students of the Scriptures have viewed Psalm 24 as having been written as a processional hymn for use on some great historical occasion. Its questions and responses would lend themselves admirably to antiphonal use, and the reference to ascending the hill of the Lord and to the coming in of the King of glory suggest a procession. The occasion of the hymn has been variously stated but frequently identified with the event recorded in 2 Sam 6:12-16 – the bringing of the ark of God into the city of Jerusalem by David. Others, however, would refer the psalm to the time when the ark was brought into the temple by Solomon a generation later (1 Kgs 8:46), while still others would refer it to Zerubbabel's temple later still (516 B.C.).

---

[57]Leslie, *The Psalms*, p. 285.
[58]Dahood, *Psalms 1-50*, p. 148f.

Following the lead of Mowinckel and Gunkel, another group of scholars consider Psalm 24 to be cultic in nature, written to be used in one of the great festivals of Jewish worship. Mowinckel related it to his proposed annual enthronement of Yahweh festival. Others have suggested the Feast of Tabernacles as a suitable occasion.

Besides these cultic and historical views of the psalm, there is yet a third approach, the eschatological, that sees here a reference to the messianic age and/or to "the last days." As J.D. Smart has shown,[59] "there is nothing whatever in the psalm to suggest the ark"[60] (and hence a procession). He also notes the absence of any priestly influence such as one would expect if this were a liturgy.[61] The psalm is more of the nature of prophetic writing and has close affinities to Isaiah.

For example, the prophet states that in the last days, from all nations many would seek to "go up to the mountain of the LORD" (Isa 2:2-3; cf. Ps. 24:3). But who could aspire to such an honor? Who could escape "the consuming fire"? the prophet asks, and then answers his question — the righteous would "see the king in his beauty" (Isa 33:13-17; cf. Ps 24:36). Furthermore, to these God would give blessings (Isa 44:3; Ps. 24:5). In Isaiah 40–66 Yahweh is the glorious king and six times is designated as "the LORD Almighty" (cf. Ps. 24:7-10). Finally, the "ancient doors" of the psalm apply more aptly to the New Jerusalem or to heaven than to Solomon's temple.

Viewing the psalm in this light we see, then, a unified production extolling Yahweh as the King of Glory. The opening verses introduce the Lord as the creator of all things, with the inference that he will bring to consummation his ultimate aim for creation. Though not expressed, we expect the culmination to be a golden age and it is to be in the last days, of which the prophets speak. The great question is who may expect to share in the blessings of that era? With the question answered, there is then envisioned the coming of the victorious Lord in glory into the holy city.[62]

---

[59]J.D. Smart, "The Eschatological Interpretation of Psalm 24," *JBL*, 52 (1933): 175-180.

[60]Ibid., p. 175.

[61]Ibid., p. 179.

[62]Alan Cooper proposes yet another interpretation of Psalm 24. (See

1. Lord over All — Contemplation (24:1-2)

24:1 The earth is the LORD'S, and everything in it. In a world where many gods were conceived of as in constant warfare, the importance of this statement is apparent. Not many conflicting gods, but one Lord is the sovereign of his creation. He had called Abraham; he had called Israel out of Egypt; he had established her as a nation as he had promised. But he had also brought up the Philistines from Caphtor and the Syrians (Arameans) from Kir (Amos 9:7). None are beyond his dominion; all come within the scope of his concern — **the world, and all who live in it.** And even though this earth is but one of millions of heavenly bodies floating through space, it is marvelous beyond imagination and amazing — amazing as one would expect the creation of God to be.

In such a world a rational creature can scarcely escape thoughtful contemplation of his own role in the total scheme of things. Who am I? Why am I here? What place in life does God have for me? Naturally, apart from belief in God, such questions have no meaning. But if "the earth is the LORD's," then they are of the

---

"Psalm 24:7-10: Mythology and Exegesis," *JBL* 102:1 [1983]: 37-60.) That the psalm depicts a procession with the ark, he considers to be a mere assumption without evidence. Consequently he rejects both the historical and the cultic approaches to its understanding. Instead, he views it as mythological in its signification. The clue to this interpretation is the presence of terminology in the psalm comparable to that found in the mythological literature of Mesopotamia and Canaan, with particular reference to warrior gods (cf. 24:8-10). The "gates" of the psalm are recognized as the gates of the underworld (the gates of death). Who dares to challenge them? The answer is *Yahweh*. He had demonstrated his power over nature in creation (24:1-2) and as Yahweh of hosts, mighty in battle, he is also able to confront the forces of death. Cooper demonstrates effectively the relationship between the psalm and the thought patterns of Canaanite mythology. He adds, however, that "the biblical evidence does not permit us to say whether those traditions (reflected in the mythopoeic language) were ever incorporated into a coherent mythological structure" (p. 54). It is possible to recognize the mythological terminology and to appreciate the connotation as it applies to the Lord, without subscribing to the mythological interpretation. Since the thought and terminology of the psalm have an affinity with Isaiah, we prefer the eschatological interpretation given above.

utmost significance and some answers can be anticipated from God, the owner and sustainer of his world.

24:2 The sovereignty of God over the earth is his by right of creation, **for he founded it upon the seas.** The description is phenomenological; that is, it depicts what appears to the sight. If one is on an island, the land appears to be resting upon the water. (In the same fashion we say, "The sun rises.") The **waters**, in the latter part of the verse, appears usually translated as "rivers." Subterranean rivers may be the meaning. (See Exod 20:4; Deut 33:13; Ps 136:6.) In any case, the earth is firmly established, and all of nature, all of humankind, owe their existence to the Lord.

2. Who May Approach God? — Preparation (24:3-6)

24:3 This concept of the universal reign of God is prominent with the prophets. It is little wonder, therefore, that their thoughts of the future would include the involvement of all mankind in the purposes of God. Thus Isaiah writes: "In the last days the mountain of the LORD's temple will be established as chief among the mountains; it will be raised above the hills, and all nations will stream to it" (2:2). Here the word for "mountain" is the same as that translated "hill" in our psalm, and in each case the reference is to the temple mount, made holy by God's presence. The prophet tells us that many will say, "Come, let us go up to the mountain of the LORD, to the house of the God of Jacob" (2:3). And the psalm asks: **Who may ascend the hill of the LORD?** or **Who may stand in his holy place?**

24:4 It is a disturbing question. Who indeed? Is it possible for the creature to be admitted to the fellowship of the Creator? Who would dare to hope so? Yet that is what the Scriptures are all about, from Genesis to Revelation. As Augustine declared: "Thou hast made us for thyself, O Lord, and our hearts are restless until they rest in thee." Yet the question remains, Who may aspire to this privilege? And the answer: **He who has clean hands and a pure heart.** In Israel the unclean were not permitted within the sacred precincts of the temple, and ceremonial washings were required before entrance was granted. But here the context makes it clear that it is not ceremonial cleanness that is in view but purity of heart and of life. Fundamental to such a life is a basic devotion to the Lord, the devotion of one **who does not lift up his soul to an idol.** To "lift up the soul" is an idiom meaning "to pray" (Ps 25:1; 86:4), and "idol" is "a thing of nothingness" (Jer 10:15). The one walking in the way of the Lord, walking with the Lord, does not pray to nor worship any other gods. On the other hand, his worship of God, with right heart and motive, helps him to keep his hands clean, his heart pure, and his tongue free of deceit. Henry Van Dyke describes these qualities in terms of their practical significance:

> An honest, earnest, true heart; a hand that will not stain itself with unjust gain, or hold an unequal balance, or sign a deceitful letter, or draw an unfair contract; a tongue that will not twist itself to a falsehood or take up an evil report; a soul that points as true as a compass to the highest ideal of manhood or womanhood – these are the marks and qualities of God's people everywhere.[63]

Notice that to be acceptable to God the requirement is not that one perform the proper ritual nor that he be a member of a proper social or ethnic group – "God does not show favoritism but accepts men from every nation who fear him and do what is right" (Acts 10:34b,35). In simple terms, if one aspires to be a child of God, then he or she should live as a child of God ought to live. What does the Lord require? In the words of Micah: "To act justly and to love mercy, and to walk humbly with your God" (6:8b). Uprightness of character is essential to fellowship with an upright and holy God.

24:5-6 He will receive blessing from the LORD. The obvious blessing is his acceptance by the Lord whose presence he has sought (v. 6), though such acceptance is to be viewed as a precursor of other blessings to follow. However, to stand in the presence of God is in itself a signal blessing! **And vindication from God his Savior.** Elsewhere, salvation is associated with this term "vindication," or literally "righteousness." (Isa 46:13). From the God of his salvation, or, properly, "from his saving God" ("his Savior"). These blessings

---

[63]Henry Van Dyke, *The Story of the Psalms* (New York: Charles Scribner's Sons, 1892), p. 66.

will accrue to those **who seek** and go on seeking (v. 6, participles) the face of the **God of Jacob** (LXX).

Although it is not stated, a logical inference from the above would be that those who do not seek the Lord, those who do not have clean hands and a pure heart, will be denied entrance to his presence. If there are those whose sensibilities are offended by this thought, it should be recognized that a righteous God cannot be morally indifferent. Whether one obeys or disobeys his precepts matters greatly. Consider also, if one is not comfortable in God's presence now, why should he expect to be hereafter? But to anyone who is concerned, the invitation comes: "Seek the LORD while he may be found; call on him while he is near. Let the wicked forsake his way and the evil man his thoughts. Let him turn to the LORD, and he will have mercy on him, and to our God, for he will freely pardon" (Isa 55:6-7). The way to God remains open to all who would enter.

3. The King Comes — Realization (24:7-10)

The prophet Isaiah wrote: "The LORD is exalted, for he dwells on high; he will fill Zion with justice and righteousness. He will be the sure foundation for your times" (Isa 33:5-6). Frightened sinners ask: "Who of us can dwell with the consuming fire?" (33:14). (J.D. Smart observes: "There is no doubt that the question is concerned with who shall stand and remain secure in the last days.")[64] Isaiah answers: "He who walks righteously and speaks what is right, . . . [You] will see the king in his beauty" (33:15-17). The reference is definitely to a future period, and we view Psalm 24 in the same light, as anticipating the coming reign of the Lord.

24:7,9 Lift up your heads, O you gates. Scholars have debated whether the reference is to the gates of the temple or of the city of Jerusalem. In either case, it is an indication of the place where the Lord will be enthroned. It may even be the heavenly Jerusalem of which the Scriptures speak — "Jerusalem that is above" (Gal 4:26); "Mount Zion, . . . the heavenly Jerusalem, the city of the living

---

[64]J.D. Smart, "The Eschatological Interpretation," p. 178.

God," (Heb 12:22) whose gates will open to receive the King of glory or, the Glorious King.[65]

24:8,10 Who is this King of glory? The question is asked twice, for emphasis. Elsewhere, *Yahweh* is shepherd. In Hos 12:1 he is heavenly father. But the same Lord who is shepherd and father is also sovereign of his creation. He to whom all creation belongs (v. 1) has not abdicated. *He* **is the King of glory.**

Isaiah is not silent about the Glorious King. "The whole earth is full of his glory," the seraphim said (Isa 6:3). Compare this with the psalm, which says, "The earth is the LORD's" (24:1). "Who may stand in his holy place?" the psalm asks. And Isaiah says, "Woe to me! . . . I am ruined; for I am a man of unclean lips" (6:5). "This (live coal) has touched your lips," Isaiah was told, and "your guilt is taken away" (6:7). "He who has clean hands and a pure heart" may stand before God, the psalm assures us, and God took Isaiah into his fellowship. **The King of glory [shall] come in**, the psalmist said. And the vision was given to Isaiah to see the Lord, "seated on a throne, high and exalted" (6:1).

Whether Psalm 24 may have been used in connection with some religious festival, or whether it served as a liturgy upon entry into the temple, it appears obvious that it envisions the coming of the Lord to reign over a kingdom, "the home of righteousness" (2 Pet 3:13). It should be noted that the prophets foresaw such a kingdom, but the king would be a descendant of David — "a righteous Branch" (Jer 33:15). But more than this, his name would be called "Wonderful Counselor, Mighty God, Everlasting Father, Prince of Peace" (Isa 9:6). In view of these Scriptures, it is understandable that the Christian views Psalm 24 as descriptive of the ascension of Christ, to the right hand of God in heaven, after his mighty victory over sin and death. Thus a new era was inaugurated and thus was ushered in the kingdom of God.

---

[65]The noun is used adjectivally, just as "the sword of gold" = "the golden sword."

VI. DRAWING NEAR TO GOD (25:1–29:11)

A. THE PRAYER OF A TRUSTING SOUL (25:1-22)

It is difficult to classify Psalm 25 as to type other than to say it is a prayer. Certain characteristics of the lament are evident — reference to gloating enemies (v. 2) and to distressing troubles (v. 17). Elements of didacticism are apparent; verses 8-10 and 12-14 would fit very nicely in the book of Proverbs. The penitential motif is suggested by verse 7. But all are incorporated in a prayer of an individual whose requests are more of a general nature than for God's blessing in regard to one specific matter. The diversity of thought that results is described by Eerdmans as "a series of pious phrases, without a leading thought" — an overstatement of the case, we believe.[66] It would seem, rather, that the psalmist is intent on trusting the Lord, whatever the circumstances of life, and so he expresses himself accordingly. Consequently, we would designate the psalm, "The Prayer of a Trusting Soul." Foes without and anxieties within, great transgression and admission of guilt — all are here. Any one of these could be devastating were it not for the mercy, the lovingkindness (the *ḥesed*) of the Lord. But having knowledge of that steadfast love, he has hope, and he can say, "Lord, I trust in you." That is the bedrock upon which the prayer rests.

The pattern of the selection is acrostic, with each verse beginning with each successive letter of the Hebrew alphabet. However, the sixth letter (*waw*) is not used. Its omission has led some to divide v. 5 in such a way as to begin a new line with the missing letter, with the belief that the text calls for some such solution. However, this is gratuitous, for Psalm 34, a similar acrostic, has the same peculiarity. Apparently the omission was intentional in both instances. A likely reason would be that, since the psalm is divided into three distinct strophes, it was desired to have an equal number of verses in each. Since there are twenty-two letters in the Hebrew alphabet, provision is made for seven verses in each strophe, with one letter remaining, and so it is omitted. Verse 22, beginning with the Hebrew letter *pe*, is not part of the acrostic arrangement, neither here nor in Psalm 34.

---

[66]Eerdmans, *The Hebrew Book*, p. 189.

Why some of the psalms pursue the acrostic pattern can only be conjectured. It is quite possible that the style was adopted, in part, as an aid to memorization. Eerdmans suggests that the psalmist was motivated by the fact that "the circle in which he moved appreciated literary skill."[67] And N.H. Sarna states as a probability that "the arrangement in alphabetical sequence from beginning to end would signify the striving for comprehensiveness in the expression of an emotion or idea."[68] (Or, as we would say, "The subject is covered from A to Z.")

Others would say that the psalmist was merely responding to the challenge that the alphabetic arrangement presented. "As a result of being bound by this somewhat artificial device," Leupold writes, "the sequence of thought does not flow as freely as is ordinarily the case in the Psalms."[69] Nevertheless, the psalmist's trust in the Lord remains as a unifying factor.

If there is no one special concern pressing upon his consciousness, then he is free, in his moments of contemplation, to consider various aspects of his life, *but all in relationship to God.* If the thoughts that a person entertains in moments of idleness are indicative of his true character, and they are, then the psalmist was undoubtedly one whose sincerest desire was to walk in the ways of the Lord. And as his thoughts moved from one subject to another, in each he found, in the words of Albert Barnes, "something to be thankful for, or to pray for, or to rejoice over, or to anticipate with pleasure, or to hope for, or to be penitent for, or to contemplate with gratitude and love."[70] In this, his experience might well be an example to us in our own moments of meditation upon the exigencies of life!

1. I Trust in You for Protection, Guidance, and Forgiveness (25:1-7)

25:1 To you, O LORD. The words are emphatic and set the tone for the entire psalm. Unto you, and to no other, for you alone are

---

[67]Ibid., p. 188.
[68]N.M. Sarna, "Acrostics," *EJ* 1:230.
[69]Leupold, *Exposition*, p. 222.
[70]Albert Barnes, *Notes on the Old Testament, Psalms*, reprint (Grand

altogether trustworthy, **I lift up my soul**, in prayer, in praise, in thanksgiving.

25:2-3 In you I trust, O my God. Opening the sentence, the pronoun again is emphatic.[71] Throughout the first seven verses the writer addresses the Lord directly. **Do not let me be put to shame** (v. 2). **No one whose hope is in you will ever be put to shame** (v. 3, see Isa 40:31). The prayer in verse 2 is for protection from the ridicule of enemies who would certainly gloat over him if his trust in the Lord resulted only in disappointment or abandonment. Verse 3, then, is not a petition but a strong affirmation of faith. Those who trust in the Lord will never regret it, but **they will be put to shame** (when they discover how wrong they have been) **who are treacherous without excuse** (in their relationship with God).

25:4-7 As the psalm continues, we feel that our own hearts can follow the pattern of the writer's meditations. "If I am to realize the blessings of God, it is necessary that I have his guidance" — **Show me your ways, O LORD.** "And since I am unworthy, I need to plead his mercy and forgiveness" — **Remember, O LORD, your great mercy and love . . . Remember not the sins of my youth.** "I know that his way is right, for he is **God, my Savior.**" **Guide me in your truth** (v. 5). All of this expresses a willingness to be instructed and a humility altogether lacking in the "know-it-all" individual. How we delight to instruct a child who trusts us and is eager to learn (see v. 9). But no one, not even the Lord, can teach one who is not willing to be taught. "But why should the Lord forgive me? Why should he teach me? Not because I deserve it, but because through countless ages he has shown himself merciful, so I will plead his

---

[71]"In you" in Hebrew begins with *beth*, as one would expect for verse 2; so we recognize it as the beginning word. If the preceding word, in the Masoretic text, belongs to verse 1, as has been suggested, then verse 2 does not begin with "O my God" (placed last in the first line of v. 2 in the NIV). It is my view that, originally in verse 1, this word was the pronoun with suffix, "on you" (do I wait all the day), a word that in the Hebrew looked somewhat like the word for "my God" and that could have been thus mistaken by a copyist, especially if the remainder of the verse had dropped out. Note also that throughout the psalm, Yahweh (LORD) appears over and over as the designation of deity, not *Elohim* (God), except in verse 22, added to the verses that comprise the acrostic.

mercy" – **according to your love** (covenant love/loyalty, *ḥesed*) **remember me** (v. 7).

2. The Lord Is Good and Will Guide in Right Paths (25:8-14)

25:8-9 The first seven verses were spoken directly *to* God; the next (with the exception of v. 11) are a meditation *about* God. He is **good and upright.** When it is said that God is good, the reference is not to passive goodness; he is actively good, promoting what is beneficial and desirable. (Happy thought! Many of the gods of the nations were malevolent.) The word "upright" (יָשָׁר, *yāšār*) means one who is straightforward (not deviating) whether in character (Job 1:1), or on a journey (1 Sam 6:12), or in the discharge of a duty (Exod 15:26). The verb form is used to indicate the making of a path that is the right path. (Do see Isa 40:3,4.) So, God is actively good, and for that reason he opens the right path. **Therefore**, consequence of this truth, he is willing to teach **sinners in his ways**. It is understood that this would be repentant sinners, of which the psalmist was one. The hardened sinner would not be interested.

25:10-14 The Lord's paths (**ways**) are **loving and faithful** for such as keep his covenant. Expressed negatively, his paths or ways are ineffectual only if I refuse to walk in them; however, sin will block my way and separate me from God. A sudden awareness of this reality is sufficient to prompt the psalmist to pray again: **Forgive my iniquity, though it is great** – so great that he can only hope for pardon from a God rich in mercy. Consequently, **for the sake of your name** I ask, for you have a name for mercy. I trust in your loving-kindness! Immediately there follows another affirmation that the Lord will instruct the God-fearing man **in the way chosen for him**, and it will be a way of blessing. Of this the writer is confident. Once again he has come to the bedrock of his faith.

3. My Eyes Are toward the Lord, Not toward My Troubles (25:15-22)

25:15-19 Nevertheless, at the moment he was suffering distress, as the remaining verses indicate. Entangled, as it were, in a net from which there was no escape, he was suffering loneliness and affliction, the latter from the hands or tongues of enemies, it would seem. He felt closed in from every side like a city under siege. And so he cries out, "O make room" (Briggs, v. 17), ("give me breathing space") — "Relieve the troubles of my heart" (RSV), **free me from my anguish.** His distresses (lit., "constraints, pressures") were many. In addition, he suffered physical pain, and the violent hatred of foes. It is readily understandable why this psalm is called a lament.

25:20-21 Throughout the psalm it is obvious that it is not possible for the psalmist to shut these things out of his mind. But he does look up to God, and he would continue to do so. Beyond his immediate surroundings he sees the Lord, and he directs his heart and soul to him. This he declared as his intention in his opening words, and to this he commits himself for the future: **I take refuge in you.** Having thus unburdened his heart, once again he utters a little prayer — **May integrity and uprightness protect me.** This is no boast that he possesses these virtues, but a request that they may become his, so that, in the words of Paul, he might be clothed with the whole armor of God (Eph 6:11ff).

25:22 The acrostic ends with verse 21. It may have been as an afterthought that the psalmist remembers that he is not the only person in Israel who has troubles, and so he offers up a prayer for his countrymen.

B. VINDICATE ME, O LORD! (26:1-12)

In Psalm 25 we observed an individual who desired to walk in the ways of the Lord and who committed himself to that end. The basis of his commitment was implicit trust, and to accomplish his purpose he asked God for two things: "Instruct me in the way that I should go and be merciful to me when I fail." In Psalm 26 the writer is asking God for a report card. He makes no claim of deserving a grade of "A," but he reaffirms his trust in the Lord and reports on the direction that his steps have taken. His desire now seems to be (expressed in a question) "Am I making any progress?"

Some have classified the psalm as a lament, but this is strange since it contains not a word of complaint. Others consider it to be the prayer of one falsely accused, on the basis of the opening word, "Vindicate me." Yet there is no reference to any accusations nor to an accuser, nor is there any petition for protection from adversaries.

As we read the psalm, we may get the impression that the writer has recently been reciting Psalm 1, about the walk of the righteous man. Compare the two. At least the theme of that psalm seems to be in his consciousness, and as he reflects thereon, he checks his own response to it. The godly man does not "sit in the seat of mockers" (1:1) — "I do not sit with deceitful men" (26:4), etc. Some would consider the writer's recitation of what he has done as the reflection of an advanced stage of self-righteousness. We view it as an attempt to make an honest appraisal, and verse 11 indicates that the psalmist was fully conscious that he still needed the Lord's mercy.

As to the occasion of the psalm we can only surmise, but obviously it was written by one who would approach the Lord, if not boldly, at least confidently. The view expressed by Craigie that the psalm was used as part of an entrance liturgy, upon entering the temple for worship, may be correct, although not fully attested. "The psalmist prays for the divine judgment" (v. 1), Craigie writes, "and testing" (v. 2) "prior to admission to worship."[72] Whether this be the case or not, it would be fitting, in preparation for worship, to reflect upon the progress one has made in his daily walk in life.

1. Examine Me (26:1-3)

26:1 If one is making a conscientious effort to attain a worthy goal, concern about his progress is natural. This would seem to be especially true of one who seeks to live a decent, godly life. To determine if any progress is being made, self examination is in order. The psalmist so examines himself, with the following evaluation: **I have led a blameless life.** He is not stating that he is sinless, but that his manner of life — his dedication to the way of God — has been from the heart and consistent. Presuming the concept of

---

[72]Craigie, *Psalms 1-50*, p. 224.

Psalm 1 to be the basis of his self-testing, we can understand his statement, "I do not sit with deceitful men, nor do I consort with hypocrites" (v. 4). He can truthfully say that he has shunned the companionship (and the advice) of the wicked. Instead, he has determined to follow the divine leadership, having put "unfaltering trust in the LORD," (v. 1, NEB). This trust he has demonstrated by continuing to walk "blameless[ly]" before God, being kept true to his purpose by his constant remembrance of the steadfast love (the *ḥesed*) of the Lord (v. 3) — "your love is ever before me."

26:2-3 Self-examination, although necessary and helpful, can never be completely satisfying, for one must realize the possibility of myopic vision when looking at himself. A person may be too critical of self or too lenient. The psalmist knew that he had chosen the way of the Lord; He had no doubt about that. But he desired some indication of his true character. Verse 2 expresses this desire. **Test me, O LORD, and try me, examine my heart and my mind,** or, "my deepest affections and innermost thoughts." Here is a request that might indicate spiritual pride, if we did not consider that it is uttered with utmost sincerity. As an unfeigned petition, the psalmist is saying: "I have stated that I have lived the life of trust; now I am ready to be put to the test, that I may know the validity of my profession."

Have we not all, at some time, wondered how we would acquit ourselves "when the chips are down" and there is no opportunity for evasion or equivocation? We are acquainted with some whose commitment to the Lord has apparently been so shallow that they have dropped out of the running at the first sign of adversity. We ask ourselves, "Would we do any better?" We desire to know. Yet it takes courage to ask that the test come, and a great deal of confidence, a confidence that must be rooted and grounded in faith.

The psalmist was asking for a thorough testing, as the verbs in verse 2 indicate. The first (בְּחָן, *bāḥan*) refers to an examination to determine the essential qualities that are present; the second (נָסָה, *nāsāh*) means "to prove, to put to the test" (as Abraham was proven, Gen 22:1); and the third (צָרַף, *ṣāraph*) is a term used to indicate the smelting process whereby precious metals are refined and the impurities removed. The writer so desired to know his true character that he was willing to submit to whatever form of examination the Lord might choose. He was fully conscious that God sees into the recesses of the heart. But he also knew that the judgment of the Lord would be a true judgment and just. With this knowledge he says, "Examine me, Lord."

2. My Commitment (26:4-8)

26:4-5 For two reasons he could seek such an examination from God with assurance. First, he knew that the way of the Lord is right, and in the second place, he knew in his heart that he was committed to that way. To have an accurate guide and to commit oneself unreservedly to following that guide is sufficient reason to give any traveler confidence in the outcome of his journey. As to the commitment of the psalmist, it is expressed, on one hand, negatively: **I do not sit with deceitful men, nor do I consort with hypocrites** — with those who plot evil in their hearts while outwardly feigning friendliness. He would not accept connivance as a way of life, whatever others might do. In a world where the word "integrity" has lost all significance, he will nevertheless not give in to "joining the crowd." Instead, he has a deep aversion — hatred even — for the company of evildoers; he will not **sit with the wicked**. This is not so much a disavowal of association, though it is that, as it is a refusal to be a participant with them in evil. Or, as Kidner notes, the matter is not one of social preference but rather of spiritual alignment.[73] He does not choose to dwell in the darkened corners of life when he can move in God's sunlight. In every community one may find those who associate together for evil. The psalmist had not, nor would he, give himself to become part of such a group.

26:6-7 Positively, his commitment was to continue to walk in the integrity of heart that he has already mentioned (v. 1). To this end he will endeavor to keep himself pure. **I wash my hands in innocence.** In the temple court there surely were lavers placed conveniently, providing opportunity for the washing of the hands before

---

[73]Kidner, *Psalms 1-72*, p. 118.

approaching the altar of the Lord.[74] Such a washing may have been in the mind of the psalmist, but more is implied than merely a ceremonial cleansing. Clean hands, in the context, means hands that are clean of any wrongdoing, and this is the cleanness that he wants, because such would be a necessary prelude to his proclamation of the Lord's **wonderful deeds**, and this he aspires to do. That this is true is indicated by the fact that verse 7 is purposive, as in the King James Version — "That I may publish, etc."[75] The understanding is: "I will cleanse my hands for the purpose of causing the sound of thanksgiving to be heard and for the further purpose of recounting all of your great deeds." Only one with clean hands could successfully do this.

26:8 The joy of the writer, though not explicit, is obvious in verse 8. **I love the house where you live; O LORD** – in contrast to the assembly of the wicked – **the place where your glory dwells.** This may be a restrained way of saying, "I love you, O LORD," although one might express his love for the house of God itself, because of the associations he has experienced there. Remember the reference in verse 5 to hatred of the "assembly of evildoers." The psalmist is saying, "I had much rather find myself walking in the fellowship of God than in the congregation of those who plot and entice to evil; to the one I am devoted, the other is abhorrent to me." The wise will surely agree that his commitment was in the right direction.

---

[74]Craigie writes: "No doubt fonts of water were located at the temple's door, similar to those on a ceramic model of a shrine excavated at Gezer." See Craigie, *Psalms 1-50*, p. 226. See also Othmar Keel, *The Symbolism of the Biblical World (Ancient Near Eastern Iconography and the Book of Psalms)* (New York: Seabury Press, 1978), pp. 123-127. "The model of a temple from Gezer shows two fonts of holy water, one at either side of the entrance. In them, everyone who visited the temple could 'wash his hands in innocence' (Ps 26:6; cf. 24:4; 73:13), then go about the altar in the forecourt (Ps 26:6b)" (p. 123).

[75]The infinitive construct with which the verse begins indicates the purpose of the action of the preceding verbs. This is evident in the KJV, not in the NIV, and Cohen's translation takes account of it (*The Psalms*, p. 76). Oesterley states the causative idea specifically (*The Psalms*, p. 192). This rendering is based on the vocalization of the Hebrew text as given by the Masoretes.

3. My Prayer (26:9-11)

26:9-10 Again recalling Psalm 1, we are reminded that "the LORD watches over the way of the righteous, but the way of the wicked will perish" (1:6). "I have committed myself to the way of the former," the psalmist says, "do not destroy me with the latter" — "Sweep me not away with sinners" (RSV). MacLaren has aptly observed that "he has had no fellowship with (evildoers) in their evil, and therefore he asks that he might be separate from them in their punishment."[76] Another thought suggests itself: If one anticipates being separated from sinners in judgment, he had better separate himself from them here and now.

26:11 Some insight into the nature of the evils of the day may be obtained from the brief description of these sinners. They are men who thirst for blood and whose hands are full of wickedness and full of bribes. Such persons — the violent, the wicked, the corrupt — are lacking in all decency and rectitude. Could anyone consciously aspire to such a life? And is it not equally odious or worse, to die as such? "Let me die the death of the righteous," Balaam said (Num. 23:10). The psalmist desired as much, and he must have realized that to die the death of the righteous, one must live the righteous life. For that reason, he again affirms his determination to walk in integrity, trusting the Lord for the outcome.

Committed to the Lord, willing to be tested, there yet remains a question such as Job might have asked. "Who can be pure in the sight of God?" Surely no one can lay claim to having earned the favor of the Lord. Some such thought must have prompted the prayer that follows: **Redeem me and be merciful to me.** For all of his resolve and dedication, he does not lose sight of his need for God's help and grace. The prayer to be redeemed is to be understood in the light of Ps 25:22 as meaning from all trouble, from the hand of evildoers, and from their fate. The prayer for mercy is the cry of a penitent heart.

---

[76]MacLaren, *The Psalms*, p. 256.

4. My Assurance (26:12)

26:12 The psalm closes on a strong, positive note. Like Paul, the writer can say, "I do not consider myself yet [to have arrived]. . . But . . . I press on" (Phil 3:13,14). Where one finds himself on the journey of life is important; the direction in which he is headed is doubly so. How good it is to be able to say, "My foot stands upon the right path."[77] One who can speak thus has hope for a better tomorrow. On the right path, he has every reason to bless the Lord **in the great assembly**; that is, in the fellowship of others who gather to praise his name. This is the anticipation, the assurance, and the joy of those who put their trust in him.

C. TRUST AND PRAYER IN THE TIME OF TROUBLE (27:1-14)

Psalm 27 consists of two parts — some would say two distinct parts. The first, verses 1-6, is a strong affirmation of trust in the Lord because of the help he has given. From trials and assaults of enemies, the writer has experienced deliverance of such nature that he can face the future with confidence — "Though an army besiege me, my heart will not fear" (v. 3). The basis of his confidence is the nearness of the Lord. Consequently, his desire is to "dwell in the house of the LORD" continually. The language is figurative, meaning that he desires God's presence at all times. To this end, he does draw near to the Lord in the temple, and there, in God's presence, he finds sanctuary in time of trouble. And the sacrifices he brings are accompanied by singing and shouts of joy.

Verse 7, by contrast, gives voice to an anguished cry for help, addressed directly *to* the Lord. (The opening verses were about the Lord.) The psalmist feels that God's face (his presence) is hidden from him, and he pleads that he not be forsaken. This plea is followed by a prayer for leading and for deliverance from cruel

---

[77]My rendering of מִישׁוֹר, *mîšôr*. Although the basic meaning of *yašar* is straight, or level, the term is fraught with ethical connotation. In the present instance, the meaning seems to be "right" in the sense of straight; that is, not deviating. But this, too, has ethical implications.

enemies. The concluding note is an admonition to wait on the Lord and to take courage.

The change in mood and subject matter in the second part is obvious. The unshakable trust in God expressed in the opening verses has given way to the cry for help by one in great distress. There is also a difference in the metrical pattern of the two parts. These considerations have led many to the view that we have here not one, but two, psalms, originally independent compositions. Weiser observes that they could not have been written in the same circumstances and, further, that "they can hardly have been composed by the same author."[78] Leupold, on the other hand, thinks it would be more unreasonable to suppose that the two parts of the psalm were from different authors. "Who," he asks, "would have dreamt of combining things that are so much at odds with one another and presenting them as a unit?"[79]

Others, too, consider the psalm to be one. Craigie, for example, cites a number of key words that are common to both sections and sees a liturgical use of the psalm that requires the inclusion of the composition in its entirety.[80] As it stands, the psalm indicates that the writer has experienced the help of the Lord in time past. He has come to have complete trust in God, and this note of confidence continues throughout the psalm. The change of mood is occasioned by the fact that he now is confronted by a new danger. The new circumstance becomes a strong test of his faith and the reason for his impassioned cry for help.

1. My Trust Is in the Lord (27:1-3)

27:1-3 Seldom does one read an affirmation of trust so sublime as we find in the opening verses of this psalm (see v. 1). Its expression may not approach the sustained grandeur of Psalm 23, but the depth of feeling is present nevertheless. There we found peace in the valley. Here is expressed a faith that could only have arisen out of deep turmoil, from which deliverance has come at the hand of

---

[78]Weiser, *The Psalms*, p. 245.
[79]Leupold, *Exposition*, p. 234.
[80]Craigie, *Psalms 1–50*, p. 231.

the Lord. These are not the words of a novice. They come from
one who has tried, and experienced, the life that is possible only
through the presence and help of God. For the writer, **the LORD is
my light**; this means that he has been in the deep shadows! **My salvation**; he has known danger. **The stronghold of my life**; there
have been enemies. And there is reason to suppose that there will
be more shadows, dangers, and implacable foes. But he will not
face them alone! In time past foes who had sought to devour him —
metaphorically, either by slander or as ravenous beasts — **stumble[d]
and f[e]ll**. And so he is prompted to say: **Though an army besiege
me, my heart will not fear.** Here is expressed deep trust, based not
upon the psalmist's own resources but upon his conviction of the
all-sufficiency of God.

2. His Presence Is My Delight and My Confidence (27:4-6)

27:4-6 This trust is more than an affirmation of the lips. It is a
basis for establishing life's priorities, for determining the **one thing**
above all others that has become the concern of his heart. The sin-
gleness of purpose that drives him is aptly expressed in Buttenwieser's translation: "Only one thing I ask . . . ever do I seek it."[81]
The first verb is indicative of completed action: I have asked, period!
I will not be changing my mind. The second is durative and inten-
sive: I will go on seeking, with diligence. Since he has known the joys
and blessings of trusting God, his consuming desire is to live in
God's presence continually — to **dwell in [his] house**, to behold his
beauty, to seek him in his temple. For him, participation in acts of
public worship would not be an end in itself, but a means of realizing God's presence in life and of experiencing his protection and
guidance. This would be his security and his desire. Trouble might
come; it *would* come (v. 5). But God's **shelter** would become his
sanctuary. The Lord would set him **upon a rock**, out of the reach of
his enemies, and give him victory over them (v. 6). Consequently, he
would show his gratitude by **sacrific[ing] with shouts of joy** before
the Lord.

---

[81]Buttenwieser, *The Psalms,* p. 494.

3. Do Not Forsake Me (27:7-10)

27:7 With this verse the psalmist begins a prayer. No longer is he telling what God has done for him; now he brings a petition: **Hear my voice when I call, O LORD.** The change of mood is unmistakable. The petitioner has not doubted the validity of the trust he has avowed, but current circumstances compel him to acknowledge his present need for help.

27:8-9a The Hebrew of verse 8 is difficult. Without violence to the text, the New English Bible renders it: "'Come,' my heart has said, 'seek his face.'" Dahood concurs in this reading, and it fits the context. What more normal thing to do than to direct his soul to him who has been his strength and stay in time past? **Your face, LORD, I will seek** (diligently). The verb, in this instance [Piel stem], conveys a mood of urgency and intensity in its meaning, and this urgency is indicated further by the other verbs in the passage: "hear, be merciful, answer" (v. 7), **do not hide, do not turn** (me) **away, do not reject me,** nor **forsake me** (v. 9), "teach me," "lead me," "do not turn me over [to foes]" (vv. 11-12).

27:9b-10 You have been my helper. The remembrance of past blessings from the Lord and the conviction of God's abiding concern are reason enough for the current appeal. He is sure that he can always turn to the Lord, and his reference to father and mother reveals just how deep his faith is. **Though my father and mother forsake me** [and they would be the last to do so], **the LORD will receive me.** What trust! Greater either than the love of mother or father is the love of God. How beautifully Isaiah expresses this truth: "Can a mother forget the baby at her breast and have no compassion on the child she has borne? Though she may forget, I will not forget you" (says the Lord) (Isa 49:15).

4. Direct My Way (27:11-14)

27:11-12 The faith of the psalmist is shown further by his desire to be directed in the way of the Lord. His enemies appear to have been numerous and violent, rising against him with lying accusations. Under similar circumstances we would be tempted to pray: "Lord, let me have my way with them." But his prayer is: **Teach me**

your way. And then, as though from the realization that in pursuing that way he would need help, he adds: **Lead me.** He dare not trust himself to walk that way alone. He may be willing to use up all the strength he has, but when that is gone, he will trust God to give him more. **In a straight path** — the Hebrew term has ethical connotations. **Because of my oppressors,** more precisely, "because of the ones watching me intently," every move I make. Buttenwieser has indicated the probable meaning of the verse in his rendering: "Lead me in the straight path to refute my foes."[82] The enemies were like beasts of prey stalking a victim. One false move and they would be upon him. (Are not men merciless in their censure of a Christian who sins?) The psalmist knew that he must walk in a way that would "give the enemy no opportunity for slander" (1 Tim 5:14b), and he sought God's help to that end.

27:13-14 When these false witnesses who breathe **out violence,** confront him, his trust in God sustains him, and he shudders to think what would have happened to him without it. **I am still confident of this: I will see the goodness of the LORD** (in this present world) — What then! The sentence is left unfinished because the eventuality is too horrible to contemplate. Already he would have become the victim of those enemies had it not been for his faith. Recalling this fact, he resolves that he will cling ever closer to God. **Wait for the LORD,** he tells his own soul; **be strong, and take heart** (courage). And so the psalm that began with a fearless trust in God ends on a similar note: **Wait for the LORD.**

D. PRAYER AND PRAISE (28:1-9)

Psalm 28, it may safely be said, is a psalm of prayer and praise. That much is obvious. Not so readily discernible is the situation out of which it arose. Wicked persons are mentioned in verse 3, and some assume that they are enemies of the psalmist. He himself does not so identify them, though that may be the case, and he does call on the Lord to deal with them. Apparently, danger of some kind threatened, but the immediate concern was that God might have turned a deaf ear to him.

---

[82]Ibid., p. 497.

Following Mowinckel, some propose that the psalmist was suffering from a life-threatening illness — others, that enemies had cast
a spell upon him, or had accused him falsely of evil deeds. Still
others consider the danger to have been national in scope — Briggs:
warfare; Kirkpatrick: pestilence, while those who seek a setting in
the life of David suggest Absalom's rebellion as a likely occasion for
the writing of the psalm. The variety of these proposals should, in
itself, urge caution in seeking to determine the motivation of the
poet. In the absence of any definite clues, the suggestion of Albert
Barnes has as much to recommend it as any: namely, that the psalmist
was facing a great temptation[83] (and was thus in danger of being
swept away with the wicked).

Whatever the occasion of the psalm, it opens with a plea that
God not be silent, and with a prayer for help. This is followed by
words of praise and thanksgiving and a prayer of intercession on
behalf of all of the people.

1. A Plea to Be Heard (28:1-2)

28:1-2 To you I call, O LORD my Rock. The opening words are
emphatic: "To you and to no other." Whatever the cause of the
psalmist's troubled heart, he is determined to turn to none other
than the Lord for deliverance. He still believes that the support he
needs to keep from sinking into despair and defeat is God, for he is
his rock. This much he is sure of. But it seems that the Lord is deaf
to his prayer, and so he prays the more earnestly so that he will not
become **like those who have gone down to the pit**; that is, like the
wicked who die and enter the grave (or, specifically, *Sheol*, — the
abode of the dead). And why should he expect the Lord to hear
him? First, because he is the Lord, Yahweh, the God of the
covenant, his rock, his helper in time past and his hope now. Again,
he can believe that God will help him because the Lord is known to
be merciful — it is to a gracious God that he addresses his supplica-
tions (lit., his "cries for mercy," plural, v. 2). The lifting up of the
hands was a common attitude in prayer. **Toward your most Holy**

---

[83]Barnes, *Notes, Psalms*, 1:243.

Place. This refers either to the Most Holy Place in the temple or to God's dwelling in the heavens.

2. A Prayer for Help (28:3-4)

28:3-4 Do not drag me away with the wicked. Why did he fear that he might suffer this fate? It may be that he was so strongly tempted that he felt helpless without God's sustaining power. Or, since the Lord seemed to be deaf to him, perhaps he had already been classified among the wicked. It could be that, in the course of affairs, he had been associated in some way with the ungodly, as in a contractual or covenant relationship. They had, however, spoken peace (**cordially**) with their lips, while **malice** was **in their hearts.** Had they done so with him? Apparently, and so now he was himself in trouble, in danger of being classed as one of them. In defense, he would disavow any such guilt by association and distance himself from such evildoers. **Repay them for their deeds.** This would demonstrate to the community that they, and not he, were the guilty ones, and his own innocence would be vindicated.

3. Assurance of the Outcome (28:5)

28:5 In verses 1-4 the psalmist was speaking directly to God: "To you . . . O LORD." Verse 5 is a response to his prayer, telling how God will deal with the wicked. They will indeed be dealt with according to the work of "their [own] hands" (v. 4) because **they show no regard for the works of the LORD.** Those who see this psalm as serving liturgical purposes suppose that this response was spoken by a prophet or priest in the temple setting, much as Isaiah brought the Lord's answer to Hezekiah when he prayed to be delivered from the Assyrians (2 Kgs 19:20). Or, the words could express a conviction of the psalmist himself. In either case, the verse is clearly a response to the prayer he had voiced, as the following words indicate. The assurance becomes a cause for rejoicing.

4. Praise and Thanksgiving (28:6-7)

28:6-7 The psalm opened on a note of despair, but that now gives way to a shout of victory; the prayer becomes praise and thanksgiving. **Praise be to the LORD, for he has heard my cry for mercy.** This is precisely what he had prayed for in verse 2. Has God been deaf to his prayers? If so, not any more. **The LORD is my strength and my shield.** Once again the *Rock* in which he has trusted has proved adequate. We do not know the exact nature of the help that was given him from the Lord, but his experience must have been memorable, judging from the depths of emotion revealed in his cry of praise. **My heart trusts in [the Lord] and I am helped**, or, with Craigie, "I am rescued." His concern is not to describe precisely what happened; he wants to let others know that God has heard his prayer. That is the reason for now lifting his voice in praise.

5. Intercession for Others (28:8-9)

The psalm, from the first, has been characterized by individual lament and individual thanksgiving. With verse 8 the scope is widened to include the people of God generally. And there is a change in meter. For these reasons some scholars consider the last two verses to be an addition to the psalm to adapt it to congregational use. This is possible, but there is good reason to consider the concluding verses as expressive of the heart and concern of the original author.

In the theology of Israel, no belief was more significant than the concept of the people of God as a community. It was not in isolation that one enjoyed the fellowship of God, but as a part of the covenant people. True, there was the recognition of individual responsibility, and individuals were specifically recognized — Noah is a prime example. But at no time in the history of Israel was the individual considered merely a fragment of the collective whole. Very definitely, the relation of the individual to God was seen as having a social dimension — there are no hermits in the OT. To be a child of God was to be related in life to the people of God, not to live apart in solitude. Every child of God an individual? Yes, definitely, and precious in God's sight, but *an individual in commu-nity*.[84]

28:8 In view of this fact, it would be natural for the one who had experienced help from the Lord to think of his people and of their needs. "The LORD is my strength," he had said (v. 7). And now he adds: **The LORD is the strength of his people.** I can praise God for what he has done for me; I also rejoice in the victories others have achieved through his power, realizing that his love and mercy extend to them also.

28:9 The prayer for the people is brief, but reflects tender concern. **Save your people** from whatever danger may threaten, for they are the **inheritance** (or, heritage) of the Lord (Deut 4:20). **Be their shepherd** (or, literally, "pasture them"). Give them the gentle care that a shepherd affords his flock. And **carry them forever** — continuing the figure of the good shepherd. The Lord will tenderly care for his own. This is the prayer of one who had found help in the Lord in the time of his own trouble.

E. THE LORD'S GLORY, HIS POWER, HIS PEACE: GOD AND THE STORM (29:1-11)

When Isaac Watts wrote, "I Sing the Mighty Power of God," he included a line: "Clouds arise, and tempests blow, by order from thy throne." This suggests that he may have had the twenty-ninth psalm in mind, for its dominant motif is the mighty power of God as revealed in a great tempest. A violent storm, with its wind, its cracking lightning and reverberating thunder, is sufficient to strike fear in the hearts of many, young and old. But for the psalmist, this great display unleashed upon the earth spoke of God and of his power, and was an occasion to sing of his glory! Accordingly the psalm is to be recognized as a hymn, a hymn praising God as Lord over the storm.

In the view of some scholars, Psalm 29 is an Israelite adaptation of a Phoenician hymn in praise of Baal-Hadad, the Canaanite god

---

[84]For more on this, see "Individual and Community," chapter 4 in *The Faith of Israel*, by H.H. Rowley (Philadelphia: The Westminster Press, 1956).

of thunder, who was responsible for the rain and for the storm. In comparing the psalm with Ugaritic literature one finds similarities of imagery, of linguistic forms, and of rhythmic patterns. From this we conclude that the psalmist utilized terminology and modes of expression that were common to his day. Scholars differ, however, on the nature and extent of Canaanite influence. Is the psalm an original production of the Hebrew writer, whose style and phraseology reflect that of the Canaanites? Or is it an adaptation of a Canaanite hymn? Since no such hymn, other than the psalm, is known to exist, the argument for the latter position is precarious at best. B. Margulis considers the reference to the wilderness of Kadesh (v. 8) to indicate the Sinai/Red Sea area, and that this fact, (with others) "leaves no room for doubting that the original subject of the poem was Yahweh, not Baal, and that its author was accordingly a Yahwist."[85]

The majestic nature of Psalm 29 is impressive, enhanced as it is by its utter simplicity of style. It opens with a summons to heavenly beings to join in praising the glory and power of Yahweh. Immediately it moves to the portrayal of these attributes of the Lord as they are manifested in the thunderstorm. Eighteen times the name, *Yahweh*, is on the lips of the psalmist — sufficient to emphasize that even at the height of the tumult it is the Lord who arrests his attention, not the storm. Even the thunder of the tempest is not thunder but the voice of Yahweh, and seven times it is cited, the (thundering) voice of the Lord — powerful and full of majesty, breaking cedars and shaking the wilderness. And then, as suddenly as the storm came, it is gone, and Yahweh is seen in his glory, sitting upon his throne, omnipotent, strengthening his people and blessing them with peace!

[85]B. Margulis, "The Canaanite Origin of Psalm 29 Reconsidered," *Bib* 51 (1970): 346. For an excellent summary of the arguments regarding the question of a Canaanite original for Psalm 29, see Craigie, *Psalms 1–50*, pp. 243f. Craigie concludes that whereas there is evidence that indicates a Canaanite background, it is insufficient to require the presumption of a Canaanite/Phoenician original.

1. Yahweh's Glory Acclaimed (29:1-2)

29:1 Ascribe to the LORD, O mighty ones, ascribe to the LORD glory and strength. The song opens with a call to angels to join in the praise of the LORD (Yahweh). An overwhelming feeling of awe and wonder, inspired by the whirling tempest, has swept over the psalmist — to such a degree that he feels inadequate in his own extolling of the deity; he must call upon heavenly beings to join him in praise. "Mighty ones" is a translation of the Hebrew בְּנֵי אֵלִים (b⁼nê 'ēlîm, "sons of God"), so designated not because they are themselves divine, but rather of their being in the heavenly domain. Since they are called upon to praise the Lord, it is clear that they are understood to be creatures subordinate to him. (Ps 89:6 makes this distinction quite clear.) In Job 1:6 they constitute a heavenly council and in Job 38:7 a heavenly chorus, singing along with the stars at the time of creation. Now the psalmist would have this same choir, who "shouted for joy" on that occasion, to continue their praise in view of the Lord's manifest power over his creation. There is no one comparable to Yahweh. He is the supreme Lord, both in the heavens and upon the earth, and in both realms should be praised.

Over three hundred years ago John Trapp commented upon this verse: "Bear an (awe-inspired) respect to the Divine Majesty . . . unless you will come short of brute beasts and dumb creatures."[86] The warning is still valid. If it is my desire and aim to glorify God in all my actions and undertakings, then my life will be guided by lofty and noble ideals, not by brute instinct. To fail to give glory to God, by word and by deed, is to accept a baser level of life, lower even than that of beasts, for even they express gratitude!

29:2 Ascribe to the LORD the glory due his name; that is the glory belonging to him by virtue of his character as it has been revealed to us. The psalmist was, at the moment, concerned with that revelation wrought through the storm. We can contemplate the continuing revelation of God through his word and consummated in Christ Jesus. Who would want to withhold praise from such a God? It is duly his, yes. But to praise him is not a chore, any

---

[86]John Trapp, *A Commentary or Exposition upon the Books of Ezra, Nehemiah, Esther, Job, and Psalms* (London: Thomas Newberry, 1657), p. 494.

more than breathing is a chore; it is a privilege and a blessing that enriches one's life.

Worship the LORD in the splendor of his holiness. This translation indicates that one in the presence of God should be wholly aware of and appreciative of his absolute holiness. (But the Hebrew text does not include the pronoun "his.") Based on a comparison with the Ugaritic, a number of modern scholars would render the line: "Worship the LORD when he appears in holiness." Craigie, however, is quite persuasive in demonstrating that this derivation is not adequately attested.[87] This leaves one other option: "Worship the LORD in holy array" (RSV, and others), or, "in holy apparel." This appears to be the preferred reading.

In showing homage to a great king, no one would enter the royal presence unless wearing court apparel, and royal wardrobes were maintained to provide guests attire that was acceptable. (Cf. 2 Kgs 10:21,22.) Jesus spoke of a king who invited guests from the highways to the wedding feast of his son (Matt 22:8-13). We may be sure that proper attire was expected — and provided. Why else would the guest who dared to enter improperly clothed be cast out? (vv. 12-13). Apparently, the holy apparel of the psalmist would be that which is appropriate for one who would stand in the presence of a holy God. In this light, Isaiah wrote: "I delight greatly in the Lord; . . . For he has clothed me with garments of salvation and arrayed me in a robe of righteousness" (Isa 61:10). From the Christian perspective, one may claim the privilege of being clothed in "the righteousness of God" (Rom 3:22).

2. His Power Displayed (29:3-9)

29:3-9 The voice of the LORD . . . thunders. The reverberation of the thunder was, in the psalmist's ears, the voice of God speaking in awesome power. The voice of God? Does not a novice in the study of physics know that thunder is the result of the explosive expansion of air superheated by a discharge of lightning? Indeed, and yet the devout physicist, the more advanced he may be in his

---

[87]Craigie, *Psalms 1–50*, p. 242f.

study, can still hear the voice of the Lord in the storm. And that glory of the Lord of which the angels sang in verse 1 is no less glorious as seen in the mighty acts of verses 3-9. **The voice of the LORD is over the waters**, or, upon mighty waters — a voice of power and majesty (v. 4). It is the Lord who fixed the limits of the sea, saying: "This far you may come and no farther; here is where your proud waves halt" (Job 38:11). The storm of the psalmist sweeps in from the sea, breaking in fury upon the land. It **breaks . . . the cedars of Lebanon**, those mighty giants of the forest, striking with such force that even **Sirion** (Mt. Hermon) and the entire Lebanon seem to skip, or dance, **like a calf**. The **flashes of lightning** are further evidences of the power of the Lord. **The voice of the LORD shakes the desert**, or, "makes the wilderness writhe (as in pain)." **The voice of the LORD twists the oaks and strips the forests bare.** This translation takes note of the parallelism involved and suits the context better, which is dealing with the awesome power unleashed by the storm. However, an alternate translation of the verse is possible. "The voice of the Lord makes the deer give birth" (as in NIV fn.). It has been asserted that the terror aroused during a violent storm causes animals to give birth prematurely.[88] Still, the former translation is preferred.

Whatever the precise meaning of verse 9, the psalmist, from the beginning until now, is singing the mighty power of God. The fury of the tempest with all of its alarming force has struck, but still he is unafraid. What he has heard and seen is not a storm only, but the voice of God and the majesty of God. It is natural to experience the nearness of God when in the stillness and solitude of a quiet forest glade or when contemplating the stars on a calm evening. The psalmist realized that nearness at the apex of the storm when the "voice of the seven thunders" broke upon his consciousness. And his reaction to the awe-inspiring experience is expressed in one word — **Glory!** Now the chorus of the angels singing God's praise in

---

[88]Job 39:1, where the meaning "the doe bears her fawn" is unmistakable, has the same Hebrew terms found here, יְחוֹלֵל אַיָּלוֹת (yᵉḥôlēl 'ayyāloth). The verb חוּל (ḥûl) means to writhe, particularly in the act of giving birth. Still, the same letters with different vocalization may sustain the alternate translation, oaks (terebinths) instead of deer (hinds). Compare also the LXX καταρτι- ζομένου ἐλάφους (katartizomenou elaphous, "strengthens the hinds").

verse 1 is joined by those on earth who have witnessed God's wonder and might.

3. His Peace Bestowed (29:10-11)

29:10 The storm ends and peace is restored since God is the Lord of his creation. The first verb of verse 10 should be rendered as past tense: **The LORD [sat] enthroned over the flood.** The reference is undoubtedly to the flood of Noah's day, since this term for flood (*mabbul*) occurs nowhere else except in the account of the flood in Genesis 6-9. It is the Lord (Yahweh) who is in control, not Baal, the supposed god of thunder and storm.

29:11 In the Septuagint (LXX) there is a note that Psalm 29 was used by the Hebrews on the last day of the Feast of Tabernacles, a celebration in the fall at the end of the dry season. Under these conditions, such a storm as the psalm depicts would be a welcome relief and a foreshadowing of God's care for another season. He who was enthroned over the flood was enthroned still, King forever, and sovereign above every tempest that should arise. The Lord whose glory is acclaimed in heaven is the eternal King in the midst of his people. He whose power and strength were displayed in the storm imparts **strength to his people.** And he who calmed the tempest brings to his people the blessing of **peace.**

It is significant that the final word in the psalm is peace — *shalom.* This is not a negative term; it does not mean the absence of something. On the contrary, it means fullness or completeness — in every respect — a state of oneness, of wholeness (with no missing parts). It is a life lived in right relationship with all others and with all else, and basic to this is a right relationship with God. Paul speaks of this as "the peace of God, which transcends all understanding" (Phil 4:7). It is a delight to know that the blessedness of this peace is a reality, even though the storms of life may rage!

PART THREE:
THE EXPERIENCES OF
THE REDEEMED (30–41)

I. EXPRESSING GRATITUDE TO GOD (30:1–34:12)

A. THANKS TO A MERCIFUL GOD (30:1-12)

Psalm 30 bears the title, "A psalm. A song. For the dedication of the temple," with the name "Of David" following to show that it belongs to the Davidic Psalter. At some time this psalm was used at a dedication ceremony. But in its origin it is a psalm of thanksgiving and praise on the part of one who has been restored after undergoing a near-fatal illness (vv. 1-3). In his jubilation he calls on others to join him in singing praises to Yahweh (v. 4). He has concluded that his brush with death was evidence that God had been angry with him, but now the Lord has shown mercy (v. 5). Upon reflection, he realizes that he has been guilty of the sin of smugness and complacency. In pride, he had congratulated himself on his self-sufficiency. "I will never be shaken," he had boasted, with no thought of dependency upon God (v. 6). But when the Lord had turned from him and left him to his own devices, calamity had beset him. Then it was that he had prayed for mercy, and God had answered his prayer.

Now he recognizes and acknowledges that it was the Lord who had sustained him. The illness that had brought him to the brink of death had been disciplinary — "But when you hid your face, I was dismayed." It was then that he decided to throw himself upon God's mercy, and that is when he called for help (vv. 8-10). The Lord had responded, turning his mourning into dancing (v. 11). Henceforth he would be thankful forever.

1. Praise to God for Restored Health (30:1-5)

30:1 I will exalt you, O Lord, for you lifted me out of the depths. The term here for "lifted me out" is elsewhere used of drawing water from a well. The psalmist had been very near death and the grave, about to descend into Sheol, or the Pit (v. 3). But the Lord had drawn him up and had restored him again to the land of the living. The **enemies** mentioned in verse 1 are not identified. The implication is that they would have been pleased to see his illness prolonged, but God had thwarted such a perverse desire; he would not let them enjoy such satisfaction.

30:2-4 O LORD, you brought me up from the grave (from *Sheol*; the abode of the dead). This deliverance from impending death had moved the psalmist to sing God's praise and to call upon the saints to join him in his song of thanksgiving. These saints were devout souls (*ḥasidîm*) to whom *ḥesed* (loving-kindness) was the way of life. **Sing to the LORD . . . praise his holy name.** The translation could be, more precisely, "give thanks to his holy remembrance." Others translate: "to his holy name" (RSV). In the Hebrew, "name" identifies all that a person is; in this sense "remembrance" is a synonym for "name." In any case, it is the Lord who is to be praised, for it is he who has shown mercy and has restored the despairing one to health.

30:5 The opening thought of verse 5 is echoed in the words of the apostle Paul: "For the wages of sin is death, but the gift of God is eternal life . . . ." (Rom 6:23). However, this is not reflected in the NIV translation: **For his anger lasts only a moment, but his favor lasts a lifetime.** This translation is using the parallel words in the context of "time." The words are clear enough, and this translation or its equivalent is universally accepted. Yet note that the opening clause is precisely parallel and should be read: "In his anger is ——," the anger and its consequence being contrasted with the favor and its consequence, "life." The translation of the KJV is appealing – "His anger endureth but a moment" (רֶגַע, *rega'*) which is similar if not the same as the NIV. But this meaning would have to be assumed from the literal "in his anger (is) a moment." But *rega'* also has a meaning of "smiting" (Job 26:12), and since it stands in antithesis to the life that is to be found in the Lord's *favor*, the translation of Craigie (and others)[1] is to be preferred — "In his anger is death, but in his favor is life." That the anger of God may be replaced by his favor is a lesson that the psalmist learned from his experience. Repentance on his part is not specifically mentioned, yet it is implied in his appeal to God's mercy (v. 10). Consequently, he could give testimony that **weeping may remain for a night, but rejoicing comes in the morning.** In his case, it was the joy of recovery and of restoration to the favor of God.

2. The Former Flight from Reality (30:6-7)

30:6 But the psalmist had not always recognized his need of God. At some time he had displayed an arrogant spirit of self-dependence, an overweening confidence in his own worth and ability, the pride that "goes before destruction" (Prov 16:18). **I said** (and the *I* is emphatic) **"I will never be shaken."** Obviously, he was suffering from spiritual illness before ever the physical malady struck him. He had not reckoned with the truth that the arm of flesh will fail, nor with the reality that "Every good and perfect gift is from above" (Jas 1:17).

30:7 Now he realized that it was only through God's favor that he had enjoyed that which had given him such a feeling of security. **O Lord, when you favored me, you made my mountain stand firm.** But he had forgotten *that* when he had taken credit all to himself for his achievements. It was then that **God hid [his] face**, leaving him to his own devices. And trouble had come.

---

[1]Some sources, among others, that favor this or a comparable translation are Dahood (*Psalms 1–50*), Eerdmans (*Hebrew Book*), Rogerson and McKay (*Psalms 1–50*), Oesterley (*The Psalms*), the DouayRheims Version, and William F. Beck, *An American Translation* (New Haven, MO: Leader Publishing Co., 1976). Leslie would recognize the prepositions in parallel and retain the traditional meaning with his translation: "For *though* a moment *passes* in his anger, life *persists* in his favor." The words in italics must be supplied in this rendering.

3. The Plea for Mercy and for Help (30:8-10)

30:8-9 When it dawned upon him that he had taken the presence of God for granted in a time when he no longer acknowledged that presence, he gave voice to his longing for God's mercy (v. 9). Apparently, his spiritual awakening had come, and with it the realization of his utter dependence upon the Lord. The threat of death added fervency to his prayers. **To you . . . I called; . . . I cried for mercy** (the verbs indicate repeated acts of intercession). As if God needed to be persuaded, the psalmist proposed a reason why his life might be spared: If he died, God would be deprived of a worshiper! (In Ps 6:5 and 88:10-11 the same argument occurs.) **Will the dust praise you?** God would be the loser if he should die. Such an attitude may appear to be naive. In addition, it suggests a lack of understanding of the nature of God's mercy, as if it were self-serving. At the same time, as Oesterley has observed, here is "a touching picture of the psalmist's childlike intimacy and communion with God."[2] When a relationship of loving trust exists between God and the creature he has made in his own image, it is not without reason to suppose that God himself would be delighted to see that relationship continued. (That is why he sent his Son into the world!)

But when the psalmist speaks of **gain**, he is intimating that in some way our relation to God is of value to him. Is it possible? Yes, indeed, when we consider that "God is love" and that the objects of his love are of concern to him. In a very real sense, God has need of each one of us. For the psalmist, prolonged life was considered to be the opportunity to declare the Lord's truth, or **faithfulness**, to others, an opportunity that would no longer be his when death overtook him.

30:10 Hear, O LORD, and be merciful to me. There is no longer a discussion of being profitable to God, only the realization of need and the willingness to trust himself to God's mercy. Thus he had prayed, and the Lord had heard his cry.

---

[2]Oesterley, *The Psalms*, p. 204.

4. God's Gracious Response, a Cause for Continued Praise (30:11-12)

30:11 You turned . . . Credit where credit is due — it is the Lord who brought joy and gladness where there had been sorrow and despair. The verb "turned" (הָפַךְ, *hāpak*) means not just a simple exchange of one circumstance for another, but an overwhelming action bringing the defeat of the one and the ascendancy of the other.[3] **Wailing into dancing.** Both of these terms, in Hebrew, denote physical activity, the former an expression of grief by beating upon the breast and the latter an outward expression of an inner happiness. The garb of mourning was sackcloth. This was replaced, metaphorically, with **joy**, the garment of festal joy. How great the change that had been wrought by the Lord on his behalf!

30:12 That is a strong purpose word in Hebrew (לְמַעַן, *lᵉma'an*), "in order that." It indicates the ultimate purpose of God's gracious dealing with him, namely, that he be restored to that fellowship with God that, in its very nature, would call forth praise. **That my heart may sing to you.** The NIV follows the LXX here instead of the MT, which is reflected in the KJV: "That my glory may sing praise to thee." **And not be silent.** Presumably, there was a time when he had been silent. How many there are who never give voice to the praise of God! But a person who never says "thanks," who never voices a compliment to another, who never finds in others a cause for praise, such a one must surely have a shriveled soul, wholly incapable of that joyousness of heart that is the gift of God to those who would walk with him and in the light that he gives.

The praise of the psalmist is a testimony to God's grace. One who had boasted of his self-sufficiency had learned through suffering his need for God, and God had responded to that need. The renewal of life that God granted awakened in him the desire to bear witness to God's goodness and mercy. Henceforth, he would delight to sing God's praise and give him **thanks forever.**

---

[3]In Gen 19:25 the term translated "overthrew" is used of God's action in transforming the cities of Sodom and Gomorrah into rubble.

B. THE CONFIDENT PRAYER OF A DISTRESSED SOUL (31:1-24)

The keynote of Psalm 31 is confidence in God in a time of great distress. Various attempts have been made to identify the situation out of which the psalm arose, but none with any degree of certainty. Buttenwieser is convinced that the psalm describes a national crisis and not a personal affliction, written at a time when the city of Jerusalem was under siege. (Reference is made in v. 21 to "a besieged city.") The "I" in the psalm Buttenwieser considers to be a personification of the nation.[4] Others would identify the psalm with David, at a time when he was fleeing from Saul (1 Sam 23:25). Whatever the setting, the theme is clear. One with a deeply rooted faith is in need of deliverance from a net that enemies have set for him (vv. 1-5). He affirms his trust in the Lord (vv. 6-8) and follows this with a description of his present distress (vv. 9-13). After the renewal of his prayer (vv. 14-18) he praises God for his goodness (vv. 19-22) and closes with a word of encouragement for those who trust in God (vv. 23-24).

It is difficult for us, when reading the psalm in security and comfort, to know either the agony of the situation out of which it arose, or the sustaining power of the faith that is reflected throughout. However, many, in times of stress and suffering, have found courage in Psalm 31. One such was Savonarola, who was writing a short commentary on it while in prison, awaiting the time when he would be executed. "I will hope, then, in the Lord," he wrote, "and soon I shall be delivered of all tribulation."[5] The psalm is a model of trust to anyone who is undergoing deep distress.

1. The Prayer for Deliverance (31:1-5)

31:1-2a The psalm begins with a prayer for deliverance, but even this is prefaced by a strong affirmation of trust, without which

---

[4]Buttenwieser, *The Psalms*, pp. 564-568.

[5]William Clark, *Savonarola, His Life and Times* (Chicago: A.C. McClurg Co., 1894), p. 340.

the prayer would not have been uttered. Faith is the seed from which the prayer grows. **In you, O LORD, I have taken refuge**; that is, in time past I have trusted you and continue to do so; consequently I have hope. **Let me never be put to shame** of having put my trust in you, or (possibly, with Dahood) "Let me not be humiliated, O Eternal One." Prompted by a confidence based on past experience, the psalmist is made bold to seek from the Lord deliverance from the present danger. His appeal is to the **righteousness** of God, to the Lord's faithfulness in keeping safe those who commit their way to him. **Turn your ear to me.** The Hebrew idiom is replete with verbs of action. Here the meaning is "hear and respond to me," but the picture is that of inclining the ear as earnestly desiring to hear the suppliant.

31:2b-3 Be my rock of refuge, a strong fortress to save me. His only hope is in God, so great is the ordeal that he faces. Yet he continues to trust, for immediately after saying, "Be my rock," he declares, "You are my rock and my fortress." This is a truth he will not let go! **For the sake of your name lead and guide me.** The life of the psalmist is God-centered, and the glory of God is ever in his thinking. The leading and guidance he asks for are not altogether for his own welfare, but that God might be glorified; they are requested "for the sake of your name." The psalmist's prayer was not wholly selfish. The working of God through his people and on behalf of his people is testimony to the world of his presence and power, and his name is thereby exalted.

31:4-5 Verse 4 indicates that the danger threatening the psalmist is in the nature of some plot or trap set for him by enemies, otherwise unidentified. Verse 5 becomes an open avowal of complete trust: **Into your hands I commit my spirit** – not my fate but my "spirit," and what a different outlook that represents! The spirit, as here used, indicates the animating principle of life, and so, life itself (see Ps 146:4). This is a commitment or surrendering of the self to the care and to the will of the Lord. On the lips of Jesus (Luke 23:46) and of Stephen (Acts 7:59) the words had similar import. **Redeem me, O LORD, the God of truth.** Here we have a request and a noun used adjectivally. As "sword of gold" means a golden sword, so here the meaning is true God; that is, God who is true to his nature, and thus a faithful God.

2. The Abiding Faith (31:6-8)

31:6-8 In sharp contrast with those **who cling to worthless idols** (worship idols), the psalmist is steadfast in his trust in God alone. It is especially the mercy of the Lord (his unfailing covenant love) that rejoices his heart — the term is *hesed*, that bond of loving faithfulness between God and his people. **I will be glad and rejoice in your love.** Confident that God is aware of his distress and will respond, he anticipates the time of joy that will be his when the Lord makes the deliverance for which he prayed (v. 1) a reality. Even now he is aware that God has not shut him up into the hand of **the enemy**, but has left him room to maneuver. With this assurance, he is now ready to give voice to the burden that is pressing so heavily upon him.

3. The Present Crisis (31:9-13)

31:9 That his distress is almost beyond endurance is obvious from verse 9, with its plea for mercy. Apparently, his anguish is both physical and mental. There is a hymn that admonishes: "Take your burden to the Lord and leave it there." Does not every person suffering affliction need someone who is understanding, someone with whom he may share the anguish of his soul? How dreadful to suffer in loneliness! But God hears when the lonely sufferer calls to him, and the very fact of the psalmist's reciting his plight permits him to view it objectively and to commit it to God.

31:10 The suffering that he endures is, first of all, physical (vv. 9 and 10), the ravages of an illness of some kind, apparently of long duration. Soul and body are wasting away. **My strength fails**, or, literally, "totters" or "staggers," as one under a heavy burden, **because of my affliction** (NIV, a reading in agreement with the Greek text of Symmachus). But to compound his agony, he has become the scorn of his enemies and "a calamity and a fright" to his neighbors and friends (Dahood), or, a "horror" and "object of dread" (RSV). More than this, he is just ignored, forgotten as if he were dead and buried, or only a broken piece of pottery on the trash heap.

31:11-13 Why this aversion to him? Perhaps his illness has made him physically repulsive. Or is his affliction viewed as punishment from God for some great sin? In any case, the physical agony he endures is aggravated by the rejection he suffers from his friends and neighbors. Abandoned, forsaken, there is no one to whom he can turn for help but to the Lord. As Weiser has observed, "Thus his suffering drives him directly into the arms of God."[6]

4. The Prayer Renewed (31:14-18)

31:14-18 Another strong affirmation of faith becomes the prelude to the continuation of his prayer. The spiritual resources of the psalmist have proven to be adequate to his need. **But I trust in you, O LORD.** In spite of illness, regardless of rejection by friends and the plots of foes, he can still say, "I trust." Therefore, I pray. **My times are in your hands.** Enemies may rise up, but I take comfort in the fact that my future is with you. Show kindness to me — **let your face shine on your servant.** The assurance of heaven's sunshine in his soul will serve to dissipate the darkness that has all but overwhelmed him. **Let the wicked be put to shame.** Let the machinations of these evil persons come to naught. Verse 18 indicates that a smear campaign, **lying lips**, had been directed against him. Nevertheless, he knows himself to be still within God's grace.

5. Praise for God's Goodness (31:19-22)

31:19-22 We have noted the theocentric orientation of the writer. He is constantly indicating his awareness of God, and such awareness will not permit him to remain long in the mire of despondency. He may look at himself and despair. He prefers to look at God and rejoice. **How great is your goodness, which you have stored up for those who fear you.** What deliverance came to him, and in what fashion, we are not told, but it was such as to strike wonder in his soul. The rendering of the NIV in verse 21 is

---

[6]Weiser, *The Psalms*, p. 278.

too weak: **for he showed his wonderful love to me.** The RSV is better: "He has wondrously shown his steadfast love." But the significance of the passage is best expressed in the New English Bible: "Blessed be the LORD, who worked a miracle of unfailing love for me when I was in sore straits." The verb describing the action of the Lord is from a root (אלפ, *pālā'*) that means to be wonderful, marvelous, or incomprehensible. Here it means to cause a wonderful thing to happen, something that God alone can do. But the emphasis is focused upon the action more than upon the deed. The latter may be incomprehensible (even a miracle). The greater marvel is that God has shown his concern in the doing of it. His action is a miracle of love, such as to inspire wonder in the heart of the psalmist. In the midst of his great suffering, confidence in the Lord has been rewarded, and for this he praises God. In a moment of alarm he had been near panic, but when he had cried for help, God had heard.

6. Encouragement of the Faithful (31:23-24)

31:23-24 It is not unnatural for one who has experienced the goodness of the Lord to bear witness to others of God's grace. Gratitude for God's mercy is accompanied in the heart of the psalmist by the desire to share his blessing with others. His confidence is unabated. He is sure that God will aid those who trust him and so he encourages them to love and faithfulness. **Love the LORD, all his saints!** The admonition is addressed to those who are devoted to God. Among them there are undoubtedly some who are distressed, burdened, suffering. To such he says, "Take heart." **The LORD preserves the faithful.** It had been so for him. It would be so for them. It is so today.

C. SIN, FORGIVENESS, AND JOY (32:1-11)

Sin is devilish — deceitful, debasing, dehumanizing. Sin is destructive, with a power of atomic proportions. In an instant it can bring devastation to one's life. At other times, sin is subtle, like a cancer, and may remain unperceived until incalculable damage has resulted, with a grip so tenacious as to defy all attempts at dislodging it. Sin takes many forms, reflecting such nonvirtues as envy, pride, lust, greed, malice, and hate. Its consequences are also many, varied, and far-reaching. (Just look all around to see the havoc sin has wrought.)

One of the results of sin upon the sinner is psychological — the experiencing of guilt. No matter though one may attempt to run away from it, to forget it, or to cover it up, it remains in the subconscious. The deed of which we must ever be ashamed cannot be undone, and the guilt of it will not just go away. Yet there is a remedy, and the joy that results when deliverance is realized is the theme of Psalm 32.

The psalmist had been living under a burden of guilt. This was not just a *guilt complex* or a manic-depressive condition induced by some imaginary offense. He had sinned. He knew he had sinned. Yet he would not admit it and seek the Lord's forgiveness — and his life was miserable. Finally, he decided to face his condition honestly, to cease his rebellion, and confess his sin to God. Apparently, God had been waiting for this, for his response was forgiveness and the removal of the guilt. The joy that resulted in the life of the psalmist was so great as to call forth the jubilant note of thanksgiving with which the psalm opens.

1. The Blessedness of Forgiveness (32:1-2)

32:1-2 Blessed is he whose transgressions are forgiven (literally, "taken away"). Transgression (פֶּשַׁע, *peša‘*) is rebellion against the will of God, disobedience, unfaithfulness, and it involves the breaking of relationship; it separates one from God. "Blessed," in this verse, means "O the joy of" or "the happiness of." The words are reminiscent of Psalm 1, except that there the joy was experienced from walking in the ways of God while here it is the happiness of being restored to God's fellowship and to his way, after having sinned against him. The theme is forgiveness. No attempt is made at self-justification. The joy is not predicated upon freedom from transgression, but upon the mercy of God in granting pardon.

It is the joy of one whose sin is covered; that is, buried out of sight for ever, no longer to be remembered against him. Note that it is God who does the covering, not the sinner in an attempt to hide his wrongdoing. "He who conceals his sins does not prosper, but whoever confesses and renounces them finds mercy" (Prov 28:13). The psalmist claimed this promise. Only thus could he experience the joy of a new life of liberation from his sin and his guilt.

Not the least among his reasons for joy was that now, at last, he stood before God in complete honesty, hiding nothing. He now knew the joy and peace of one **in whose spirit is no deceit**, no attempt any longer at a deceptive life.

2. The Necessity of Honesty before God (32:3-7)

32:3 The psalmist would never have known the forgiveness of his sin and the joy of forgiveness if he had not come before the Lord without deceit. There was a time when any thought of penitence was completely foreign to him. He chose instead resolutely to ignore his sin. But life became unbearable, and he suffered untold anguish, physically, mentally, and spiritually. Awareness of what he had done would not go away, and any attempt at self-deception could only aggravate his condition. **When I kept silent, my bones wasted away**. Not until he was ready to admit his sin and his need was he in a position to seek deliverance from the Lord.

32:4-5 For day and night your hand was heavy upon me. It may be that adversity had been his lot in world affairs and that he considered this to be the hand of the Lord upon him. Or, more likely, the sense of guilt and condemnation that burdened his soul he attributed to God. In any case, the hand that he felt so heavily upon him served to bring him to repentance. **Then I acknowledged my sin to you.** This was the beginning of his release. He would be honest with God and no longer deny nor try, on his own, to cover up his **iniquity**. At last he had dared to look at himself squarely and he did not like what he saw. But rather than give way to despair, he would seek God's mercy: **I will confess my transgressions to the LORD.** Being conscious of his shortcomings and wanting to confess them (and, abandon them — understood) was half the battle, yet altogether necessary if he would have any hope of release from his burden of guilt. The other half of the victory was from God: **You forgave the guilt of my sin.**

In commenting on verse 5, Perowne was quite discerning:

> The clauses of this verse stand in beautiful contrast with those of vv. 1,2 in an inverse order. The sin is acknowledged that it may not be imputed, the iniquity is uncovered that it may be covered, the transgression is confessed that it may be taken away (forgiven), this last being emphatically expressed. 'Thou didst take away (forgive),' etc., and going back to the opening clause of the Psalm. The pronoun *thou* is emphatic; it was *God's* doing. To Him he made his confession; He forgave. The same words are used here of sin and its forgiveness as in ver.1.[7]

32:6-7 Therefore, since the connection between penitent confession and divine forgiveness has been clearly revealed in my own experience, let others among the godly who have sinned be encouraged and instructed to **pray to [God] while [he] may be found**; that is, while the opportunity for grace remains, a way of saying, "Now is the time of God's favor, now is the day of salvation" (2 Cor 6:2). They, too, may then anticipate the forgiveness of God and have no fear of being overwhelmed when the judgment of God overflows the land like a flood. The security that is found in God is elaborated upon in verse 7 — **You are my hiding place**, etc. With my life submitted into your hands, I am forever secure.

3. Instruction in the Way (32:8-9)

32:8 Opinion is divided as to whether the words of verse 8 are spoken by the Lord to the psalmist or by the latter to his compatriots. Since they are addressed to one person — **I will instruct you** — it would seem that God is speaking to the psalmist. Just recently restored, he is not abandoned to the necessity of floundering as

---

[7]J.J.S. Perowne, *The Book of Psalms*, Third London Edition (Andover: Warren F. Draper, 1901), 1:262.

best he can in his newly given freedom but can anticipate that the direction his life should take will be illumined by the Lord who promises: **I will instruct you and teach you.**

32:9 Verse 9, on the other hand, is addressed to a group, (You [pl.]) **do not be.** The psalmist had himself been obstinate for a time, with a stubbornness and pride that had prevented his turning to the Lord. He would now urge his hearers to show more maturity than he had done. **Do not be like the horse or the mule.** These animals, not having understanding, must be curbed and directed by **bit and bridle.** God has ordained something better for humankind. He could compel our obedience but does not. He wants us to walk in that way of uprightness that brings blessing, but he desires for us the joy and dignity of a free, willing, and joyful obedience, not one of compulsion.

4. The Wicked and Those Who Trust in God — A Contrast (32:10-11)

32:10 In verse 10 the psalmist is bearing witness to what he has learned by experience. As many have noted, the words are in the style of wisdom literature. (The verse could fittingly be incorporated in the book of Proverbs.) But there is more here than proverbial wisdom. These are the words of one who has experienced deep agony because of his self-will and stubbornness of heart but has also known the joy that resulted from turning to God. Only one who has had such an experience could know the magnitude of the contrast. In reality, there are only two choices open to the one who has rebelled against God. In order that others might gain from his experience and choose wisely, the poet states the contrast simply but clearly: **Many are the woes of the wicked, but the LORD's unfailing love surrounds the man who trusts in him**; that is, the one who trusts in his mercy and commits himself to walk in his way.

32:11 If there is any question about the earnestness and sincerity of the psalmist, it is completely dispelled in the last verse of the Psalm, a call to jubilant praise. Here three terms are used to indicate joy and its expression. **Rejoice in the LORD.** The verb (שִׂמְחוּ, śimḥû) indicates joy that involves the whole heart and soul — deep-

felt joy, we would say. **And be glad, you righteous.** This term (גִּילוּ,
gîlû) suggests joy that is given expression enthusiastically. **Sing**
(from רָנַן, *rānan*) is a call to jubilant vocal expression of praise to
God, whether by shouting or singing.

The call to be glad in the Lord is addressed to the **righteous** as
contrasted to the wicked of verse 10. As the Psalm demonstrates,
these righteous are not the absolutely perfect, but those who trust
in the Lord's mercy for forgiveness and deliverance from sin and
turn to him with upright heart. These are the ones who will find
abundant cause to rejoice in the Lord.

D. A JOYOUS CALL TO PRAISE GOD (33:1-22)

Psalm 33, from beginning to end, is one sustained, exuberant
shout. With a fervency and energy seldom equaled, the writer sets
forth the nature and character of God and cites his word and work
as more than sufficient reason why he should be reverenced and
praised. One might almost say that what the Hallelujah Chorus is to
Handel's *Messiah*, Psalm 33 is to the Psalter. It extols the righteousness and justice of God, his marvelous creative power, his awareness of the needs of his people and his willingness to meet those
needs. Who would not be moved by all of this to sing his praises?

In its presentation, the Psalm is in the nature of a persuasive
speech; the writer is bursting with zeal to have others know the joy
of trusting God and to join him in praising him. It is worthy of
note that, in the pursuit of this aim, the psalmist follows a pattern
not unlike one that might be taught in a class in oral communication today — 1) Get attention, 2) State a proposition, 3) Prove it,
and 4) Call for action.

1. The Proposition — Praise of the Lord Is Fitting (33:1-3)

33:1-2 The psalm opens with a ringing cry, its challenge to attention. **Sing joyfully to the LORD, you righteous.** This is immediately
followed by a statement of the proposition. Some things are not
suitable — snow in summer (Prov 26:1), lying lips on the part of a

prince (Prov 17:7). But **praise** (of the Lord) **is fitting for the upright**; that is, it is suitable, appropriate, even beautiful, for the upright person to praise God. All of the adjectives just used are helpful to express the content of the Hebrew term for "comely, fitting" — נָאוָה (nā'wāh). One does not expect the godless to glorify God. They may, on the contrary, heap ridicule and abuse upon those who do. But for the person who is dedicated to walking in "integrity of heart" (1Kgs 9:4), it is altogether fitting to be zealous and joyful in the praise of the Lord. Praise (תְּהִלָּה, tehillāh) in this clause indicates the expression of sincere and heartfelt thanks. In **praise the LORD with the harp** we have a different word (הוֹדוּ, hôdû, from יָדָה). Its basic meaning is to "acknowledge" or "confess." It is the verb appearing in Ps 32:5 — "I will confess my transgressions." (We would hesitate to render it "praise" in this instance!) It is the acknowledgment of the exalted character and goodness of God, a confession with an intellectual dimension, based on the recognition of who and what he is and what he has done for us. This praise, defined by Patrick D. Miller, Jr., as "a declarative act,"[8] is to be uttered with our lips. We are to declare openly who God is and what he has meant to us, and to emphasize the truths expressed and the joys experienced, instruments of music may be employed.

33:3 Sing to him a new song. One may be fond of the old hymns and the grand truths they express, but each new day brings new manifestations of God's love and power and the occasion for new songs. **Play skillfully, and shout for joy.** The term for "shout for joy" (תְּרוּעָה, t⁰rû'āh) indicates a shout (whether of joy or of alarm), or a blast on a trumpet or ram's horn. When the foundation of the second temple was laid, the people "gave a great shout of praise to the LORD" (Ezra 3:11), and the sound could be heard at a great distance (3:13). The challenge in the psalm is to jubilant praise.

---

[8]Patrick D. Miller, Jr., *Interpreting the Psalms* (Philadelphia: Fortress Press, 1986), p. 72.

2. Because of His Righteousness and the Integrity of His Word
(33:4-9)

33:4-5a Having issued the call to worship God, the psalmist proceeds to adduce one reason after another why the people should do so. First of all there is the moral perfection of God. His word is **right and true** – "direct" (Dahood), "upright" (RSV), "truthful" (Leslie). The basic concept is that it never deviates. His word, therefore, is wholly dependable — a worthy consideration! In addition, **he is faithful in all he does.** The New English Bible has caught the significance of אֱמוּנָה (*'ĕmûnāh*) with the translation: "All his work endures." The root אָמַן (*'āman*) means "to be firmly established, certain." (From this comes the word *amen*.) What we call "the laws of nature" are but evidence of the immutability of God's work. It is firmly established. But there is more: **The LORD loves righteousness and justice**, not only because of their ethical import, but also because they provide the foundation for a just and stable social order. Can there ever be stability and peace in the life either of an individual or of a nation without righteousness and justice? How good it is that these are concerns of God and how vital that we make them ours as well.

33:5b It is noted further that the concern of God is not subject to geographical limitations. True, the Lord (Yahweh) chose a particular people (Israel), for a particular purpose — that through them "all the families of the earth might be blessed" (Gen 12:3). But this is no mere tribal God: The (whole) earth is full of the goodness of the LORD; **full of his unfailing love.** And so all humankind is included in the summons to acknowledge and praise him.

33:6-9 That God's word is indeed "right" is seen preeminently in creation. **By the word of the LORD were the heavens made.** Consider the wonder of it! "Let there be light," God had said, and light was — just like that! (Gen 1:3). We may marvel at the mighty oceans, covering three-forths of the surface of the earth, but with God the gathering of the great deeps into their confines was no more than pouring water into a bottle. In considering a creator who can speak worlds into existence, should not **all the people of the world revere him?** Verse 9 lingers upon the wonder of God's creative power by divine fiat. **For he spoke** (the pronoun is emphatic) **and it came to be.**

The above should be reason enough to call forth the joyful acclaim of the Lord, but there are yet other reasons to praise him.

3. Because God's Counsel Stands Forever (33:10-12)

33:10-11 In the day of the psalmist as today, kingdoms and nations made alliances. They plotted and planned, to conquer and to dominate. The little strip of land along the eastern Mediterranean was the crossroads of the world. Up and down this narrow corridor passed the armies of Assyria, Egypt, and Babylon. Later there would be the Persians, the Greeks, and the Romans. And still later, the Crusaders, the Byzantines, the Ottoman Turks, the French under Napoleon, and the British. And to what end? All the movements of history will not serve to contravene the purposes of God, and only that which is in accord with his will will endure. **The LORD foils the plans of the nations**. Gamaliel realized this truth when he said: "For if their purpose or activity is of human origin, it will fail. But if it is from God, you will not be able to stop these men" (Acts 5:38,39). The honored rabbi was speaking of the evangel, of the proclamation of the good news in Christ Jesus, and the passing centuries have rendered their verdict — God's work continues in spite of what men may do. **But the plans of the LORD stand firm forever.**

33:12 In view of the foregoing truth, because God's counsel stands, **Blessed is the nation whose God is the LORD.** Theirs is a blessed condition, obviously, because of the unfailing power and steadfast love of God. But no less significant is the blessing that is theirs because such a nation finds direction in the divine counsel. These are indeed a chosen people, but not so much as a privilege as to responsibility and to purpose. It is in the meeting of that responsibility and the fulfilling of that purpose that the greater blessing comes — as to a people living within the will and purposes of God. God's counsel is sure. It stands forever. Praise his name.

We have remarked on the righteous nature of God, the integrity of his word, and the immutability of his counsel, but there is more. The Lord, from the exalted location of his throne in heaven, is sovereign of his creation. God is no recluse! He could abandon humankind to their own devices. However, heaven's concern is not idle bliss, but rather involvement. History is not only a record of the deeds of men; it is also His story!

4. Because God Sees and He Reigns (33:13-19)

33:13-15 From heaven the LORD looks down and sees all mankind. He sees the evil in the world that is done by those who choose to do evil. But he also sees and knows when even a cup of water is given in his name. More significantly, he is aware of the motive that directs us, since it is he who has fashioned the hearts of all. We need never fear that the Lord misunderstands us. He knows us completely — and still he calls us into his love, his fellowship, his life!

33:16-19 We praise God because he does take note of the affairs of this world and, moreover, is concerned and involved. For example, when nations feel threatened one by another, they inevitably seek the protection of massive armaments, knowing, at the time, that these do not ensure survival. It was true in David's day, and especially true today, that **a king is [not] saved by the size of his army.** "The race is not to the swift, or the battle to the strong" (Eccl 9:11). The battle is "to the Lord," the outcome is in his hands. **But the eyes of the Lord are on those who fear him . . . to deliver . . . and keep them alive in famine.** The writer was certain of this. The people of Israel had experienced it. They were delivered from the hands of their oppressors, and in the wilderness wanderings their hunger had been satisfied with manna (Exod 16:15). Later, in a time of famine, the widow of Zarephath who shared her last bit of food with Elijah was provided for by the Lord (1 Kgs 17:7-15).

It is an act of faith to believe that the eye of the Lord is upon his people for good. Yet there are thousands who will testify to the providence of God in the working out of events in their lives. To those who have not known such an experience may be directed the challenge of Ps 34:8 — "Taste and see that the LORD is good; blessed is the man who takes refuge in him." No amount of theorizing will convince a skeptical soul of this truth. The proof must be a matter of experience. As one encounters the presence and help of God in his life, he finds that it is so. And he finds himself also moved to join in the chorus of those who praise the Lord.

5. We Trust in Such a God, Realizing He Is Our Hope (33:20-22)

33:20-21 The theme of Psalm 33, as we have seen, is joyful praise; that such praise is fitting to humankind has been fully demonstrated. The Lord loves what is right and just and he acts accordingly. His word is *right* and is with power. He is our creator and the sustainer of our lives. The counsels of men are subject to failure; his counsel and purposes are sure. He is the sovereign of this world and of our lives, and as such he is concerned to deliver and to keep those who put their trust in him. Therefore, **in him our hearts rejoice.**

33:22 But to what end is this praising of the Lord? Has the psalmist participated in some service of worship that now comes to a close? Is it time for the benediction and dismissal until the next such occasion? There is a benediction — **May your unfailing love rest upon us, O LORD.** But there is more. There is commitment of life, not just by the psalmist but by the whole congregation. **Even as we put our hope in you.** The verb carries the meaning of trust, of waiting with an attitude of joyful expectation and confident hope. It is as if the worshipers cannot wait to begin anew the life of trust in such a God. "He is our help and our shield." What confidence! What incentive to victorious living! With such a God as this, his people can go forth with joyful hearts, since they do put their trust in him.

E. TASTE AND SEE THAT THE LORD IS GOOD (34:1-22)

In Psalm 34 one who has been saved from his troubles, having experienced God's goodness, invites others to join him in his praise and in his enjoyment of the Lord's blessings. Throughout the psalm the saving power of the Lord is emphasized (vv. 5,7,10,18,19, 20). "Make the venture," the writer is saying. "Begin the journey."

"Taste and see that the Lord is good." These words are addressed to the *afflicted* (humble) (v. 2), since the proud would scarcely be interested though the writer had experienced a dozen salvations.

The selection is an acrostic, in the pattern of Psalm 25. (See our introductory remarks relative to that psalm.) Such a pattern imposes restrictions upon an author since he must choose words beginning with the proper letters to form the acrostic. This necessity, in the eyes of some, has resulted in a composition rather loosely put together with no precise continuity. Moreover, the psalm does not lend itself to easy classification according to any one of the usually recognized types. The first part includes praise and thanksgiving, whereas verses 11-22 are didactic in nature, in the pattern of wisdom literature. (Ps 25 shared this characteristic also.) Even so, we do find in the psalm, in addition to praise, (vv. 1-3), testimony to God's goodness and help (vv. 4-7), a challenge to try the Lord and to fear him (vv. 8-10), and instruction in what it means to fear him (vv. 11-22).

1. Invitation to Praise (34:1-3)

34:1-2a This psalm, like Psalm 33, opens on a note of jubilant praise. **I will extol the LORD at all times.** The translation is accurate, although the implication, "no matter what happens," is valid. The psalmist is going to make an appeal to others to commit themselves to the way of the Lord, but first he will declare his own stand, unequivocally and for all time. He will ever bless the Lord. *Blessing*, in the Scriptures, is usually from the greater to the lesser. When otherwise, as here, it is praise that acknowledges the greatness of the one so acclaimed. The next verse makes this clear: **My soul will boast in the LORD.** Not in self, not in any other, but in God alone shall be my glory. These are the words of one who would place God, not on the periphery but at the very center of his life, and therein find blessing.

34:2b Let the afflicted hear and rejoice. The "afflicted" (עֲנָוִים, *'ănāwîm*, translated "humble" in KJV) are such as may have been victimized by others and thus, humiliated. The term may, therefore, signify a state or situation in life. That seems to be the primary significance here, and to those thus afflicted the psalmist offers significant hope. But the term may also indicate a state of mind — humility instead of arrogance. In Prov 16:19 the "lowly in spirit" are contrasted with the proud. These shall be glad, for they will see the great deliverance that the Lord provides.

34:3 Glorify the LORD with me. From a root (גדֹּל, *gādal*) meaning "to be great," the verb does not imply that the psalmist would add anything to the Lord's greatness in magnifying him. Rather, he calls upon his hearers to recognize and to acclaim that greatness and to sing God's praises with him. **[L]et us exalt his name together.** He desires the joy of praising God in fellowship with others. John Henry Jowett has commented on the joys of corporate worship: "The praise that lifts its voice in solitude is beautiful, but it is far more beautiful when heard in communion with the praise of one's fellows. God's praises sound best in concert."[9] The joys of the psalmist he cannot keep for himself alone. They must be shared with others.

2. Testimony to God's Saving Grace (34:4-7)

34:4 In only six words (in Hebrew) the psalmist gives his reason for praising God. It is really quite simple. **I sought the LORD, and he answered me; he delivered me from all my fears.** In context, the verb *to seek* (דָּרַשׁ, *dāraš*) means "to ask" or "to inquire." Sometimes inquiry was made through a prophet (Jer 21:2), and those who see a cultic setting for the psalm would propose that the psalmist had come to the sanctuary for that purpose. But verse 6 (which see) seems to indicate a direct, personal approach to God. And the Lord "answered me"; more specifically, he responded, by delivering him, not just from his troubles (v. 6) but from all of his fears, and that is a greater blessing! As Jowett observed, "There are many people who are not afflicted by calamity, but who are greatly burdened by the fear of it."[10] But to those who are in fellowship with the Lord there comes "the peace of God, which transcends all

---

[9]John Henry Jowett, *Thirsting for the Springs* (London: H.R. Allenson, 1902), p. 201.

understanding" (Phil 4:7). To love God and to trust him is to be rid of fear (1 John 4:18).

34:5 The verbs in verse 5, as in some Hebrew manuscripts, are best considered as imperatives: "Look towards him and shine with joy; no longer hang your heads in shame" (NEB). This means look to the Lord. Eerdmans, however, accepts the translation, "They looked at him," as indicating the notice of the psalmist taken by others, the inference being that they are delighted by the great deliverance that has come to him. Eerdmans bases his conclusion on the biblical assertion that no man can look upon God and live (Exod 33:20), adding that the verb "to look at" (נָבַט, *nābaṭ*) is never used in a metaphorical sense.[11] This may be true, yet one can look to the Lord *to the extent that he has revealed himself*, and that is sufficient to gladden one's heart and to enlighten the countenance. It should be noted that the imperative, "look" to him, does not mean a casual glance only, but a fixing of the eyes upon him. See! and have cause for rejoicing!

34:6 This poor man – the psalmist identifies himself as one of the "afflicted" of verse 2 – **called, and the LORD heard him.** Before seeking the commitment of others he testifies to his own experience. God had **saved him out of all his troubles.** Note that he was not spared from troubles – the righteous may have their share of them. His was not an "easy" faith, stemming from years of tranquility, but a faith that had been forged in the crucible of adversity, by which process its power to sustain had become evident. The psalmist does not describe the nature of his difficulties, but he does bear witness to the deliverance that came when he sought the Lord.

Actually, "troubles" is not an exact translation of the Hebrew, צָרַר (*ṣārar*). The verb means "to be restricted" or, as we would say, "in a tight spot." In Ps 4:1 we may read, "You gave me relief from my distress." It was the feeling of helplessness that was alleviated. Dahood catches the meaning when he translates: "From all his *anguish* [Yahweh] saved him" (italics supplied).[12] Troubles, as we know them, may have remained, but the deep distress that he had known was gone. People long for security in a very insecure world.

---

[10]Ibid., p. 203.
[11]Eerdmans, *The Hebrew*, p. 213.
[12]Dahood, *Psalms 1–50*, p. 204.

They experience disappointment, accidents, suffering, rejection, loneliness, sickness and death. They are burdened with guilt and assailed by various phobias. Such are the anxieties of life and we have to live with them. Indeed, we may feel hemmed in to the point of suffocation. Is there no deliverance? From his own experience the psalmist says, "Yes!" His was not a Pollyanna existence with everything always rosy — far from it. But, because he knew the Lord, when there was no way to look but up, this he did and found a security in God that could not be shaken, bringing relief from all anxiety, and *deliverance*, as his attestation in verse 7 indicates.

34:7 The angel of the LORD encamps around those who fear him, and he delivers them. The writer may have had Elisha in mind, when the prophet had assured his servant that "those who are with us are more than those who are with them" (2 Kgs 6:16-17). This scenario is not tenable if the superscription is historically reliable. Otherwise, David's experiences must be the background. However, it has already been suggested that the superscriptions, while ancient, were added to the even more ancient psalms and it is difficult to determine whether the לְ (l°) in l°Dāwid means "belonging to," "for the sake of," "on behalf of," etc. In any case, he recognized that divine aid had been his and that it was available also to others who fear (who reverence) the Lord. In Ps 35:5-6 the angel of the Lord is seen as a force with whom the wicked also will have to deal in their wickedness.

3. Challenge to Try the Lord (34:8-10)

34:8-9 Not until he has given his testimony of God's redeeming power in his own life is the psalmist ready to call on others to trust in the Lord. Now he issues the challenge. **Taste and see that the LORD is good.** The goodness of God here indicated is not moral perfection (though that is not excluded) but is, rather, good in the sense of being productive of that which is beneficial. It is a way of saying that the way of the Lord is the good way and that God will do you good as you walk in that way. Try it and see. Only by personal experience does one discover the reality of God's goodness. Like the child learning to walk, every soul must venture the first step with the Lord if he would know that joy. "Taste and see!" The writer is not proposing a creed for adoption nor suggesting a debate of various value systems, but only a simple pragmatic test through a commitment to God. Trust in the Lord and be blessed. He is not supporting a philosophy but a manner of life, with the promise, **Blessed is the man who takes refuge in him.** This trust is to be accompanied by an attitude of godly fear; that is, of reverence, an awesome wonder that will lead naturally into a manner of living in accord with the will of God and thus appropriate to a child of God (Deut 17:19-20; 31:11-13). To **fear the LORD**, in this sense, is not to cringe in terror but rather to feel dismay at the very thought of wrongful acts. So the fear of the Lord is actually synonymous with right living. And a venture into this territory is what is meant by tasting that the Lord is good. One who fears the Lord, in this sense, will "seek the LORD." (compare verses 9b and 10b: fear and **lacking nothing**, "seek" and "lack no good thing.")

34:10 God provides for his own. Strong young lions seem naturally to occupy an enviable position in the scheme of things. By stealth and craft and brute force they take what they want. Yet, for all this, they may suffer want and hunger. However, **those who seek the LORD lack no good thing.** We may agree with Rhodes when he writes: "The psalmist surely knew of exceptions, but they do not concern him here."[13] He is speaking from experience. He had sought and God had responded (v. 4). The emphasis, both in verse 4 and in 10, is upon the verb "seek." One does not just drift into the life of trust. It is for those who actively engage in seeking the way of the Lord; they are the ones who find that he is good. They also find that nothing else that is called good has any real significance, any meaning, apart from him. He alone is good (Matt 19:17). If we miss this reality, then all true goodness is gone from our lives; they have become a mere shell, with no real existence; they are as though they had not been. Taste God and see.

---

[13]Rhodes, *The Book of Psalms*, p. 66.

4. Instruction in Godliness (34:11-22)

34:11-12 We have noted that to possess the *fear* of the Lord is to live a godly life. Verses 11-22 make this abundantly clear, for we are told specifically: **I will teach you the fear of the LORD.** The writer then proceeds to describe the manner of life that one who is seeking God will follow (what it means to fear the Lord). At the outset, he makes clear that this is the formula for **life**, for long life, for the good life. The instructions are not detailed nor extensive, but are inclusive. They have to do with right speech (v. 13) and right conduct (v. 14). One should note the absence of reference to any cultic requirements. The concerns are moral and ethical. The Scriptures do not proscribe "religious" activities. In fact, public worship, with appropriate ritual, is part of biblical teaching. But this is not an end in itself but a means to an end. The end is right living, and until a person has made this his aim and goal, he has not learned "the fear of the LORD."

34:13-16 Keep your tongue from evil. This is the negative aspect. There are certain things that should be shunned and guarded against by the person seeking God (and the good life) and the evil use of the tongue is one of them. Be careful what you say. **Turn from evil.** When confronted by evil, *turn* aside. Don't do it. Doing evil makes the good life impossible, so evil must be shunned. Very frankly, **the face of the LORD is against those who do evil.** This is because of the nature of evil. We associate the meaning "wickedness" with the term and rightly so. But the Hebrew root (רָעַע, *ra'a'*) carries the basic concept of that which is harmful, detrimental, calamitous, injurious, or destructive. Any injury or detriment caused another is evil, in the biblical sense of having affected him adversely. It is when such injury is inflicted deliberately and maliciously that it becomes wickedness and the perpetrator becomes guilty of sin. Thus it is against the person who willfully harms others that God sets his face, his countenance, while his eyes and ears are attentive to the righteous. God desires good for humankind — for all humankind.[14] Those who would abuse others in any way can only incur his wrath.

---

[14]There are Scriptures that indicate that God sends disaster (evil) upon humankind (e.g., Jer 25:29). In Isaiah it is recorded: "I form the light and

But the fear of the Lord does not call for a negative response only. To shun evil is not the end of the good way but only the beginning. Some persons may pride themselves in what they do not do. "I do not lie, cheat, or steal." Neither does a fencepost! But what do you do? This is as much a measure of commitment to God as the other. **Do good; seek peace and pursue it.** One's attitude in life is involved. Does he look upon others as objects to be exploited? Or, fellow human beings with whom life is to be shared? In verse 12 there is the question, "Whoever of you loves life and desires to see many good days?" And here is the answer, startling in its simplicity — "Turn from evil and do good." In this fashion, a person learns to live at peace with himself, with others, and with God. This is what it means to seek peace. Indeed, there is no other way to peace except through righteousness. So closely are the two related that elsewhere it is written: "Righteousness and peace kiss each other" (Ps 85:10). So pursue this goal. To live otherwise is destructive of one's own person as well as of those around us, and this can only incur the wrath of the Lord.

34:17-22 Conversely, as verses 17-19 remind us, the favor of God rests upon the **righteous, the brokenhearted**, the **crushed in spirit**. In every eventuality of life, the Lord is near. Here we note again that the psalmist is well acquainted with reality. Those who trust in God are not shielded from all *troubles* – **A righteous man may have many troubles, but the LORD delivers him from them all.** Is this categorical statement to be taken as absolute? What of those who have been persecuted or martyred for their faith? What of the execution of Jesus of Nazareth? What deliverance was theirs? Our psalm indicates, as Craigie has observed, that "God's presence is experienced within these crisis situations; there is no divine guarantee that the righteous will escape the crises and trials of mortal existence. The divine presence . . . made possible triumph in the

---

create darkness, I bring prosperity and create disaster; I, the LORD, do all these things" (45:7). The NEB reads: "I make the light, I create darkness, author alike of prosperity and trouble." But this trouble that God brings is not malicious. Rather, it is as just judgment upon the wicked who will not turn from their wickedness, or else within the permissive will of God, which may be beyond our understanding.

midst of trial."[15] From the NT disclosure of resurrection we are aware of the reality of deliverance beyond death. Whether or not this was in the mind of the psalmist we cannot tell, but in verse 20 he speaks of the physical protection that God provides for his people — "He guards every bone of his body" (NEB). Throughout, the emphasis is upon the contrast between the fate of the wicked and that of the righteous. Destruction comes to the former, deliverance to the latter. **Evil will slay the wicked.** Those who do evil will be slain by evil, but **the LORD redeems his servants; no one will be condemned who takes refuge in him.** This was the experience of the psalmist. He believed that it could be that of others as well.

II. DEALING WITH PROBLEMS (35:1–39:13)

A. A THREEFOLD PRAYER FOR DELIVERANCE (35:1-28)

In a study of Psalm 35 one is faced initially with the question of whether the selection is a unit or a composite of three originally independent psalms (as Psalm 108, for example, which is a combination of 57:7-11 and 60:5-12). Its threefold nature is obvious, with each component composed of a complaint, a prayer or petition, and a promise of praise. The complaint in the first section is directed against those who seek the psalmist's life (v. 4), in the second (vv. 11-18) against vicious "witnesses" whom he has previously befriended (vv. 11-12), and in the third (vv. 19-28) against those who are his enemies without cause (v. 19). One might suppose that the psalm reflects three separate occasions when the author suffered abuse. We note that the enemies in the first case seek his death; in the second they are intent on bringing about his condemnation, and in the third they would gloat over his misfortune. (It is possible, of course, that one group of enemies could be cast in all three roles.)

Rotherham associates the first two stanzas of the psalm with events in the life of David. "The governing note of Stanza 1," he

---

[15]Craigie, *Psalms 1–50*, p. 281.

writes, "is indignation: that of Stanza 2 is wounded love. The indignation is fiery, and finds vent in imprecation — nothing is too bad
to ask from Jehovah in avengement of the wrong the petitioner has
received from his enemies at court."[16] In Stanza 2 there is no call
upon the Lord to punish the adversaries, some of whom the psalmist
apparently had held in deep friendship. He only asks that God
rescue him from them. The fiery indignation felt against the first
foes here "melts into a wail of anguish"[17] because of his betrayal by
the former associates in the court of Saul. Stanza 3 Rotherham
would attribute to *Prince Hezekiah*, whose godly manner, it is
asserted, aroused the hatred of the corrupt court of his father
Ahaz. This is a possibility, but in the absence of any specific indication of such must remain a conjecture at best. Certainly the superscription would indicate that the original psalm was by David,
whether later edited or not. (See the detailed comments on Ps 3:7.)

Three psalms or one? Leslie treats it as a unit, as do many
others.[18] Oesterley considers it to be one psalm dealing with two
episodes and he does not see all of it written at one time. Taylor
favors the view that three separate authors are responsible for the
three stanzas.

The general approach has been to view the psalm as the plea of
an individual for personal deliverance. As such, it could be designated as the prayer of one falsely accused, an individual lament.
Briggs, however, considers it to be national in application, a prayer
for deliverance from the enemy nations that harassed Israel after
the return from exile in Babylonia. Following Briggs, Mowinckel
puts Psalm 35 in the category of "I" psalms "which are apparently
quite personal, but in reality are national (congregational) psalms."[19]
The "I" is understood to be used collectively for the nation (a
conclusion Leupold considers to be "strained").[20] Buttenwieser,

---

[16]Rotherham, *Studies I*, p. 272.

[17]Ibid., p. 273.

[18]Among them, Stuhlmueller; Rogerson and McKay; Ash; Dahood;
Leupold; Donald Williams; Weiser; A.A. Anderson; Gerstenberger;
Brueggemann; Cyril S. Rodd, *Psalms 1–72* (London: The Epworth Press,
1963).

[19]Mowinckel, *The Psalms in Israel's Worship*, I:219.

[20]Leupold, *Exposition*, p. 285.

however, agrees with Mowinckel that the "I" is the nation personified. He cites the warlike opening verses of the psalm as evidence,
also the reference in verse 20 to those who "lay dark plots against
the peaceful people of the land."[21] The foes, in his view, are the
foreign population dwelling in the land among the Jews after the
return of the latter from exile.

Eaton views Psalm 35 as a royal psalm, with the "I" being the
king, beseeching the Lord to take up arms and join him in battle
against the enemy.[22] The reference to the Lord's servant (v. 27)
could well indicate the king. That one king might have shown
brotherly concern and have prayed for another (vv. 13-14) is a possible implication of 2 Kgs 20:12. Furthermore, the false witnesses of
verse 11 could be testifying in political matters, rather than personal. Craigie concurs in this matter, admitting that the designation
individual lament or *prayer* is generally appropriate, but that the
psalm should be interpreted in an international context. But rather
than oppression by a local foreign population, he sees a national
military threat as the likely occasion for the complaint.[23] He proposes that the psalm may have been used in a service of worship
prior to the king's departure for battle.[24] The king is desiring
victory both on the diplomatic front — "Plead my cause" — and the
military — "fight against them" (v. 1). Craigie presents a strong case.
Nevertheless, the only really positive clue that the distress may have
been national in scope is in verse 20. Here the enemy are pictured
as deceitful "against those who live quietly in the land," and Craigie
considers this to refer to the peaceful people of Israel. Perhaps, but
overall the psalm seems to be so very personal in nature that it
would seem better to consider it in that light.[25]

Whatever the situation out of which it arose, Psalm 35 is an
example of an impassioned plea to God by one who is facing the

---

[21]Buttenwieser, *The Psalms*, p. 448.

[22]Eaton, *Kingship*, p. 41f.

[23]Craigie, *Psalms 1–50*, p. 285.

[24]Ibid., p. 286.

[25]This is not to place restrictions on the uses to which the psalms were
put throughout the history of Israel subsequent to their original composition. One should remember that there is a sequence of several centuries
between the inception of the psalms and their final collection in the psalter
as we know it.

false charges and evil plots of ruthless enemies. An impassioned plea? One might even conclude the language to be impertinent: "O Lord, how long will you look on" – and do nothing (implied)? "O LORD, you have seen this; be not silent" (v. 22). But rather than being a reflection of impertinence, the language is more an indication of bewilderment. The psalmist knows that God is aware of his condition. He also knows that the Lord "rescue[s] the poor" (v. 10), vindicates the righteous (v. 24), and "delights in the well-being of his servant" (v. 27). Knowing these things he cannot do otherwise than to call on the Lord with fervency of spirit, presenting his plea, or pleas, for deliverance.

1. A Plea for God's Help (35:1-3)

35:1 With what confidence the author opens his prayer! **Contend, O Lord.** The verb may be translated "plead," as in a court of law (Job 9:13), "argue," as Jacob with Laban (Gen 31:36), or "strive," as when one man attacks another (Exod 21:18). The context must determine the precise meaning. Here the term is used parallel with "fight," the language of combat (vv. 2-3), and the enemy is seeking the life of the psalmist (vv. 4,7). This would tend to the view that he, therefore, desires the Lord to oppose force with force. Some, however, consider that it is a case of a false indictment that is the core of the complaint. Leslie translates: "Conduct my case."[26] But Craigie cites the reference to weapons as an indication that the psalmist (the king) is seeking God's assistance in battle,[27] and Dahood has: "Attack them that attack me."[28] The neutral verb "contend" is used in some translations (RSV, NASB, Berkley Version, Weiser, NIV). This allows the reader to decide for himself the nature of the contending, whether on the field of battle or in a court of law. What is clear is that the psalmist is in dire circumstances because of enemies and is crying for God's help.

35:2-3 Take up shield . . . . Brandish spear. Addressed to God, the language may sound a bit crass to our ears. But this is not a

---

[26]Leslie, *The Psalms*, p. 370.
[27]Craigie, *Psalms 1-50*, p. 286.
[28]Dahood, *Psalms 1-50*, pp. 208, 210.

reflection of a concept of some warlike primitive god, as some have suggested. It is but a representation of the divine activity in human thought patterns — anthropomorphic language. As such, it is not to be taken literally but metaphorically. As Pius Drijvers has noted, since Israel perceived God as personal, not as an "unmoved prime mover who had withdrawn himself from any interest in man,"[29] the use of *personal* (anthropomorphic) terminology became a practical necessity. We know that God is *spirit* (John 4:24). Yet he is, above all, personal, and we can only think in human terms as we contemplate his personality and his acts.

2. Imprecations against Enemies (35:4-8)

35:4-6 May those who seek my life be disgraced and put to shame. The basis for the series of imprecations is the unjust treatment shown the psalmist by his enemies. They would be satisfied by nothing less than his very life. So, let them **be turned back in dismay; may they be like chaff before the wind; may their path be dark and slippery, with the angel of the LORD pursuing them.** Reference to the "angel of the Lord" in the psalms, appears only here and in Ps 34:7. There the angel was to deliver those who fear the Lord. Here, he is to drive out the wicked as chaff and to pursue them in slippery places!

35:7-8 The bitterness of the psalmist against those who desire his ruin is apparent. He calls for their **ruin,** (such as a tornado might cause — Prov 1:27). He considers this to be their just desert, in view of the fact that their attacks upon him are **without cause.** And if he is devoid of any thought of forgiveness, we should note also the absence of any desire to take personal revenge against his enemies. He is willing to leave the matter in the hands of a just God. Furthermore, if he is concerned that he be delivered from their unjust attacks, he is concerned also that godly people be preserved, (and thus also the integrity of a moral universe) to the end that God's name not be dishonored. Delitzsch declares flatly that "all the imprecatory words in these psalms come from the pure

---

[29]Drijvers, *The Psalms*, p. 116.

spring of unself-seeking zeal for the honor of God."[30] This may be an overstatement, yet it does focus upon a significant aspect of the imprecatory prayers in the psalms. Underlying them all is the desire to see the name of the Lord vindicated.

Seemingly, a similar spirit was in Martin Luther when he prayed for God to deal with his adversaries. While he was at Coburg, during the Diet of Augsburg, his friend Dietrich overheard him while he was at prayer and later wrote the following to Melanchthon:

> One day I had the privilege of overhearing him pray. Great God! What a spirit, what a faith in his words! He prays with all the devotion of a man before God, but with all the confidence of a child speaking to his father. "I know," said he, "that Thou art our good God and our Father; that is why I am persuaded that Thou wilt exterminate those who persecute Thy children. If Thou dost not do it, the danger is to Thee as much as to us. This cause is Thine: what we have done, we could not have done otherwise. It is for Thee, merciful Father, to protect us." When I heard him from a distance praying these words with a clear voice, my heart burned with joy within me, because I was hearing him speak to God with altogether as much fervor as liberty; above all he supported himself so firmly upon the promises in the Psalms, that he seemed fully assured that nothing he asked could fail to be accomplished.[31]

3. Anticipation of Joyful Praise (35:9-10)

35:9-10 Having called upon the Lord for help, and having asked him to deal with the enemy, the psalmist anticipates victory even before it comes. More than anticipation, he makes a promise, a vow. **Then my soul will rejoice in the LORD and delight in his salvation.** And this joy he will express as praise to the Lord, not with the tongue alone, but with his **whole being will exclaim, "Who is like you, O LORD? You rescue the poor. . . ."** What God indeed is like the Lord? Not any. He alone is the living God, creator, all-

---

[30]Delitzsch, *Biblical Commentary*, I, p. 418.
[31]Quoted in *Adolphe Monod's Farewell*, tr. Owen Thomas (London: The Banner of Truth Trust, 1962, first published in 1874), p. 79.

powerful, and all-knowing. But he is distinct also in his moral attributes, as, for example, in his concern for the poor, the weak, the needy, and we reflect the spirit and nature of God when we show a similar concern.

4. The Perfidy of Ruthless Witnesses (35:11-16)

For a moment, in the anticipation of victory, the thought of the psalmist was taken away from the current problem. But he does not close his eyes to the reality of his condition. Throughout the psalms of lament we find graphic and sometimes extensive recital of the troubles endured. The writer is aware that God knows what is going on (v. 17). Yet he is intent on unburdening his heart before the Lord. (See especially Psalm 102.) And in this very act catharsis is achieved, his burden is lightened, and his courage is renewed, because he knows that the Lord understands. With this confidence, he brings again a statement of his complaint.

35:11-16 Assuming that the enemies of verse 11 are the same who sought his life (v. 4), we learn that they would accomplish their aim as **ruthless witnesses**, "malicious witnesses" (NEB), "violent" (Craigie) — accusing him of **things [he] kn[e]w nothing about.** In Exod 23:1 the warning is given: "Do not help a wicked man by being a malicious witness." Truth and justice are of no concern to such a person; there is only the venomous desire to do evil to the one who is under attack. In the case of the psalmist the experience was all the more bitter because the perpetrators of the crime he himself had prayed for in time past as a friend (vv. 12-14) are now, however, among those who are hounding him. **But when I stumbled, they gathered in glee.** Not only so, they joined together in attacking him, verbally or actually. Literally, the text states: "Smiters whom I did not know gathered against me; they tore me to pieces and would not quit" (like a lion tearing its prey — Hos 13:8). Metaphorically the verb means "slander," as it is rendered in numerous versions, including the NIV.

5. A Plea and a Promise (35:17-18)

35:17 The second petition and promise of praise are included in verses 17-18. **O Lord, how long!** This expression is quite common in psalms of lament, a phrase described by Leslie as "the sure mark of lamentation."[32] **How long will you look on?** Compare verse 23: "Awake!" Is this impertinence? Who dares to speak to God in such a manner? Only one who is confident that the transcendent God is also near at hand, concerned about his people, one who may be addressed as an intimate friend. **Rescue my life** (literally, "my soul") **from their ravages,** from their mischievous designs, **my precious life from these lions.** Used parallel with נֶפֶשׁ (*nepheš*, soul), יְחִידָתִי (*yᵉḥîdāthî*, "my only one"), "my darling" (KJV) is obviously a synonym for the self — "my life" (RSV), "my precious life" (NEB, NIV), "my own treasure" (Leupold). The expression means one of its kind. (The term appears also in Ps 22:20.) The reference to the lions indicates again that his enemies are tearing him to pieces, whether literally or figuratively (by slander).

35:18 I will give you thanks in the great assembly. Praise of God in Israel was not a solitary event. One may have prayed in secret, but having known the blessings of God's response to his prayer, he could no more refrain from the public praise of the Lord than he could refrain from breathing. Should not the praise of God be a shared experience? One may honor him in his heart and praise him in solitude, but it would seem that a heart overflowing with adoration for God could not restrain itself from the public declaration. This was true, at least, for the psalmist. He would declare the goodness of God to the whole world (Ps 22:25-27).

The chiasmus of verse 18 (see discussion of parallelism in the Introduction) enhances both the literary beauty and the thrust of the verse and should be retained in the translation. Compare the following:

I will give you thanks in the great assembly;
Among throngs of people I will praise you.

Here we have a simple, prosaic repetition of a statement, the writer emphasizing the point that his praise of God will be given before the largest crowd he can achieve!

---

[32]Leslie, *The Psalms*, p. 372.

6. The Deceit Practiced against the Peace-loving (35:19-21)

35:19 The third statement of lament emphasizes the deception of his foes, not only as practiced against him but against others as well. Their charges are malicious lies, with no basis in fact. They rejoice over him as if he were a criminal, but do so wrongfully. The winking of the eye suggests, on the part of the enemies, "We have him where we want him." It is the injustice of it all that bothers him.

35:20-21 They do not speak peaceably. That is, there is no peaceable intent in what they say, even when they talk of peace. They **devise false accusations.** "They invent lie upon lie" (NEB), and then declare, **Aha, aha, with our own eyes we have seen it;** that is, we have witnessed the things that we have charged against him.

7. A Final Plea for Vindication and Judgment (35:22-26)

35:22-26 Lying witnesses can be very damaging if their perjury is undetected. But the Lord is not deceived. When it is said, **O LORD, you have seen this,** it is an acknowledgment of the fact that here deception is impossible. The psalmist knows that false charges have been brought against him. He also knows that God is aware of this. Therefore, it is with confidence that he can pray: **Vindicate me in your righteousness, O LORD my God.** Let justice be done because you are just. **Do not let them gloat over me,** by permitting them to triumph in their evil.

8. An Invitation to Joyful Praise (35:27-28)

35:27-28 There are times when a person may feel that he is all alone in his suffering of injustice, that no one is concerned about his troubles. He may even feel that there are some who "rejoice at my calamity" (v. 26, RSV), But if this be true, there are also many who do desire to see justice and goodness prevail (v. 27). "Let them not be disappointed, Lord," the psalmist is saying. His petition to God is phrased as an invitation to them to join him in praising the

Lord for the triumph of justice. **Shout for joy.** The word for
"shout" (*rānan*) here indicates an expression of *holy joy*, the kind of
shout that is raised upon the consciousness of God's greatness. In
the present case, this greatness would be seen and lauded when the
enemy is defeated. God is to be praised, because he **delights in the
well-being of his servant.** Shalom (שָׁלוֹם, *š˘lôm*, "well-being" in this
verse) is often translated "peace" (as in v. 20), but other translations
are "prosperity" (KJV), "welfare" (RSV), "salvation" (Weiser). This
variety of renderings indicates the breadth of the term, the basic
meaning of which is "completeness" (in every detail), or "fulfillment" (completely). This God desires for and provides for his
people. Note that *shalom* ("well-being" or "prosperity") in this verse
is parallel with **righteousness.** A.A. Anderson observes that the
terms "are probably synonymous; in OT thought the one could
hardly exist without the other."[33] The way to peace, to fulfillment,
to completion, is the way of righteousness. This is the basis of the
confidence expressed in Psalm 35.

B. EVIL UNBOUNDED AND INFINITE GOOD (36:1-12)

"Evil Unbounded and Infinite Good." This title for Psalm 36 is
taken from Richard Moulton's *The Literary Study of the Bible*,
because it so accurately describes this gem of Scripture.[34] The
psalm is a study in simple contrast, somewhat after the pattern of
Psalm 1. There we find the antithesis of the righteous man and the
wicked, a difference that we equate as between wisdom and folly.
Here the same distinction may be made, except that the contrast
now is between the unbounded evil of the wicked man (vv. 1-4) and
the immeasurable goodness and mercy, not of another man, but of
the divine Lord (vv. 5-9). In the first four verses we find "a picture
of character so utterly corrupt that evil has become a law unto
itself; and then abruptly, without connecting links (the psalm) sets
against the dark background of supreme evil a supreme good – a
lovingkindness as wide as the heavens, a righteousness as high as

---

[33]Anderson, *Psalms 1-72*, p. 285.
[34]Moulton, *The Literary Study*, p. 488.

the mountains, judgments as profound as the sea, beauty as diffused as the light."[35]

Following the above, there is a prayer for blessing upon those who know the Lord (the upright) and for their protection from the wicked (vv. 10-12). Upon reading the psalm, only a modicum of wisdom should be necessary to lead one to determine whether he should cast his lot with the wicked or with the Lord.

The contrast in Psalm 36 is not limited to the content of its two parts but extends also to style. The first part is in the nature of the wisdom literature of the OT (didactic) and would be suitable in a psalm of lament. The second is a hymn of praise. The difference in style and content has led some to consider the psalm to be a joining of "two distinct, unrelated psalms."[36] But psalms of mixed type are not uncommon, and the two parts of this one constitute a unity in their diversity. To omit either would be to tell only half of the story. The first, in a few words, sets forth the reality of sin and its depravity. This is the problem confronting the psalmist, and even though some will not admit to the reality of sin, none can deny that there are forces of evil in the world that threaten our existence, evil as real as the daily headlines. But there is a solution to the problem. There is another, greater reality, and that is God.

The unity of the psalm is evidenced also by its structure, as Craigie makes quite clear. The theme of the first stanza, "the wicked" (רָשָׁע, rāšāʻ), in verse 1 and that of verse 2, "love" (ḥesed) in verse 5 are treated in verses 10-11 in reverse (chiastic) order.

A v. 1 *the wicked*   B v. 5 *love (ḥesed)*

B v. 10 *love (ḥesed)* A v. 11 *the wicked*

Stylistically, therefore, the psalm begins and ends with reference to the wicked. The problem introduced in the opening verse has been decisively dealt with and the reference to the wicked at the close emphasizes this fact. The opening and closing word, "wicked," therefore, constitutes an "inclusio," an indication that the subject introduced has been followed through to its conclusion. Verse 12, then, becomes a positive statement to that effect.[37]

---

[35]Ibid., p. 101.
[36]Buttenwieser, *The Psalms*, p. 521.
[37]Craigie, *Psalms 1-50*, p. 291.

1. Evil Unbounded (36:1-4)

We have noted that the psalm opens with a description, stark and foreboding, of the wicked person for whom evil has become a way of life. His depraved nature is clearly delineated, from his arrogance toward God, to his boast of impunity, to his lying and deceitful tongue, and his continual plotting of the evil he will do. He is a person who "has ceased to be wise" (v. 3), having spurned the way of wisdom for a life of evil.

36:1 The picture is clear, even though the translation of verses 12 poses some difficulty. A key word is נְאֻם (nᵉ'um) with which the psalm begins, unmistakably a noun meaning "utterance." The NIV retains the nominal form in its translation, **an oracle is within my heart.** Usually, however, translators verbalize the term and render it as "says," or "speaks." Many times the term appears with God as the source of the utterance, and we find "Thus says the LORD" in our translations — usually at the end of the remark (Jer 1:8). In our verse here the second word is "transgression," (**sinfulness** in NIV) and so the proposal, "Thus says transgression." But no direct quotation follows. Furthermore, the personification of evil (acceptable to the Greek mind, perhaps) is not met with elsewhere in the OT and seems extraneous to Hebrew thought. Following the lead of Craigie, I would render the verse, quite literally, as follows: "An oracle. Transgression, (as related) to the wicked, (is) in the midst of his heart."[38] This emphasizes the marked contrast between the wicked and the godly. The latter says, "I have hidden your word in my heart that I might not sin against you" (Ps 119:11). The former, refusing to be directed by the word of the Lord, lives his life solely according to the inclinations of his evil heart.

There is no fear of God before his eyes. This says it all. He can stand with his hand in the cookie jar and look God in the face with a smile, believing that he is free of all culpability. With no feeling of

---

[38]This translation ignores the Masoretic pointing of the noun construct, but to do so simplifies the translation. As for "his heart" instead of "my heart," Dahood has demonstrated conclusively that in some circles the Hebrew suffix ִי (î) may indicate either person, my or his. Craigie's translation is: "An oracle. Transgression belongs to the wicked person; it is in the midst of his heart" (*Psalms 1–50*, p. 433).

awe and respect for a righteous God, he recognizes no moral absolutes and no obligation to submit himself to ethical restraints when it is to his profit to do otherwise. There is no hint of atheism here. This is a person who would not hesitate to identify himself with the 94% who "believe in God." It is just that his "belief" in God does not make one iota of difference in his life, and so his sin is the greater! It wells up from his transgressor's heart, not from his intellect.

36:2 He flatters himself. Instead of having his eyes focused upon God, he suffers from the myopia of an overweening pride in himself. As Spurgeon observed, "He who makes little of God makes much of himself." [39] This exalting of the ego is proof *ipso facto* that such a person has no fear of God "before his eyes." One ray of recognition of the just and righteous Lord would suffice to reveal his own perverted nature. But "men loved darkness instead of light because their deeds were evil" (John 3:19). None is so blind as he who will not see. And his own self-deception makes it impossible for him **to detect or hate his sin.**

36:3 The tongue of such a person is directed by the evil heart to iniquity (wickedness) and deceit, to stirring up trouble and to treachery. Pursuing this course, **he has ceased to be wise and to do good.** The equation of goodness with wisdom implies the folly of doing evil. Sadly it is said that he *ceased* the way of wisdom. This suggests that at one time it had been otherwise. The poet has written: "Of all sad words of tongue or pen, the saddest are these, 'It might have been.'" But equally sad are the words, "I used to" when they are used in reference to the walk with God that one has experienced in years gone by but has long since abandoned. One who has "left off" his relationship with God is in a sad state indeed.

36:4 Even on his bed he plots evil. Perhaps nothing is more indicative of the character of a person than what he thinks about when upon his bed at night. In his daily walk, a godly person may fall into temptation — Satan is always seeking to ensnare him. But the wicked would make Satan his bedfellow! He plans deliberately to pursue the way of evil, plotting how he can best seduce, defraud, or destroy. **He . . . does not reject what is wrong.** Rather than feel

---

[39] Spurgeon, *Treasury*, 1:2:163.

COLLEGE PRESS NIV COMMENTARY

a revulsion toward wickedness and indecency, he embraces it and without apology makes it a pattern of life. Unless one abhors sin, unless it is repugnant to his sensibilities, there is always the danger that he will succumb to it. Here there can be no middle ground, no neutrality. This is not to have a condemnatory spirit toward the sinner, but it is to entertain such a revulsion toward evil as to prohibit any compromise with it in one's own life.

2. Infinite Good (36:5-9)

The picture of wickedness that has been shown us could scarcely be darker or more foreboding. And it is an accurate picture, an oracle of God. It is the kind of picture that, at times, causes one to despair of the human race, especially of those who boast that their humanism is sufficient for all things. How far have we come on the road to Utopia for all our technological and intellectual progress? We had better ask: How much fraud, how much bribery with dope money, what percentage of crooks in high places until a nation's morals collapse entirely? How much violence, how much immorality, until the law of the jungle alone remains? And what of the person who has been caught up in all of this, whose life is directed by a heart of evil? Is there any hope that it may be otherwise? Indeed the picture is grim and depressing. But — and this is the joyous note of the psalmist — it is possible for this terrible darkness to be dispelled and overcome by the light that comes from a loving Lord. Again, it is a matter of wisdom or folly, the wisdom of walking in God's light or the folly of living in the darkness we have created for ourselves. It must be one or the other. There are no alternatives.

36:5-7 The opening assertion of verse 5 gives us the basis for hope. **Your love, O LORD**, or, your lovingkindness, your steadfast love (*ḥesed*), **reaches to the heavens**, or, "extends to the heavens" (RSV). That is, the love of God is as broad in expanse as the heavens, and that is limitless. Moreover, his **faithfulness** (dependability) is as high as the sky (the clouds), his **righteousness** is as firm as the mountains, and his **justice** is as deep as the ocean. Over against the evil, the darkness in the heart of men, there is set the light of God's mercy. Covenant love, faithfulness, righteousness, and justice, all in such manner as to be wholly adequate for his entire creation, for he **preserve(s) both man and beast.** The ecology as established by the Lord is a marvel to behold. So also is the design of God for his people. Ignorance, greed, and abuse on the part of man can turn even a garden of Eden into a wasteland. God's way is best! For God has made adequate provision for every need of humankind, be it physical, spiritual, or emotional. How excellent — indeed, **how priceless is [the] unfailing love** of God that provides this for those who put their trust in him; that is, who seek the refuge he affords.

36:8-9 For with you is the fountain of life. It does not need to be said that apart from God there is only death. But here the emphasis is not so much on the contrast with death as upon the quality of life that the Lord provides. And how far removed it is from the life that gets its kicks only from evil! Here is a life abundantly satisfying and filled with genuine delights. **In your light we see light.** In the light that God has revealed we have knowledge unattainable in any other way — certainly not through speculation, postulation, or meditation. Has God spoken? A more important question could hardly be imagined. The Scriptures tell us that he has, and the corroborative evidence is abundant. When we affirm, "Yes, God has spoken," admittedly it is a statement of faith, but it is a faith based on evidence! And millions today will still testify to the truth: "The unfolding of your words gives light" (Ps 119:130). If this be not true, and the picture of human depravity in verses 1-4 is a valid one, then ominous indeed is the darkness that engulfs this earth. We are devoid of any light that will make any difference. It is enough to cause even the skeptic to cry out: "I do believe; help me overcome my unbelief" (Mark 9:24). And to such the answer comes back: "Taste and see that the LORD is good" (Ps 34:8).

3. Prayer for Continued Mercy (36:10-12)

36:10 Since it is through the mercy of God that deliverance from evil comes, it is natural for the psalmist to conclude with a prayer for a continuance of that mercy which he had already experienced. **Continue your love.** But he thinks not only of himself, his prayer includes others as well — **to those who know you.** He is praying that the wickedness that threatens may be overcome by the divine mercy as God works on behalf of, and through, those who know him; that is, those who have that knowledge of God that comes through walking in his way (see Jer 22:15-16). These are **the upright in heart**, those whose inclination of heart is to what is right — right morally and practically. This desire dominates their thinking, becoming the motivating principle of their being. Confidently the psalmist can expect the mercy of God to fall upon such as these and to manifest itself through them.

36:11-12 There remains the reality of the evil that exists, but there is confidence that this, too, may be overcome by the grace and power of God. And so he prays God's protection against such as would seek to trample him into the ground or bring about his defection from the way of righteousness. The psalm closes with a cry of victory as though it had already been achieved. The problem introduced in verse 1 has been settled. The darkness, great though it was, has been dispelled by the light that is from above.

C. THE VALIDITY OF THE DEVOTED LIFE (37:1-40)

Psalm 37 falls unmistakably within the class of Old Testament writings designated wisdom literature. It is an acrostic with (basically) every other verse beginning with the succeeding letter of the Hebrew alphabet. Each pair of verses is a complete proverb in itself. (like those in Prov 10:1–22:16). Nevertheless, the verses are not like so many beads strung on a necklace. A more apt comparison is that of Ash who sees the psalm as "an overall tapestry with a dominant pattern."[40] The threads composing the theme are interwoven from start to finish rather than appearing in any formal design. But the impact of the words of the psalm is by no means diminished thereby; it is actually heightened! If one may be granted another comparison, it would be that of a clear voice being heard reechoing through the canyons of some mountain fastness — again, again and again, the same voice, the same message: "The life devoted to the Lord is the blessed life."

---

[40]Ash, *Psalms*, p. 135.

Wisdom literature, by its very nature, is designed for instruction and guidance. The present psalm was written by one well advanced in years (v. 25). Apparently he is concerned that those less experienced in their walk with God may be tempted, in times of adversity, to turn away. His aim is to admonish and to encourage them to steadfastness, especially when they are tempted to envy evildoers who enjoy great prosperity.

Any concern for theodicy ("Why do the wicked prosper?" "Why do the righteous suffer?") seems not to trouble the psalmist's mind. Of course the questions are there, but if they were put to him, he would probably answer: "I am altogether willing to leave that matter in the hands of God." It is not his intent to give a lesson in theology but to present a challenge to live the life of trust in God, with the firm conviction that such a life will bring untold blessings from God, whereas a life of evil will result in ruin. As to the prosperity of the wicked he would answer: "Do not let what happens to others interfere with your own faithfulness to God nor to your commitment to what is right."

The psalmist does not close his eyes to reality. He is aware of what life is like in the "real world." But for him the greatest reality is that God will bless the life that is committed to him. Or, in the words of MacLaren, his is "the certainty that well-doing will lead to well-being."[41] This is the lesson that he would teach, the theme that echoes and reechoes throughout the psalm. Never does the author have a shadow of a doubt about *the validity of the devoted life*.

This emphasis is evident in the number of times that key words are repeated. For example, "Do not fret" (vv. 1,7,8), the wicked will be "cut off" (vv. 9,22,28,34,38), the righteous will "inherit the land" (vv. 9,11,22,29,34).[42] Furthermore, they will "dwell in the land"

---

[41]MacLaren, *Psalms*, p. 359.

[42]Instead of "inherit the land," the KJV has "inherit the earth" (except in verses 29 and 34, where it is "land"). אֶרֶץ (*'āreṣ*) may be translated either "earth" or "land" according to context. The basic meaning of the verb יָרַשׁ (*yāraš*) is "to possess" or "to take possession of." When this possession is conceived to be the consequence of God's promise, the term may properly be translated "to inherit." Some see eschatological significance in the psalm and read "inherit the earth." Others, remembering God's covenant with Israel, prefer "possess the land."

(v. 3) "forever" (vv. 27,29). Other significant expressions are: "Trust in the LORD" (v. 3), and "commit your way to the Lord" (v. 5). As to theodicy, the psalmist advises only: "Wait patiently" (v. 7), and "Hope in the LORD/Wait on the LORD" (vv. 9,34). In his own good time God will deal with the wicked and he will provide security for the godly.

The constant repetition of the theme of the psalm defies attempts to reduce it to a precise outline. However, it is possible to suggest one that is indicative of the general development of the psalmist's thought. There is a challenge to unreserved commitment (vv. 1-11), the promise of divine help (vv. 12-26), and the assurance of the ultimate outcome — the righteous will be preserved, the wicked will be cut off (vv. 27-40).

1. The Unreserved Commitment (37:1-11)

37:1-2 The psalm opens with a strong appeal to the godly to be constant in their trust in God. At the outset, however, there is a warning. **Do not fret because of evil men**, or "do not be all burned up, hot with anger." The godly who may have to live in humble circumstances must not fall before the temptation to envy the ungodly in their prosperity and in their lives of indulgence (v. 7). In the first place, such envy certainly does not enhance the life of the one thus disturbed. Again, it is an indictment of God's rule of his earth. But further, the position of the ungodly is not one to be envied, for they will not endure — **like the grass they will soon wither** "evil men will be cut off" (v. 9).

37:3-11 The patriarch Job had evidently observed exceptions to this, in ungodly persons who reveled in their wealth, advanced to a ripe old age, enjoyed a "flock" of happy, carefree children (and grandchildren) and, with no lingering illness, went "in a moment" peacefully to their graves (Job 21:7-13). "How often is the lamp of the wicked snuffed out?" Job asks. "How often does calamity come upon them?" (21:17). Job may have been overly cynical, but his questions do suggest that the law of retribution is not always speedily executed. But our psalmist implies as much. He tells us that God quickly brings the ungodly to account (v. 2). Still, he does indicate the possibility of delayed action when he advises the ungodly to **wait patiently** (v. 7).

In Psalm 49, where the matter is of considerable concern, the inevitability and finality of the death of the ungodly is emphasized. No amount of riches on their part can stay the hand of death (49:5-9) and all of their glory is laid aside when death summons them (49:16-20). The alternative is far more attractive. **Trust in the LORD and do good.** When one becomes aware of the reality of God, trust in him becomes a natural response, and by choosing to do good (instead of evil) we show that we trust him. We will not resort to devious, deceitful, wicked means to achieve our aims; we will not have to embrace evil in our search for the joy of life. When we trust God, we discover that his way is the way to complete fulfillment, the way of fulness of joy. To walk in this way is to **delight . . . in the LORD**, to experience that felicitous relationship with God that was intended by our Creator. How simple is the formula: "Trust God and do good." For the psalmist it is not a matter of searching for God, no attempt to be transported into heavenly realms. He is not engaged in some mystical exercise, not in search of the transcendental. He is, rather, trusting in God and in the good way he has revealed, and seeking to walk in that way. So there is a choice. One may follow the way of the wicked, the way to certain destruction, or the way of the Lord. Loudly and clearly the challenge comes: **Commit your way to the LORD.**

2. The Promise of Help (37:12-26)

The committed life is the blessed life, but it must be lived in a world that includes hostile forces. The honest, the law-abiding, the good often become the victims of evildoers. The psalmist recognizes this but he does not despair, because he knows that God is concerned and that he will act.

37:12-21 The wicked plot against the righteous and gnash their teeth at them. If the moral aberrations of a wicked people affected themselves alone, then they might be looked upon either with disdain or with compassion. But it seems that the wicked take a fiendish delight in attacking and harassing the righteous. No evil is too heinous in their sight when directed against the objects of their animosity. They will resort to deceit, dishonesty, fraud, slander, violence, or even murder, in forwarding their plots against those who desire only to live peaceably and justly before God. But the Lord will deal with them. "For all who draw the sword will die by the sword," Jesus said (Matt 26:52). Violence begets violence; greed begets greed; evil begets evil, treachery, and death, even for the one who practices it. **Their swords will pierce their own hearts.** In one way or another, the evil that men do will return to haunt them and to destroy them. **The wicked will perish.** They are the **enemies of the LORD** and their end is destruction.[40] They are **like the beauty of the fields**, in blossom today, tomorrow withered; they **vanish like smoke.** For all of their riches, they **borrow** and then find that they cannot meet their indebtedness whereas the righteous seem always to have enough to share!

37:22-26 A further contrast is seen in that the sustaining power of the Lord is experienced by the righteous; they are sustained (v. 24) while the wicked are **cut off** (v. 22). Verses 23 and 24 quite clearly reveal the nature of the help that God affords the righteous. We may translate literally: "By the LORD the steps of a (righteous) man are made firm (secure), and he (God?) takes delight in his way. Even though he should fall, he will not be hurled prostrate, for the LORD continues a firm grasp of his hand." He may fall, but he will not stay down. It is not that he has some superhuman strength or courage or wisdom; not that he is especially meritorious, that he should face life with such confidence, but because God is at his right hand to sustain and to strengthen him. God is his helper, and "if God is for us, who can be against us?" (Rom 8:31).[44] Both the psalmist and the apostle Paul found that the help of God was sufficient in any eventuality.

---

[43]A Qumran fragment of Psalm 37 reads for verse 20: "The ones loving" (*w'hby*, instead of "the enemies" — *w'yby*) the LORD are like the preciousness of lambs." But this is strange within the context of this verse. See J.M. Allegro, "A Newly Discovered Fragment of a Commentary on Psalm xxxvii from Qumran," *Palestine Exploration Quarterly*, vol. 86 (1954): 69-75.

[44]The eighth chapter of Romans is one of the most jubilant of Scriptures. It opens with *no condemnation*: "Therefore, there is now no condemnation for those who are in Christ Jesus, ... who do not live according to the sinful nature [flesh] but according to the Spirit." And it closes with *no separation*:

3. The Ultimate Result (37:27-40)

The final word is stated quite clearly in the contrast that is shown between the fate of the godly person and that of the ungodly (vv. 27-40). These verses could well be an elaboration of Psalm 1:6 — "For the LORD watches over the way of the righteous, but the way of the wicked will perish."

37:27-36 Verse 27 opens with three imperatives: (literally) **Turn from evil and do good [and] dwell . . . forever** (dwelling upon the earth is understood, v. 29). Here we are presented with both a negative and a positive: Shun all evil, and do what is right and good. And the promise is that one is blessed here and now when he thus directs his life, because the Lord loves justice, and he **will not forsake his faithful ones.** By contrast, "The unrighteous are forever destroyed, and the posterity of the wicked cut off" (v. 28b).[45] For a time the wicked may harass the righteous person (v. 32), but God will deliver him (v. 33). Consequently, the righteous needs to learn patience and perseverance: **Wait for the LORD and keep his way.** This is the way of victory. **I have seen a wicked and ruthless man** (like Hitler?) **flourishing.** Yet he passes on and **was no more.**

37:37-40 The theme of the psalm is reiterated in the closing verses. **There is a future** (אַחֲרִית, 'aḥărîth, not "posterity," RSV) **for the man of peace,** whereas the transgressors (those rebellious against God) will be altogether destroyed; there is no future for them (v. 38). Psalm 37 reflects unmistakably the theme of the book of Deuteronomy. There it is written: "I have set before you life and death, blessings and cursings. Now choose life, so that you and your children may live and that you may love the LORD . . . listen to his voice, and hold fast to him" (Deut 30:19-20). And why not? He

---

"Who shall separate us from the love of Christ? Shall trouble or hardship or persecution . . . . neither death nor life, neither angels nor demons, neither the present nor the future, nor any powers, neither height nor depth, nor anything else in all creation, will be able to separate us from the love of God that is in Christ Jesus our Lord" (Rom 8:35-39).

[45]This translation is based on a proposal in *Biblia Hebraica* and the LXX. Concurring in this basic reading are: Briggs, Kirkpatrick, Leslie, Oesterley, Weiser, Rogerson and McKay, Buttenwieser, Kraus, et al.

is our salvation and strength in trouble (v. 39), our helper and deliverer, if we put our trust in him (v. 40). The life fully devoted to him is life indeed — *valid life.*

D. PRAYER FOR GOD'S MERCY (38:1-22)

In many of the psalms designated *individual lament* it is the evil of enemies that is the source of the psalmist's grief. They bring false accusations against him, and he prays, "May my vindication come from you" (Ps 17:2). They are like ravenous beasts — "Rescue me from the mouth of the lions" (22:21). Without cause they seek his death — "May the net they hid entangle them" (35:8). And they lay plots against his life — "Confuse the wicked, O Lord, confound their speech" (55:9). Because, in these cases, the psalmist is suffering unjustly at the hands of evildoers, he prays for deliverance from their power. In Psalm 38, however, we have a different prayer. Enemies are mentioned, but not as the cause of the psalmist's distress. They do seem to take delight in his misfortune, and so he voices the prayer, "Do not let them gloat or exalt themselves over me when my foot slips" (38:16). But he does not cite them as responsible for his miserable condition.

In the psalms of the unjustly accused one finds declarations of innocence, but not in Psalm 38. Here no attempt is made at self-justification because the writer knows himself to be a sinner. Some in Israel believed that all suffering is punishment for sin. Whether or not the author of Psalm 38 believed this, in his own case he would not question the matter. He lays no claim to being an innocent sufferer and would place the blame for his condition on no one else, much less upon the Lord by asking, "Why do I suffer?" He accepts his punishment as justly deserved.

Still, sinner that he is, he prays, not out of audacity, but with a contrite heart, and out of necessity. Consider his condition. His body is ravaged with disease; pain and misery beset him, and his mind is burdened by a sense of God's displeasure. He knows that what he has done is an offense to God. Now he finds himself stricken by the hand of God, condemned by his own conscience, rejected by his near kin and by his friends, ridiculed by enemies. He is in the depths of depression, and most depressing of all is the consciousness that he has brought it all upon himself by his own sin. What hope remains for one in his condition? Hope in God's unfailing goodness and mercy! As Delitzsch has observed, he may despair of himself but he does not despair of God. The penitent sinner may have hesitated, but now he will present himself at the feet of him who is not only a righteous judge, but also a merciful savior.

1. An Impassioned Plea (38:1)

38:1 O LORD, do not rebuke me in your anger. The verb יָכַח (*yākaḥ*, "rebuke," "judge," "reprove," "correct") indicates fair and deserved judgment, especially between two parties, in this case between the Lord and the sinner. The psalmist is confessing that he deserves to be rebuked,[46] and he can accept the fact that his suffering is a consequence of his sin, retribution. But it is disciplinary also, as indicated by the remainder of the verse: **or discipline me in your wrath.** The chastening was recognized, not as a meaningless calamity that had fallen upon him, but as discipline from God. In modern terminology, the Lord was "trying to tell him something." Such discipline is not pleasant, but sometimes one may not in any other way be brought to confront his sin. And if affliction, whatever its nature, leads us to God, it is a gain in the end.

The psalmist is penitent. It is quite clear that, in all of his suffering, the consciousness of his sin weighs as heavily upon him as his physical pain. His first petition, therefore, is not that he be spared all pain, but that God's anger might soon pass. Only then could he have peace in his anguished soul. He would throw himself upon God's mercy.

2. Suffering Physically and Mentally (38:2-10)

38:2 The second verse opens with the Hebrew particle כִּי (*kî*), a term that is both conjunction and interjection: "For surely indeed!"

---

[46]For further discussion of this verse, especially of the wrath of God, see the comments on Ps 6:1, a verse practically identical.

Speaking with the utmost earnestness, the psalmist unburdens his heart, his lips overflowing with reasons why he so urgently seeks God. First of all, he has felt the chastening of the Lord. (Most assuredly) **your arrows have pierced me.**[47] They have not fallen off as they might do from one with a heart of stone, heedless of God's call to righteousness. He is receptive of God's message and is now responding in faith and in hope. He is saying, "I have sinned, but now I hear you, Lord."

38:3-10 Again, he would ask God's mercy because of the greatness of his suffering. Surely no one is in greater need of pity than he. With what pathos he pours out his agony to God! Smitten by disease, **there is no health in [his] body; his bones ache.** Festering **wounds** torment him. His **back is filled with searing pain.** And the tumult within him can only be expressed with groanings (v. 8). His heart palpitates, his strength "has ebbed away, and the light has gone out of his eyes" (v. 10, NEB).

Such a catalog of ailments seems, in the view of some, to be too much as a description of the afflictions of one individual. It is proposed, rather, that the entire psalm is metaphorical, with reference actually to the suffering that the nation of Israel was undergoing.[48] Others see the psalm as having been composed for the general use of any who suffer the guilt and consequence of sin. Yet it is difficult to dismiss the feeling that originally the psalm had its origin in the life experience of one who had suffered deeply, in pain and despair — "the genuine cry of a brother's tortured soul" (MacLaren). And on the basis of the magnitude of his suffering, he would ask the Lord's mercy.

---

[47]In the Canaanite pantheon, *Resheph* the Archer was the god of pestilence whose arrows spread sickness and disease. "Oh, no," the psalmist says, "it is not some demon god but the Lord who has afflicted me. I acknowledge it to be so. It is his arrows that I feel."

[48]The Jewish scholar Rashi (1040–1105 A.D.) held this view. In more recent times it has been shared by Briggs, Buttenwieser, and others.

3. Lonely and Abused (38:11-14)

38:11-13 The physical suffering is augmented by an overwhelming feeling of rejection and loneliness. He is abandoned by friends and loved ones alike. Perhaps they fear that his disease is contagious (v. 11). But also they entertain the view that he is "stricken of God," receiving the just punishment for his sins — surely the magnitude of his suffering proves his guilt. Thus they add condemnation to their rejection of him. And those antagonistic toward him "spread cruel gossip and mutter slanders all day long" (v. 12, NEB).

38:14 Even so, he remains emotionless and speechless before them, as one who is both deaf and dumb, as one **whose mouth can offer no reply**. After all, what can he say? Conscious of his guilt, the once-devout soul who has fallen in sin, how can he speak up in rebuke of his adversaries?

4. Daring Yet to Hope in the Lord (38:15-20)

The guilty, suffering soul, object of scorn of those about him, still dares to hope in the Lord! How can this be? He does not merit such consideration. How then dare he hope for it? Why does he still cling to God? Because in the past he has known of God's mercy and forgiveness. Has not God shown mercy to sinful Israel in days gone by? And may he not, coming to God in penitence, share in that mercy? This is his confident hope, expressed emphatically in verse 15.

38:15-20 I wait for you, O LORD; you will answer, O Lord my God. The "you" in both statements is emphatic, implying "you, and you alone." Others would only mock him. **O Lord my God.** Here is indicated the only basis for a claim for mercy. Though he has sinned, he recognizes that the Lord is still his God, and he is a God of compassion! And so he is saying, "Lord, you are my God. Help me, because of the greatness of my suffering, because I accept your discipline, and because I do look to you for mercy. In verse 19 he adds the additional reason that his enemies hate him wrongfully. He is not denying his own wrongdoing here: He has confessed his guilt or **iniquity.** Yet he has done nothing against these adversaries, having done only what was **good** toward them.

5. A Final Appeal (38:21-22)

38:21-22 The psalm closes with a final appeal. The psalmist has recognized his suffering as just retribution for evil that he has done. He has confessed his iniquity and has expressed sorrow for his sin. He has unburdened before the Lord the suffering that he has endured in body and soul, including his rejection by his acquaintances. And, most importantly, he has declared his continued trust in the Lord! "I wait for you, O LORD" (v. 15). All of this becomes the basis for his final prayer.

O LORD, do not forsake me, although all others have done so. **Come quickly to help me.** The urgency of his situation is apparent. **O Lord my Savior.** It is the certitude that salvation is with the Lord that has brought the psalmist back to God. The psalm that opened, therefore, with the plea, **O LORD, do not rebuke me in your anger**, closes with confident hope in the Lord who is his salvation.

E. TRUST WHEN HOPE IS GONE (39:1-13)

Brief though it is, for sheer poignancy of expression Psalm 39 has few equals and no superior. In the words of Cyril Rodd, the writer "wrestles with hopelessness,"[49] an apt figure! The precise cause of his distress is not revealed. He admits to having been rebellious against God (v. 8) and considers that he is suffering chastening as the consequence of his sin (v. 9). Sorely afflicted, he faces the prospect of impending death (vv. 4,5,13). The frailty of human existence weighs heavily upon his consciousness, and the pursuits of men, such as the accumulation of wealth, seem especially futile (v. 6). At one time, although he had resolved to remain quiet, he had given voice to his complaint, in a burst of passion (v. 3). Some suppose that he was upset and perturbed because of the health and wealth enjoyed by the ungodly while he suffered the exact opposite. But this is only conjecture. We really do not know the cause of his outburst. But now, in a calmer mood he assesses his condition — obviously very critical — and asks God's help (v. 4ff.).

---

[49]Rodd, *Psalms 1-72*, p. 80.

Of great significance is the fact that he clings to God even in the midst of deep depression. "My hope is in you" (v. 7). He then seeks deliverance from sin (v. 8), and closes his prayer with a petition that he may again experience cheerfulness before he dies (v. 13).

1. A Resolution Broken (39:1-3)

39:1-2 The opening verses of the psalm are a reminiscence. At the present time the psalmist, although distressed, is calm, perhaps even resigned as he talks with the Lord (vv. 4-13). But he had not always been so. In his opening remarks he recalls that he had made a resolution to keep silent about his sufferings. He would bear his burden with grim fortitude, if not with patience, for he was determined to keep himself under control. **I said, "I will watch my ways and keep my tongue from sin."** He realized that, in his grievously distraught condition, he might say something he would later regret. Especially, while the wicked, the ungodly, were before him, he felt the constraint of silence, lest he bring dishonor to God and by his example cause others to stumble. Hence his resolution. He would demonstrate strength of will and of spirit, perhaps anticipating that God would intervene on his behalf. However, no relief came. He kept himself **silent**, as silent as death, as one would still the waves of a raging sea,[50] but all of this was, literally, "from good," that is, without any good resulting. His **anguish** grew worse, as must always be the case when deep feelings of grief and guilt are suppressed.

39:3 My heart grew hot within me. The attempt to silence his tongue only served to increase the tension he experienced, for he could not quiet his heart. MacLaren uses a fitting metaphor to illustrate the point: "It is the heart, not the mouth, that has to be silenced. To build a dam across a torrent without diminishing the sources that supply its waters only increases weight and pressure, and insures a muddy flood when it bursts."[51] The torment in the heart of the psalmist was such as no earthly physician could quiet.

---

[50]The above gives the nuance of the words for "silence" that appear in the Hebrew text of verse 2. See also Ps 107:29.

[51]MacLaren, *The Psalms*, 2:3.

As he **meditated** (moaning, muttering under his breath), **the fire burned** until he could no longer keep it in.

Then I spoke with my tongue. We can only surmise that he spoke rashly, with words of bitterness and complaint (such as Job used when he finally began to speak in the presence of his three friends).[52] In any case, the psalmist broke the promise that he had made to himself that he would keep silent about his distress. We conclude that his words were an outburst in sharp contrast to those of verses 4-6. His may have been the complaint of many who suffer: "Why me, Lord?"

2. A Consciousness of Life's Frailty (39:4-6)

39:4-6 But now, in calmer mood, he faces the reality of his condition, with stark awareness of the brevity and of the frailty of his life, and asks God to grant him a degree of understanding. **Show me, O Lord, my life's end and the number of my days.** Any outrage that he may have expressed earlier has given way to acceptance. The consciousness of life's frailty gives him a better understanding of what is truly significant, at least that is what he hopes for and prays for (v. 7). He realizes that there is no meaning or real significance to what mankind so often seeks in life. Man **bustles about, but only in vain,** and his wealth he leaves to others. The basics, not the vanities of life, are now the concern of the psalmist as he contemplates the brevity of his existence on the earth.

3. A Faith That Persists (39:7-11)

39:7 The question that the psalmist asks of the Lord indicates that in his wrestling with hopelessness he has been the victor. **But**

---

[52]The thought and language of Psalm 39 bear a similarity to that of the book of Job, as Buttenwieser notes. The professor cites points of comparison; for example, 39:13 — Job 10:21-22, and lists terminology common to both, such as "moth" (39:11, Job 4:19). He concludes that both the psalm and the book of Job are from the same author, the psalm being the earlier of the two — an interesting proposal (*The Psalms*, pp. 545-550).

now, Lord, what do I look for? "Look for" is too mild a translation for the Hebrew קִוָּה (*qāwāh*). The verb means "to wait expectantly," or "with confidence." "Lord, what do you have in store for me?" **My hope is in you!** How could anyone in his condition have such confidence? He has just stated that all human life is fleeting. Now he will confess that he is a sinner, an object of scorn even to the ungodly ("fools," v. 8), that he has not a word to say in his own defense (v. 9),[53] that he still suffers bodily affliction (v. 10), and that what he possesses has no more permanence than a moth! (v. 11). Nevertheless, with undaunted confidence he says, "My hope is in you!" Here is faith that persists in spite of all!

39:8-11 Save me from all my transgressions. This prayer springs from the realization that the key element to his plight is his sin, standing as it does as a barrier to his fellowship with God, a barrier that must be removed. Verse 9 is properly understood as having reference to the present, not the past, as Craigie's rendering of the Hebrew indicates: "I have become silent. I will not open my mouth, for you have acted." This is not a silence imposed by the will (as in verse 1), but a silence that issues from an inner change of heart. It is the psalmist's way of saying, "Not my will, but yours be done." He acknowledges his guilt and thrusts himself upon God's mercy. How much he understood of God's grace we do not know, but he asks for it: **Remove your scourge from me.** This is apparently a plea for the healing of illness — **I am overcome**, from a distressing affliction. Urgency is given to his appeal by the thought once again of the transient nature of human **wealth.** It is of no more permanence than a moth (v. 11).

5. A Final Petition (39:12-13)

39:12-13 What do I look for? The question was asked in verse 7, but what could the psalmist expect? He would hope, at the least, for deliverance from his transgressions and the peace of mind that

---

[53]He cannot blame others for his condition for it is God's doing (v. 9), and he cannot blame God, because he recognizes that he is chastened for his own transgressions (vv. 10-11).

a sense of forgiveness would bring. Beyond this he asks only that God will respond to his tears and to his prayer. He lays no claim to deserving such consideration, but, like a sojourner who is altogether dependent upon his host, he would seek God's tender concern. **Look away from me**; let the period of discipline end. He obviously does not anticipate any great extension of his life. He asks, instead, only that he may experience a bit of cheerfulness once again before he dies — **before I depart** to Sheol **and am no more** upon this earth.

III. CONCLUSION (40:1–41:13)

A. GOOD NEWS OF DELIVERANCE (40:1-17)

In the opening verses of Psalm 40 the writer bears testimony to the great deliverance God has wrought for him in answer to his prayer (vv. 1-3a). This, together with the many other wonderful works of God, is cited as reason why one's trust should be in the Lord, with no thought of joining with those who would serve false gods (vv. 3b-5). The response of the psalmist to his great deliverance follows (vv. 6-10). He finds delight in doing the will of God (v. 8) and in proclaiming to others the good news of salvation (vv. 9-10). The note of joy and of praise and thanksgiving ringing throughout these verses is unmistakable. A "new song" is on the lips of the psalmist and he cannot refrain from singing it!

However, beginning with verse 12 the mood changes — most abruptly, some would say. "Troubles" are encountered, "sins" take hold, the "heart fails." There is a fervent plea for the Lord's help (v. 13), for deliverance from enemies who threaten (vv. 14-15). The song of joy has become a cry of despair, or so it would seem.

In view of the above, many scholars state categorically that Psalm 40 actually is a combination of two originally separate pieces, the first a psalm of thanksgiving and praise, and the second a lament. Verses 13-17 are found also, with some variations, as the whole of Psalm 70, and the latter is assumed to be the original source. According to this view, verses 11 and 12 were inserted to provide a transition from the theme of joy to that of lamentation. If the question is raised as to the why of this combination of disparate elements, it is answered that the setting of the psalm is in a time of grave difficulty, and that the inclusion of the reminiscence of former deliverance is a fitting prelude to the present plea for God's help. But why could the psalm not be a unit? Could not the original psalmist have included the two themes as readily as a compiler? Psalm 70, then, would be an independent preservation of the latter part of Psalm 40.

In opposition to this conclusion some find the transition from the one theme to the other (v. 12) to be incongruous (and therefore, not original?). Oesterley, for example, states: "This verse is so entirely out of harmony with the whole spirit of the preceding psalm that it cannot have been part of it . . . . It must, therefore, have been inserted by the redactor."[54] Eerdmans, however, in recognizing verse 12 as a conditional sentence, indicates its relevance most convincingly; indeed, it becomes the key to the understanding of the psalm.[55] "If (or when) troubles (evils) come upon me (in the future)," the psalmist is saying, "I pray that you will deliver me (as in the past)." The fact that the psalm, in its heading, is assigned "for the director of music" indicates that it was incorporated into the worship of Israel. What would be more natural, then, than to sing of the deliverance the Lord had provided in the past preparatory to a prayer for his continuing care?

J.H. Eaton recognizes the psalm definitely as a unit — "a deliberately organized whole."[56] He views it as a royal psalm of lament, the first part being preparatory and necessary to the second. Identifying it as a royal psalm places its date in the preexilic period, not late postexilic as some would claim. Whether or not the psalm was used at an annual enthronement, as Eaton suggests, its words would fit well upon the lips of a king, whether of David or of some other. The psalmist bears witness to the deliverance God has afforded him (vv. 1-3a), believing that many of his people will be led to trust in him also (vv. 3b-4).[57] In his role as a witness he speaks of the wonderful works of the Lord "for us" (v. 5). He pledges

---

[54]Oesterley, *The Psalms*, p. 236.

[55]Eerdmans, *The Hebrew*, p. 231.

[56]Eaton, *Kingship and the Psalms*, p. 43.

[57]Brueggemann calls attention to "very close linguistic ties" between the first and the second parts of the psalm, listing several Hebrew terms that

himself to go beyond the offering of sacrifices to devote himself to doing the will of God, by honoring the *torah* of the Lord – the God-given directive for king and for people (vv. 6-8). All of this, as God's appointed leader, he shares with his people as the good news that indeed it is (vv. 9-10). Then, in view of new dangers that threaten (Eaton), or that may threaten, he offers his petition for continued protection.

1. The Deliverance Experienced (40:1-3a)

40:1-3a We begin with reference to the psalmist's past experience. **I waited patiently for the LORD.** Patiently? Perhaps, because the Hebrew (literally, "waiting, I waited") may indicate "I continued to wait." But since the verb *qāwāh* also carries the connotation of expectancy or hope, we may translate, "I waited earnestly for the Lord" (and not for any other). It is those who have the confidence and the patience to wait thus for the Lord who "will renew their strength. They will soar on wings as eagles" (Isa 40:31). We cannot know the exact nature of the distress which the psalmist suffered, but, from his own testimony, he was rescued by the Lord from the "slimy pit." In Ps 30:3 the pit appears parallel with Sheol, the abode of the dead. It is from the threat of death, apparently, that deliverance has come.

The Hebrew here speaks quite explicitly of what the Lord had done for the writer. God was not some numinous influence working within the consciousness of the psalmist but a very active participant in his victory over his despair. He was his "refuge and strength, an ever present help in trouble" (Ps 46:1). First of all, **he turned to me,** stooped to hear my prayer. He **heard, he lifted me out, he set my feet, he gave me a firm place to stand, he put a new song in my mouth!** So many things the Lord does for those who wait for him!

---

occur in both. "It appears," he writes, "that the lament is composed with precise reference to the thanksgiving song so that the thanksgiving song adds weight to the complaint" (*Message*, p. 131). Gerstenberger demonstrates rather conclusively the unity of the psalm and cites various German scholars who concur in this view (*Psalms*, Part 1, p. 169f.). See also, Craigie (*Psalms 1–50*, p. 314).

The psalmist, having "waited on the Lord," has indeed mounted up as on eagles' wings. He has been brought from despair to hope, from the miry clay to the solid rock. Henceforth, his way that had been so insecure and uncertain is now firmly established. No wonder he sings a new song! The psalmist sang because he had something to sing about. God, by his grace and power, had brought to him deliverance from despair.

2. Trust in God (40:3b-5)

40:3b-4 Biblical faith is not a leap in the dark; it results from the acquaintance with and the belief of evidence. The conviction that the hand of God had wrought his deliverance was sufficient to put a new song in the mouth of the psalmist. And he had reason to believe that what the Lord had done for him would be evidence for others to consider also. His life would become a testimony to them. **Many will see and fear and put their trust in the LORD.** The saving power of God would inspire awe and wonder in their hearts and faith would be kindled. The very thought of this brings additional joy to the psalmist and he cries out: **Blessed is the man who makes the LORD his trust** (v. 4a). His life finds focus in God, so he will not defect by turning aside with the **proud**, those who with arrogance denounce God and continually solicit him with entreaties to join them. He will have no part of their falsehoods or false gods (v. 4b). "[He] does not walk in the counsel of the wicked" (Ps 1:1).

40:5 Many, O LORD my God, are the wonders you have done . . . . too many to declare. We are reminded of the words of the apostle John about the wonderful works of Jesus: "If every one of them were written down, I suppose that even the whole world would not have room for the books that would be written" (John 21:25). "But these are written" he said earlier, "that you may believe" (20:31). Reflection upon the acts of God is the way to faith and truth.

3. The Believer's Response (40:6-10)

40:6-8 The ultimate proof of faith is to be seen, not in what one says, but in conduct. The psalmist demonstrates his trust in God by bearing testimony to others of the deliverance he has experienced. More than this, he pledges himself to walk in the way of the Lord. **Sacrifice and offering you did not desire.** This is not to repudiate the offerings and sacrifices as a part of worship, but they are not to become an end in themselves. In context, the thought is that more is desired by our God than these.[58] **But my ears you have pierced,** or, literally, "ears you have dug for me," so that I can hear you (and obey).[59] This is a concrete way of saying that God has so constituted humankind that we are capable of receiving and comprehending revelation of the divine. It is up to us then to determine what our response will be. There is no more important question a mortal can ask than, "Has God spoken?" Has he revealed himself to us? But an affirmative answer, astounding as it is, is self-condemning if one does not heed what he has said. For the psalmist the response was acceptance and obedience. **Then I said, "Here I am, I have come — it is written about me in the scroll. I desire to do your will, O my God."** That the speaker is the king seems to be indicated by the reference to the scroll ("book") in which "it is written about me" a reference to the scroll of Deuteronomy. There instructions are given to the king, charging him to be faithful in the study of God's *torah* and in his obedience thereto. This he will do, not alone because it is written in a book, but because **your law is within my heart.**

40:9-10 In addition, a significant part of his response is the sharing of the good news with others. **I proclaim righteousness in**

---

[58]The attitude toward sacrifice is said to indicate a late, postexilic date for the psalm. However, the same attitude is found expressed in 1 Sam 15:22 and even though the latter is said to be from a late source, it is clearly preexilic.

[59]In Heb 10:5 this verse is quoted in reference to Jesus but is rendered by the New Testament author to the Hebrews: "A body you prepared for me." While the LXX is faithful to the Hebrew text (MT), the New Testament has apparently interpreted the Hebrew idiom as an example of synecdoche, with *ears*, a part, representative of the whole, *a body*.

the great assembly . . . your righteousness. I have declared to all
the people the goodness of the Lord in providing salvation, his
faithfulness, his love (*ḥesed*), his truth (reliability). The psalmist has
become an evangelist!

4. A Plea for Continued Help (40:11-17)

40:11-13 Verse 11 is a petition that the goodness and mercy of
the Lord may continue to be shown in the future (as in the past). **O
LORD . . . always protect me.** Verse 12, then, may properly be translated as a conditional sentence, as, Eerdmans proposes. The
opening particle *kî* is here viewed as of temporal significance —
when (or, *if*), a common usage in Hebrew. (The NIV takes *kî* as a
simple conjunction, *for*, with result or cause implied.) "If troubles
without number have encompassed me, my iniquities have caught
up with me . . . more than the hairs of my head, and my courage
has failed me" — **Be pleased, O LORD, to save me; O LORD, come
quickly to help me.** This petition for the future, then, is recognized
as the occasion for the psalm, without supposing that there is a
sudden turn to gloom and lament. The whole tenor of the psalm is
joy and confidence.

40:14-17 This is so of the verbs of verses 14 and 15. They may
well be future, with the request for the Lord's help in dealing with
enemies. These words, then, are not so much an imprecation as an
expression of confidence that the Lord will deal with any such in the
manner that their conduct deserves. In contrast, a blessing is pronounced upon those who seek the Lord (v. 16). As for the psalmist,
he has indeed experienced a great deliverance, but he will never be
beyond his need of help from the Lord. Thus he may properly
describe himself as **poor and needy**, at the same time cherishing the
conviction that God is still his **help and** his **deliverer**!

B. THE PRAYER OF ONE WHO IS SICK (41:1-13)

Many and varied are the opinions of the scholars relative to the
original setting and significance of the psalms. In this regard,

perhaps no psalm has elicited a greater variety of proposals than the one with which Book One closes, Psalm 41. Briggs views it as a prayer for national deliverance. He sees Israel as suffering severely from enemy nations, one of which is a treacherous neighbor "who, violated treaties of alliance and friendship."[60] Briggs would date the psalm after the exile at a time when the walls of Jerusalem were still rubble.

Eaton recognizes the writer as a king, blessed for his wise and benevolent rule and protected by the Lord from his enemies (vv. 1-3). In his present illness the king anticipates the time when he will be raised up to punish those who have plotted against him (vv. 4-10), believing that God will honor him for his just rule (v. 11) and restore him to the divine presence forever.[61] Others, without attempting to identify the writer except as a very sick man, see the psalm simply as a prayer for healing, containing elements of a didactic poem and of a lament. Buttenwieser accepts this view, though he considers verses 1-3 to be unrelated to what follows and so a separate psalm.[62]

The view of many others, perhaps a majority, is reflected by Arnold B. Rhodes when he identifies the psalm as "the thanksgiving of a man who has been delivered from a critical illness and from the reproach of malicious enemies."[63] According to this view, verses 4-10, in the lament pattern, are not a complaint but a recital of the condition of the psalmist before he received healing, for which he now expresses gratitude. The psalm closes, then, with a note of thanksgiving and praise.

Stuhlmueller proposes that Psalm 41 was originally a lament "adapted to the instructional part of the temple liturgy."[64] The instructional aim is seen in the inclusion of the didactic strain with which the psalm opens. Craigie also finds the form of the Psalm to be liturgical, stating that "the text must be interpreted as a liturgy (or a part of a liturgy) for use within a ritual in which a sick person

[60]Briggs, *Book of Psalms*, 1:361. Eerdmans states categorically that there is no evidence to support this theory (*The Hebrew Book*, p. 239).
[61]Eaton, *Kingship*, p. 45.
[62]Buttenwieser, *The Psalms*, p. 815.
[63]Rhodes, *Psalms*, p. 74.
[64]Stuhlmueller, *Psalms I*, p. 221.

comes to the temple in quest of healing."[65] He sees the ritual beginning with the words of a priest, addressed to the sick person,
describing the type of person God will bless (vv. 1-3). This is
followed by the sick person's confession of sin and his lament,
"framed in a prayer for healing" (vv. 4-10). The suppliant then
closes with a statement of confidence (vv. 11-12). Craigie is rather
convincing in his presentation. However, a weakness with this
analysis is the absence of any transitional bridge from the lament to
the thanksgiving. To satisfy this lack Craigie would suppose that a
priestly oracle from God would have been given at the close of
verse 10, thus prompting the words of the sick man, "I know that
you are pleased with me."

It is altogether possible that Psalm 41 was incorporated into the
liturgy of the temple worship. Yet in its inception it appears that
the psalm was a lament, with an appeal for healing not yet realized.
It is a prayer for help by one suffering grave illness who has confidence that his prayer will be heard and answered. His expectation
is based on the belief that a devout, compassionate person is
blessed (vv. 1-3). Consequently, he freely addresses his lament to
God (vv. 4-9) and prays confidently for deliverance, since he has
maintained his integrity before the Lord (vv. 10-12).

1. The Compassionate Are Blessed (41:1-4)

41:1-3a The opening verses, far from being irrelevant, enunciate
a principle that becomes the basis for the psalmist's appeal. The
words could well be the expression of common knowledge, such as
is found in Prov 22:9: "A generous man will himself be blessed, for
he shares his food with the poor." It is the part of wisdom to be so
concerned. The blessedness here involved is like that of Ps 1:1
(which see). It means genuine happiness. And the "poor" are not
only such as may be destitute, but the weak, the miserable, those
whom the world may consider of little importance. It is a joy to be
able to help such persons. But that is not all. The compassionate
soul may anticipate blessings from the Lord as well. **The LORD**

---

[65]Craigie, *Psalms 1–50*, p. 319.

delivers him . . . will protect him and preserve his life. He will **not surrender him to the desire of his foes.** Furthermore, he **will sustain him on his sickbed.** In all of this the psalmist is stating the principle. And although the words are didactic in nature, he is not attempting to persuade others to the view that the way of compassion brings its reward. Of course he would not preclude such a response, but his purpose is to state the basis for the appeal he will make to the Lord. The compassionate are blessed of God (see Matt 25:35-40), and on this principle he dares to approach the Lord with his petition.

41:3b It is significant that in verse 3b God is addressed directly: "You" (Hebrew text, see KJV. The NIV does not follow this reading.) We need not attribute this to a corrupt text, as some propose. Rather, it is at this point that the psalmist ceases to speak of the blessedness of the compassionate and directs his discourse to God relative to his own situation, showing that his condition is altogether in contrast to that he has just described. "Thou wilt make all his bed in his sickness" (KJV). The King James is quite literal, but the use of the future tense and the translations "make" and "bed" may be questioned. The verb is perfect (completed action) (or, precative — a request, wish or supplication) and thus may be translated as past tense or as a request. Its root meaning (from הָפַךְ, *hāpak*) is "to overturn"or "to overthrow," not "to make" (God overthrew the cities of Sodom and Gomorrah — Gen 19:25. He also overturned the curse of Baalam — Neh 13:2.) The term translated "bed" (מִשְׁכָּב, *miškāb*) does bear that meaning but it also means "lying down." Is there not more significant meaning in "all his lying down," meaning, "all his repose"?[66] Considering the foregoing, one

---

[66]Sensing the difficulty, many translations omit the word "all" (כֹּל, *kol*). Dahood would vocalize the term differently (כֻּל, *kūl*), making it a verb, "sustain" — "Sustain his confinement, overthrow the sickness itself" (*Psalms 1-50*, p. 248). Following the lead of Gunkel, Oesterley would, through emendation of the text, read: "All his pain thou turnest to strength" (*The Psalms*, p. 238). However, Kraus observes that "the alterations of the text frequently undertaken have no foundation" (*Psalms 1-59*, p. 430). Leupold translates: "Thou hast changed his whole lying down in sickness into health" (*The Psalms*, p. 330). And Cohen submits: "Mayest Thou turn all his lying down in his sickness," but finds it necessary to explain this obtuse statement in the words of Cheyne: "As oft as he lies down, Thou recoverest

may appreciate Eerdmans's rendering: "Thou hast overturned his repose in bed by his sickness."[67] The "his" refers to the psalmist himself. He has been deprived of all rest, this one who has shown compassion to others. This becomes the basis of his appeal.

41:4 I said, "O LORD, have mercy on me; heal me, for I have sinned against you." The speaker is a man dedicated to God, but he makes no claim to sinless perfection; he confesses himself to be a sinner. Since this is true, he asks for mercy and, by implication, for forgiveness, realizing that unforgiven sin may be the occasion of God's wrath. His dire need he then sets forth before the Lord.

2. Despite His Integrity, the Psalmist Suffers (41:5-9)

41:5-9 My enemies say of me in malice. These enemies are not depicted as vicious, actively seeking his death. They are actually acquaintances who come to visit him upon his sickbed. They do not speak evil, *against* him but *of* him; that is, with long faces, they have only words of doom to utter. (The malice of the NIV and RSV is probably not justified.) Obviously, they feel there is no hope for him. **"When will he die and his name perish?"** they ask. Whatever his ailment, the nature of which is not disclosed, they consider that his doom is certain and do not hesitate to say so. And, if they are like Job's friends, they have concluded also that his suffering must be from God as punishment for some hidden sin; he has brought it upon himself. They are certain that death is imminent, so they have no message of comfort or of encouragement for him, only **false** words. In their hearts they have room for only one thought, and it is of disaster (v. 6 – not "slander," NIV; "iniquity," KJV; or "mischief," RSV; but "calamity"). The New English Bible conveys the thought precisely: "All who visit me speak from an empty heart, alert to gather bad news." And then they go out to spread their message of doom about him in the community. **They imagine the worst for me,** he says. And, from his sickbed, to see them huddled

---

him his sickness" (*The Psalms*, p. 127). Ash notes that the passage is obscure (*Psalms*, p. 150).

[67]Eerdmans, *The Hebrew Book*, p. 235.

together whispering among themselves only adds to his agony. And, if this were not enough, he experiences even greater distress because even his trusted friend **has lifted up his heel against** (him) by joining the ranks of those who have "written him off" as one abandoned by God (v. 9). (The words of this verse were quoted by Jesus with reference to Judas, in the upper room, the night of the last supper with his disciples — John 13:18). As the Greater Son of David, Jesus identifies with the Davidic psalm, experiencing the same betrayal as David long ago. It is considered by Jesus a fulfillment of Scripture.

3. Prayer for Healing and Vindication (41:10-12)

41:10 All alone, abandoned and forsaken by all, the psalmist will not believe that he is abandoned by God. **But you, O LORD** (in sharp distinction from all the rest) **have mercy on me; raise me up, that I may repay them**. This is definitely a prayer for recovery. Is the psalmist reminiscing (vv. 4-10) about a previous experience, telling what happened, telling of his prayer? Or is he at this moment suffering from his illness and his rejection? The answer to this question depends largely upon the precise meaning of the Hebrew text of verse 11, soon to be considered. But first, what of his desire to "repay" his enemies, his erstwhile friends and neighbors? Is this the expression of a desire for vengeance? Vengeance seems to be too strong a word. The Hebrew term, שִׁלֵּם (*šillēm*), does mean "to get even" or "to recompense." But in context, it appears that vindication is what is desired. They were sure that he was suffering because of sin and that he must certainly die. He, like Job, refused to accept their conclusion. His recovery would settle the matter, proving them to be wrong. In this way he would get even.

41:11-12 The correct rendering of the text of verse 11 is determinative of whether the psalm is one of thanksgiving for healing already experienced or a prayer for recovery from an illness still endured. Many translations are consonant with the NIV: **I know that you are pleased with me, for my enemy does not triumph over me**. The deliverance has already been experienced. But an alternative is to recognize v.11 as a conditional statement. A typical rendering is that of Dahood: "Then shall I know that you love me if my foe does not triumph over me."[68] The difference in translation is due, in part, to the treatment given to the Hebrew particle *kî*. Translated "for" in the NIV, "because" in the KJV, it is rendered "if" by Dahood ("when" would be acceptable also). Both usages are quite common, with the choice to be determined by the context. This I consider to favor the conditional nature of the verse and would translate as follows: "Raise me up, that I may requite my enemies (v. 10). By this (then) I will know[69] that you are pleased with me and that my enemy will never[70] shout in triumph over me." This is followed by a prayer: **In my integrity you uphold me[71] and set me in your presence forever.** By "integrity" is meant his lasting commitment to the Lord and to his way. That has not changed even though he has acknowledged that he is a sinner (v. 4). His desire now is the assurance that he has been forgiven and restored to fellowship with God. We believe that he uttered his prayer from a sincere heart, in confidence that God would hear and respond.

4. Closing Doxology (41:13)

Each of the five books into which the psalms have been collected ends with a doxology ("word of praise"). It would seem, therefore, that verse 13 is not a part of the psalm proper, but a fitting close to Book One. Even so, as the psalms were incorporated into the worship of Israel, this verse would surely have been used with Psalm 41. **Praise be to the LORD, the God of Israel, from everlasting to everlasting.** When God blesses humankind, it is to provide some beneficence or to impart the potential for achieving a desired aim or goal. For man, however, the lesser, to bless God, the

---

[68]Dahood, *Psalms 1–50*, p. 249. Of 27 translations reviewed, nine were compatible with that of Dahood. These included the NEB, Moffatt's translation, The Jerusalem Bible, and Eerdmans. Eighteen Bible versions rendered the text in accord with the NIV, including the KJV, ASV, and RSV.

[69]The perfect of certainty.

[70]לֹא־יָרִיעַ (*lō'-yārîya'*) is a strong negation.

[71]Precative perfect (a perfect verb form in Hebrew indicating a wish, request, or entreaty from the context).

greater, is to appreciate, honor, and praise him.[72] But even though we may believe that God is pleased with the praise we offer, is his pleasure not due to the fact that, in doing so, we are blessed more in the act of worship than he? Pity the man who has no one to thank for the blessings that he enjoys!

---

[72]See comment on Ps 34:1.

BOOK TWO: PSALMS 42-72

Beginning with Psalm 42 one may observe the predominance of the use of *Elohim* (God) rather than *Yahweh* (LORD) in reference to deity. This is evidence that at one time this group of psalms existed as a separate collection. Persons identified with these psalms are: the sons of Korah (42-49), Asaph (50), David (51-65, 68-70), and Solomon (72). Psalms 66, 67, and 71 are unattributed. Since Book Three contains additional psalms of Asaph and of the sons of Korah, it would appear that at one time Books Two and Three were a unit. If one considers Psalms 42-83 (Book Two through the Asaph collection of Book Three), he will find *Elohim*, appearing 200 times, compared to only 43 appearances of *Yahweh* (The count for Book One was 272 for *Yahweh* and only 19 for *Elohim*.)[1] As was mentioned earlier, the restraint in the use of the divine name *Yahweh* could be an indication that Psalms 42-83 constitute a collection used by the exiles who would avoid uttering the divine name among heathen. We cannot be certain of this, but additional evidence is the fact that these psalms, not in their entirety but as a whole, are national in scope, and thus the concern of an exiled people, whereas the Psalms in Book One are more personal. This is not to say that these were necessarily written in the exile. We speak only of their incorporation into a collection.[2]

---

[1]See discussion on pp. 41-44 of the Introduction.

[2]A more detailed introduction will be given by the editor in volume two of this series concerning the theory of the collection of the Psalms, its history and theological structure. Volume two will cover chapters 73-150 in commentary and include an updated bibliography.

PART ONE: DELIVERANCE FOR THE ESTRANGED (42–51)

I. INTRODUCTION (42:1–43:5)

A. LONGING FOR GOD (42:1–43:5)

In some ancient manuscripts Psalms 42 and 43 are written together as one psalm. That this was their original state is indicated by the fact that the refrain that occurs in 42:5 and 11 also appears in 43:5 to close the psalm. Why it was divided we do not know, although it has been proposed that it was to serve some particular use in synagogue worship. But the psalm consists of three stanzas, reflecting great depth of feeling, and all three are necessary to its expression.

Generally, the psalm is classed as an *individual lament* (or, *prayer*, if you prefer). Those who consider its use as liturgy, however,[1] would classify it as a *communal lament*, with the worshipers speaking as a group but giving voice to individual concerns. The setting of the psalm cannot be determined definitely. If it were written purely as liturgy, as some suppose, then no specific setting is to be sought. Yet the very urgency of the language seems to reflect an actual experience of the speaker, about whom we can ascertain at least this much: He is a musician (43:4) who has known the joy of worship in the house of the Lord (42:4) but is now denied that privilege (42:2). Where we now find him is not clearly evident. Many conclude that the reference to "the land of Jordan" (42:6) indicates his present abode, but this is not absolutely clear. It is altogether possible that he is among the exiles in Babylon, reminiscing about the land of Jordan from which he has been removed. In any case, he is away from Zion, the "holy mountain" (43:3), in the midst of a Gentile

---

[1]Gerstenberger, for example (*Psalms*, p. 181f.).

people (43:1), who taunt him in his present distress. Here he experiences a deep longing for the fellowship he had known with God in worship in bygone days. Sweet (or, painful?) memories of the past lead him to contemplate his present dire straits. Yet faith triumphs, and the psalm closes on a glad note of hope for the future.

1. Memories of the Past (42:1-5)

42:1 The psalm opens on a melancholy note. How long has the speaker been an exile? A year? Two years or more? Whatever the time, his soul is troubled. Is this because of his exile from home? Undoubtedly, but that is not the burden of his lament. His distress is occasioned by his being cut off from access to worship in the house of God — for him a loss most devastating, keenly felt. **As the deer pants for streams of water, so my soul pants for you, O God.** What a picture of the longing of the soul for God! One can visualize the deer, in a parched land, neck outstretched, seeking to get the scent of water, without which it will surely perish. So is the thirst for God.

42:2 But why must he seek? Is not God with him in the exile? Surely, for he is addressing God in this verse, and he will direct his prayer to him (43:1). But somehow he does not experience the nearness to God he had once known. **My soul thirsts . . . for the living God** — "living," in strong contrast with the gods of the heathen, among whom he now finds himself. They are "nothings." The mighty works of God in the lives and destiny of his people had been testimony that he lives, and the psalmist feels a special need of his presence now. When shall I come and appear before God? What he desires is to worship God with the people of God in the house of God (v. 4). Undoubtedly he had known the presence of God on such occasions in the past.

42:3-4 The grief he experiences from the emptiness he now feels robs him of appetite, and so his tears become his food. **While men say to me all day long, "Where is your God?"** "Men" are identified in verse 10 as "foes" or "adversaries." The latter is the better term. There is no hint that they seek him harm. But they do not hesitate day or night to taunt him. Undoubtedly he, like Daniel,

318

had made no secret of his devotion to the Lord (Dan 6:10). Surely he knew that one exposes oneself to the possibility of ridicule when he declares or exhibits his faith. (However, if faith remains unexpressed, does it not cease to be faith?) The foes ask, "Where is your God?" However, they are not speaking with the voice of skepticism but of derision. Seeing his condition — an exile (perhaps suffering a dread illness) — they conclude that his god has forsaken him (as Job's friends thought about him). This is not the query of the atheist. They are deriding him, not his deity. It is one way of saying, "You God-forsaken wretch. Your god has abandoned you." And what can he say? But then thoughts come to him of the happier times he has known: **how I used to go with the multitude, leading the procession to the house of God.** The term, "leading the procession," means "to move slowly" (or, "walk humbly," Isa. 38:15), and the type of verb may indicate that he led the procession in worship.[2]

How joyous those occasions had been, those times of worship in the assembly! Perhaps he had not fully realized their significance at the time, but now that he is cut off from this worship, he senses a great loss. And yet, even the memory will lead him once again to have hope. "It is great wisdom" wrote Spurgeon, "to store up in memory our choice occasions of converse with heaven; we may want them another day."[3] The glow of that light in the soul, once experienced, can serve to illumine one's way when he must walk in the dark shadows of the present. Pity the child who has no such memories of God!

42:5 The fond recollection causes the psalmist to question his own dejected spirit and challenges him to renewed hope. He has a serious dialogue with himself. **Why are you downcast, O my soul?** Here we find faith coming to grips with fear, and faith conquers. Over against his condition of distress he can set hope. Can he not? He can, and does, but not without a struggle.

---

[2]This possibility led Kent to state as probable that the psalmist was "a high priest or a Levite banished from Jerusalem at the time when Jehoiachin (597 B.C.) was carried into captivity" (*The Songs*, p. 184).

[3]Spurgeon, *Treasury*, 1:2:273.

2. The Present Woeful Reality (42:6-11)

42:6-8 Memories of the past may be pleasant, but we cannot close our eyes to the present situation. Face up to it! Then one may determine, in view of the past, how best to meet the current ordeal. **My soul is downcast within me.** There is no denying the reality. The mind even of a saint of God may at times be burdened with deep apprehensions. Consider the case of the prophet Elijah (1 Kgs 19:4,14), and of Job! It is not to be considered strange, the apostle Peter noted, that one devoted to the Lord should suffer fiery trials (1 Pet 4:12). The psalmist found it so, but at such times he was not without recourse: **Therefore I will remember you** (and trust you in the present crisis). True, it appears that the depths of the ocean itself have conspired against me – **all your waves and breakers have swept over me.** But they are still *your* waves and *your* breakers, Lord, not some demonic forces unleashed against me! At any time you can say to them, "This far you may come and no farther," and the proud waves will be stayed (Job 38:11). The anguish is over-whelming, but Lord, your **love** (*ḥesed*) continues, and even the darkest night cannot silence the song that is in my heart or the prayer that is on my lips, for you are **the God of my life.**

42:9-11 As we read these words we can sense something of the struggle that is going on in the heart of the psalmist. He cannot doubt the goodness of God. God is and always will be his **Rock**, the strong base and support of his life. But has God indeed forgotten him? So it seems. His distress at the hands of his **foes** or adversaries continues; their taunts still ring in his ears: **Where is your God?** Again he must search his own soul: **Why are you downcast?** But hope continues, and faith affirms that he will again have cause for rejoicing.

3. Commitment and the Renewal of Hope (43:1-5)

43:1-3 Vindicate me, O God. Such a prayer can be offered in sincerity only by one who has committed himself to God and to the ways of God. This the psalmist has done, but now he is suffering abuse as a result of that commitment. The abuse comes from **an ungodly nation**, the gentile world into which he has been taken. They who ridicule him say that he has been rejected by his God,

and it certainly seems to be so: **Why have you rejected me?**
Vindication will come when they have been shown to be wrong.
The darkness and gloom that they project must be displaced by the
light that comes from heaven's throne. Instead of their deceit, he
prays for God to send his **truth.** The coming of this **light** and the
working of this truth will be evident when the Lord restores him,
bringing him again to the **holy mountain,** (Zion, in Jerusalem)
where he may once again have access to the house of God. This is
the burden of his prayer.

43:4-5 Then will I go to the altar of God. This, the continual
desire of his heart, is now his confident expectation. The joy he had
once known when he was free to join in the public worship of God
would be his once again. This is not to say that he could not draw
near to God where he is now residing. Is he not now talking with
God? But he has remembered the occasions in time past when his
spirit was refreshed, his heart made to rejoice, and new life and
strength given to him through the fellowship with God he had
experienced with other believers. And so, for the third time, he
questions himself: **Why are you downcast, O my soul?** Why,
indeed, when one recalls the many blessings he has known from
the Lord, when he remembers God's steadfast love, when the
melody put there by God continues to sound in his heart? And so
again he admonishes himself: **Put your hope in God,** certain now
that this is precisely what he will do. Consequently, when he says
again, **for I will yet praise him,** it is with a confidence that entertains no doubts. We do not know if this one who held such a
longing for the house of God ever returned to experience there
again the former joys. But we can believe that wherever he found
himself, his awareness of God's presence was never diminished.

II. THE REVELATION OF GOD'S POWER
(44:1–45:17)

A. PERPLEXED, SMITTEN, STILL PRAYING (44:1-26)

There is no mistaking Psalm 44 as a *national lament.* It may have
been utilized in the liturgy of worship in times of national distress,
but in its origin it surely is the response of a greatly troubled soul

to an overwhelming national tragedy. The people of God have suffered a devastating military defeat, being slaughtered like sheep.
They have had to flee from the enemy, who have plundered the
land, taken captives, scattering them among the nations, making
them slaves (vv. 10-12). It is all so perplexing and devastating to the
spirit, for although the people have been constant in their loyalty to
God, they have become the laughingstock of the nations (vv. 13-16).

The above portrayal of the conditions of the times is clearly
revealed. Not so obvious is the exact historical moment that is
reflected in the psalm. The view, once widely held, that it stems
from the Maccabean period (ca. 178 B.C.) during the persecution
of the Jews by Antiochus IV is now abandoned, as that era is now
known to be much too late. Leslie, among others, places the psalm
in the time of savagery unleashed against Phoenicia (Palestine),
Syria, and Egypt by the Persian ruler Artaxerxes III (Ochus) about
350 B.C.[4] Harold M. Parker, Jr., holds this view also and adduces
considerable evidence in its support.[5] He notes especially the brutality of Ochus. When a hundred men of Sidon came out of the city
to negotiate a surrender, he had all of them killed, thrust through
with javelins. Later, when five hundred came out, bearing olive
branches, they suffered a similar fate, whereupon the 40,000
remaining in the city, realizing they would be shown no mercy,
destroyed Sidon with fire, perishing in the flames. Parker cites
archeological evidence to indicate the probability that Jerusalem
also was sacked by the Persians at this time. (One may wonder why
Josephus, in 95 A.D., made no reference to this persecution, but
historical records of the period are quite scarce.)

Many consider the psalm to be preexilic, even though it does
contain a reference to Israel's being "scattered . . . among the
nations" (v. 11). Some find the setting in the time of Jehoiakim.
In 606-605 B.C. this king of Judah submitted to the yoke of
Nebuchadnezzar, at which time a number from the king's household were taken to Babylon (Dan 1:14). These were followed by an
additional 10,000 in 598-597 B.C. (2 Kgs 24:14). However, there is

---

[4]Leslie, *The Psalms*, p. 227.
[5]Harold M. Parker, Jr., "Artaxerxes III Ochus and Psalm 44," *JQR* 68
(1978): 152-168.

no indication of a wide-scale slaughter at this time. Others would place the psalm in the days of Hezekiah when Sennacherib's forces overran the land (701 B.C.). But at whatever point in history, the agony suffered by the people was monumental.

Noteworthy of this particular time of suffering is the fact that it was considered to be undeserved. In several psalms it is acknowledged that evil has come as a consequence of the nation's sins. But these people have been loyal to God, and yet they suffer! Why? They can only conclude that God has rejected them. This leaves them perplexed, perhaps embittered. Their perplexity arises from the fact that they are aware that God had provided deliverance for their fathers while they, even though loyal, continue to suffer. Apparently, they dare to hope, though no word of hope is recorded. The psalm does open, in the Hebrew text, with direct address to the Lord: "O God!" And the last word is "your unfailing love," as the basis of an impassioned plea for help.

1. God's Deeds in Time Past (44:1-8)

44:1 Our fathers have told us what you did in their days – and that is why they are now talking with God! How fortunate they were to have fathers who would tell them about God. (We could hope that there would be such a father in every family.) These people did have a spiritual dimension to their lives, a faith in the living God, a faith not inspired by a recitation of creeds but by the record of deeds – the mighty acts of God at definite points in time. The particular act in the present instance was the giving of the land of Canaan to Israel for their possession (in keeping with God's promise to Abraham, Gen. 17:8).

44:2-3 With your hand you drove out the nations. God is not capricious, nor unjust. When the land of Canaan was first promised to Abraham, its people were not immediately driven out because, though sinful, their sin had "not yet reached its full measure" (Gen 15:16). In other words, God granted them time for repentance. But they did not repent. Consequently, when judgment did finally descend upon them, it was "on account of (their) wickedness" that God drove them out (Deut 9:4). And in their place God planted the people of Israel – not because they were a superior people (Deut 7:7) but as an act of love and grace; he showed favor to them. This was history. God had blessed the nation, and it had grown accordingly.

44:4-8 The psalmist knows this. Furthermore, he does not hesitate to declare his allegiance to this one who has "commanded Jacob's victory" (v. 4, Craigie) as his own God and King. Naturally, then, he and his people have come to trust in the Lord's help and protection, not in the bow or in the sword, and they have continued to praise him. (vv. 5-8).

2. The Present Distress (44:9-16)

44:9-16 Still they endure bitter suffering, and verse 9 opens with a strong adversative, introducing the sharp contrast between what has happened in the past and their lot in the present. **But now you have rejected and humbled us.** Our armies are defeated in battle, as they turn their backs and flee; we are objects of scorn and contempt. Our possessions are seized as the booty of war. Many are slain without mercy; others are scattered among the nations, sold as slaves. **You sold your people for a pittance** — "for a trifle, demanding no high price for them" (v. 12, RSV). You don't even bargain for them! You gain nothing (no prestige) in their ignominious defeat! The people of God have become the object of derision. They must endure the taunts (and God the blasphemy) of those around them (v. 16).

3. A Faithful and Loyal People (44:17-22)

44:17-22 Verse 17 gets to the heart of the agonized perplexity of the psalmist. "If we suffered because we were living wickedly, we would understand and have no complaint," but **all this happened to us, though we had not forgotten you.** We are your covenant people, loyal to you and faithful. Why then do we not experience the deliverance that was accorded to our fathers? Instead, **you crushed us and made us a haunt for jackals** — in some out of the way, deserted place — **and covered us over with deep darkness.** If we had shown devotion to false gods, we would deserve your rebuke and expect to be punished for our faithlessness, but it is **for**

your sake (or, "on account of you"!) that we suffer slaughter! Is this the reward for our loyalty? Have we misunderstood? Were we not told that when one turns to God, skies turn to blue, ills and troubles vanish, and peace and tranquility remain uninterrupted?

If this were the thinking of the psalmist and his people (as it seems to be of many today), then they had yet to learn the deeper meaning of faith. They were now painfully aware that one may suffer even though he trusts in God — suffering *in spite of* his faith — and that in itself was disconcerting. They were learning, also, that one may suffer *because of his faith*, and that was devastating. They had yet to learn that *faith would make the suffering bearable*, (and that is a wonder of wonders!). Consequently, they questioned the ways of God. However, they would not abandon him, as some do under similar circumstances.

4. Wake Up, God! and Help Us (44:23-26)

44:23-25 Awake, O Lord! Why do you sleep? Is the psalmist rebuking God? It would seem to be so. One does not dare to speak in such fashion to an earthly monarch, but here God's subject speaks in remonstrance with his Lord! This, however, is not effrontery or impudence. It but reveals how close the relationship is between the psalmist and his God. He speaks as to an intimate friend in open frankness of thought and spirit.[6] Is God asleep? The words are not to be taken literally. Elsewhere it is stated that "indeed, he who watches over Israel will neither slumber nor sleep" (Ps 121:4). The words here express the desperation of the speaker. Surely, he reasons, the plight of the afflicted people must be because God is either asleep to their condition or else has deliberately turned his face from them (v. 24). Obviously, there are depths to the mystery of suffering that the psalmist has not plumbed. But among ourselves is there any who would claim to have a complete understanding? Every child of God has likely been perplexed at

---

[6]Jeremiah addressed God in a similar vein: "O LORD, you deceived me, and I was deceived" (Jer 20:7). The New English Bible renders the verse: "Thou hast duped me, and I have been thy dupe"!

times by the fact that the people of God may be called upon to undergo suffering for which there is no apparent explanation. However, since the experience of Jesus on Calvary, we know that suffering, far from being a negation of God's love, may be the deepest expression thereof, and that nothing "will be able to separate us from the love of God that is in Christ Jesus our Lord" (Rom 8:39).

44:26 The psalmist must have felt this continued relationship with God, even though the thought is not articulated, for he prays: **Redeem us** (not because we deserve it, but) **because of your unfailing love.** In his innermost heart he knows that God is not asleep nor has he ceased to love his own. "For your sake we face death all day long," he had said (v. 22). And he wonders that one should pay such a price for his loyalty to God! Still, he believes himself yet to be within the circle of God's love. The apostle Paul takes one step further. He quotes verse 22 of the psalm and makes it a cry of victory, declaring that "in all these things we are more than conquerors through him who loved us" (Rom 8:36,37).

B. THE MARRIAGE OF THE KING (45:1-17)

The heading of Psalm 45 defines it as "a wedding song," "a song of loves" (KJV), or "a love song" (RSV). The psalm was obviously written to celebrate a marriage, ostensibly that of a king. Consequently, the psalm is usually identified as a royal psalm, written as an ode (or as a liturgy) for a royal marriage. T.H. Gaster, however, considers that it was composed for ordinary wedding occasions, in which bride and groom were arrayed and addressed as royalty, becoming king and queen for a day. "In the Near East, as elsewhere," Gaster observes, "it is common convention to treat a bride couple as royalty."[7] It has not been established that this was true in OT Israel, but if this view is accepted, then the psalm is recognized to be secular in nature, and this raises the question as to why it

---

[7]T.H. Gaster, "Psalm 45," *JBL*, 74 (1955): 239. R.H. Alexander, in commenting on *shir yedidoth*, "a song of loves," says: "The plural form probably indicates the broad use of the psalm as a wedding hymn" ("Yedidoth," *TWOT*, p. 364).

should be included in the Scriptures.[8] As a matter of fact, some question whether even a song for a royal wedding should be a part of the holy writings. The problem is then resolved by recognizing the psalm as messianic. Thus Spurgeon writes: "'The King,' the God whose throne is for ever and ever, is no mere mortal . . . . This is no wedding song of earthly nuptials, but an Epithalamium [a nuptial song or poem in honor of the bride and bridegroom] for the Heavenly Bridegroom and his elect spouse."[9]

The messianic nature of the psalm has been recognized from earliest times, both in Jewish and Christian circles. For example, the Targum renders verse two thus: "Thy beauty, O King Messiah, exceeds that of the children of men; a spirit of prophecy is bestowed on thy lips."[10] The marriage of the King (Messiah) was recognized as "an allusion to his redemption of Israel."[11] (This theme is incorporated, in part, in the book of Hosea, chapters 1–3.) In Christian circles (as in the NT) the psalm is seen as prophetic of the relationship between Christ and his bride, the purified church. It is, as Spurgeon said, the Heavenly Bridegroom and his spouse who are being extolled. But did the psalm have no pertinence to any known king at the time of its writing? That is, was it purely and simply referring to the future King? To answer the question, it would help to know the date of writing. If it should be postexilic, after the kingship had ceased in Israel, the psalmist (if referring to

---

[8]A similar question may be raised in reference to the *Song of Solomon* (*the Song of Songs*). That it speaks of love between man and woman is clear, but to feel that an apology is therefore necessary is to reflect an ungodly concept of marital love as ordained of God in creation. The lesson to be gained from the book is twofold: the blessing and delight of the married state (as God intended it) and, by inference, the greater blessing of the covenant love between humankind (the creature) and God.

[9]Spurgeon, *Treasury*, 1:2:315.

[10]The Targums were translations (or interpretations) of Hebrew Scriptures in Aramaic ("Chaldee") made necessary when Hebrew ceased to be the spoken language of the Jews. For years, it is believed, the Targums were oral explanations, only to be put in writing at a later date. Their existence in the first Christian century is attested by their use in the NT. For example, Christ's quotation from Ps 22:1, in Mark 15:34, is from the Aramaic Targum, not the Hebrew.

[11]Cohen, *The Psalms*, p. 140.

an actual king) would undoubtedly have in mind one who would yet arise to occupy the throne of David, thus the Messiah King.

On the other hand, if the psalm is preexilic, coming from a time when kings still reigned in the land, it is difficult not to assume that any reference to a king would be understood as indicating the reigning monarch. Many scholars favor the preexilic setting, but there is a wide difference of choice as to whom the king may have been. The various proposals include: Solomon, on the occasion of his marriage to the daughter of the king of Egypt; Ahab, king of Israel, who married Jezebel of Tyre; and Jehu, king of Israel.[12] In the absence of any certain identification, we must content ourselves that here we have a wedding song of a king and bride now unknown. At the same time, we recognize the messianic import of the psalm, for it does indeed provide a number of threads in the tapestry that, completed, depicts the Christ who was to come.[13]

The theme is simple but developed with great depth of feeling, as by one who rejoices greatly in the happy occasion. After a superscription stating his delight in writing (v. 1), the psalmist extols the beauty, gracious character, and valor of the king (vv. 2-5). He follows this with a reference to the righteous nature of the kingdom, blessed of God because of that righteousness (vv. 6-7). The king, arrayed in royal wedding garments redolent of aromatic spices, is gladdened by the wedding music that announces the coming of the bride, the daughter of a king (vv. 8-9).

The bride is then addressed, admonished to forget her people and bow to the king, assured that the wealthiest persons, including

---

[12]Briggs makes an extended correlation between references in the psalm and what is known of Jehu as recorded in 2 Kgs 9–10 (*Psalms*, 1:384ff.). His conclusion, however, has not been widely accepted.

[13]Spurgeon wrote: "Some here see Solomon and Pharaoh's daughter only — they are shortsighted; others see both Solomon and Christ — they are cross-eyed; well-founded spiritual eyes see here Jesus only, or if Solomon be present at all, it must be like those hazy shadows of passersby which cross the face of the camera, and therefore are dimly traceable upon a photographic landscape" (*Treasury*, 1:2:314). According to Spurgeon's equation, the present writer must be cross-eyed — not that I see Solomon necessarily, but some king known to the psalmist and in whose honor the psalm was written. At the same time, I recognize the psalm as rich in messianic import. Herein is a part of the mystery that was revealed in Christ and about which Paul wrote in Rom 16:25 and Eph 3:4-5.

the rich merchants of Tyre, would honor her and court her favor with gifts (vv. 10-12). Then there is given a description of the bride and her trousseau, the wedding procession begins, and the bride enters to the king, accompanied by her maidens of honor (vv. 13-15). The psalm then closes with the assurance to the king that his sons will become princes "in all the earth," his name will be remembered "in all generations," and his praises be sounded "for ever and ever" (vv. 16-17). In view of the fact that we do not know the name of the king, we may recognize the latter statements as poetic hyperbole. In their fulfillment in Christ, however, they are quite literal!

1. The Jubilant Poet (45:1)

45:1 From his opening words, the jubilation of the psalmist as he contemplates his theme is evident. **My heart is stirred by a noble theme!** There may be somber themes for other days, but this is a day for rejoicing, and he is filled with joy as he recites the verses he has prepared in regard to the king. On such an occasion his is not a laborious task, but the words flow from his tongue as effortlessly as words from the pen of an accomplished writer. His song treats of a noble theme, and he delights to sing it. The melody and joy in his heart must find expression.

2. The Royal Bridegroom (45:2-9)

45:2 As the psalmist addresses the king, his words of praise are brief but significant for their content. **You are the most excellent of men**, or "You are more beautiful than all mankind." That physical beauty may here be indicated cannot be denied, but the reference may equally be to inward beauty or beauty of character. The latter seems to be indicated by the second clause of the verse, which may be translated, "Grace is poured out by your lips"[14] in contrast to the NIV's: **your lips have been anointed with grace.** (It is a bit awkward to say that grace was poured *upon* your lips.) The king has proven to be a gracious person, considerate, not devoid of sympathy. On account of this he has received God's blessing.

---

[14]Recognizing the Hebrew preposition with *lips* as instrumental dative.

45:3-5 A gracious king? Yes. A weakling? No! **Gird your sword upon your side.** Verses 3-5 do not necessarily infer that armed conflict is impending. The preparation is for a wedding, not for a military campaign. He is to champion the cause of truth, humility, and justice. It is in this direction that his strong right arm should do **awesome deeds.** Since he is the champion of just causes, it is proper to ask that his arrows find their mark in disposing of the enemy (v. 5). It is his responsibility to maintain justice and righteousness among God's people, and he is to be commended for doing so.

45:6a That the address to the king continues in verse 6 would seem to be beyond dispute. If it is read in the context of the verses preceding and following it, no other conclusion seems possible. Yet its wording is puzzling to many: **Your throne, O God, will last for ever and ever.** Accepting this translation — and it is the most natural rendering of the Hebrew — the first thought is of God's heavenly throne. Otherwise, if it is the throne of the bridegroom of the poem, then this individual is being addressed as *Elohim*, God. An alternate translation is possible: "Your throne (is) of God, for ever and ever." The New English Bible reads: "Your throne is like God's throne, eternal." However, although infrequent, the use of *Elohim* in reference to men or to heavenly beings is not unknown in the Scriptures. For example, God would make Moses to be a "god" to Pharaoh (Exod 7:1 — "Like a god" may be understood, but the text does not include the preposition. See also Exod 22:8,9; 1 Sam 28:13-14; and Zech 12:8). The king was the God-sent ruler and for that reason may have been addressed by the term *Elohim*. (Never, however, would a devout Yahwistic Hebrew consider the king to be deity.)[15] Yet as a king ordained by God, he is heir to an eternal throne.

45:6b-9 Noteworthy, at this point, is the nature of his kingdom. His **scepter,** the symbol of his authority to rule, is a **scepter of justice**; literally, "upright," "straight" (not crooked). His concern for **righteousness** has resulted in great joy, indicated by his being

---

[15]Dahood, not without some validity, would recognize the noun "throne" in verse 6 to be a verb. Thus: "The eternal and everlasting God has enthroned you" (*Psalms 1-50*, p. 269). Craigie concurs. However, the translation of the NIV stands as the normal reading of the text as it has come to us. This is the rendering also in Heb 1:8.

anointed with the **oil of joy**. Happiness, elusive to so many, has been his by the simple expedient of doing what is right in the sight of God! And now, on this joyful occasion, attired in robes bearing the fragrance of **myrrh and aloes and cassia** (perfumes of the choicest kind), he is greeted with music as he enters the palace – **From palaces adorned with ivory the music of the strings makes you glad.** (Ivory palaces were palaces having wall panels and furniture inlaid with ivory.) At this moment, "A princess takes her place among the noblest of your women, a royal lady at your side in gold of Ophir" (v. 9, NEB). On the basis of the Syriac version this translation is justified, the two parts of the verse thus being in synonymous parallelism.

3. Counsel for the Bride (45:10-12)

45:10-12 The psalmist offers words of counsel to the bride, assuring her that hers will be an honored position. **Listen, O daughter,** The words that follow are in the style of wisdom literature (cf. Prov 5:1; 7:1). **Consider and give ear** – "be attentive." In keeping with other Scripture relative to marriage, the summons is to **forget your people and your father's house.** From this time, she is to have a new loyalty, a new allegiance. Naturally, she will not cease to be a daughter, but now she is entering into a new relationship, one in which she is to be queen in her own household. It is understandable that the beginning of this new experience would stir feelings of trepidation in the heart of the bride (not to mention the nervousness of the groom). Yet she is assured that, in return for her loyalty, the union will be a happy one; she will be accepted by the king; he will **be enthralled by [her] beauty.** Her response is to **honor him.** "Since he is your lord, bow to him" (RSV). This is a literal translation and, taken literally, would mean to follow court protocol. But in context, the phrase appears to mean, "respect his wishes." The result would be that her place in the court would be one of honor and respect, and one of influence. Consequently, she would be approached by persons bringing requests and gifts. **The Daughter of Tyre will come with a gift.** (The Hebrew, "daughter of Tyre," is recognized as idiomatic, indicating "the people of.") Tyre was noted for its wealth in all manner of precious commodities

(Ezek 27), and even this richest of cities would delight to secure the favor of the new queen.

4. The Bridal Procession (45:13-15)

45:13a The precise rendering of verse 13a eludes us. Literally, it may be translated, "All glorious a princess within." Craigie is just as literal: "A princess is all honor within." This would indicate the quality of her character, matched outwardly by the splendor of her gold embroidered robes. Others would supply an object (as understood, so the NIV) for the preposition "within." Thus, "All glorious is the princess within *her chamber*" (NIV, cf. RSV). The New English Bible assumes that the "within" refers to the palace: "In the palace honour awaits her; she is a king's daughter." We may well accept the verse as in the King James Version: "The King's daughter is all glorious within," and leave the reader to resolve the ambiguity (if it exists) for himself or herself.

45:13b-15 The general content is clear enough. The bride is decked in her royal wedding garments and is led to the king, accompanied by her bridesmaids, **her virgin companions** (perhaps, closest friends). It is a time of great joy and merriment, the wedding of the king and his bride.

5. A Promise to the King (45:16-17)

45:16 Verses 16 and 17 are addressed to the king. This is clear from the Hebrew text, for the pronouns are masculine in gender. **Your sons will take the place of your fathers.** It is good to be acquainted with history to have an appreciation of the legacy that is ours, especially of the spiritual legacy that is bequeathed us. In addition genealogies may instruct and inspire us. But the inexorable march of time assures us that the future lies with the children God may be pleased to give us. How gracious of God to make such provision! The elderly among the people of God find joy when they witness the devotion, the talent, the dedication to the Lord, and the accomplishment of good by the succeeding generation.

The king in the psalm would rejoice to hear that his marriage would be blessed with children. These he would establish as **princes**, or governors, over the various provinces (cf. 2 Sam 8:18), **throughout the land.** (Also NEB.) Or, the translation may be, "in all the earth" (KJV, RSV). Here is an instance where inspiration may provide a term in Scripture with a double significance. For the immediate king, "throughout the land" may be the meaning, but for the Messiah King, "all the earth" is appropriate, since his realm was to be all the world (Matt 28:18-20).

45:17 I will perpetuate your memory through all generations. It is natural to suppose it is the psalmist who is speaking. Throughout the psalm his exuberant spirit has been evident. Now he assures the king that through the poet's efforts his renown will be perpetuated. **Therefore the nations will praise you for ever and ever.** This is high praise, indeed, because "nations," literally, "peoples," is a term that usually means Gentile nations. Evidently the poet expected widespread and continued regard to accrue to the king. To what extent did this follow the marriage of the king and his bride? If the king were Solomon, his fame is well attested. If some other, we do not know. For the King who was to come to establish an everlasting kingdom, the Messiah King, the prophecy was fulfilled to the letter.

As to the ultimate significance of the psalm, whatever king the psalmist may have been addressing, the Christian sees here the Messiah, the heavenly bridegroom, the bride being the church (that is, the totality of the redeemed and purified). The relationship is stated most clearly by the apostle Paul: "Husbands, love your wives, just as Christ loved the church and gave himself up for her to make her holy, cleansing her by the washing with water through the word, and to present her to himself as a radiant church . . ." (Eph 5:25-27).

Some consider the psalm to be an allegory. If so, one should be cautious in attempting to make every word a prediction. (It has been proposed, for example, that the "daughters of kings" of verse 9 indicate the various national groups that are drawn to the Messiah.) What is clear is that the figure of a marriage indicates the closeness of the relationship and the depth of the love existing between Christ and the church. And since it is a royal marriage that is celebrated, the significance of the allegory is heightened.

III. THE PRAISE FOR THE REDEEMER (46:1–48:14)

A. GOD AS HELP AND REFUGE (46:1-11)

The inspiration of Luther's grand hymn, "A Mighty Fortress Is Our God," this psalm, from beginning to end, speaks of God's awesome power and sustaining presence.[16] He is sovereign over the cataclysmic forces of nature — earthquake and raging sea (vv. 1-3). His presence with his people provides refuge from the threats of warring nations (vv. 4-7). He brings the schemes of mighty empires to nought — "breaks the bow and shatters the spear" — bringing wars to an end (vv. 8-9). In view of the above, the psalm has been designated a Hymn of Praise, although it does not fall into the general pattern of praise hymns. It is better to think of it as a hymn of confidence (as Craigie identifies it).

The psalm has an affinity with the "Songs of Zion" (48, 76, 87). These are psalms that extol Zion (Jerusalem) as the dwelling place of the Lord, the place specially chosen by him for his abode, the temple being his sanctuary. Here God reigned, and for that reason his people experienced the protection due to his presence. (See Ps 78:68-69.) Gunkel accepted this classification, defining the psalm more specifically as an "eschatological Song of Zion" (concerned with future manifestations of God's sovereignty). Events of the future may be incorporated in the psalm, but it seems basically to be an acknowledgment of the power of God and of the protection he has afforded his people in delivering them from some recent great crisis that would have destroyed them. And so we consider the setting to be some definite historical round of events.

This view is widely held. However, there is no unanimity of opinion as to what historical moment may be the setting of the psalm. Often cited is the invasion of the land in 701 B.C. by

---

[16]Whether it be Demetrius, Grand Prince of Russia, when confronted by the rapacious Tartars on the banks of the River Don (A.D. 1380); Martin Luther, who, when feeling his courage ebb, would say to Melanchthon, "Come, Philip, let us sing the 46th Psalm" (ca. 1520); or American Prisoners in North Vietnam, the psalm has been a source of courage to many through the ages. See Prothero, *The Psalms in Human Life*, pp. 83, 123.

Sennacherib, when Jerusalem was spared destruction only by God's intervention on her behalf (2 Kgs 19:35-36). But the psalm praises God as much for protection from catastrophic natural forces as for deliverance from attacking armies (vv. 2-3). Unless both dangers threatened at one time, we need not find the setting of the psalm in one solitary historic episode. This is not to say that the psalmist does not refer to actual moments of deliverance by the Lord, some of which he and his people had witnessed (v. 9). However, he may be reciting history as well as recording it, referring to more than one deliverance that God had provided. In any case, we agree with Eerdmans when he says, "This is not a psalm from dreamland . . . . It is founded on reality. 'Go and see what devastation Jahu has made!'"[17] Whatever the setting, the relevance of the psalm transcends any local situation, pointing to the universal nature of the sovereignty of God (v. 9).

Even a casual reading will reveal that Psalm 46 bears a close relationship to Psalms 47 and 48 that follow. All three are concerned with a single theme: God is sovereign and is the refuge of his people, the latter thought, especially, being the focus of Psalm 46. This theme is stated in the opening words and repeated in the refrain (vv. 7,11).

1. No Cause for Fear (46:1-3)

46:1 God is our refuge and strength. A twofold significance is evident in these words. There is a tacit and unashamed admission of a need for help. There are some who go through life never admitting such a need, so confident are they of their own self-sufficiency. But inevitably the moment of truth will come, the realization of one's ultimate insecurity and the confession of his innate need for companionship and help. In the psalm, these people had experienced their need. More significantly, they knew themselves to possess a security that was from God.

One should note the plural pronoun "our" in the verse. There are times when the child of God rejoices in saying, "The Lord is my shepherd," expressing his own personal relationship with God. But

---

[17]Eerdmans, *The Hebrew Book*, p. 254.

there is enhancement of the joy when he can stand with others and glory in "our refuge and strength." The Scriptures place great emphasis upon the individual as the object of God's concern and of his mercy, and it is as individuals that we enter into God's fellowship. But always it is "individual in community," as we have noted, not in isolation. (This was true of the Jewish community. It is equally true of the church as the family of God.) In expressing confidence in God, one's joy is increased when it is a shared experience.

The latter part of verse 1 may be translated, literally: "A help in troubles (God) has been found to be, exceedingly." These are not words of speculation; they are testimony to that which has been the experience of these people, a song they delight in singing.

46:2-3 Verse 2 begins with an emphatic **therefore.** Since God is present to help us, therefore, we will not fear. It is as simple as that! There is no assertion here that difficulties will not arise, that times of testing will not come. But "when the earth is changed" (this is the meaning of the Hebrew) "even to the point that the mountains fall into the sea," the people of God will not fear! Roaring waters and shaking mountains will not avail to dislodge their confidence in God.

2. Cause for Great Gladness (46:4-7)

46:4-6 The book of Hebrews refers to "what can be shaken" and to "what cannot be shaken" (12:27). This contrast is incorporated into the psalm. Here we find three uses of the Hebrew word מוֹט (môṭ, meaning "to totter," "to stumble," "to reel," or "to fall"). In the volatile realm of nature, "mountains" may "fall" (v. 2). In the continuing march of history, **nations are in uproar, kingdoms fall.** So be it. But – in bold contrast – the city of Zion with God in her midst **will not fall.** "God's solid foundation stands firm" (2 Tim 2:19).

There is a river whose streams make glad the city of God. Here the river and its streams provide a metaphor of the life-sustaining and refreshing power of God in the midst of his people. Perhaps it is only those whose lands have been deprived of water for an extended period of time who can fully appreciate an ever-flowing stream. The psalmist envisions no treacherous wadi, but a perennial fountain flowing in the city of God. This city is not identified, but Jerusalem is to be understood. (In Ps 48:2 Zion is called "the city of the Great King.") Here stood the temple of God, and some in Israel were certain of their security because of that fact (Jer 7:2-8). The psalm makes clear, however, that it is not the temple but the presence of God that provides security. God is in the midst of her; she shall not be moved. What confidence! As a city, Zion is really not that impressive. In the days of King Hezekiah her walls encompassed less than one hundred acres! Indeed, "God chose the weak things of the world to shame the strong" (1 Cor 1:27). And even though the whole world conspire against him, he need only speak the word (**lifts his voice**) and **the earth melts.** In context, the melting seems to be on the part of the nations and kingdoms that rage. As God brings judgment, their hearts melt in fear and they themselves melt away.

46:7 The confidence and joy that all of this inspires is enhanced by reflection on the nature of the God who does this for his people. Two significant attributes of God are indicated in verse 7. When the people say, **The LORD Almighty is with us**, they are recognizing God in his unlimited power to accomplish his will. The designation "LORD Almighty" (literally, "Yahweh of hosts" or "Yahweh Sabaoth") is used many times in the Scriptures. (In the NT it appears as "Lord Almighty," Rom 9:29, Jas 5:4. See the explanation of this usage in the Preface of any NIV Bible.) It means that God has at his disposal sufficient forces, whether it be the armies of Israel (1 Sam 17:45) or angelic hosts (1 Kgs 22:19) to ensure victory. If such a God is the refuge of a people, why should they fear? But there is a further consideration. He is also the God of Jacob, the God who has chosen to enter into covenant with his people. It is, then, the omnipotent God, who has also shown himself to be a God of grace and mercy, who has become **our fortress**, or "the stronghold" of his people. How simply verse 7 states this! **The LORD Almighty is with us; the God of Jacob is our fortress.** As a refrain, the words are repeated at the end of the psalm, and there is reason to believe that they once stood also at the close of verse 3. (Note that the word *Selah* appears at all three places.) The words cannot fail to bring reassurance to the hearts of any people who can speak them in truth.

3. The God Who Acts (46:8-11)

Verses 8 and 9 adduce the evidence of God's governance in the world. This is no God on the periphery of life, or beyond, no distant deity totally removed from the affairs of humankind, but a God active in the world he has created and among the peoples of that world.

46:8 Come and see the works of the LORD. This is a jubilant invitation, not to a forensic bout but to a consideration of the nature and purposes of God as revealed in what he has done and in what he does. And what are those works? **Desolations . . . on the earth?** Perhaps. The Hebrew שַׁמּוֹת (*šammôth*) signifies "appalling" or "marvelous" things, and in the context of verses 8 and 9 may speak of God's judgment upon warring nations. Whatever direction the judgment may take, it will be brought about in marvelous ways (or, appalling). (This was especially true of the decimation of the Assyrian army encamped about Jerusalem in 701 B.C. — 2 Kgs 19:32-36.)

46:9-10 Verse 9 opens with a participle and may be rendered: "(He is) the one making wars to cease throughout the world" (in an ongoing process). We may see here reflected the message of the prophets as they envisioned a time of universal peace that is to come (see Isa 2:4). In the meantime, it is possible for the people of God to experience peace in their own hearts now. **Be still, and know that I am God.** The summons of verse 8 was for a purpose, as revealed in verse 10. "Come and see" in order that you may "be still and know." In other words, God is calling the raging world to "Stop! Be quiet! Stop your babbling and warring! Know that I am the one and only God!"

From time immemorial there is evidence of the inborn longing of the human soul to know God. Here is the bold assertion that it is possible to know him. However, the assertion is not made on philosophical grounds; neither is it an *a priori* assumption. Rather, it is based on observable evidence that convinced those who sang this psalm (along with myriads of others who give their witness throughout the Scriptures) that God is active in the affairs of men. How may one know God? "Come and see." Examine the evidence and then pursue the course it marks out. Then one will know experientially its validity.

46:11 How else does one propose to cope with all of the factors in modern life that multiply tension? One who has come to know God will suppress the impulse to scream, will relax and know a "peace . . . which transcends all understanding" and find a strength to help in time of need. Then he can lift his voice and join with others in singing the chorus: "The Lord of hosts is with us; the God of Jacob is our refuge" (KJV wording).

B. GOD AS BENEFACTOR AND SOVEREIGN LORD (47:1-9)

Unmistakably Psalm 47 is a praise hymn extolling Yahweh as God Most High and King over all the earth. It would appear that the psalm arose as the overflow of joy following some national triumph, a companion piece to Psalm 46. There we have a song of confidence as the response of the people of the Lord to the realization of God's sovereignty over the world — "We will not fear." Here the circumstances are similar, but the response is an outpouring of praise — "Sing praises to God, sing praises" (v. 6).

Mowinckel considered Psalm 47, along with Psalms 93, 96–99, to be a clear example of an *enthronement psalm,* prepared for cultic use, and incorporated into an annual celebration of the kingship of the Lord over his people. The recital of verse 5, "God has ascended amid shouts of joy," is thus said to signal God's reenthronement at the moment in the festive procession when the ark of the Lord, as the shrine of God, was brought into the temple, accompanied by shouts of homage from the people and blasts from the trumpet. That such a procession did take place in the time of David is recorded in 2 Sam 6:17, and that religious processions were a part of the practice of Judaism is beyond dispute. (See Ps 132:7-8.) But that there was an annual reenactment of the enthronement of Yahweh is greatly questioned by many.[18]

An "historical" view of the psalm seems better to account for its origin. Eerdmans states, quite simply, "The psalm is a reflection of

---

[18]See the discussion of Enthronement Psalms on pp. 55-57 in the Introduction.

recent events."[19] He views the occasion as an assembly in Jerusalem of volunteers from all the tribes of Israel, preparatory to being led to victory by the Lord — "He subdued nations under us" (v. 3). In his view, verse 9 indicates that the princes of the people (with their troops) were then in Jerusalem, ready to march. The psalm was thus a hymn of praise preparatory to battle.

It seems rather that the psalm is a reaction to a victory, or victories, already achieved. It is a worship hymn, with special emphasis upon the universal reign of God, celebrating what he has accomplished — and will yet accomplish — for his people. J.J.M. Roberts sees a "religio-political" background as the provenance of the psalm, viewing it as "a cultic celebration of Yahweh's imperial accession" (not reenthronement).[20] The gathering of the princes, in verse 9, he sees as a cultic assembly. Roberts finds the psalm to be "based on the relatively recent victories of David's age, which raised Israel from provincial obscurity to an empire of the first rank."[21] The subjugation of surrounding nations would be an indication that Yahweh is not a provincial deity, but ruler over all nations.

Claus Westermann recognizes the psalm as incorporating the historical motif, with its recognition of the Lord as the God of history. However, he would date it in the postexilic period and describe it as "historical-eschatological" in nature.[22] Assuming his dating to be correct, his conclusion would be justified. At a time when Israel had been reduced to a subordinate position, with no king of her own, still faith triumphed. Based on God's dealings in the past and with confidence in the future, the (eschatological) reign of God over all of the peoples of the earth is spoken of as an accomplished fact although it is yet in the future. (Westermann identifies the verbs of verse 8 as prophetic perfect, i.e., referring to a future event as if it has already taken place.)

However, in the reading of the psalm, one cannot miss the note of jubilation that is present throughout. This would seem more to

---

[19]Eerdmans, *The Hebrew Book*, p. 255.

[20]J.J.M. Roberts, "The Religio-Political Setting of Psalm 47," *BASOR*, No. 221 (Feb., 1976): 132.

[21]Ibid.

[22]Claus Westermann, *Praise and Lament in the Psalms* (Atlanta: John Knox Press, 1981), p. 147f.

be the response to some recent great victory Israel had experienced than to the anticipation of a future triumph. This is not to say that the psalm is without eschatological significance but would make a preexilic date to be preferred. In this case, the psalm would be a hymn of praise for God's care for his people and of proclamation of his universal sovereignty. The theme of the psalm, repeated in its two stanzas, is quite simple: "Sing praises to God" (vv. 1,6) because he is "a great King over all the earth" (vv. 2,7). The first stanza declares God's kingship in relation to his choosing to establish Israel as a people, the second in relation to his reign as sovereign over all nations.

1. Praise God Who Has Blessed Israel (47:1-5)

47:1-2 We believe the psalm was intended for use in the worship of God in Jerusalem. Consequently, the call to worship with which it opens would be addressed to the people of Israel, assembled for worship. Eerdmans's translation of verse 1 is in keeping with this view: "O clap your hands, all ye clans" (that is, clans of Israel).[23] This is in distinction from the translation, **Clap your hands, all you nations** (NIV). True, the noun עַמִּים (*'ammîm*) is plural — "clans," "nations" (NIV), "peoples" (RSV), and in verse 3 it does refer to people of other nations. But it seems too ironic to invite these nations to join Israel in praise because God subjugates them to Israel (v. 3)! As for the latter, they have abundant reasons for joyful praise, five of these being evident in verse 2. **How awesome is the LORD Most High, the great King over all the earth!** Note, first of all, that this God whom they praise is the "LORD" (Yahweh), the God who revealed himself to Moses personally as the God of Israel (Exod 3:6-15), and ever faithful. Again, he is the LORD "Most High," "exalted far above all gods" (Ps 97:9). (The title "Most High" is a translation of עֶלְיוֹן (*'Elyôn*), the name of God as honored by Melchizedek — Gen 14:18-20.) Third, he is **awesome**; that is, holy fear takes hold of the one beholding him; awe-inspiring by his appearance. Fourth, he is a "great King," one whose rule is with

---

[23]Eerdmans, *The Hebrew Book*, p. 254.

complete authority and power. And fifth, his dominion extends "over all the earth." This is his nature. Who would not worship such a God as this? The psalm need not add that he is the living God; that fact was the foundation stone of Israel's faith.

47:3-4 But there are other reasons why Israel sings his praises, reasons centered in God's mighty acts on behalf of his people. The verbs describing these acts in verses 3 and 4 may be translated past (NIV, RSV), present (ASV), or future (KJV), indicating experiences in Israel's past, the present reality, or help anticipated in the future. The translation, "He subdues nations under us," would convey the full scope of meaning, describing as it does God's continuous concern for his people. A special reason for praise was God's fulfillment of his promise to Abraham that his descendants would become many and inherit the land of Canaan (Gen 13:14-16). With confidence they can say, **He chose our inheritance for us.** This "inheritance" they call **the pride** (also RSV) **of Jacob,** "the excellency" (KJV) or, that is, Israel's cherished possession. In the psalm there is no attempt to explain why God has favored Israel except to recognize that his providing them with this inheritance is a demonstration of his love for Jacob; that is, for Jacob and his descendants.

47:5 At this point the thought of the first stanza is completed. The call has been to praise God for who he is — his great majesty, sovereignty, and power — and because he has delivered Israel and bestowed upon them their heritage. The term **Selah** marks this close. Now, **God has ascended amid shouts of joy.** The Most High God ascends on high. (The Hebrew terms for "most high" and for "ascends" are similar.) Having given victory to his people, the Lord now returns to his heavenly domain. This is the understanding of the phrase by many. In this case, the "shouts of joy" and **sounding of trumpets** would seem to be descriptive only and not to be understood literally. However, when the psalm is viewed as incorporated into a worship ceremony, the shouts and the sounding of the trumpets will be seen to be the natural accompaniment of the announcement of God's ascension. This would be true whether the ascension is symbolized by the transport of the ark of God in a procession into the temple, or we have simply a public proclamation of the fact.

2. Praise God Who Reigns over All Nations (47:6-9)

47:6-7 The call to worship is repeated and intensified in verse 6 with its fourfold use of the plural imperative (and again in verse 7). **Sing praises!** From the root זָמַר (*zāmar*) from which we get the word for "psalm" (*mizmôr*), the basic meaning is "to make music," but the term is used almost exclusively in the Scriptures to indicate singing praises to God. (An exception is found in Ps 149:3. Here the very same verb appears and is properly translated, "*Making melody* to him with timbrel and lyre," RSV, italics added). In verse 7 the admonition is to sing praises "with understanding" (a possible translation), or "skillfully" (recognizing the adverbial use of the final noun). The inference is that the excellencies of God are of such a nature as to call for one's praise in the most skillful manner of which he is capable.

47:8-9 At the moment it is awareness of God's universal dominion that has stirred the hearts and emotions of the people. The object of Israel's devotion is no tribal deity, but the God who is over all. This much they are convinced of. God said it (see Amos 1:3-2:3) and their experience and observation had confirmed it. So they declare: **God reigns over the nations**; that is, over the Gentile nations.[24] Whether or not people of other nations were then in Jerusalem praising the Lord along with Israel cannot be determined with certainty. Verse 9 is the key, but unfortunately the rendering of the text is not universally agreed upon. A literal translation would be: "The princes of peoples assemble, people of the God of Abraham" (compare KJV). This would seem to exclude the people of other nations. Many, however, would insert "as" (NIV):

---

[24]All people are thus accountable to God. How far his permissive will extends to those who would rebel against his sovereignty we may not know until his judgment falls upon them. But because of his sovereignty, all human attempts to absolutize power have been and will be brought to failure. As to human rule, the concept in the Scriptures is that the king on the throne in Jerusalem is God's servant, anointed as God's representative, and responsible to God to rule with righteousness and equity. It is in this light that we should read Paul's words to Titus: "Be subject to rulers and authorities" (3:1). The only "divine right of kings" in the Scriptures is the right to do the holy will of the God who sits upon his holy throne.

The nobles of the nations assemble as the people of the God of Abraham; or "with" into the verse[25] (NEB): "The princes of the nations assemble with the families of Abraham's line." Craigie views the text in this light but describes such joint participation in the worship of the Lord as "a limited reality, which was present for only a short period in Israel's history" (perhaps at the height of David's reign).[26]

However, the present writer believes the call to worship of Psalm 47 to be directed to Israel alone (see comment on v. 1). This being true, we have then in verse 9, a joyous assembly of Hebrew peoples because they have had recent evidence that "God reigns over the nations," that **the kings** (literally, "the shields" = rulers) **of the earth belong to God.** Yet the thought that Gentiles would join with the seed of Abraham in the praise of God was not foreign to Israel. God had promised Abraham that in his seed all of the nations would be blessed (Gen 12:3). "Foreigners" would come to "love the name of the LORD," and God would "give them joy" in his house, which would become "a house of prayer for all nations" (Isa 56:6-7). Eventually, the plan of God uniting the peoples of all nations in the worship of the one God would be revealed. Beginning with Jesus, it would be consummated at that time when "the kingdom of the world has become the kingdom of our Lord and of his Christ, and he will reign for ever and ever" (Rev 11:15). Then it may be said with deeper meaning than of old, **he is greatly exalted!**

C. PRAISE GOD AND REJOICE IN ZION, HIS HOLY CITY (48:1-14)

We have observed in Psalm 46 that the reaction of God's people to his presence in Jerusalem is confidence — "We will not fear; . . . God . . . is with us." In Psalm 47 the response is jubilant praise —

---

[25]In the unpointed Hebrew text the word for "with" and the word for "people" are exactly the same, עַם, and would have appeared side by side. This may have resulted in an inadverdent omission of the preposition by a copyist.

[26]Craigie, *Psalms 1–50*, p. 350.

"Shout to God with cries of joy," for Jerusalem's King is "King of all the earth."

In Psalm 48, another of the "Hymns of Zion," the key word would seem to be "appreciation." The beauty and the glory of the city, deriving from the presence of God in her midst, are not to be considered commonplace. Thought is given also to the stabilizing influence of God's "right hand," which is "filled with righteousness" (v. 10). The love or loving-kindness (ḥesed) of the Lord is especially significant and is worthy of one's deep meditation (v. 9). From the reading of the Psalm one cannot but notice the joy (and excusable pride?) with which the city is viewed. Yet, from first to last, there is the tacit acknowledgment that the greatness of the city is not inherent; it is God in her midst that gives her greatness. "Great is the LORD" is the theme, not "Great is Jerusalem." The city is great because God is great. And when one has come to know and to appreciate the beauty (and the security) of Jerusalem, he is to go and tell the following generation, not that it was great, but that it has a great God (v. 14).

Many consider Psalm 48, like 46, to be a celebration of a recent deliverance of Jerusalem from a powerful attack; either this, or a praise song growing out of a long history of the city's preservation by the mercy of God and by his power. In either case, it is a deep awareness of the Lord's love for Zion, and of his care; that is the basis for the psalm. Mowinckel, however, does not interpret the psalm in an historical light. (He speaks of it as "quasi-historical.")[27] In keeping with his cultic approach to the psalms he sees this as a drama, presented by the worshipers. The attack of the kings (vv. 4-6), as part of the drama, is indicative of "all the kings and nations of the earth."[28] But they are crushed by the Lord. This, Mowinckel would say, is not a recital of history nor a prediction of things to come (eschatology) but is, as drama, a visible presentation by the worshipers of "what faith knew to be happening."[29] Afterwards they could say, "So have we seen in the city of the LORD Almighty" — they had just witnessed the victory — "God makes her [the city]

---

[27]Mowinckel, *The Psalms in Israel's Worship*, 1:110.
[28]Ibid., p. 151.
[29]Ibid., p. 181.

secure for ever" (v. 8). The deliverance, Mowinckel says, "in an 'ideal' and real sense is [a reality] repeated whenever Yahweh appears as king, victorious in the festival."[30] Should any dare attack the city, it was then believed that the 'ideal' would become empirical reality, with the certain defeat of any nation so presumptuous. This view would make of the psalm, basically, a ritual to ensure the continual preservation of Jerusalem.

However, the psalm reflects such a state of joy and enthusiasm that it seems to be the expression of what has been experienced rather than an acting out of what might be. It is in the nature of a glad song of a dweller in Jerusalem, such as he might sing to a pilgrim visiting the city. From the opening declaration of God's greatness (v. 1) to the description of the flight of enemy kings (vv. 4-6), to the invitation to "walk about Zion" (vv. 12-14), the psalm appears to be the reflection of the attempt of someone to share his faith, not to dramatize it. In doing so the focus is, first of all, upon God, as the object of praise, then, upon the city that is graced by his presence. This is followed by a meditation on God's goodness, addressed to God (vv. 9-11) and a call to observe the city in order to share with the next generation the glory of Jerusalem's God.

1. God, the Object of Praise (48:1a)

48:1a Great is the LORD, and most worthy of praise. The greatness of the Lord is everywhere proclaimed in the OT as it was realized and experienced by his people. Here it is his greatness as sovereign and protector of Jerusalem that is in view. In Ps 47:2 he is "the great King over all the earth." Elsewhere he is great in his works (Deut 11:7), great in his mercy or compassion (Isa 54:7), and his faithfulness (Lam 3:23). The glory of Jerusalem is extolled in this psalm, but there is no shadow of a doubt that it is a reflected glory. To God, and to him alone, belongs the true glory and the praise. Nevertheless, the beauty and security he has brought to the city is worthy of acclaim.

---

[30]Ibid., p. 151.

2. The Beauty, Joy, and Security of Zion (48:1b-8)

48:1b The high esteem of the psalmist for Jerusalem is indicated in the titles that are used designating it. First, and most significantly, it is **the city of our God**, this being its chief glory, that God is in its midst. It is **his holy mountain**, the site of his holy temple, where he may be approached in prayer and supplication. But this is no localized deity. Solomon marveled that God would dwell upon planet earth at all. "The heavens, even the highest heaven, cannot contain you," he said. Yet he could pray that God's eyes be open day and night toward this place and expect that his prayer would be answered (1 Kgs 8:27-29). Any place where God meets man is holy, and this was true of the temple in Jerusalem.

48:2a Again, the city is **beautiful in its loftiness** (a possible translation). Also, it is **the joy of the whole earth!** In what sense the psalmist means this we cannot say. It is possible that in his exuberance he makes use of hyperbole. Potentially, the designation may be taken most literally. The word of the Lord, bringing salvation and life to humankind, was to go out from Jerusalem (Isa 2:3) and would bring joy to all who would receive it.

48:2b-6 One of the most cherished designations of the city was Mount Zion, designating Jerusalem as the place where God chose to dwell (Isa 8:18), "on the sides of the north," (KJV) or, "in the far north" (RSV). These are translations of צָפוֹן יַרְכְּתֵי (yark*thê ṣaphôn*). In Hebrew *ṣaphôn* came to be commonly used to indicate the north. But the term is also a proper name and is so translated in the NIV: **heights of Zaphon**. This name is quite common in Canaanite mythology, designating the place of the assembly of the gods (comparable to Mount Olympus in Greek mythology), and is so used in Isa 14:13. (In Isaiah the NIV translates, "the utmost heights of the sacred mountain.")[31] However, the psalmist's interest is not with mythology but with reality. "It has been stated," he might say, "that the gods dwell in the far north, in Zaphon. Then you should know that Jerusalem is 'Zaphon,' because this is where God is; this is the place where he has chosen to 'dwell,' and there is

---

[31]The Hebrew is the same in the psalm and in Isaiah, except that the latter includes the preposition "in."

347

nothing mythological about it." **God is in her citadels; he has shown himself to be her fortress.** And this forthright statement is followed by an example of the effectiveness of this defense (vv. 4-6), expressed most succinctly in the Hebrew: "Kings assembled, advanced together. They saw, were astonished — they were terrified! They fled."

48:7 We have no way of identifying the kings here spoken of. Some believe them to have been Canaanite kings of the coastlands (kings of Tyre and Sidon?). These peoples engaged in sea trade and amassed great wealth. But any designs they may have had upon Jerusalem were doomed to failure. Their seagoing vessels, **ships of Tarshish**, whereby they acquired the means to wage war, were no match for the devastating **east wind** of the Lord. It is possible, however, that the reference to the "ships of Tarshish" is a metaphor (some Hebrew manuscripts insert the preposition "like," which the NIV follows). This meaning is also conveyed by the rendering of the NEB: "[The kings] are seized with trembling, they toss in pain like a woman in labour, like the ships of Tarshish when an east wind wrecks them" (vv. 6-7).

48:8 In verse 8 the pronoun "we" appears as the subject of the verbs. The words may well be those of a group of pilgrims who have come to Jerusalem. They had heard of its wonders and of the wonders of its God, and now they give their testimony. **As we have heard, so have we seen.** The response of these pilgrims is in sharp contrast to that of the kings who had come with hostile intent. These latter had seen the city and had been panic-stricken. (We must conclude that it was something more than the sight of the city walls that struck terror in their hearts. In some way they must have seen evidence that the Lord was Jerusalem's "sure defense" — v. 3, RSV.) The pilgrims saw the same city and recognized it as a place of refuge for the same reason that the kings had been filled with fear; they recognized that God was in this place. Now they feel drawn to the city's inhabitants in praising God for the mercy and care he has shown the holy city.

3. Meditation (48:9-11)

48:9 The words of the pilgrims continue in verses 9-11, words of praise and thanksgiving addressed to God. **We meditate on your unfailing love.** A precise translation of the verb in this instance is elusive, but it means something more than merely "thinking" about something.[32] The root idea of the Hebrew דָּמָה (*dāmāh*) is "to be like." (The noun "likeness" is from this root.) The form of the verb in our text appears in Isa 40:18 — "To whom, then, will you *compare* God?" The verb at times connotes the process of forming parables. Quite literally, then, Eerdmans translates the present verse: "We make epigrams on thy kindness."[33] If this appears to be a bit too literal, the following may be the general understanding of the verse: "Here in the hour of worship, Lord, we take the time to ponder your steadfast love, have considered what it may be likened to, and find it to be incomparable." The lovingkindness (KJV, usually translated "love" in the NIV) of God is an inexhaustible theme for meditation.

48:10 Like your name, O God, your praise reaches to the ends of the earth. The name of God is a symbol of his person, of his nature and character as they have been established. The name is also a symbol of his presence and power. The praise accorded God to the ends of the earth is "praise (his) name deserves" (v. 10, NEB), because he may be relied upon. He is as trustworthy as his name indicates.

Your right hand is filled with righteousness, "filled with victory" (RSV), "charged with justice" (NEB). All three translations contribute to an understanding of the phrase. The Hebrew term צְדָקָה (*ṣᵉdāqāh*) means conformity to an established standard or norm (not deviant). When used of God, it has a twofold dimension. It means not only that the deeds of his powerful hand are morally pure and clean, but "charged with justice," they are so designed as to promote and to maintain right relationships, as a demonstration

---

[32]Briggs chooses "ponder" for his translation. Other suggestions: "reflected" (Craigie, Dahood), "consider" (Buttenwieser), "think about" (Kraus). The NEB uses "re-enact," reflecting the view that the psalm is drama.

[33]Eerdmans, *The Hebrew Book*, p. 256.

of his righteousness. By his right hand he brings deliverance and vindication to his people and punishment or retribution ("judgments," v. 11) to the wicked. Thus is his hand "filled with victory."

48:11 Thoughts of God's steadfast love, reflection upon who he is and what he has done for his people, leads to an overflowing of praise. **Mount Zion rejoices, the villages of Judah are glad because of your judgments.** Now those who have joined in the praise of God and of the city of God are ready to be commissioned.

4. Appreciation and Proclamation (48:12-14)

48:12-13 Walk about Zion . . . consider well . . . that you may tell. The pilgrims have found ample reason to praise the Lord, especially for the glory that he has bestowed on Zion, the holy city. It is beautiful and, with God in its midst, secure. Enemies have threatened but have retreated in panic, giving reason why God should be glorified. Now those who have seen and who have thrilled to this must return to their various villages. And that all may keep the memory fresh in their minds, they are instructed to take one more walk around the city, appreciating fully its beauty and its security as the city of God.

48:14 It may have been to take part in a religious procession that the invitation was given. However, since we believe that the psalm arose out of an actual experience (or experiences) of God's deliverance, we consider the careful inspection that is enjoined to be significant. By noting closely the condition of the walls, the towers, the ramparts, the citadels, it will be seen that the enemy has left them unscathed. Zion stands firm. Yet even as the pilgrims evaluate the excellent condition of the city's fortifications, they realize that these could not, of themselves, have withstood the onslaught of the battering rams of an enemy such as the Assyrians. No, it was not the walls alone that provided the security of Jerusalem but the presence of God in her midst. This is the message that they must share with their children, the next generation. **For this God is our God for ever and ever.** Tell of Jerusalem? Yes, the glorious city, but be sure to make it clear that there can be no Jerusalem, no holy city, apart from the presence within it of the God of righteousness and holiness.

IV. THE REDEMPTION OF GOD'S PEOPLE
(49:1–51:19)

A. MORE PRECIOUS THAN RICHES (49:1-20)

In the parable of the sower Jesus refers to the "deceitfulness of wealth" (Matt 13:22) that keeps people out of the kingdom of God. Psalm 49 deals with the same theme, although in not quite such a definitive manner. The psalm may be classified as belonging to the *wisdom* group. Verses 3 and 4 make this quite clear (cf. Prov 1:2,6). As such, it approaches its subject as an *enigma* to be solved, a *puzzle* that may be designated the *riddle* of life. Of significance is the observation that men who trust in their wealth (v. 6) are only like the beasts that perish (v. 12). It is not said that they perish *because of* their wealth. The point is that they perish *in spite of* it, thus indicating the ultimate failure of riches (and of the god Mammon) to meet the needs of humankind. One element of the riddle, then, is this: If wealth, which is so universally pursued as the *summum bonum* of life, is in actuality such a deceitful goal, and its possessor is only to perish with it in the grave, is there an alternative? The psalmist believes that there is and that he has found it. Instead of putting his trust in riches, he will trust in God, confident that God will redeem him from the power of Sheol.

Not surfacing to any great extent, but present nevertheless, is another factor in the riddle, namely, the existence of gross inequalities in life. The psalmist is surrounded by "wicked deceivers" (v. 5) who, nevertheless, enjoy great riches and a sumptuous life. Underneath the surface is the ages-old question, "Why do the wicked prosper? Why do the righteous suffer?" The problem of the inequities of life on earth is expressed so poignantly by Job. God himself had declared this man to be "blameless and upright" (Job 1:8). Even so, he lost all of his possessions and all of his children. In addition he was afflicted with a painful and distressing ailment. How fraught with feeling, then, his question: "Why do the wicked live on, growing old and increasing in power?" (Job 21:7). "They see their children established around them" (he had lost ten), "their homes are safe and free from fear," their herds productive. They "spend their years in prosperity and go down to the grave in peace"

— no lingering illness, no pain. And these are persons who have openly denounced God! (Job 21:8-15). Is not the way of life on this earth puzzling indeed?

True, certain blessings do accrue to the righteous and penalties fall upon the wicked. There is no denying the truth that "a man reaps what he sows" (Gal 6:7). Psalm 1, dealing with the righteous man and the wicked, speaks specifically to this matter. And elsewhere it is written: "Blessed is the man who fears the LORD. . . . Wealth and riches are in his house, . . . Surely he will never be shaken, . . . The wicked man will see and be vexed" (Psalm 112:1,3, 6,10). Yet often the ungodly seem to escape the punishment due them for their evil. Not only so but, as Job noted, they enjoy their wealth and good health, the richest pleasures of life. Sometimes retribution is exacted of them, but the exceptions are too numerous to allow the formulation of any rigid equation of desert and fortune in this life. The inequities existing between "the low and the high, the rich and the poor" continue all the way to the grave.

From the psalm it becomes obvious that there were many in that long ago day, as there are now, who were certain that the closest approach to an answer to what life is all about lies in the accumulation and enjoyment of wealth. The psalmist sees this approach as woefully inadequate. First of all, the life that is so motivated is easily enticed to evil (see vv. 5,6). In addition, the hard reality remains that all of the money in the world cannot ransom a soul from death. Twice it is stated that man "in his pomp" (RSV), "despite his riches" (NIV), perishes like the beasts (vv. 12,20).

The psalmist knows that there is a better solution to the enigma and he calls upon all the world to hear his words. His words are addressed to humankind, not to God. That is the nature of wisdom literature, in contrast with most of the psalms. Elsewhere, God may be called upon to see, and to act on behalf of the petitioner, but at no point in this psalm is the deity addressed. The problem is a dilemma confronting humankind, that must be dealt with by every individual, and the writer would share with all who would hear its solution.

1. Words for All to Hear (49:1-4)

49:1-2 Truth is universal; it knows no racial barriers. This is no less so with spiritual truth. Note, then, that the psalm is not directed to Israel alone, but here is wisdom for all the world to hear. No distinction is made in its relevancy because of class; it is applicable to all – **both low and high, rich and poor alike.** The poor will be encouraged to know that God will redeem. The rich will be warned that they cannot evade death, the "great leveler." Both will learn that there does not exist a solution to the puzzle of life apart from God.

49:3-4 My mouth will speak words of wisdom. The term for "wisdom" is plural, hence, the NIV's translation: "words of wisdom." The speaker promises a full measure of wisdom on the matter. **The utterance from my heart will give understanding**; that is, will give light on the problem and provide its resolution. This promise is no expression of egotism but comes from the speaker's assurance that this wisdom is from God. This we gather from verse 4 – **I will turn my ear.** "I will listen attentively to what I hear" (from God, being understood). It is this that will attest to the validity of his message. **With the harp I will expound my riddle.** The problem, together with the solution, will be recited in song, to the accompaniment of stringed instruments.

2. The Problem (49:5-6)

49:5-6 The problem is stated in verse 5, **Why should I fear when evil days come, when wicked deceivers surround me.** The writer implies that he suffers unjustly from the evil deeds of others, from men **who trust in their wealth and boast of their great riches**. However, he does not ask, "Why do the righteous suffer?" Apparently he accepts the state of affairs as one of the facts of life (or as the will of God). But his question is of a different sort. **Why should I fear?** The inequity is real enough and the evil is real enough. But that is not the whole story. Upon reflection, the writer knew that he had no cause to envy those who trust in riches nor to fear because of them. He has a much better foundation for life than they.

3. The Inadequacy of Wealth (49:7-12)

49:7-12 The general meaning of verses 7 and 9 is clear enough, although textual variants have resulted in a variety of translations (v. 8 is parenthetical). The opening word, in the Hebrew, may be the emphatic particle, rather than the word for "brother" (KJV). Thus, we would translate: "A man cannot by any means redeem himself; he can never give to God his price of redemption, that he should go on living and not see death." Wealth has no power over the grave. Whether they consider themselves to be wise or foolish or stupid, all die, and **leave their wealth to others.** Those who trusted in their riches are now destitute. They had acquired more and more. **They had named lands after themselves.** We would say they affixed their names to the deeds. But however vast an estate had been theirs, now each will have only a six-foot plot — no more! What irony! And **their tombs will remain their houses forever.** Verse 12, then, is to be understood in light of the preceding. **Man, despite his riches, does not endure; he is like the beasts that perish.** This is the ultimate futility.

4. The Gift of God (49:13-15)

49:13-14 Verses 13-15 draw a sharp contrast between this fate of the unscrupulous rich and that anticipated by the one who puts his trust in God; namely, the psalmist. Here again is presented **the fate of those who trust in themselves.** Verse 14 depicts this, but this verse has received varied treatment at the hands of translators.[34] Even so, the verse speaks clearly to the effect that Sheol is the destiny of these people, a destiny from which there is no escape.

---

[34]One without a knowledge of Hebrew may wonder how there could be such a variety in the translations that are proposed. Notice: "Like sheep they will be put into Sheol. Death will be their shepherd. When they descend into his gullet like a calf, their limbs will be devoured by Sheol, consumed by the Devourer" (Dahood). Craigie is more in keeping with the KJV. "Like sheep shipped to Sheol, Death shall graze on them. The upright shall rule them at dawn, their forms for Sheol's consumption, rather than their lofty abodes." Eerdmans renders the latter part of the verse: "One

49:15 The one trusting God anticipates a far different destiny. That verse 15 presents the contrast is clear. However, the exact nature of the alternative is debated. The verse opens with an emphatic adversative — **But . . .** We would translate thus: "But God will redeem me (not, "my soul," from the KJV) from the power of Sheol (the abode of the dead, i.e., **grave**), for he will take me." The NIV is very close to this. What is the nature of the deliverance here spoken of? Many see only that the writer is protected at this time from some threat of death from his foes, that he is "ransomed" from a premature death. But what kind of ransom, what kind of victory is this? The others also are spared the grave until their "time" comes. If Sheol is the final destiny both for them and for him, they have the decided advantage, for they have had, in addition, a lifetime of affluence in which to delight themselves. No, the contrast must be greater than this, as the emphasis upon the permanence of Sheol as their abode would indicate. In some way (the *how* not being considered) the writer is certain that his redemption will free him from Sheol forever. It is not from some illness but from the power of death itself that he would be ransomed or redeemed. And when he says of God, **He will surely take me to himself**, he is using precisely the same term that describes God's taking of Enoch, who did not see death because "God took him" (Gen 5:24). As Kirkpatrick observes, "God will do for him what all his wealth cannot do for the rich man."[35] He who is the source of all life will sustain in the hereafter his own, even as he sustains them here. Death is no challenge to the power of God.

---

morning their bowels shall be worn out and Sheol shall be his habitation." And Kraus avers that "the text in v. 14 is irreparably corrupt. Only the first words can tentatively be reconstructed." He leaves the latter part of the verse untranslated (*Psalms 1–50*, p. 480). Compare other translations.

The difficulty of this verse and its treatment by the scholars is a rather extreme example. For the most part, the Hebrew of the OT is quite understandable, though rendering it with the proper nuances into another language presents a challenge. As a translator, Martin Luther expressed the frustration he felt somewhat as follows: "How difficult it is to make the primitive Hebrew writer speak German!"

[35]Kirkpatrick, *The Book of Psalms*, Book II, p. 268.

5. Thought to Remember (49:16-20)

49:16-17 The point has been made. The rich who are oppressive are not to be feared. **Do not be overawed.** Whatever they may do cannot affect the inheritance that the righteous have from God. Neither is the oppressor to be envied, **for he will take nothing with him when he dies.** He will have lost the one thing in life to which he has dedicated his entire existence. Such a one is not to be envied, but pitied, pitied not because of his wealth, not because of what he has, but because of what he has deprived himself of. In placing his full confidence in wealth, he knows nothing of the confidence that one may have in God. Instead of perishable treasure, his could have been a hope that does not fade away nor perish.

49:18-19 The irony is that while the rich man lived, he congratulated himself. He blessed his soul, **counted himself blessed.** We remember the words of the rich man in the parable of Jesus: "And I'll say to myself, 'You have plenty of good things laid up for many years.'" (Luke 12:19). Congratulations were in order, because he had so many goods. The tragedy is that he did not have "many years." There is an alternative. This has been shown. God provides that which is beyond the price of earth's riches, the life of trust. Here is a hope that does not end in the grave.

49:20 The psalm closes with one more reminder of the alternatives, with the final verse focusing upon the ultimate futility of riches. Here we have a repetition of verse 12, but with a slight yet important difference. The verse, as restated, is at the same time a solemn warning and an invitation. Perishing as the beasts does not have to be any man's end. With a bit of subtlety the wise one now says, **A man who has riches without understanding is like the beasts that perish.** Note the words, "without understanding." We may believe that the writer entertained the hope that they who would read his words would *have* understanding and thus choose the alternative, namely, that they cease to trust their lives to possessions and put their trust in the Lord instead.[36]

---

[36]The thought that devout Jews (Ezra?) from the exile would add a verse to David's penitential psalm (Psalm 51) should not bother the Christian's view of inspiration of the text. After all, there are signs of similar editing found not only in the Psalms but in other OT texts. Surely God is able to

B. GOD JUDGES HIS PEOPLE (50:1-23)

Man is a responsible being and must answer to a righteous God. This is the stark reality that underlies the development of Psalm 50. However, nothing is said here of future judgment. It is one's standing in the eyes of God here and now that is in the view of the psalmist. In essence, the psalm is concerned with the kind of life (and of attitude) that is acceptable to God, or, we might say, that is befitting a child of God. It is assumed, without mention, that the good life can be experienced only in fellowship with God. What, then, is required of one who would enjoy that fellowship? In the psalm, it is the people of God themselves who are called to judgment in regard to this matter.

In the terminology of today, we would say that the psalm is concerned with what constitutes true religion (understanding religion to mean that which binds one to God).[37] It is true that the psalmist uses no such abstract term, but he is, nevertheless, concerned to know on what basis one may stand before a righteous God and be assured of his favor. (Is this not what all of us desire to know?) For the psalmist, the basis of that relationship was recognized as being the covenant that God had made with his people, a covenant to which the people of Israel had committed themselves. But in the psalm it is the covenant people themselves who are called to account, as noted above. Apparently, to be in fellowship with God requires something more than just a formal or perfunctory relationship. That is what this psalm is all about.

So significant is the judgment of the people in this matter that God calls both heaven and earth as witnesses. And — surprisingly, as some may think — the judgment would include both "saints"

---

guide the hands of those who put together the "final shape of the Psalms," including making certain psalms expressly relevant to their day, although it was not necessary. It will be seen in volume two of this commentary that the final shaping of the psalter has a "theological message," one that is just as inspired in its canonical shape as it is inspired for each individual psalm.

[37]This is the significance of the term, according to its derivation, understanding it to be from the Latin *relig(are)*, "to bind," + ion, the suffix indicating an action.

(v. 6) and "sinners" (v. 16). The danger confronting the former was
that of formalism, of supposing that in bringing the proper sacrifices and in observing the proper holy days, they had met their
responsibilities toward God and were deserving of his favor. Such
empty worship is rejected. The "wicked" (v. 16), on the other hand,
are those among God's people who speak of the covenant and
quote God's statutes and then proceed to violate every one of
them. Upon both classes, therefore, upon those who are satisfied
merely to go through the forms of worship, and upon the hypocrites openly engaged in evil, the judgment of God must come.

The psalm is not concerned for judgment alone, however, but
for "instruction in righteousness," as Paul would say (2 Tim 3:16). It
makes clear that God desires more of his people than ritual or the
hypocritical mouthing of the proper doctrines and beliefs. In a
word, that desire is for a spirit of gratitude toward God (recognizing him as the true source of all our blessings — v. 14), and for the
keeping of his law (walking in the way of God with integrity, not
just giving assent to it — v. 23).

The psalm refers to Israel as the covenant people of God (v. 5).
This suggests the possibility that it was used in a covenant renewal
celebration, during which the worshipers would reexamine their
relationship with the Lord. There is no definitive knowledge of
such a festival, but such may have been the occasion of the psalm.
In such a case, the celebration would have been to Israel something
like the Lord's Supper is to the Christian, with the words of the
psalm providing a liturgy for the occasion. God, who had inaugurated the covenant at Sinai, speaks again to bring renewal. But
whatever may have been the occasion of the psalm, its message
remains evident.

1. The Summoning of Witnesses (50:1-4)

50:1-3 The Mighty One, God, the LORD, speaks. Literally, "El,
Elohim Yahweh has spoken" (or, "speaks"). *El* signifies God in his
power. In conjunction with *Elohim* it may be rendered, "The God
of gods" (comparable to "King of kings," and "Lord of lords"), and
meaning the God who is above all that are called god. Such is
Yahweh the God of Israel (Deut 10:17; Josh 22:22; Dan 2:47). And

now he summons the whole earth, from the rising to the setting of the sun. The devout Israelite, reading these words or hearing them recited, might think that God is summoning the Gentile nations to judgment. "Let our God come," verse 3 may be translated, "and not remain silent."[38] By contrast the NIV presents the verbs as a statement of fact, not permissive: **From Zion, perfect in beauty, God shines forth. Our God comes and will not be silent; a fire devours before him, and around him a tempest rages.** In verse 4 the summons is widened. Not only the whole earth but the heavens are called before God.

50:4 However, these are not summoned to be judged. Instead, they are assembled to be witnesses of God's judgment of **his people.** It is not here the heathen but Israel who stands before the tribunal of God. (See Isa 1:2.) The judgment of the world is clearly taught elsewhere in the Scriptures (Acts 17:31). But also we read that "judgment [is] to begin with the family of God" (1 Pet 4:17). So it does in Psalm 50. Israel stands in judgment before God, and that judgment involves both her relationship with God and her relations with others.

2. In Israel's Relationship to God (50:5-15)

50:5-7 Beginning with verse 5 the text speaks of those who, presumably, stand in a very close relationship with God. **"Gather to me my consecrated ones, who made a covenant with me by sacrifice."** The "consecrated ones," (the "saints," KJV), ("faithful ones," RSV), are those who have committed themselves to God in response to his covenant offer. "By sacrifice," that is, by bringing the sacrifices that God had stipulated, they had acknowledged the right of God to state the terms of the covenant, and they had met those terms. They would be present at all of the religious gatherings and ever careful to fulfill the requirements of sacrifice. Today they would be classed as those who are actively and openly religious. Still, they stand in judgment, and not capriciously, for God's righteousness (his "justice," NEB) is fully attested (v. 6). He does not err nor is he unfair. Yet, why should he judge such as these? Have they

---

[38]A plausible translation. See Kidner, *Psalms 1-72*, p. 186.

not been faithful in fulfilling the stipulations of sacrifice that God
had prescribed through Moses? Yes, indeed. Were they wrong in
doing this? No, this is not the charge.

50:8-13 I do not rebuke you for your sacrifices, God says.
Sacrifice was a factor in their covenant with God and it could not
be lightly dismissed as unimportant or inconsequential. Apparently,
however, their approach to God had become a form only. They
were indeed religious, but theirs was a "mindless" religion, as aptly
described by Kidner. Now they are called to judgment and they can
think only of offering more sacrifices. It is as if they believed they
were doing God a favor in bringing the sacrificial animal! Such an
attitude calls for the strongest rebuke. **I have no need of a bull
from your stall or of goats from your pens**, God says. The sacrificial system had not been designed to provide food for God. How
ridiculous! It was not for God's benefit but for theirs that the sacrificial system had been instituted. To forget this was to miss entirely
the significance of what they had been called upon to do.

50:14a Sacrifice thank offerings to God. The KJV has perhaps a
better reading: "Offer unto God thanksgiving." The noun, תּוֹדָה
(tôdāh), may indicate a thank-offering, but that is a derived meaning.
No one word in English is sufficient to express the term, but basically it indicates "confession," such as of the goodness and greatness of God and his works, or of one's own sin and unworthiness.
It also has connotations of thanksgiving and praise associated with
the confession. In the present case the notion of thank-offering
would seem to be excluded since the context indicates the inade-
quacy of the offering, *per se*. If worship consists only of bringing
and offering the specified sacrifices (or performing the prescribed
ritual), it is seen to be futile. True worship involves the heart and
the mind, a recognition of the majesty of God and a response to his
goodness. Such consciousness can only result in our praising him
in a true spirit of thankfulness. In all of this, it is not that God
needs our praise. But we need to know and to honor him as God.
Our praise then becomes the overflow of this recognition. How
empty must be the heart of the person who has no one to thank for
the blessings he has enjoyed!

50:14b-15 Fulfill your vows to the Most High. Vows, in the OT,
were not mandatory, but voluntarily one might make a promise to

the Lord. (See the example of Jacob at Bethel, Gen 28:16-22.) If one
is not led to do this, the matter should not be taken lightly. He
should do what he has promised to do. **Call upon me in the day of
trouble.** What gracious words! In difficult times, one might feel that
he should seek God's favor by bringing an offering (or by more
regular attendance at church!), as though he could influence God by
such actions. But no! Instead, God says simply, "Call upon me." To
do this would be to demonstrate faith. But not only is God willing to
help; he is desirous of doing so for those who ask. Perhaps many of
us have shared the sentiment of the person who said: "I do not go
where I am not wanted." Nor does God intrude. He who would
ignore God may go his own way. (That is his God-given privilege!).
But he who would respond to God is invited to call on him, in the
assurance that he will be heard: **I will deliver you.** One submits
himself to God's care and experiences the deliverance provided by
him. It is in this way, God says, that his people bring glory to him
(and not by the multiplication of animal sacrifices).

3. In Relationship to Others (50:16-21)

50:16-17 One honors God by an unfeigned, grateful trust in him,
also by a blameless character in his treatment of others. It is to this
second truth that the latter part of the psalm speaks, and we must
be reminded again that it is God's people, Israel, who stand in judgment. To be sure, they are called **the wicked** — that is because they
are! Even so, they are in the ranks of those who profess to believe in
God and to be partakers of his covenants, but because of their
conduct in their dealings with others, such profession becomes
sheer hypocrisy. **What right have you to recite my laws or take my
covenant on your lips?** God asks. They speak freely of the covenant
as though they recognize its terms. Yet they hate the instruction or
direction for life that God's *torah* provides; they "turn [their] back[s]
while [God is] speaking!" (v. 17, NEB). They give lip service to the
word of God, but refuse to be guided by its teaching.

50:18-20 Specific violations of the Ten Commandments are
cited in verses 18-20. The three alluded to are: "You shall not
commit adultery. You shall not steal. You shall not give false testimony . . ." (Exod 20:14-16). All of the people would have known

the *Ten Words* (commandments). They also knew the command to "love your neighbor as yourself" (Lev 19:18). But, either in open rebellion, or by some means of rationalization, they were able to become the companions of thieves and adulterers (v. 18) and to give their mouth to evil and slanderous use (vv. 19,20).

50:21 These things you have done, and I kept silent. God was long-suffering with his people, but there is always the danger that one may interpret his patience as indifference, or even as acceptance. I sin, and I am not immediately stricken dead, and so I conclude that, after all, God is not all that concerned about issues of right and wrong. To think in this fashion is to deny the God of righteousness as he has been revealed to us and to make God in our own image. — **You thought I was altogether like you.** Refusing to strive for the level of godliness as revealed, humankind would debase God by attempting to bring him down to our level. This we do in a subtle fashion when we equate our own concepts as truths of God. The human conscience, unenlightened by God's Word, is a deceptive guide, both in matters of religion and of conduct. Every religious doctrine, every practice, is approved by someone's conscience (by someone supposing God to be like himself). But to the one who would substitute his own concept of what is right for what the Lord has given, God says: **I will rebuke you.**

The verb "rebuke" is from the root יָכַח (*yākaḥ*), which has the basic meaning of an action (or verdict) determined on the basis of what is right and true. Here it speaks of an indictment, with a verdict to be established upon the true facts in the case, and here there can be no subterfuge, no rationalization. **But I will rebuke you and accuse you to your face.** These people could not plead ignorance of the will of God. They, like some in Paul's day, had, in the law of God, the "embodiment of knowledge and truth" (Rom 2:20). They even bragged about the law! (Rom 2:23). Yet they could defame a brother, deal in stolen goods, and condone adultery, while all the time claiming to be the people of God, abiding by his covenant. Theirs was the sin of hypocrisy, a sin that made it impossible to walk in the fellowship of God. In order to live in a right relationship with him, they must be right in their relationships with others. That is God's judgment upon the wicked who claim to be his people.

4. Admonition (50:22-23)

50:22 It is encouraging that the psalm does not end with verse 21 on this note of judgment. There can be no compromise, and the judgment must not be lightly dismissed. The warning could not be stated more forcefully: **"Consider this, you who forget God, or I will tear you to pieces, with none to rescue."** (Even the prophet of God's love, Hosea, uses this figure indicating the execution of God's judgment — Hos 5:14.) But there is an alternative. It *is possible* for human beings to live in harmony with God and with one another. This is the result of the salvation that God provides, a salvation greatly to be desired.

50:23 The way to the enjoyment of that salvation is simply stated in verse 23. **He who sacrifices thank offerings honors me.** It is essential that we worship God — not for his benefit (who can benefit God?) — but that we might recognize our own place in his universe. Life in its fullness of meaning cannot be realized apart from him. Worship, therefore, to him who would truly know life, is not an option. It is essential. To one who comes to know God worship does not have to be commanded; it but becomes the natural overflowing of his heart and soul. In regard to such worship, Adolph Monod stated: "God, from whom all good proceeds, who does not need us, invites us to add something to his glory by giving testimony to Him before His creatures, thus contributing in our own way to the hallowing of His name."[39] This kind of worship does indeed honor God at the same time that it enhances the life of the worshiper.

However, the relationship with God cannot be maintained when one's conduct toward others is evil. Attention must be given therefore to the way in which one walks (the way he lives). This is the apparent meaning of verse 23b. The Hebrew is a bit cryptic, stating simply, "he set (or "established") a way," or, "(the one) establishing a way." A way in accord with the way of God may be understood from the context. The one who thus directs his life will cherish God's Word as guide and will do no ill to others. To such a one God will show — "go on showing" — his salvation.

---

[39]Monod, *Farewell*, p. 24.

C. A SINNER'S PLEA FOR FORGIVENESS, CLEANSING, AND RENEWAL (51:1-19)

Except for Psalm 23, Psalm 51 has been perhaps the most often recited of the Psalter. Every soul that has ever felt remorse for sin and the need for God's forgiveness can identify with this psalm. Called the *Miserere* (from the first word in the Latin version – "have mercy") this is the most famous of the penitential psalms (the others being 6, 32, 38, 102, 130, and 143). Because of the intensity of feeling revealed in the psalm, it has been widely recognized as an individual lament, the words of one whose soul carries a heavy burden of sin and a sense of alienation from God. On the other hand, some hold that it is a communal lament, the cry of the nation. Leslie would identify it as an individual lament, "because of sin," at the same time recognizing it as providing a liturgy to accompany ritual acts of worship by any penitent approaching God.[40] Cohen would concur in this, holding that "originally, the Psalm was a personal *cri du coeur* – (cry of the heart).[41]

Mowinckel recognizes that "the psalm is deeply personal" but adds that it "may have been written with a view to the public cult of the concerns of the congregation."[42] In this case, the "I" of the psalm would represent the nation, not an individual. Kirkpatrick sees the possibility that the psalm, originally personal, was later adapted and used as a congregational confession and plea for pardon.[43] That the psalm was used in public worship is indicated by the assignment **for the director of music** in the superscription. Still, it is difficult to believe that it was written by any other than the person who had experienced the remorse and need for forgiveness so evident in its composition.

The superscription identifies the author as David, **when the prophet Nathan came to him after David had committed adultery with Bathsheba.** There are some who dismiss this heading of the

---

[40]Leslie, *The Psalms*, p. 399.
[41]Cohen, *The Psalms*, p. 161.
[42]Mowinckel, *The Psalms in Israel's Worship*, 2:17.
[43]Kirkpatrick, *The Book of Psalms 42–89*, p. 284. The author cites the differences in Psalm 53 as given in Psalm 14 as an example of the changes a psalm might undergo before the text of Scripture became finally fixed.

Jewish scribes as without validity. However, unless we could know the history of the tradition they sustain, it should not be summarily put aside without adequate reason. To be sure, some scholars cite various grounds for rejecting David as the author, and these are not to be lightly dismissed. Still, to say that David could not have written the psalm is to be a bit dogmatic.

This is, however, the view of some. For example, it is alleged that the spiritual and moral level expressed in the psalm are much too advanced for the era of David. Some of the terminology of the psalm is shown to be like that found in Isaiah 40–66, which came several centuries after the time of David. For example, only in Ps 51:11 and Isa 63:10,11 do we find reference to God's holy Spirit. But God had put his spirit upon David (1 Sam 15:13), and it should not seem strange that David would think of the spirit of God as being holy when he was contemplating his own sinfulness.

Again, it is said that in David's time no one would denounce sacrifice as being of "no delight" to the Lord (v. 16), since in that primitive era, sacrifice was considered to be the sure way of access to God. The repudiation of this view, it is said, came in the eighth century B.C. with Isaiah (1:11-15), Hosea (6:6), and Amos (5:21-27). Yet Samuel, even before the time of David, rejected the sacrifice offered by King Saul, because of that monarch's disobedience (1 Sam 15:22).[44]

It is noted that no mention is made in the psalm of David's offenses, adultery and murder. Why this omission, it is asked, if the psalm is from David? But as Leupold notes, "All the nation knew of these crimes . . . . The obvious was too sordid for mentioning."[45] Yet how could David say to God, "Against you, you only, have I sinned" (v. 4)? Because the terms for "sin" and "transgression" indicate rebellion against God and violation of his commandments. It is in this that the offense is against God. We would say that David was

---

[44]Verses 22 and 23 are poetic in form, inserted into the narrative, and according to H.P. Smith, their author (too) is remote from the era of Saul (and David). "The passage is a summary of later Jewish theology," Smith states (*Samuel*, ICC, p. 137.) Still, Saul had offered sacrifices and he was rejected. Obviously, the acceptability of such sacrifices was questioned.

[45]Leupold, *The Psalms*, p. 398.

guilty of crimes against others but this was sin against God, and only God could grant forgiveness.

One other factor is of importance in the eyes of those who aver that David did not write the psalm. This is the petition of verse 18: "Build up the walls of Jerusalem," and the assertion of verse 19: "Then there will be righteous sacrifices, whole burnt offerings to delight you." The words of the former verse are understood to indicate a time after the destruction of Jerusalem in 587 B.C. — long after David — and before its walls were rebuilt. And verse 19 is said to be a corrective of the (alleged) renunciation of sacrifice found in verse 16. With this understanding, the verses could not have come from David. Some who recognize the Davidic origin of the psalm, acknowledging this apparent incongruity, consider the concluding verses to be an addition by devout Hebrews who would use David's psalm to give voice to their own penitence, adding the prayer for the welfare of Jerusalem. It is suggested that Nehemiah, who led in rebuilding the walls of the city, might himself have added the prayer.

On the other hand, it would seem natural that David, king that he was, would be concerned about the great harm he had brought upon his people (upon the people of God) through his sin. True, that sin was perpetrated with a high hand, with utter disregard for others. But once stricken with remorse, having finally recognized the enormity of his crime, his prayer for restoration would naturally include a prayer for the city for whose welfare he was responsible.

All in all, there is insufficient reason to deny the Davidic origin of Psalm 51. Eerdmans, although recognizing that tradition is the basis for the superscriptions of the psalms, after treating the evidence extensively, states that "it seems quite probable that this time the historical note [in the superscription] is right and that we should ascribe the psalm to David."[46] The present writer agrees.

In the psalm there are really two themes that dominate. On the one hand there is the overwhelming burden of guilt that has crushed the very life out of the writer. This heart-consciousness of sin is accompanied by the twin realization of his own uncleanness and of his alienation from God as a consequence. It is this double jeopardy of his soul that wrings from him his plea for help. But

---

[46]Eerdmans, *The Hebrew Text*, p. 278.

where or from whom can he find any alleviation for his suffering? Is there any hope for such a one as he? With desperate trust he dares to believe that there is! And this is the second major thrust of the psalm. He recognizes not one glimmer of hope in himself, nor in anything that he can do, standing guilty, as he does, and without excuse. But there is the recollection that the God who rises in wrath against sin is also a God of grace and mercy, and this becomes the coordinate theme of the psalm. Here is hope. On one side there is the reality of the sin. (In verses 1-9 words for "sin," "transgressions," "evil," and "sinning" appear ten or more times, and God is mentioned only once.) But on the other side is God's mercy. (In verses 10-17 sin is gone; God appears six times.) David, like the prodigal son, is ready to arise and go to the Father, declaring, "I am no longer worthy," trusting himself alone to God's mercy.

The opening words of the psalm include this cry for mercy and also for forgiveness and for cleansing (vv. 1-2). This is followed by a confession of guilt (vv. 3-6). The plea for cleansing is then resumed (vv. 7-9), and a prayer uttered for moral and spiritual renewal (vv. 10-12). The psalm then concludes with a vow of commitment (vv. 13-17) and the prayer for Jerusalem (vv. 18-19).

1. A Plea for Mercy, Cleansing, and Pardon (51:1-2)

51:1 Have mercy on me, O God. What other plea can a sinner make before a righteous God? **According to your unfailing love.** And this is the only basis for that plea. Elsewhere it is written that the Lord is "not wanting anyone to perish [because of sin], but everyone to come to repentance" (2 Pet 3:9). **Blot out my transgressions.** The noun "transgressions" indicates sins deliberately committed, acts of conscious rebellion against God, described elsewhere as sinning "with a high hand." The law of sacrifice did not include any offerings for sins of this nature (see v. 16). The expression "blot out" means "to wash away," as from a record (see Num 5:23). This is not a plea for cleansing; that comes in the next verse. Here David is asking that the record of the sin be obliterated, that the charge no longer be held against him, that the "slate be wiped clean." Similar language appears in Isa 43:25.

51:2 Wash away all my iniquity. Here is the prayer for cleansing of the soul, expressed in figurative language. (Elsewhere the verb כָּבַס [kābas] is used only of the washing of clothing, by rubbing, treading, or pounding in water, as in Exod 19:10.) "Iniquity" is from a root that means "to bend" or "to distort," "a twisting of moral standards" (Leupold). Intense washing is called for — thoroughly; the evil in the soul is deeply ingrained. **Cleanse me from my sin**, or "make me pure." The verb is used of purifying metals (Mal 3:3). It also appears in regard to the cleansing of lepers, reflecting a concern that the uncleanness not spread to others (Lev 13). The sin that is here in view is a defection from what is right, "missing the mark" in life, a failure. It is like taking the wrong fork in the road — with no possibility of retracing one's steps. How truly John Galsworthy spoke when he said, "There is nothing more tragic in life than the utter impossibility of changing what you have done." Once the deed is committed, it is beyond recall. How significant the appeal, then, that God cleanse us of the propensity to do the evil thing, to take the wrong turn in the road, to miss the mark. It is a great thing that David asks of God — that the record of sin be blotted out, that the polluted heart and soul be cleansed, that the moral and spiritual deviation be negated, and the life be put back on track.

2. Acknowledgment of Guilt (51:3-9)

For nine months or longer David refused to acknowledge his sin (2 Sam 11:27-12:13). No one in the kingdom would accuse the king. So, somehow, he went on living with his conscience — and apart from God — until confronted by Nathan the prophet. Then he confessed, "I have sinned" (2 Sam 12:13). That it was a genuine outcry of the heart, however, becomes evident from the psalm.

51:3 I know my transgressions. The verb is durative, introduced by an emphatic particle: (literally) "Because my transgressions I, even I, know (or acknowledge continually)." We can imagine the succession of sleepless nights and troubled days, without respite. **My sin is always before me.** There is no attempt at evasion; it is transgressions, my sin. He might have said, "I am only human,"or "this is the way God made me." But there are no excuses offered, just an open confession of a heart suddenly conscious of its actual condition before God. Such an acknowledgment of transgressions is difficult for a stubborn will, but it is the first step of the sinner back to God. And it is made easier upon our realization that God is waiting for our return — "But from everlasting to everlasting the Lord's love is with those who fear him" (Ps 103:17).

51:4 Against you, you only, have I sinned. Crimes against others are sins against God. For this reason, the forgiveness of sin is a religious matter and must come from God alone. This means that for the irreligious there is no forgiveness. Those who deny the reality of sin as an offense against God may seek psychiatric counseling to rid themselves of a guilt complex. But only those who, like David, recognize themselves to be sinners against a loving and righteous God will seek and find cleansing for their sins and his forgiveness.[47] For who else can forgive sin except God?

So that you are proved right when you speak. The "so that" is hardly introducing a purpose clause, that David sinned on purpose, *so that* God would be proved right. The verse is better rendered by Dahood: "And so you are just when you sentence, and blameless when you judge."[48] In other words, "I have confessed my sin; now you are justified in any sentence you may pronounce," **justified when you judge.**

51:5 Surely. ("Behold" KJV), הֵן (*hēn*) introduces a significant truth. **I was sinful at birth.** David is not casting any aspersions upon the character of his mother nor implying that his sin is related to some genetic influence. He is born of flesh, yes. And subject to the temptations of the flesh. But to say, "I was born a sinner" would be to excuse the sin. "The [verse] implies no doctrine of 'original sin,'" Mowinckel notes; "it is the strongest possible expression on the part of the author of the consciousness that as a weak and frail man he has never been without sin."[49] In our terminology one would say, "I have been a sinner all my life." Nor is this an anthropological state-

[47]This is the message of the gospel as made known in the NT. There it is written, "The blood of Jesus, his Son, purifies us from all sin" (1 John 1:7).
[48]Dahood, *Psalms 51–100*, p. 1.
[49]Mowinckel, *The Psalms*, 2:14.

ment about the depravity of the human race. David speaks of his
own condition, not that of others.

51:6 The fact of his sinful nature having been admitted, the
psalmist now states another significant truth, one that could be
cause for alarm. It, too, is introduced by "Surely" or better "Behold,"
making it parallel to the preceding. **Surely you desire truth in the
inner parts.** "Truth," although inherent in its meaning, is scarcely
adequate to express the breadth and depth of the Hebrew term
אֱמֶת (*'ĕmeth*). It means also "adherence to the truth," "faithfulness,"
"trustworthiness," "dependability," "reliability," and such like. See,
then, the dilemma in which David found himself. Behold, on the
one hand, his sinful condition (v. 5). And on the other, behold that
God requires truth in the inner being (v. 6). So what is he to do?
Ask God to instill that truth within him. **You teach me wisdom in
the inmost place.** Only in the wisdom of God can the disparity
between a heart inclined to sin and a steadfast heart be resolved.

51:7 That the disparity is very great is indicated by David's
renewal of his plea for cleansing. **Cleanse me with hyssop.** When a
leper was healed of his leprosy, he would undergo a ritual of cleansing in which the plant hyssop was used (Lev 14:4,8). David sees his
sin as uncleanness and prays that the impurity be removed. (Remember Isaiah's concern about his "unclean" lips that must be
purified – Isa 6:5-7). The second half of verse 7 is parallel to the
first, repeating the same request with a different figure. **Wash me,
and I will be whiter than snow.** (See Isa 1:18.)

51:8-9 Let me hear joy and gladness, or, "Cause me to hear."
The thought of the KJV should be retained, for the verb is causative.
All of the joy had gone out of the life of the sinner, and only God
could restore it, **Let the bones you have crushed rejoice.** The
"broken bones" are not to be understood literally (cf. Ps 42:10). It
is possible that some physical ailment had developed as a consequence of his guilt. Such things do happen. The psalmist dared
hope for God's forgiveness of his sin, realizing that healing for the
soul would bring bodily blessing as well. In verse 9 is repeated the
plea that his sins no longer be held against him.

3. Prayer for Moral and Spiritual Renewal (51:10-12)

51:10 Forgiveness lifts a heavy burden from the heart, and to be cleansed, to be restored to a state of purity must result in wonder and unspeakable joy. But what if the cleansed life should revert again to its former sordid condition? (See 2 Pet 2:22.) David must have realized this possibility, and so he offers a prayer of another kind. **Create in me a pure heart, O God.** The adjective is used of *pure* gold, as being without any dross, and of clean clothing. The verb for "create" (בָּרָא, *bārā'*) indicates the bringing into existence of something that did not exist before, a new heart that has been transformed by the power and grace of God.[50] Since the verb, in the sense of create, is used only of the activity of God (as in Gen 1:1), it indicates something that only God can do.

It should be noted that "heart," in the OT, is an inclusive term, referring to the inner being in its fullness of function — feeling, thinking, and willing. The plea, then, is that all three, the emotions, the thoughts, and the will, be kept pure, directed by a **steadfast spirit**. In a way, David is saying, "Let me think pure/clean thoughts, respond with pure/clean emotions, and make pure/clean decisions."

51:11 Do not cast me from your presence. These are the words of one who has walked with God but who knows that the relationship has been shattered. For a year, or thereabout, David's unrepented and unforgiven sin has been an impregnable barrier between himself and God. Now he hopes, by God's grace, that the barrier be removed and that he may once again be brought into the fellowship of the Lord. To be cast away forever from God's presence is too dreadful to contemplate. **Or take your Holy Spirit from me.** Just as David had walked with God, so had he known the presence of God's Spirit in his life. When Samuel the prophet had first anointed him as a youth to become the future king, "from that day on the Spirit of the LORD came upon David in power. . . . Now the Spirit of the LORD had departed from Saul" (1 Sam 16:13-14). In the psalm David recognizes that spirit as holy, and naturally so, in

---

[50]The verb does not necessarily mean creation *ex nihilo* ("out of nothing," see Isa 41:17-20). But it does mean something new.

view of his own unholiness.[51] In our verse the *spirit* of God is parallel to the *presence* of God, so if the spirit departs, God has departed.

51:12 Restore to me the joy of your salvation. There is no joy in sin, but how great is the joy that comes with forgiveness, cleansing, and reconciliation. "He went on his way rejoicing" is recorded of the Ethiopian, after he came up from the waters of baptism at the hands of Philip (Acts 8:34-39), and his experience of joy has been that of millions since. It was the joy of salvation for which David's heart yearned, and in order that he might never again lose it, he asked one more thing of God: **Grant me a willing spirit, to sustain me**. It is the sustaining presence of God's Spirit that David desires and asks for.

4. Commitment (51:13-17)

51:13 Verse 13, without explicitly giving voice to confidence, does seem to reflect it. That which David had been praying for he now dares to hope will become a reality. **Then I will teach transgressors your ways**. Was it presumptuous to feel that he would be forgiven? If he laid any claim to forgiveness, yes. But if such assurance is a reflection of confidence in God's redeeming mercy, it is a demonstration of faith, and this it seems to have been. It is almost as if David had already received word of forgiveness, and the glimmer of hope brought forth this promise of commitment. **And sinners will turn back to you**. When a soul destined to ruin because of sin has been redeemed, cleansed, turned around and given a new life, his experience will be an encouragement to others to trust in God's saving power, and they, too, will turn to God. Notice that the verb is active: "Sinners will turn back to you." God is waiting to show mercy, but the sinner does the turning, as an act of volition. The KJV has "sinners shall be converted," as though some outside force must turn their faces to God. But the verb is not in the passive voice.[52] God calls, we respond (or refuse to do so). He leads, we follow.

---

[51]*Holy Spirit*, or *holy spirit*, occurs only in the verse before us and in Isa 63:10-11, in the OT. The capital letters, where they appear, are supplied by translators or editors of our printed editions of the Bible.

[52]The KJV makes the same error in translating Acts 3:19 — "Repent and be converted." The Greek has: "Repent and turn."

51:14-15 Save me from bloodguilt, O God. This, in reality, is another confession of his sin by David. He makes no attempt to evade the truth that the blood of Uriah is on his hands. He pleads that he may be spared the death penalty for having committed the crime. **O Lord, open my lips.** If David had attempted to praise God so long as the unconfessed and unrepented sin was on his conscience, it would have been sheer hypocrisy. Evil in the heart and life stifles praise and seals the lips. But when God in his mercy forgives the sin, the lips are opened. Indeed, they cannot remain silent any longer! **My mouth will declare your praise.**

51:16-17 You do not delight in sacrifice. This verse must be read as the antithesis of verse 6 that speaks of truth in the inner being as that which God desires. This is no repudiation of sacrifices; however, no offering is acceptable to God if one's heart is not right with him (and, in Matt 5:23-24, right with one's fellowman). Moreover, the sacrificial system made no provision for any offering to atone for willful, deliberate sins, such as David had committed (see Num 15:22-31). For these two reasons God desires no sacrifice from David, else he would give it. All he has to offer is **a broken and a contrite heart.** And this (amazing grace!) God will not despise because it is precisely the kind of heart that he can bless and forgive, giving it a new life and beauty. Someone has advised: "Submit your life to God. He can do more with it than you can." This is what David had to do. David the sinner! David the murderer!

5. Prayer for Jerusalem (51:18-19)

51:18 It would be fitting for David to close his plea to God with a prayer for Jerusalem. However, the request, **Build up the walls of Jerusalem,** or "rebuild," (the verb may be translated either way) may seem a bit strange coming from his lips. After he had captured the city from the Jebusites, he strengthened its fortifications, and there is no evidence of any necessity, during the remainder of his life, for them to be rebuilt. Some, including Leupold, would view the words as figurative language, referring to the spiritual devastation the city had suffered because of the king's sin, hence a prayer that God would restore it in a spiritual sense.[53] However, unless there is a compelling reason to interpret a clearly worded statement figuratively, it is better to retain its literal meaning.

51:19 When we do this, the language suggests a time in the history of the city after its walls had been torn down (587 B.C.) and before they were rebuilt in the days of Nehemiah (445 B.C.). During the exile there were devout Jews who realized that the nation had suffered because of sins committed, and they "made David's penitence their own,"[54] and added this prayer at the close. If God would restore their city, **then there will be righteous sacrifices, . . . to delight you**, the sacrifices offered with a pure heart and a penitent spirit, such as they would bring. In the days of Nehemiah the walls were completed. "And on that day they offered great sacrifices, rejoicing . . . . The sound of rejoicing in Jerusalem could be heard far away" (Neh 12:43). The joy of a penitent and forgiven David had become the joy of a penitent people.

---

[53]Leupold, *The Psalms*, p. 408.
[54]Kidner, *Psalms 1–72*, p. 194.

PART TWO: THE FAITHFUL AND THE FAITHLESS (52–60)

I. THE FAITHLESS EXPOSED (52:1–53:6)

A. THE FOLLY OF WICKEDNESS (52:1-9)

The title "Wisdom and Folly" that we gave to Psalm 1 would be equally suitable to Psalm 52. Here again the contrast is drawn between evil and good, more particularly between one who trusts in riches and in his ability to do mischief and one whose trust is in God and in his steadfast love. The former relies upon his own cleverness in lying, deceiving, and slandering to advance himself or herself at the expense of others. He is one who would embrace the doctrine of the survival of the fittest and make sure, by fair means or foul, that he is one of the "fit." He entertains never a thought that the judgment of God will come upon him and that his wealth will be of no avail when the blow falls. This is his folly. The psalmist, by contrast, makes no boast. He simply bears testimony to the blessed quality of life that is his — he is "like an olive tree flourishing in the house of God — and affirms his abiding trust in God. This is wisdom. Since, however, the position of the psalmist is given in a single verse as an alternative to the preceding (v. 8), we consider it more precise to designate the psalm *The Folly of Wickedness*.[1]

The situation depicted in the psalm is clear. A "mighty man," essentially godless, rich, and apparently of some reputation, is causing great damage to others with his wicked, lying tongue. Trusting "in his great wealth." He even "boasts" of the "evil" that he causes. But his boasting is premature, for God will deal with him. Of this the psalmist is certain and predicts his downfall.

---

[1]This is the title suggested by Ash and Miller, *Psalms*, p. 185.

The superscription assigns the psalm to an event in the life of David involving Doeg, an Edomite and Saul's chief shepherd (1 Sam 21:7). However, although Doeg did bring havoc by the use of his tongue, it was not through lying or deceit (1 Sam 22:9-23). Nor is anything said in the account of Doeg to suggest that he was rich. What is recorded of him is his savage slaughter, at Saul's command, of the priests of Nob, all eighty-five of them, plus their families and livestock. But this is not alluded to in the psalm. For these reasons, some would question the identification of Doeg as the villain in the psalm.

According to Buttenwieser, the psalm is a denunciation of foreign rulers who were inimical to Israel,[2] after the time of Alexander the Great, around 310 B.C. Few, however, would concur in such a late date. Because of similarities between the psalm and the prophetic literature of the 8th and 7th centuries B.C., some would assign it to that period. Actually, there are no compelling reasons why it could not have come from David, whether or not the Jewish fathers who added the superscription were right in assigning it to the incident concerning Doeg.

Those who hold that the Psalms were written originally to serve cultic purposes would identify Psalm 52 as a liturgy used upon the occasion of the expulsion of an evildoer from the community, or else as a defense of the godly, using the psalm as a means of warding off the ungodly. Apparently, the strictures of the psalm have been applied to various persons, groups, or occasions. This but illustrates the versatility of the psalms in confronting the human situation.

In general, this psalm has been identified as a combination of an individual lament (vv. 1-7) and a personal thanksgiving (vv. 8-9). But it is not a lament of the usual pattern, addressed to God. Instead, the psalmist confronts the adversary (in the style of the prophets; see Isa 22:15-18 and Jer 21:13-14). And the contrast between the godly and the ungodly (vv. 5-7) is in the style of wisdom literature. The psalm illustrates, therefore, the difficulty of classifying all of the psalms according to precise literary types, prepared for particular cultic purposes. This does not, however,

---

[2]Buttenwieser, *The Psalms*, p. 764.

prevent our grasping the message of Psalm 52, with its comparison of the insecurity of the wicked man whose trust is in his wealth and the blessedness of the righteous who trust in God.

1. The Boasting of the Evil Man (52:1)

52:1 Why do you boast of evil, you mighty man? The term גִּבּוֹר (*gibbôr*) often indicates a mighty warrior, a champion, and may be spoken here in sarcasm. "You consider yourself mighty? You are only mighty in doing evil, which is nothing to brag about." "Infamous tyrant" is Buttenwieser's translation.

Widely variant translations of verse 1b reflect the difficulty that it presents, and one's understanding of the context becomes an important factor in determining the meaning and intent of the author. The Hebrew text has literally: "The covenant love/loyalty of God all the day." The NIV follows a variant reading from the MT, thus making the following phrase a continuing denunciation of the "mighty man"; i.e., **Why do you boast all day long, you who are a disgrace in the eyes of God?** Since we consider the main thrust of the psalm to be the contrast between the fate of an evil man and that of the godly, we would retain the general meaning of the KJV for this verse. "You boast of the mischief you can do; my boasting is in the steadfast love of God" (v. 8). "Your boasting is for but a while, but" — "The goodness of God endureth continually." "Goodness" here is a rendering of חֶסֶד (*ḥesed*), God's covenant love, and the same term appears in verse 8, where it is translated "unfailing love" (NIV). It is enduring. Furthermore, the final word of the psalm is a form of the same root (*ḥsd*). Translated "saints" (*ḥasidîm*), or "the godly'" (RSV), "thy faithful servants" (Buttenwieser), it indicates those who are faithful in their love of the Lord. Thus the psalm opens and closes with this term, the final use providing an *inclusio*. From first to last it is *ḥesed* that endures forever — God's love in verses 1 and 8, and the accompanying covenant love of his people in the concluding verse. How transient the boasting of men! It is the *ḥesed* of God that continues — period! A modern commentary and translation of verse 1b concurs with this assessment. Marvin Tate translates the verse: "Why brag about evil, you hero! — God's loyal-love does not cease —"[3]

2. The Nature of an Evil Man (52:2-4)

52:2 The wickedness of this particular character is perpetrated by the use of his tongue, although the underlying cause is his heart (v. 3). The old saying, "Sticks and stones may break my bones but words can never hurt me," is true only in a most literal sense. They may not inflict bodily pain, but words can cut to the heart. And malicious words can destroy a reputation and a life. The tongue is indeed as sharp as a razor. It is an irony that the gift of speech, that gift of God to man that distinguishes him so markedly from the animal creation — a fabulous gift that we take for granted — can be and often is prostituted to produce evil and not good.

52:3-4 You love evil rather than good expresses the Hebrew idiom just fine, "evil from good." The root of the lying and slanderous tongue is the perverted soul or heart that actually prefers what is wrong to what is right. "For out of the overflow of the heart the mouth speaks," Jesus said (Matt 12:34). The nature of one's speech is determined by the nature of his heart. Therefore the words of a slanderer or a gossip may reveal far more about the one speaking than of the one spoken against. It is the nature of an evil man to have an evil tongue; in fact, he loves an evil tongue (the meaning of verse 4b).

3. The Judgment of an Evil Man (52:5)

The wicked do not hesitate to resort to unscrupulous behavior — lying especially — in their assaults upon the righteous. Since the latter would not stoop to such low behavior, they would not seem to have even a chance of survival. But it is the wicked who stand in jeopardy since they must answer to God for their wicked deeds.

---

[3]Marvin E. Tate, *Psalms 51–100*, Word Biblical Commentary (Dallas: Word Books, 1990), 20:32.

52:5 "You love evil," the psalmist has said (v. 3), and "false-hood." Verse 5, then, opens with an emphatic particle in Hebrew, **Surely God.** There is the emphasis. Why should the wicked man boast? For a while he may take delight in evil, but God will not permit him to endure in his wickedness, He will **bring you down to everlasting ruin.** The other verbs in this verse, **snatch up, tear,** and **uproot** indicate the suddenness, completeness, and finality of the judgment upon him. This fate of the wicked is contrasted (in v. 8) to that of the one whose trust is in God.

4. The Laughter of the Righteous (52:6-7)

52:6 The righteous will see and fear. A similar statement appears in Job 22:19, with a difference: "The righteous see . . . and rejoice." The Syriac and three Greek manuscripts have a similar rendering in the psalm, and some (Weiser, for example) would sub-stitute "rejoice" for "fear" here. This would provide a parallel for the second clause, which has **laugh at him.** However, in the Hebrew there is a play on words (intentionally?) that attests to the validity of the traditional text. Words having the same sounds are used, as the psalmist says, "The righteous yir'u [יִרְאוּ, "see"] and yîrā'u [יִרָאוּ, "fear"]." They are filled with awe and wonder as they witness the outpouring of God's justice upon the evildoer. The wickedness that is done on earth is not beyond God's notice! What a thought! Enough to fill any heart with awe, and with holy fear lest he, too, be tempted to evil.

52:7 But then the fear gives way to laughter. Yes, laughter, reflecting the joy that comes from the realization that God has acted with retributive justice. The way of the wicked will have been seen to be the way of destruction and not of triumph. Stated positively, it is the triumph of righteousness and truth over wrong and falsehood that is the occasion for the joy. For this reason, it is not to be inferred that the laughter of the righteous over the demise of the wicked is indicative of a malicious or perverse joy. Prov 24:17 con-demns such: "Do not gloat when your enemy falls; when he stum-bles, do not let your heart rejoice." Verse 7, as it is contrasted with verses 1-4, indicates the nature of the merriment. **"Here now is the man who did not make God his stronghold, but trusted in his**

great wealth and grew strong by destroying others!" He denied any
need of God in his life, trusting instead in what he had accumulated.
However, the mighty man of verse 1, the *gibbôr*, is now just an ordinary male, a *geber*. The man who "grew strong by destroying others"
is now himself destroyed, completely and irrevocably.

5. The Security of One Who Trusts God (52:8-9)

52:8 The wicked one, in the height of his infamy, finds himself
suddenly snatched up, torn up [from his tent], uprooted – this, in
contrast with the one who trusts in God, as shown in this verse. **But
I** (a strong adversative) **am like an olive tree flourishing in the
house of God**; that is, I find perennial life and sustenance. The
olive tree is evergreen; it is noted for longevity, and it is productive
of good (instead of evil). The house of God here is not a reference
to the temple, but to the Lord's dwelling place. "I live continually in
God's presence." Trust in riches (and in wickedness) is certain to
bring ruin. **But I trust in God's unfailing love.** Here again is the
"unfailing love" of God (*ḥesed*) as in verse 1, enduring forever
because God is forever. This latter thought seems to be the
meaning of the final clause. Dahood so understands the text in his
translation: "I . . . trust in the love of the eternal and everlasting
God."[4] Elsewhere the psalmist writes: "I will sing to the Lord all my
life; . . . as long as I live" (not "for ever and ever") Ps 104:33.[5] It is
God who is forever and ever in this text.

52:9 Verse 9 also contains the word **forever** or "eternal." With
good reason Dahood recognizes it again as a reference to God, and
translates: "I will praise you, O Eternal (One), because you acted."[6]
The text calls for a vocative at this point. For "acted" the NIV has
what you have done. But there is no reference in the psalm to what
the Lord has done. What he will do to the wicked one is stated in

[4]Dahood, *Psalms 51–100*, p. 17.
[5]Cohen (*The Psalms*, p. 167) would render Ps 52:9: "I will praise you
as long as I continue to live." This surely is too great a limitation of the
Hebrew "for ever and ever." The dilemma disappears when we adopt the
translation provided by Dahood.
[6]Dahood, *Psalms 51–100*, p. 17.

verse 5. Even so, the verb in verse 9 is correctly rendered as a verb perfect (past tense in English) though it refers to future time. The fact that God will deal with the one who "grew strong by destroying others" in the manner described is so certain of fulfillment that it is spoken of as already having been done.

In your name I will hope; that is, "wait expectantly, have hope." This is a possible translation. However, "I will proclaim thy name" (RSV) is to be preferred, on the basis of a second meaning of the verb (See the Hebrew word, קָוָה, *qāvāh*).[7] It is not unusual in the Psalms for the psalmist to pledge himself to making known to others the good news of God's mercy and salvation. The name of God is used as the equivalency of God himself, so the clear meaning is: "I will proclaim your name, because it is good (= you are good) to your saints." Verses 8 and 9 thus become the crowning statement of the psalm. The man who trusted in his wealth and in his own capacity for evil is destined for ruin. The one who lives the life of trust in God, in the unfailing love of God, will come to know as a reality the goodness of God toward his saints. Does not the name of such a God need to be proclaimed to the world?

B. AS A MAN THINKS, SO IS HE (53:1-6)

Psalm 14 and Psalm 53 are generally recognized as variants of the same original. This being true, it will not be necessary to repeat our general treatment of the psalm, referring the reader instead to the earlier chapter and suggesting a rereading of it at this time. Since the psalm deals with the theme of wisdom and folly — such an important consideration in the sapiential writings of the OT — it should not be surprising that it was preserved and utilized in more than one circle of the people of Israel. This would seem to be the obvious reason why it appears twice in the Scriptures.

The psalms have a few insignificant variations, primarily the use of *Elohim* only to designate God in Psalm 53 while *Yahweh* is prominent in Psalm 14. In verse 1 we find "deeds are vile" (14) and **ways are vile** (53); in verse 3, "all have turned aside" (14) and **everyone**

[7]See Dahood, *Psalms 1-50*, p. 121f. and *Psalms 51-100*, p. 17.

has turned away (53). Verse 4 has "all" in Psalm 14 (though this is not reflected in the NIV), omitted from Ps 53:4. These minor variants do not change the meaning in the least. They are mentioned only as typical of such as may appear whenever we have multiple copies of ancient documents. Dahood, who recognizes northern Israel as the provenance of the Elohistic Psalter, would account for some of the variants as dialectical differences.[8]

Of a different nature is verse 5. Here Psalm 14 has: "There they are, overwhelmed with dread, for God is present in the company of the righteous" (only six words in Hebrew). That is, the godless will fear when they observe that God is with the righteous. But Psalm 53 gives an entirely different cast to the text, referring apparently to the deliverance of Israel from an enemy encamped against her. If this was the case, it is easy to see how the psalm was adapted to fit the occasion. Often suggested is the view that the situation could well have been God's overthrow of the Assyrians who besieged Jerusalem in the days of Hezekiah and Isaiah (2 Kgs 18:9ff.). Verse 5 would lend itself to such an application: **There they were, overwhelmed with dread** (the Assyrians), **where there was nothing to dread** (they had been most arrogant). **God scattered the bones of those who attacked you.** If it is not the Assyrians who are the object of God's action here, then the psalm could apply to some other historical deliverance of Israel (or of the psalmist king) from the attacks of a godless foe.

Obviously the adaptation of a psalm to meet a subsequent need was not considered taboo. Some would suggest that the Psalter is a living book (whatever that means!) and that a psalm could be refashioned by the Holy Spirit to meet the needs of a new occasion.[9] Others, from a different viewpoint, would say that a subsequent writer felt free to rework the psalm. The present writer would suggest that what had previously been fashioned by an inspired writer could subsequently be used and refashioned by another who was equally inspired. This, he believes, is what happened, and accounts for the existence of Psalm 53.

---

[8]Dahood, *Psalms 51-100*, p. 19.
[9]See Donald Williams, *Psalms 1-72*, p. 376.

II. THE FAITHFUL ENCOURAGED (54:1–56:13)

A. A CRY FOR HELP (54:1-7)

Amazing in its brevity (fifty words in Hebrew) Psalm 54 never-theless contains all of the elements of an individual lament. The psalmist (1) calls on God, (2) affirms his innocence (or, infers as much, by asking to be vindicated, v. 2), (3) describes the distressing situation (v. 3), (4) declares his confidence (vv. 4,5), and (5) makes a vow which he will fulfill because of his deliverance (vv. 6,7). For any among us who seek help in learning how to pray in times of distress, the psalm, so simple in form, could be a model, so far as the structure of the prayer is concerned.

From the psalm itself there is no certain clue as to the occasion on which it was written. Some writers consider it to be the prayer of one falsely accused, in view of the request for vindication. Others see it as a prayer for deliverance from oppression (v. 3). And still others believe it to be the prayer of a king for deliverance from foreign enemies. There is an indication, however, that whatever the occasion, the psalm was written at a time when the psalmist was already experiencing an answer to his prayer. This is determined by verse 4, which states jubilantly, "Surely God is my help," and by verse 7, with its positive statement, that "he has delivered me."

The superscription sees the setting as a time when David was fleeing for his life from Saul, after the Ziphites had betrayed David's whereabouts to the king (1 Sam 23:19). At one time Saul and his men had David surrounded (1 Sam 23:26), but a messenger to the king brought tidings of an invasion by the Philistines and Saul turned away to meet the threat. Thus David was spared. This could have been the occasion of the psalm. Having experienced this respite from danger, David then may well have uttered his prayer for complete deliverance from those who sought to kill him. There is a difficulty posed by the reference in verse 3 to his oppressors as "strangers," a term that elsewhere refers to non-Israelites. There is good reason, however, to rely upon an alternative text of this verse, which has "arrogant" instead of "strangers."

1. The Appeal (54:1-2)

54:1a Save me, O God. That is, deliver me from the danger threatening my life. **By your name.** This is added because the psalmist is not expecting God to appear corporeally on his behalf! That would not be necessary. "By your name" is not the same as saying, "by your spirit," but with similar connotation. The name was recognized as having operative powers — as indicative of God's active presence — and as representative of all the divine attributes.[10] Anticipating God's response, in verse 6 the pledge is given to praise the name. This provides a definite tie to verse 1 and provides an *inclusio* to the psalm.

54:1b-2 Vindicate me by your might. Knowing that his assailants have no just cause against him, his plea is for God to see that justice is done. **Hear my prayer, O God.** The call goes through! Whatever the enemy may do, whatever assaults he may launch, he cannot sever the communication lines between the devout soul and his God. And so long as that channel is open, the call for reinforcements will be heard and answered.

2. The Peril (54:3)

54:3 Strangers are attacking me. This verse appears almost verbatim in Psalm 86:14, and there adversaries are "arrogant ones" (זֵדִים, *zēdîm*) instead of "strangers'" (זָרִים, *zārîm*). In Hebrew, the *D* (ד) and the *R* (ר) letters are in appearance so nearly alike that, when not carefully written, they are indistinguishable. It is possible, therefore, that the word for strangers is a copyist's error and that originally the term here was the same as in 86:14, a conclusion reflected in some manuscripts of the text. These are **ruthless men** (also RSV) who **seek** the **life** of the psalmist (the *nepheš*). Their arrogance and their ruthlessness seem to be heightened by the fact that they are **men without regard for God.** That is, they neither take

---

[10]When Peter and John would help the lame man at the gate of the temple, Peter said to him, "In the name of Jesus Christ of Nazareth, walk" (Acts 3:6b). That is, by the authority and by the power of that name.

God into consideration nor care one whit about any moral or ethical principles as being divinely established.

In any age, the peril from those who deny divine righteousness is very great, even when they have the best of intentions. When a people deny the existence of any God-given concepts of right and wrong, they are left without any adequate basis for their ethic. Then "all a man's ways seem right to him" (Prov 21:2). But when all follow this dictum, the result can only be the equivalent of anarchy, in one state or another. A powerful king (or a dictator) may impose rules as he may see fit, but the ethic may change with the change of monarchs and so is no real ethic at all. Many recognize democracy as much more preferable, but whoever would claim that what is right and what is wrong can be determined by a majority vote? The inference of our text is that if these men had "regard for God," they would not rise up against another. Is not this the better way?

3. The Confidence (54:4-5)

54:4 The psalmist has called upon God. He has stated the cause of his concern — godless men threaten his life. Now he makes a confession of faith and expresses confidence that God will deliver him. **Surely God is my help.** At the very time the enemy threatens, the psalmist acknowledges help from God. "Look!" he says, or "See!" (הִנֵּה, *hinnēh*) "God is helping me" (the Hebrew participle). Continuing the verse, we would translate: "The Lord (*Adonai*) is my sustainer of life." This is preferable to "the sustainer of my life" since it focuses more upon the essential nature of God as the sustainer of life — of all life and not just my own: **the Lord is the one who sustains me.** That I am sustained is cause for personal rejoicing. That it is the universal sustainer of life who sustains me is the emphasis and the cause for greater wonder and praise.[11]

---

[11]The Hebrew בְּסֹמְכֵי (*b⁹sōmkê*) consists of a preposition *b⁹* plus a plural participle and could be rendered "among (the ones) sustaining." But surely this is not descriptive of God. Dahood proposes as a possibility the recognition of the participle as a plural of majesty, in apposition to the Lord, and the *b⁹* as an emphatic particle (*Psalms 51-100*, p. 25). Stuhlmueller recognizes the *be*, not as the preposition "among," but as *beth essentiae* indicating

54:5 This verse asks that just retribution may be the lot of the enemy. **Let evil** (that they intend me) **recoil on those who slander me** (waiting to ambush me). Since they plot my destruction, let them be destroyed, in keeping with your character — **in your faithfulness** (literally, "truth"). That the writer wishes to be rid of enemies who threaten his life is understandable. Yet this need not be interpreted as a cry for vengeance; it is a plea for justice and for the vindication of God's good name.

4. The Promise (54:6-7)

54:6-7 Having expressed his confidence in God's deliverance, the psalmist turns his mind to thoughts of how he may best express his gratitude. **I will sacrifice a freewill offering to you** — not out of compulsion, except from the compulsion of a joyful and appreciative heart. **I will praise your name, O LORD, for it is good.** "Save me . . . by your name," was the request of verse 1. Here the name *Yahweh* is spoken, a name to be honored and praised because it is good. Specifically, **he** (we would say It — the name) **has delivered me from all my troubles.** Since verse 5 is a request that justice will be done, the statement of verse 7 that "he has delivered me" must be understood to mean that the anticipated deliverance is so certain to become reality that it may be spoken of as already accomplished, this being, in the Hebrew, the *perfect of certainty*, or *prophetic perfect*. **And my eyes have looked in triumph on my foes** — such would be the interpreted translation of the Hebrew literal: "And upon my enemies my eye has looked upon" meaning "I have looked (in triumph) upon them."[12] This is a continuation of the declaration of what is certain to come about. The soul that looked to God for deliverance has found God to be his helper in his hour of need.

---

an essential quality of God's character (*Psalms 1–50*, p. 264). See also *Gesenius' Hebrew Grammar*, 119 I, p. 379.

[12]The same idiom appears on the Moabite Stone in the inscription of king Mesha, dating from about 830 B.C. Mesha states that in relation to king Ahab of Israel, "I looked on him" — that is, "I looked with triumph upon him" (line 7).

Consequently, he can look with anticipation to his ultimate triumph and proceed, with a trusting and thankful heart, to worship God with a sacrifice, praising him for the deliverance he has provided.

B. DISTRESSED BUT NOT IN DESPAIR (55:1-23)

One can scarcely imagine a person enduring emotional stress greater than that which is reflected in Psalm 55. The writer describes its nature in verses 3-5. Enemies have launched such an unjustified, slanderous attack against him as to be overwhelming, causing him actually to come face to face with the "terrors of death." In his deep distress, his first reaction is to flee (vv. 6-8), but such escape is denied him. He must remain in the city, a place that is filled with violence and strife (vv. 9,11). But the agony, distressful as it is, is intensified by the discovery that a trusted friend, a bosom companion, has betrayed that trust by joining those who conspire against him (vv. 12-14).

What is he to do? In his innocence and in the integrity of his soul, he cannot fight evil with evil. So he gives these antagonists over to the judgment of God, asking that they might be stricken (v. 15). Having done this, he confesses his faith that God will deliver him and deal with the enemies (vv. 16-19). Then his thoughts revert to the friend who has turned against him (vv. 20-21). The psalm then closes on a solid note of confidence. His trust in God remains unshaken (vv. 22-23).

If the above constitutes an accurate analysis of the psalm, then its coherent soundness is established. Even so, it may be admitted that the ideas expressed are not always sharply in focus. We do notice abrupt changes of thought and of the persons considered "the wicked; for they" (v. 3), "you" (v. 13), "them" (v. 19), "he" (v. 20), and "their" (v. 23). These, together with the frequent change of mood and the apparent repetition of ideas, lead some to conclude that we have here not one psalm alone, but one to which has been appended part of another.[13] Only in this way, it is said, can the confusion that is reflected in the psalm be accounted for.

---

[13]See, for example, Kraus, Leslie, William R. Taylor.

However, it is very obvious that the psalm reflects great emotional strain, and under such circumstances a person may not be concerned for an orderly and disciplined presentation. Beset by enemies, betrayed by his friend, the psalmist is not writing for the benefit of curious exegetes attempting to probe his mind but crying out to a God whom he recognizes as his only hope. Such circumstances may well account for any irregularities of style or presentation that are encountered. In any case, the matter does not preclude the possibility of our recognizing in the author a person who, although sorely tried, never succumbed to despair, because of his confidence in the Lord. It is to the Lord that he makes his appeal, to the Lord he declares his distress, and in the Lord he trusts for his deliverance.

1. An Appeal for God's Help (55:1-2)

55:1-2 Like many psalms of the lament pattern, this one opens with an appeal for God's help. The agony of soul of the speaker is reflected in the very touching way in which he makes his appeal. **Listen to my prayer, O God.** The first of four verbs that are included in his plea, "Listen" means "please listen." **Do not ignore my plea.** (The Hebrew literally says: "Do not hide yourself.") This may seem to be a strange request, but in Israel the expression had a special significance. "Do not hide yourself," the law of Moses said, if you are tempted to withhold help from a neighbor when it is in your power to do it (Deut 22:14); do not ignore (the NIV rendering) the need that you can fulfill. This is the request that the psalmist is so bold as to make to God. **Hear me and answer me** or "listen and respond to me!"

2. The Complaint and its Cause (55:3-8)

55:3-8 The root of the psalmist's troubles seems to be a loud and life-threatening verbal attack against him. Slander, vituperation, false accusations, threats all may be involved. "I am panic-stricken at the shouts of my enemies" (v. 3, NEB). **They bring down suffering upon me;** "heap invective" (Dahood), **and revile me in**

their anger. (Remember the mob before Pilate's judgment seat and their cries, "Crucify him! Crucify him!") Under the circumstances we can understand the psalmist's desire to escape. **"Oh, that I had the wings of a dove! I would fly away and be at rest."** Who has not felt such an urge as this at some time? The prophet Elijah actually did flee, for a while, until God returned him to active duty (1 Kgs 19:3-18). Also Jeremiah, perhaps more than once, longed for a lodging place in the wilderness, to get away from it all (Jer 9:12). If these stalwarts of faith had such experiences, it should not surprise us too greatly when we, too, are tempted to flee. (Did not even Jesus pray: "Father, if it is possible, may this cup be taken from me" [Matt 26:39]?)

3. A Cry for God to Act (55:9-11)

55:9a Lying, deceitful, accusing tongues (in this day of mass communication, how the evil is multiplied!) these are the source of the psalmist's troubles. And the remedy? **Confuse the wicked, O Lord, confound their speech.** "Destroy (them, the tongues) O Lord." This appears to be the meaning of verse 9. Dahood clarifies this with his translation, "Destroy . . . their forked tongue;"[14] (literally, "the cleft, or division, of their tongue." Division is thus recognized as a noun and not as a verb — "divide" (KJV), "confuse" (RSV), "confound" (NIV). The psalmist is not asking that the tongue be divided, but that it be destroyed. They are already speaking with a split tongue. This source of the evil he would have God destroy. (In Ps 58:6 he asks God to break the teeth of those who would devour him.)

55:9b-11 The remainder of verse 9 and verses 10 and 11 describe the havoc that is wrought by these evil tongues. **Violence and strife** follow when those skilled in rabble-rousing inflame the masses. **Day and night the malice** continues, and the **abuse** that it brings. **Destructive forces are at work in the city** or "ruin" (RSV), or "pernicious deeds" (Dahood). **Threats and lies never leave its streets** — a reference to specific wrongs that are the work of an evil

---

[14]Dahood, *Psalms 51-100*, p. 33.

tongue. To combat such evils as these the psalmist would, as we have indicated, have God destroy the instrument of the wicked, the treacherous tongue.

4. A Treacherous Friend (55:12-14)

55:12-14 As rampant as the evil is, there is another reason for the distress that weighs so heavily upon him. He can withstand the slurs of his enemies, he believes, no matter how vicious. But, he declares, it was not **an enemy insulting me.** He expects to be the object of scorn of those who hate him, and can bear it (v. 12a). He can take measures to avoid (or, to "hide himself from") his adversaries (v. 12b). But now it is one who has been the closest of friends who rails against him (the verbs being in the present tense). **A man like myself**; literally, "a man of the (same) rank as myself" not a thug, any more than I am! A friend with whom he **once enjoyed sweet fellowship**, has conversed with about things dearest to their hearts. To be betrayed by such a one is the height of infamy (or should we say the lowest depth?). For he has been my **companion, my close friend,** meaning "bosom companion," inseparable. More than this, we have known the spiritual blessing of worship together in the house of God (v. 14) we have prayed together! Now all of this is suddenly forgotten and cast aside, as though by a bitter enemy. One's reaction to such perfidy could never be expressed more poignantly than in the words of Jesus to Judas. After the traitor had kissed him, Jesus addressed him by the term of endearment, "Friend" (Matt 26:50) – and then put the question that wrenched his heart, "Judas, are you betraying the Son of Man with a kiss?" (Luke 22:48). "Friend" – with what sad bitterness Jesus must have uttered the word.

5. An Imprecation (55:15)

The context suggests that the one-time friend has joined the conspirators against the psalmist in their unjustified attack. Now his thoughts revert to the entire group of enemies, and he asks that they fall under the judgment of God.

55:15 Let death take my enemies by surprise. The request is not such as a Christian would make. "Love your enemies," Jesus said, "and pray for those who persecute you" (Matt 5:44). Yet vindictiveness is not the motive for the psalmist's plea. Rather, he would have these who are bent on destruction to be destroyed instead as a fate befitting their evil design and as an act of justice. **Let them go down alive into the grave [Sheol]**. He would like to have some visible demonstration to indicate that swift justice has prevailed.

6. Confidence in God (55:16-19)

55:16-19 But I, verse 16 begins, **call to God**; literally, "I, unto God I call" ("unto God" is emphatic – not upon anyone else). When unscrupulous enemies threaten, one may naturally turn to the Lord. Why not, also, when friends fail? This the psalmist does, with assurance. **The LORD saves me.** *Yahweh* is the God who is in covenant with his people. **Evening, morning and noon I cry out in distress.** Whether he has these set times for prayer we cannot determine; he does renew his prayer throughout the day. (As the day for Israel began at sundown, "evening" is mentioned first.) **He ransoms me unharmed**. He had not been able to fly away to find rest. The enemies, apparently, had not been stricken dead. But he is willing to leave their fate in the hands of God, who will surely deal with such as these who are not going to change their evil behavior because they do not reverence God (v. 19). Or else, they feel no compulsion to fear God because they have experienced no changes in their daily fortune. Nevertheless, his confidence has proven to be justified, for he has known the sustaining power of God's deliverance.

7. More Treachery (55:20-21)

55:20-21 The betrayal by the friend is so grievous that the mind of the psalmist is filled with thought of him again. He is one like Brutus, lifting his hand to stab Caesar in the back. One by whom a solemn covenant of friendship may be summarily broken, or **he violates his covenant** (v. 20). The Hebrew root, חָלַל (ḥālal, translated "broken," "violated") has a basic meaning of "to profane" or "to desecrate," indicating that there is a sacred quality to the covenant of friendship — sacred at least to the psalmist but not to the one who would betray that friendship. The metaphors of verse 21 give a vivid image of the baseness — **speech is smooth as butter**, from one who harbors **war in his heart**; **words more soothing than oil** but used as **drawn swords**, not to heal but to destroy. It is understandable that the psalmist cannot get such thoughts out of his mind!

8. Trust and Confidence (55:22-23)

55:22 The psalm ends, however, on a note of confidence. To appreciate this, one needs to recall the psalmist's experience — his appeals to God; the oppression, the iniquity and the wrath of his enemies; the terrors, the fear; trembling and horror he has known; his desire for flight that was denied him; and especially his betrayal by his friend. Through all of this he has come. But instead of having been crushed by the ordeal, he has a testimony to give — glorious good news to share. **Cast your cares on the Lord and he will sustain you.** The "cares" is better understood as "your given lot," meaning your portion in life. Of course, such may have become a "care" or "burden." And note that the promise is not that the burden is sure to be removed, nor that God will carry it for us. But he will sustain the one who trusts in him, enabling him to bear it. Understandably, this opening statement of verse 22 has become one of the most cherished found in the Psalms.

55:23 In sharp contrast with those who look to God for sustenance, **bloodthirsty and deceitful men will not live out half their days.** "For all who draw the sword," Jesus said, "will die by the sword" (Matt 26:52). The psalmist would not disagree, but he anticipates the exercise of God's judgment in the matter. As he utters the words **deceitful men**, we can only wonder if his heart is pained once again by thoughts of the friend who has proven deceitful. In any event, his closing word to the Lord is one of confident commitment: **But as for me, I trust in you.**

C. THE CONQUEST OF FEAR (56:1-13)

From first to last, Psalm 56 breathes confidence in God. At the outset the psalmist focuses upon the onslaught of enemies who press upon him continually — all day long (vv. 1-2). The nature of their attack is not made clear, whether they threaten him bodily or accuse him of a crime that would exact the death penalty. In any case, he does not blush to admit that he is afraid, as if death were staring him in the face. But he has found the secret of dealing with fear. "When I am afraid, I will trust in you" (v. 3). These words to the Lord constitute the key verse to the psalm. Because of his confidence in God, he can admit that "I was afraid, truly I was, but I will not be afraid (any longer)" (v. 4). Although the enemy have not ceased their daylong attacks (v. 5) and, like beasts of prey, continually stalk him (v. 6), he knows that God is aware of his need (vv. 8-9). And he has overcome his fear (v. 11). By faith he has viewed the situation from a perspective that includes God. The enemy may be numerous and vicious. He is aware of this. But God's answer to his call will thwart their plans. This also he knows, as he says with confidence, "God is for me" (v. 9). (With Paul he could say, "If God is for us, who can be against us?" — Rom 8:31.) Consequently, he pledges himself to offer the praise and sacrifice that will honor God for the deliverance he knows will come (vv. 12-13). And he will continue (unafraid) to walk before God. Faith has conquered fear.

1. God Be Merciful! (56:1a)

56:1a Be merciful to me, O God. In a simple and forthright manner the need is expressed and the petition directed to God. That it is *Yahweh* who is addressed is indicated definitely in verse 10 — the God revealed to Moses, the covenant God of Israel upon whom his people are free to call. And the cry is to "be merciful," or to "be gracious." The verb expresses a request that one grant a favor that is within his power to do, out of kindness. Because he recognized both the power of God and his kindness, David did not hesitate to call upon him.

2. The Fear — Its Cause and the Response (56:1b-7)

56:1b The need is immediate and pressing: **for men hotly pursue me.** In Hebrew, literally "man," here in the singular (אֱנוֹשׁ, *'ĕnôš*), indicates humankind, for the enemies are many (v. 2). The verb has been variously translated: "hotly pursue" (NIV), "swallow up," "trample upon" (RSV), "persecute, harass" (J.W. Rogerson), "snap at" (Leupold), "lie in wait for" (Weiser), "desire to catch (me)" (Kraus). The person uninitiated in the Hebrew language may wonder how such a proliferation of meanings can be derived from a single word! All find their significance in the root, שָׁאַף (*šā'āph*), which means literally "to pant" or "to pant after" (as dogs in pursuit of their prey). Dahood has aptly chosen a nondefinitive term which would incorporate most of the above concepts in his rendering: "How men hound me!"[15] Obviously their pursuit of David is to subject him to their power and to their will. And that pursuit is relentless: **all day long they press their attack.**

56:2-4 The cry for mercy ends on a note of urgency: **many are attacking me in their pride.** That last phrase, "in their pride," is taken from the Hebrew מָרוֹם (*mārôm*), which can mean "from a lifted up (spirit)," i.e., "pride," understood as an adverbial phrase. (See NIV and RSV.) It could also refer to God as the "most high," in this case used as a vocative (to God) but placed at the beginning of verse 3 where it would most naturally be.[16] It would balance the vocative in verse 1 if placed at the beginning of verse 3 (also, see NRSV). Thus: "O Most High, when I am afraid, I will trust you." Think of that for a moment. This simple statement is a testimony to what faith is all about. The psalmist does not say, "When all is peaceful, I will trust you." (Is not that the measure of faith for many?) But, "when I am afraid"! He has learned that it is in adversity that one discovers the true meaning of faith. If it is not right for me to trust God "when I am afraid," what is faith for? The response to fear is not despair but trust — trust in God and in his

---

[15]Dahood, *Psalms 51-100*, p. 40.
[16]Dahood, *Psalms 1-50*, pp. 44f., *Psalms 51-100*, p. 43. See also Marvin Tate, *Psalms 51-100*, pp. 65,66, who supports Dahood and Tesh for *marom* as an address to God: "O Most High!"

word (v. 4). Thus the fear is dispelled, and the psalmist can ask: **What can mortal man do to me?** Note the progression: afraid — trust in God — not afraid any more. So simple and yet so profound is the formula that it is repeated in verses 10-11.

56:5-7 Having asked what the enemy could do, the writer proceeds to describe their strategy. **They twist my words.** If we were permitted a personification, we would translate: "They cause my words to writhe in anguish!" (They distort them unmercifully.) **They are always plotting to harm me. They conspire, they lurk,** seeking opportunity to take my life. Some difficulty of translation is occasioned by the next verse, as the variety of versions will show. The reference to **nations** is particularly puzzling since the enemies of the psalmist have, apparently, been individuals. Some would suggest that the inclusion of nations indicates a later adaptation of the psalm as a national prayer against the abuse of Israel by foreign nations. In the LXX the superscription includes the words, "For the people far removed from the sanctuary," indicating Jewish exiles in foreign lands. However, even as a personal lament, the psalm may include a reference to nations, as in the following proposed translation: "Deliver them (my enemies) over to trouble; by means of the anger of nations bring them down, O God."[17] Thus the psalmist would leave the judgment of the enemy in the hand of the Lord.

3. The Faith That Overcomes Fear (56:8-11)

56:8-11 The writer cherishes the assurance that God is aware of his plight. Not only this, but also that he has taken note of it. This is the substance of verse 8. **Record my lament.** (The term "lament" means to toss the head, or to nod, or to move to and fro in grief.) God had noticed. **List my tears on your scroll.** This figurative language expresses the desire that the full extent of his grief be entered into the record. When this is done, he anticipates that God will come to his defense. **Then my enemies will turn back.** This will occur when he calls on God for help. This is his faith, a faith that

---

[17]Eerdmans renders this verse: "Let them be free to calamity, make them to descend into the anger of nations: (*The Hebrew Book of Psalms*, p. 391).

has triumphed over fear. And again he can sing: **In God I trust; I will not be afraid. What can man do to me?**

4. A Cause for Praise and Commitment (56:12-13)

56:12-13 The assurance of God's deliverance elicits a promise — rather, a joyful declaration — that he will bring thank-offerings and praise to the Lord. **I am under vows to you, O God.** This is an acknowledgment that he has pledged himself to special offerings and worship. Now he will gladly keep that promise, not alone because of the vow, but because deep within his heart is the urge to express his gratitude. He realizes that he owes his very life to God — **For you have delivered me from death and my feet from stumbling.** And he recognizes God's purpose in such deliverance![18] "You have delivered me," he says, "in order that I may walk before God in the light of life." And to that walk with God he commits himself.

III. THE FAITHFUL ENCOMPASSED (57:1–60:12)

A. PRAYER AND PRAISE IN A DEN OF LIONS! (57:1-11)

Psalm 57 is similar to Psalm 56 in that each expresses confidence in time of danger. In each the writer appeals to God when suffering at the hands of his enemies and in each he affirms his assurance that he will be delivered. Psalm 57 accompanies its plea for God's help (vv. 1-6) with a song of jubilant praise and thanksgiving (vv. 7-11). Thus it cannot be classified either as a lament or as a song of thanksgiving only, but is a combination of both. This suggests to some that the psalm consists of two (or parts of two) originally separate poems, a view that is confirmed, it is said, by the fact that verses 7-11 appear also as Ps 108:1-5. However, the abrupt change from the plea of one facing great peril to the proclamation of thanksgiving may be due to the rekindling of faith within him even as he prays. Verse 7, with its

---

[18]In the Hebrew the infinitive "to walk" is used indicating purpose.

reference to the dawn, suggests the possibility that the night has been spent in prayer. With the break of day, faith has triumphed, the spiritual victory has been won. The two parts of the psalm are thereby shown to be closely related.

The superscription refers the psalm to the period in David's life when he was being pursued by King Saul, who sought to kill him. On one such occasion David hides in the cave of Adullam southwest of Jerusalem (1 Sam 22:1). Later, he is in a cave near En Gedi, in the wilderness overlooking the Dead Sea (1 Sam 24:1-10). It was on this occasion that Saul unwittingly entered the cave where David was hiding and David could easily have killed him. However, he would not do so, saying, "I will not lift my hand against my master, because he is the LORD's anointed" (v. 10). At such a time his confidence in the Lord and his joy over his own deliverance would have been a fitting motive for a psalm such as this.

1. A Plea for Mercy (57:1a)

57:1a The psalm opens with a simple petition: **Have mercy on me, O God, have mercy on me.** The twice spoken plea for mercy is the psalmist's sole request. It seems that, having made it, there is no necessity to ask for more. He is sure that God is aware of his need. And he knows that it is the nature of God to show mercy in response to the prayers of his people. Now he has voiced his petition and he is content. With simple trust and confidence he will leave the matter in God's hands.

2. A Confession of Trust (57:1b-3)

57:1b-c For in you my soul takes refuge. The conjunction "for" is significant. It indicates the reason *why* the psalmist asks to receive God's mercy — not that he deserves it or has earned it. He is saying, "Have mercy on me, Lord, because I do trust in you." The first use of "refuge" in this verse is in the perfect tense, emphasizing the act itself. The second use is imperfect (or incomplete) indicating continuation to the present and even into the future. David had found temporary safety in a cave, but he knew that this was no adequate refuge. For that he would look to God — **until the disaster has passed.** He is certain that they will pass! In the meantime, as long as the storm rages, he will put himself in the care of the Lord.

57:2-3 I cry out to God Most High. "Most High" is *Elyon*. By this name God was known to Abraham (Gen 14:18ff.), and the psalmist would call upon the same God, the **God, who fulfills his purpose for me.** David is confident that God's purpose for him will be fully realized. He knows that he can count on God's **love and his faithfulness.**

3. Ravenous Enemies (57:4-6)

57:4-5 All of this is not to ignore the very real danger that the enemies threaten. Verses 4-6 vividly portray that reality. He is like one cast among lions, among **ravenous beasts — men whose teeth are spears and arrows** — weapons of death — and **whose tongues are sharp swords,** slaying with lies and slander. But these grim threats to his life do not leave the psalmist in despair; rather, they serve to turn him to God. **Be exalted, O God, above the heavens;** that is, to the furthest reaches of creation. This is a way of saying, "Let justice be done and let your righteous will prevail, because in these you are exalted and glorified." It is the psalmist's way of asking God to bring to nothing the plans of evil men.

57:6 Now the figure of the enemies changes from that of savage animals to clever hunters who would catch their prey by deceit and trickery. The writer admits that his soul **was bowed down in distress.** But then those who schemed against him were caught in their own machinations. **They dug a pit in my path — but they have fallen into it themselves.** The verb "fallen" may, as Dahood suggests, be the precative perfect (a request or entreaty), in which case we would translate, "May they fall into it themselves." Even so, the psalmist is no longer worrying about them, so certain is he of God's response to his need.

4. The Song of a Steadfast Heart (57:7-11)

57:7 An old spiritual states: "I shall not be, I shall not be moved." This is the testimony of the psalmist. Danger threatens

him, yet from the beginning he has resolved to abide in the shadow
of God's wings until the storm is past. Now he can say, **My heart is
steadfast, O God.** And for emphasis he repeats the words. With his
faith firmly fixed, he is unwavering in his trust. And the result? **I
will sing and make music.** Just like Paul and Silas in the prison at
Philippi! (Acts 16:25).

57:8-11 Awake, my soul! The NIV and many other versions
smooth over a puzzling Hebrew word with the translation of "soul."
The Hebrew word is כְּבוֹדִי (*kᵉbôdi*), which on the surface means
"glory." It is suggested that "glory" is equivalent to "heart" or "soul"
and the change is made: "Awake, my soul!" This explanation is a bit
strained.[19] However, the root *kbd*, "glory," also means "liver," and
Dahood would identify it thus in this verse.[20] For us to say, "Awake,
my liver," would perhaps be unintelligible. To the ancient Hebrew
it meant the stirring of one's deepest feelings, for the liver was considered to be the seat of the emotions (the heart being more the
center of the will). However, to make the translation palatable to
English ears, perhaps we should retain "soul," "spirit," or "heart" in
our translation, but with the understanding given above. (Dahood
uses "my heart.") The meaning of the expression is clear enough.
The psalmist is rousing himself to jubilant praise. "Wake up, my
soul!" **Awake, harp and lyre! I will awaken the dawn. I will praise
you, O Lord, among the nations.** (Here the term for Lord is
Adonai. In the same verse in Ps 108:3 it is *Yahweh.*) Such jubilation
must have a very special cause. Indeed it does. The psalmist has
prayed for mercy, because he trusts in God (v. 1). He has stated his
unfaltering confidence in the Lord's mercy (covenant love/loyalty)
and truth (faithfulness) (v. 3). Now he sings praises, for that confidence has been justified — **For great is your love [*ḥesed*], reaching
to the heavens; your faithfulness [*ĕmeth*] reaches to the skies.** The
only fitting close for such a psalm is the repetition of the desire

---

[19]The same word "glory" appears in Ps 30:12. There the RSV is consistent in substituting "soul." The NIV there uses "heart."

[20]In the Hebrew text of Lam 2:11 the term is clearly "liver" — "My liver is
poured upon the earth" (KJV). But there the change is made to "heart" —
"My heart is poured out on the ground" (NIV). The NEB would capture
the significance of the figure — "In my bitterness, my bile is spilt on the
earth," as expressing the strongest emotional experience imaginable.

expressed earlier (v. 5). **Be exalted, O God, above the heavens; let your glory be over all the earth.**

B. A CRY TO GOD AGAINST CORRUPT LEADERS
(58:1-11)

Psalm 58 is classed by scholars as a lament — a national lament decrying the injustice heaped upon the innocent at the hands of unjust rulers. As to whether these are foreign oppressors or corrupt national leaders there is a difference of opinion. But in either situation, the psalm provides encouragement for the oppressed. As a lament, it does not follow very closely the accepted pattern. Gerstenberger declares it to be of "a different genre," intended as instruction for the early Jewish community.[21] In any case, the tenor of the psalm is clearly discernible. It is a call for the righteous judgment of God to fall implacably and decisively upon wickedness in high places. This theme is reflected in the title that Cohen would give the psalm: "Unjust Judges Condemned," and Kidner's "Tyrants on Trial."

The psalm opens with a summons and indictment of wicked judges (vv. 1-2). This is followed by a description of their evil nature, constituting, as it were, a verdict — guilty (vv. 3-5). Thereupon the psalmist calls upon God to execute justice upon the wicked (vv. 6-9), and concludes with a reference to the joy that will prevail among the righteous when they see God's rule vindicated (vv. 10-11).

Just who it is being summoned to judgment in the opening verse has been widely debated. That the Hebrew text is difficult is generally admitted. Especially among scholars who see the culture and religious ideas of Israel as following a pattern comparable to that of the nations around them, the view is widely held that the psalm begins with an address to lesser gods to whom the Lord has entrusted the guidance of the nations. Note, for example: "Do you indeed decree what is right, you gods?" (v. 1, RSV; a footnote says, "Or 'mighty lords'"). The implication is that they do not promote justice, and thus the people who have been their subjects (their

---

[21]Gerstenberger, *Psalms, Part I*, pp. 233,235.

worshipers?) have become corrupt and wicked. The psalm continues then with a call for God's judgment upon the wicked people
and concludes with an affirmation that God is in control.

There are several difficulties with this view. First of all, the word
for "gods" (*ĕlohîm*) does not appear in verse 1. Instead, the term is
אֵלֶם (*'ēlem*). This is said to be a misspelling of אֵלִים (*'ēlîm*), as found
in Ps 29:1 and translated "mighty ones"(KJV) or "heavenly beings"
(RSV). Some refer also to Ps 82:1 — "God . . . gives judgment among
the 'gods.'" But in 82:1 the term is *ĕlohîm*. Furthermore, the judgment of Psalm 58 falls upon evil men on earth (vv. 2ff.). This is not
warfare in heaven; the psalmist is not addressing the gods, either
literally or figuratively. The term under discussion appears only in
58:1 and in the heading of Psalm 56. There some leave it untranslated but transliterate it as *elem* (KJV, ASV). Others omit it (NIV,
RSV). Both treatments indicate that the term, as given, is "of
unknown significance" (Eerdmans). Some would derive it from the
(assumed) root אָלַם (*'ālam*, "to bind"). As referring to a group
bound by a common bond, the term is translated "congregation"
(KJV) but this meaning is rejected by the NKJV, which has "you
silent ones" (those whose tongues are bound). This concept of
silence is recognized by others as the basic meaning of the term; by
Leupold, for example: "Do you, indeed, by silence speak righteousness?"[22] The meaning is understood to be that justice is nonexistent
in the land because the judges are so unconcerned and negligent as
not to lift a voice against evil. They wink at evil; they tolerate it, and
may even be in collaboration with the perpetrators. Thus they are
condemned for their silence.

However, the opening verse appears to be a summons, by name,
directed to a specified group and not to an indeterminate "you"
who have remained silent when they should have spoken. If these
are not "gods" or "silent ones," who then? There is broad concen-
sus that the indictment of the psalm is directed against unjust
judges or corrupt leaders in general. Even among those who see
"gods" in the term *'elem*, there are some who say it is a sarcastic
reference to leaders who exalt themselves above the people. Consequently, we find such translations as "you rulers" (NIV, NEB),

---

[22]Leupold, *The Psalms*, p. 436.

"mighty lords" (RSV, margin). We accept this as the significance of the term, though on the basis of a different etymology,[23] and as the basis of our title for the psalm, *A Cry to God against Corrupt Leaders.*

1. The Summons and Indictment (58:1-2)

58:1-2 On the basis of the lengthy consideration above, we would translate verse 1 as follows: "Do you, O rulers, indeed dispense justice? Do you judge fairly between man and man?" The vocative, "O rulers," is a summons, and the question as stated calls for a negative answer, thus becoming an indictment. This is expressed clearly in verse 2: "Indeed not! In your hearts you devise evil deeds." The latter word is plural — injustices, "all kinds of wickedness" (NEB). The charge is not that of an occasional dereliction of duty. These men plot to circumvent justice to their own evil purposes. They are called upon to mete out (or "weigh") justice in the land but instead measure out the violence that they have plotted.

2. The Condition — Unrestrained Evil (58:3-5)

58:3-5 When there is wickedness in high places, corruption among a nation's leaders, evil among the people follows — the "trickle down" effect! Verses 3-5 portray the depravity both of the leaders and of those who are partners together with them in their atrocities, corruption such as was often denounced by the prophets of the OT. "I know how many are your offenses and how great your sins," Amos declares. "You oppress the righteous and take bribes and you deprive the poor of justice in the courts" (Amos 5:12).

The psalmist describes persons who are incorrigibly wicked — **Even from birth the wicked go astray; from the womb they are wayward and speak lies.** This verse makes no statement as to the depravity of the human race. (See comment earlier on Ps 51:5.)

---

[23]Following Dahood I would recognize *'ēlem* (אלם in the unpointed text) as the plural noun אֵילִם (*'êlîm*), written defectively, meaning "rams," a term used metaphorically to indicate leaders (of the flock; that is, of Israel).

The psalmist is here speaking of a particular group whom he designates as "wicked." Obviously he does not include himself and all humankind as equally depraved; that would be to nullify his appeal to God. But these persons are indeed corrupt and have been so all their lives. (The language is figurative since newborn babies do not usually speak lies. The meaning is that they have always pursued evil.) They are venomous creatures, dealing out pain and death. The poison of their tongues — perjury, slander, cursing, false sentencing of the innocent — is like the poison of serpents. And so inured are they to pleas for justice that they turn a deaf ear to any voice of reason or of conscience, like a serpent that is deaf, **that will not heed the tune of the [snake] charmer.** And so they continue to dispense their deadly venom without restraint, incorrigibly evil. Is there no recourse for those who suffer at their hand?

3. A Cry for Judgment (58:6-9)

The answer of the psalmist is a petition directed to God, a prayer of vilification, a cry for judgment. In essence he is asking God to eliminate the menace, to pull the fangs of the reptile. Some see in these verses an attempt to put a curse upon the enemy, that by the mere uttering of the words forces would be set in motion that would overthrow these wicked ones. But no, the psalmist is not casting spells, and is not just pronouncing "a sevenfold curse" as some have said. He is not relying on magic but on the actions of a just God. Living in a time when there seem to be no earthly powers to put *a rein* on the excesses of evil men, and witnessing the injustice, the violence and death that are suffered by the innocent, he has no other recourse than to God.

58:6-7 Break the teeth in their mouths, O God. The figure has changed from serpents to lions, ferocious in their assaults. The meaning of this verse is clear — destroy their power to do evil. The Hebrew of verses 7-9 presents difficulties of translation, yet here, too, the general thrust is discernible — **Let them vanish** or "let them be as if they had never been," just as swiftly and completely as waters in the sands of the desert. In contrast to the NIV for (v. 7b) — "Like grass trodden down, let them (soon) wither." Such a translation provides a fitting parallel for the first line of the verse, expressing as it does a wish for the speedy demise of the vicious ones.[24]

58:8-9 Parallelism in verse 8 would favor the translation of the NEB: "(May they be) like an abortive birth which melts away or a still-born child which never sees the sun!"[25] That is, may all traces of such wicked ones be blotted out — negate their existence. Verse 9 continues the call for the wicked to be dealt with speedily, although the translation is elusive.[26] Our text says: **Before your pots can feel [the heat of] the [burning] thorns — whether they be green or dry — the wicked will be swept away.** With some emendation of the Hebrew the following is proposed: "Before they can discern (what is happening) may they be torn up like a thornbush; like a weed may he sweep them away in anger." Some may decry this as the language of violence. But the writer knows that wickedness will not go away of its own accord, that the evil forces operating in the world are powerful beyond human means of redress. We would do well to share his apprehension! (And rejoice that there is a divinely given way of deliverance — not a deliverance wrought by the destruction of evil persons nor by bringing them under the restraint of a police state nor by locking them away in prisons, but by the power of the gospel to redeem from sin, from its guilt, its power, and its practice, and to bring one to a new life as a child of God.) If the words of the psalmist be severe, it is because the wickedness he witnesses in the land is out of human control. And because of this wanton evil he entreats God to exercise judgment.

---

[24]The NIV must supply a couple of words to make its translation intelligible, thus: "(When) they [he] draw (the bow), let their arrows be blunted." The term for "draw" (דָּרַךְ, *dārak*) is, literally, "to tread upon" (as when stringing a bow). But when, with slight change, the word for "arrow" (חֵץ, *ḥēṣ*) may be "grass" (חָצִיר, *ḥāṣîr*), and the final verb מָלַל (*mālal*) equally "wither" as well as "blunted," the translation that we present is quite plausible.

[25]This translation is based on the suggestion of G.R. Driver that the word שַׁבְּלוּל (*šabbᵉlûl*, from בלל), appearing only here in the Scriptures, may indicate "miscarriage" rather than "snail," ("Studies in the Vocabulary of the Old Testament," *JTS* 34, 1933, pp. 41-44). A.A. Anderson concurs (*Psalms 1–72*, p. 413) as do also Rogerson and McKay (*Psalms 51–100*, p. 45).

[26]Dahood, with complete honesty, admits: "The Hebrew of the verse is unintelligible to me," (*Psalms 51–100*, p. 72) and leaves it untranslated.

4. The Rejoicing of the Innocent (58:10-11)

58:10 When that judgment falls, it will be a cause of rejoicing on the part of those who have suffered injustice and abuse. **The righteous will be glad when they are avenged.** For those imbued with the spirit and teaching of Jesus the word "vengeance" may have a disagreeable sound. It may connote a spiteful attitude. But in the Scriptures it has no such connotation. There vengeance appears in parallel with retribution, with the justice of the return of the evil of the evildoer upon his own head. Deut 32:35 sets the scene for the rejoicing mentioned in the psalm. "It is mine to avenge [says the Lord]; I will repay. In due time their foot will slip; their day of disaster is near and their doom rushes upon them." When that happens, when those guilty of brutality have been rendered powerless and incapable of further harm, justice will have been done, God will have been vindicated, and the righteous will rejoice, **when they bathe their feet in the blood of the wicked.** This is usually interpreted as figurative language, meaning that the righteous will walk off the bloody battlefield as victor. The battle will be over and the victory won.

58:11 The final verse states the consequence of the preceding. The wicked, who had given no consideration to their victims, have come under the judgment of God; they have suffered just retribution. So that a man shall say, **Surely the righteous still are rewarded.** The cry of the psalmist has been answered. Corrupt leaders may arise but inevitably they must fall. God is still the judge of all the earth.

C. "DELIVER ME FROM MY ENEMIES, O MY GOD!" (59:1-17)

This psalm, in the view of some, was an original individual lament that was later expanded for national use as a lament of the people. That the desperate plight of an individual is depicted in the psalm is evident. Reference is made to "my enemies," bloodthirsty men who lie in wait for my life. The description of the assailants would fit the situation in the life of David indicated in the superscription to the psalm. Yet reference is made in verses 5 and 8 to "all the nations," presumably as enemies of Israel, not of the individual, thus pointing to the use of the psalm collectively, and not as a private lament. There is no record of any national threat to the reign of Saul at this time, except on the part of the neighboring Philistines. But they could scarcely be described as "all the nations." It would appear that in Psalm 59 we do indeed have a psalm of David that was later expanded for community use. Rotherham suggests that such a use of the psalm may have occurred in the reign of Hezekiah, when Sennacherib and his Assyrians overran the land, or a hundred years later in the time of Jeremiah when Nebuchadnezzar and the Babylonians took prominence, or later still at the time of the return from exile when the pagan peoples harassed the repatriated Jews.[27]

As with other psalms of the lament pattern, this one breathes confidence that God will deliver those calling upon him. It opens with the call for help (vv. 1-7). It continues with the expression of trust (vv. 8-10). This is followed by a cry for judgment upon the evildoers for their wickedness (vv. 11-13). The psalm then closes on a note of triumphant praise (vv. 14-17).

1. A Prayer for Deliverance (59:1-7)

59:1-2 Other psalms may begin with an entreaty, such as "Hear me, O Lord," or "Have mercy upon me." This one, at the outset, is an urgent plea for help. **Deliver me from my enemies, O God.** The urgency is noted in the fact that the request for God to act is expressed four times, three different verbs being used — **deliver me** (snatch me away from them, rescue me), **protect me** (defend me, put me out of their reach), **save me** (preserve my life). The enemies are workers of iniquity; literally, "doers of evil." Mowinckel considers them to be sorcerers, casting evil spells upon Israel, but there is no real evidence that this is the case. Note that the term for "workers" or "doers" does not mean simply to perform a task. It is a word with moral implications, indicating acts that are willfully perverse and evil in their outcome, deeds of wickedness pure and simple.

---

[27]Rotherham, *Studies in the Psalms*, I:428.

59:3-5a Arise to help me. The psalmist does not hesitate to ask God to deal with such evil men, especially since their attacks are not justified by any wrong that he has done. With a conscience clear of offense he can seek the Lord's help with boldness. The manner in which God is addressed in verse 5 is significant. **O LORD God Almighty, the God of Israel.** *Yahweh* is the covenant name of God as revealed to Moses (Exod 6:1-4). As the God "Almighty" ("of hosts"), he is the one to whom victory belongs, and as the God "of Israel," he will be attentive when a child of Israel calls upon him. This is the confidence of the psalmist.

59:5b-7 If the appeal for God to **rouse yourself to punish all the nations** refers to national enemies, as mentioned above, then this verse may come from such time as the psalm was used as the nation's petition to God. The following verse then would be a continuation of the personal lament of David. **They** (the bloodthirsty men of v. 2) **return at evening, snarling like dogs, and prowl about the city.** Such animals are not neighborly pets but scavengers, seeking to satisfy their depraved appetites. **See what they spew from their mouths.** Kraus suggests, "They foam at the mouth." The same verb appears in Prov 15:28 — "The mouth of the wicked gushes evil." **They spew out swords from their lips**; that is, their words are as devastating as a lethal weapon and are blasphemous also, for contemptuously they ask, **Who can hear us?** (implying that not even God will know). Truly, from such vicious and irreverent ones as these one may pray to be delivered.

2. An Expression of Confidence (59:8-10)

59:8 And the writer is confident of God's help. He is conscious of the plotting of his enemies, of their malicious intent, of their false accusations and threats. **But you, O LORD, laugh at them** — as though their threats could intimidate the Lord! The very idea of these evil men that their deeds could escape God's scrutiny and his judgment can only call for derisive laughter.

59:9-10 O my Strength, I watch for you. Some, as here, would alter the text of verse 9 to have it conform, thus: "O my Strength, I will sing praises to thee" (RSV). However, instead of being an exact repetition, verse 17 represents a progression of thought. In verse 9 the concern is the strength of the enemy — "his strength" (Hebrew text!). It is overpowering so far as the psalmist is concerned, but in confidence he will leave the matter in the hands of the Lord. He thus discovers that God is his own strength, and this becomes the theme of his song in verse 17 — "my strength." [28]

3. A Cry for Judgment (59:11-13)

From the affirmation of his trust in God the psalmist moves to a cry for judgment against the wicked enemies, a cry that reveals deep emotion. As with the imprecatory psalms, this appeal to God to destroy the adversaries may shock the sensibilities of those who delight in speaking of God's mercy. But God's mercy is for penitent sinners who are conscious of their sin, not for those who go on in their evil ways. Since a penitent spirit is totally lacking on the part of these men, it should not be thought strange, therefore, that his appeal is to God's justice and not to his mercy.

59:11-13 The heart of that appeal is clearly expressed: **Consume them till they are no more** (v. 13, also RSV) "Get rid of them!" In view of such clear language, the usual translation of verse 11 is suspect — **But do not kill them, O Lord our shield, or my people will forget.** This is interpreted to mean, "Do not exact the death penalty but prolong their punishment as an object lesson to my people, an example of the fate of those who defy God." But even in this verse there is the cry, **Bring them down,** and the connotation is, to bring them down to the grave (to *Sheol*). (See Ps 55:15,23). In verse 5 we read: "Show no mercy to wicked traitors." The context presumes such an understanding here. Some would emend the text to read, "Show no compassion" (תְּרַחֲמֵם, *t⁾raḥămēm*) instead of "Slay

---

[28]Eerdmans translates the text: "I leave to thee his strength." The crux of the passage is the verb שָׁמַר (*šāmar*), meaning "to watch," "to guard." Granting Eerdman's interpretation "to leave," his translation is quite acceptable. He derives the meaning from a consideration of Job 2:6. There Satan is told that Job is in his hands, but "you must *spare* his life." Eerdmans equates this with "leave." Thus, in the psalm he arrives at a translation comparable to the KJV (*The Hebrew Book*, p. 302). Thus is the argument against the NIV reading at verse 9a.

them not" (בָרֵם, tahar²gēm).²⁹ Others read it as a question: "Wilt thou not kill them?" (NEB). Dahood, however, has a simpler solution, one not requiring any emendation of the consonantal Hebrew. He would recognize the opening word as אֵל (ēl, "God") instead of אַל (al, "not").³⁰ (In the unpointed Hebrew text there is no distinction between the two terms.) On this basis, we would translate, "O God, slay them." The words, then, are in accord with the rest of the appeal, an appeal, it should be noted, that is not a call for vengeance but for judgment. And this is so God's people will not forget that he administers justice in the earth. God's punishment of wickedness is one way of teaching morality that all may understand! "Do not be deceived," Paul would write, years later, "God cannot not be mocked. A man reaps what he sows" (Gal 6:7). And Ps 7:15 tells of the man who himself fell into the pit he had dug for another. (Notice my comment on Ps 58:10 relative to retribution. And consider especially the fate of Haman in Esther 7:9-10.)

When God brings judgment upon the wicked, this not only stirs the memory of those among his people who forget his concern; it also sends a message to all the earth that God rules in Jacob. This thought was expressed by David when he confronted Goliath: "This day the LORD will hand you over to me . . . . and the whole world will know that there is a God in Israel" (1 Sam 17:46). In Psalm 59 the administering of justice by the Lord is calculated to have the same effect.

4. A Song of Triumph (59:14-17)

59:14-17 Some consider that verses 14 and 15 are an intrusion at this point,³¹ either as the result of a copyist's error or as the addition of both verses 6-7 and 14-15 by a later hand. However, it is

---

²⁹George Baur first made this proposal some 200 years ago. The view was held also by Briggs (*Psalms II*, p. 56) and Kent, *The Songs* (p. 232).

³⁰Dahood, *Psalms 51–100*, p. 71.

³¹Buttenwieser, e.g., who sees disorder in the verses, a disorder he would correct by rearranging the text (*The Psalms*, p. 714f.). So, also, with Leslie (*The Psalms*, p. 557f.). The *New English Bible* omits verse 14 and moves verse 15 to a position following verse 6.

better to attribute these repetitions to the progression of the thought of the writer. The pack hounding him comes in the evening, howling like dogs (v. 6) and God laughs at them! (v. 8). Each evening they come back, continuing their howling and scavenging (vv. 14-15). But the psalmist sings! (v. 16). He is confident that God will see him through the night and deliver him from these assailants who seek to do their evil under cover of darkness. He does not minimize their strength. This he has recognized earlier (v. 9). But then he had affirmed his trust in the Lord. Now he sings because of God's strength. **O my Strength, I sing praise to you**.

None among us, it may be, has ever needed protection from bloodthirsty men seeking our destruction. Yet however safe one may consider himself to be, there come times when he finds himself in need of strength from outside of himself, of power that only God can give. The apostle Peter warns of a deadly foe who is ever in search of victims. "Be self-controlled," he says, "and alert. Your enemy the devil prowls around like a roaring lion looking for someone to devour" (1 Pet 5:8). And, as Martin Luther wrote, "His strength and power are great." And everyone who has succumbed to a temptation to do evil knows this to be true. But, when I am appalled by such devilish power, I can look to God and to the strength to overcome that He provides. With the experience of the psalmist in mind, it is conceivable that many who will do this may also attain the victory and join with him in the refrain: **O my Strength, I sing praise to you; you, O God, are my fortress, my loving God.**

D. THE LAMENT OF A PEOPLE REJECTED OF GOD AND DEFEATED (60:1-12)

The occasion for Psalm 60 is depicted quite graphically in the opening verses. God, angry with his people, has thrown the land into convulsions as devastating as an earthquake! Later in the psalm there is reference to war with Edom, and it becomes evident that Israel has suffered a crushing and demoralizing defeat because God has not gone with her into the battle (vv. 9-10). Psalm 44 is recognized as having a similar background. There, too, the forces of Israel are defeated (and slaughtered). There is also some similarity of expression. But there are differences. In the former psalm the people of Israel are scattered among the nations, taunted by her neighbors, and the plea of faithfulness to God is voiced in their petition. Furthermore, Psalm 44 is ascribed to the sons of Korah while Psalm 60 is ascribed to David.

Buttenwieser designates the present psalm as 60A and 60B, considering them to be two genuine, but separate psalms of David.[32] That a psalm may be composite we have noted (cf. 57:7-11 and 108:1-5), and the meter of 60:6-8 varies from that of the rest of the psalm. However, this portion appears to be the quotation of an oracle of God already given. As such, it is not extraneous, and so we may view the psalm as a unit, not as two psalms in one. Oesterley states that "Psalm 60 is a single whole and suggests neither compilation (with the possible exception of the middle section) nor mutilation."[33]

Two references in the heading of the psalm provide data relative to the time of composition. One is to David's war against Syria, involving Aram-Naharaim and Aram-Zobah, in a conflict that took him to the northern reaches of Canaan and beyond, as far as the river Euphrates (2 Sam 8:3). The other reference is to Joab, David's commander-in-chief, who returned and accomplished a striking defeat of the Edomites in the valley of salt in the vicinity of the Dead Sea. Evidently, while David and the bulk of his forces were engaged with the Syrians, the Edomites had waged a war of aggression against Judah, with devastating results. It was while the people were suffering from this oppression, and before the ensuing defeat of Edom by Joab, that the psalm was written.

On the *Moabite Stone*, the inscription of King Mesha of Moab, dating from about 830 B.C., that monarch records: "In my days . . . I have triumphed over (King Ahab) and over his house and Israel has perished forever" (lines 6,7). Mesha obviously exaggerated a bit, since Israel exists 2800 years later. Even so, the defeat that Mesha inflicted upon Israel, though two centuries after the time of David, would have brought with it a time of despair comparable to that depicted in Psalm 60. More than once Israel knew the agony of foreign oppression!

---

[32]Buttenwieser, *The Psalms*, p. 67.
[33]Oesterley, *The Psalms*, p. 297.

To be a subjugated people is reason enough for agony, but
Israel's distress was compounded by the realization that God had
rejected his people (v. 1). The only recourse of the people was to
seek to be reconciled to him, with the hope that God would have
respect to their plea, and would raise a banner around which the
devout might rally (v. 4). So they presented their petition and asked
that God rescue them. In doing this they were heartened by the recollection of God's promises (vv. 5-8). On behalf of the people, David
then spoke, acknowledging that only by divine help could victory
come, and expressing confidence that God would respond (vv. 9-12).

1. Rejected and Defeated (60:1-4)

60:1 To many it may seem that the psalm opens more as a complaint than as a lament, as if God is to blame for the distressful
conditions that have befallen the land. There is no statement of
assaults by enemies. There is no confession of wrongdoing to
suggest that the suffering in the land is deserved. The opening
words speak only of what God has done and may be translated as
follows: "O God, you have rejected us, you have broken us, you
have been angry with us again and again." The KJV concludes the
verse with "O turn thyself to us again," and the RSV with the NIV
with "Restore us" (cause us to return). But the verb is not imperative. From the root שׁוּב (šûb, "turn," "return") it is often used to
indicate returning to do a thing a second time, or again, in accordance with our translation given above. God has repeatedly shown
his displeasure.

This, however, is no complaint. The people recognize that the
anger of God is aroused by evil in the land. Their cry thus becomes
an agonizing way of confessing to wrongdoing. They do not consider their plight as merely the fortuitous unfolding of events around
them, but as evidence of God's displeasure with his sinful people. It
is this realization that compounds their agony. To live in a godless
world, as the atheist must do, can culminate only in futility. But to
live in a land that has known the blessings of God, to be given the
privilege to share in his love and care, and then to so live as to
incur God's wrath and to forfeit it all, is this not more dreadful yet
to contemplate? (See 2 Peter 2:20-22.)

Thoughts of the anger of God may never occur to some who delight to speak of his love and mercy, but his anger against deliberate and continued evil is real, nonetheless. We rejoice to read that he is "a forgiving God, gracious and compassionate, slow to anger and abounding in love" (Neh 9:17). But the mercy and pardon are for the penitent.

60:2 You have shaken the land. The description is of an earthquake, devastating in its effect, but the language is metaphorical, a figure of the horrors and aftermath of war (see Isa 14:16-17). It is noteworthy that although it is people who wage war, it is God who makes the earth to quake, throwing down the high towers and mighty schemes of men. When the Lord called the youth Jeremiah, he gave him a specific assignment "to uproot and tear down, to destroy and overthrow" (Jer 1:10). It was not a capricious assignment, however, but one that was to make possible another — "to build and to plant." God may often use the events of this world to bring down mighty strongholds of evil, in order that "what cannot be shaken may remain" (Heb 12:27).

The latter part of verse 2 has commonly been viewed as an entreaty — **mend its fractures.** More likely, the appeal does not begin until verse 4, the first three verses being wholly concerned with a description of the devastation suffered from the hand of an angry God. The word translated "mend" as an imperative of רפא (*rāphā'*), could also be the adjective of רפה (*rāphāh*), a different root meaning "to sink down," "to languish," "to be weak." Thus Dahood would translate verse 2b: "Weak from its fractures, much did (the land) totter."[34] The NEB reads: "It (the land) gives way and crumbles into pieces." Such a meaning fits the context of the verse.

60:3-4 You have shown your people desperate times, literally, "You caused (us) to see (or, to endure) hard things." The reference to wine in this verse is a figure of the helpless condition of the nation as though it had been make to drink potent wine — **wine that makes us stagger.** The verb of verse 4 should be read as a precative perfect, not as the indicative.[35] "Give to the ones fearing

---

[34]Dahood, *Psalms 51-100*, p. 78.
[35]So Dahood, *Psalms 51-100*, p. 79; Leslie, *The Psalms*, p. 232; and Buttenwieser, *The Psalms*, p. 81.

you a banner to be unfurled in confronting the bow." The meaning
is to provide a rallying point for God's people who must face the
enemy bowmen.[36] With this request to rally those devoted to God,
the cry of distress ends. **Selah.** And thus the way is opened for a
specific appeal to the Lord.

2. A Plea for Deliverance (60:5-8)

60:5 That this verse belongs with those that follow is indicated
by its inclusion with these verses in Ps 108:6-13. And verse 9 of the
present psalm indicates that the speaker here is an individual,
undoubtedly David. His plea is direct: **Save us and help us with
your right hand.** But first the reason for the request is stated: **That
those you love may be delivered.** David is interceding on behalf of
his people. God has been angry with them, but they are still his
people, his beloved! The need of the moment is for reconciliation,
but this can only come by the grace of God. The psalmist does have
hope that God will hear and respond to his plea, a hope that is
awakened when he remembers what God had promised.

60:6-7 Some believe verses 6-8 to be a quotation from an earlier
source but they could well be a summary of promises God had
made to Israel earlier. **God has spoken from his sanctuary.** This
translation, "from his sanctuary," is a possibility, the sanctuary being
his heavenly abode. But the reading, "in his holiness," is to be preferred, for, indeed, a holy God will be true to his word. The NIV
translates the same word as such in Ps 89:35: "Once for all, I have
sworn *by my holiness* — and I will not lie to David."

The words that follow reflect the sovereignty of God over the
nations, with specific reference to the portion of the world related
to his people. **Succoth,** east of Jordan, and **Shechem** to the west
represent both sides of the river as belonging to Israel. **Gilead** and
Manasseh identify the territories east of the Jordan; **Ephraim** and

---

[36]The word for bow (קֶשֶׁת, *qōšeṭ*) is rendered "truth" in some versions, but
appears only once in the Scriptures with that meaning (Prov 22:21, as
qōš°ṭ). The usual meaning "bow" (variant of קֶשֶׁת, *qōšeth*) is better suited to
the context in our psalm.

Judah those of the west. "Ephraim," as the most powerful of the northern tribes, represents **my helmet. Judah**, then, is **my scepter!** or "ruler's staff" (not "lawgiver," KJV). (David was of the tribe of Judah.)

60:8 Moab and **Edom**, east and south of the Dead Sea, and **Philistia** on the sea coast, had all at some time made war on Israel, Edom being the current adversary. But they are not beyond God's power to control. **Moab is my washbasin** — not destroyed, but the proud nation will learn humility (Isa 16:6). **Upon Edom I toss my sandal**, like Boaz who took off his sandal and gave it to his *kinsman redeemer* in order to *legalize* the transaction of acquiring the land of Elimelech (Ruth 4:7). Thus, God *acquired* Moab. The reference to Philistia is better understood in the light of Ps 108:9 — **Over Philistia I shout in triumph!**

3. The True Hope of a Nation (60:9-12)

60:9-11 The recollection of God's sovereignty over the nations is sufficient to rekindle hope in the heart of the psalmist. It also awakens him to the realization that only God can provide the help that is needed, and that with God's help victory is assured. But will God help? David is not so presumptuous as to take such assistance for granted. He does make it the burden of his prayer. **Who will bring me to the fortified city?** The chief city of Edom was Petra (or, Sela, 2 Kgs 14:7). Except over mountains, the only approach to the site is through a narrow gorge, over a mile in length and descending between high, overhanging cliffs. David is aware of the difficulty of overcoming this stronghold of the enemy of his people. But he faces a dilemma, a perplexity reflected in a literal translation of verse 10: **Is it not you,O God, you who have rejected us and no longer go out with our armies?** And without God's help, future defeat could be anticipated. It is with this realization that David makes his plea. **Give us aid against the enemy, for the help of man is worthless.**

The prayer is simple but revelatory of the spirit of the one who prays it. He has learned humility, admitting his own insufficiency. He is confident of the universal sovereignty of God. He is willing to put his cause in the hand of God, believing that things impossible to man are not impossible to him. And underlying all of this, there is a belief in the mercy of God toward a people who seek him in the right spirit. How else would he be moved to approach the God who has been angry with his people, who has rejected them and caused them to suffer hard things? (vv. 1-2). He can make no demands upon God, but he can pray to him for help.

60:12 The psalm ends on a note of confidence. **With God we will gain the victory.** The preposition may be "through," "in," or "with," the meaning being "by the help of God." The statement is a commitment to cooperation with God. He enables, we *do*; he empowers, we *do victoriously*! This expression reflects the basic meaning of the Hebrew, which indicates acts of strength, power, or valor. This is no prayer to be excused from the conflicts of life, but that God be ever present to help. With the assurance of his presence one may face the future with confidence, do valiantly, and leave the outcome to him, for he it is that shall tread down our enemies. God has not abandoned the cause of the just.

PART THREE: DAVID AND THE GREAT KING (61–72)

I. THE KING'S NEED (61:1–64:10)

A. EARNEST PRAYER, CONFIDENT EXPECTATION (61:1-8)

Like many others, Psalm 61 has been variously classified by different writers, sometimes in widely divergent fashion. In general, it is said to be a lament of an individual "hard pressed by trouble." Mowinckel, however, considers it a *national* lament, but more a prayer for protection from impending disaster, offered before a battle.[1] Others believe it to be the lament of a king, perhaps on a distant campaign,[2] or, in the face of approaching death, offering a prayer for "admittance to the celestial dwelling of God,"[3] or being gravely ill, feeling himself to be at "the ends of the earth" confronting the "chasm of the underworld, the realm of the dead."[4] Weiser recognizes the lament motif, but on the basis of the general spirit of the writer he would identify the psalm as a thanksgiving song, praising God for having answered a petition formerly given. Weiser sees the psalmist as a soul separated from God, desiring to be brought back again to the divine presence. In his view the separation is not by miles distant but by "an unbridgable gulf that in the helplessness and misery this causes, he pictures himself at the other 'end of the earth'" (metaphorically).[5] But he is restored to God's fellowship (through worship in the temple) and desires to dwell in

---

[1]Mowinckel, *The Psalms in Israel's Worship*, I:226.
[2]See Eaton, *Kingship and the Psalms*, p. 48.
[3]Dahood, *Psalms 51–100*, p. 84.
[4]Leslie, *The Psalms*, p. 268.
[5]Weiser, *The Psalms*, p. 443.

God's house for ever, where he is beyond the power of the enemy (vv. 3-4). Eerdmans does not consider the psalm to be a lamentation at all but the prayer of an official "a great distance from Jerusalem," a prayer for the king.[6]

From the above may be seen the great diversity of opinion relative to the nature of the psalm and to its setting. It is also evident that eminent scholars can be in error, for obviously all of the above cannot be correct. Whatever be the true provenance of the psalm, diverse positions will have to be rejected. (This obvious conclusion does not impugn the scholarship of any, but it should be cause for humility on the part of all.)

There remains to be considered the traditional view of the Jewish fathers that this is a psalm of David. The period to which it is generally assigned is the time of Absalom's revolt. Until the rebellion was crushed, David had to flee from Jerusalem to Mahanaim (2 Sam 17:27ff.). In the view of some who hold to the Davidic authorship, the prayer for the king (vv. 6-7) was inserted in the psalm at a later time when it came to be used in public worship. It would not have been unusual, however, for David to have prayed such a prayer on his own behalf. Because of its personal nature, and to avoid the appearance of egotism, he prays for himself in the third person: "Increase the days of the king's life," not "my life." The promise to sing praises to God (v. 8) is expressed by a verb that means "to make music" (whether vocal or with an instrument) and its use is in keeping with the image of David as one skilled in playing the harp.

With due respect for all of the views regarding its origin, to the present writer it seems best to consider Psalm 61 to be what it appears to be, the prayer of one some distance from home, experiencing heartfelt distress, caused, in part at least, by an unnamed enemy. Awareness of God's faithfulness and goodness in the past kindles a longing for the experience once again of the security he had formerly known. Thoughts of home include concern for the king's welfare, for whom or by whom a prayer is offered. On a note of thanksgiving then the psalm concludes with a promise to sing God's praise for ever. The psalm may well have come from David.

---

[6]Eerdmans, *The Hebrew Book of Psalms*, p. 307f.

1. Hear My Cry (61:1-4)

61:1-2 The psalm opens with an expression of deep anguish. **Hear my cry, O God.** The Hebrew indicates a shrill cry, sometimes of jubilation but here of sorrow, an outcry of distress. That he calls **from the ends of the earth** leads some to suppose that he is an exile in a distant land. But the translation could be "from the end of the land," meaning "from the border." In this case, it is the separation from home that is decried — not necessarily a matter of great distance. And his **heart grows faint**; that is, distressed, meaning that he is exhausted (as from some illness). Yet he takes hope in recourse to God. **Lead me to the rock that is higher than I.** A strange request? What does it mean? First, there is the recognition that there is such a rock, such a refuge from the storm or from the harassment of the enemy. The very fact that there exists a haven of rest should inspire hope in the heart of the despairing. Secondly, the psalmist has reason to believe that God will bring him to that place of security. True, the rock is "higher than I," but God can bring him hither. Each person who looks to God may believe that "the Lord is not done with me yet," and will lead me in the way of faith to new heights of peace and confidence.

61:3-4 For you have been my refuge. The verb is perfect, the "perfect of experience,"[7] describing an action or condition in the past that extends into the present. God has continually been the refuge of the psalmist, even though he does not enumerate the occasions. (Can not each of us, from our own experiences, recall times of God's deliverance through the passing years?) The recollection of God's help in the past gives the psalmist confidence for the present and hope for the future. Perhaps it was such a thought as this that inspired Robert Browning when he wrote: "Grow old along with me; the best is yet to be."

In saying that God has been his refuge, the psalmist is acknowledging that God himself is the Rock in which he finds security. The personal nature of this relationship is reflected in verses 3-4 in the progression from the sheltering rock to the **strong tower. I long to dwell in your tent,** God's tent, offering hospitality and protection, and

---

[7]Kautzsch, Gesenius' *Hebrew Grammar*, 106k, p. 312.

finally to **the shelter of your wings.** It is the very presence of God that is the refuge of the psalmist. His is the confidence later expressed by Paul: "If God is for us, who can be against us?" (Rom 8:31).

Verse 4 may be a request: "Let me dwell in thy tent for ever!" (RSV). Or, an anticipated future: "I will dwell, etc." In either case, there is the confidence that the security in God that is the burden of his prayer will be realized. The NIV opts for request above by adding the word "I *long* to dwell," a strong hope!

2. You, O God, Have Heard (61:5)

61:5 This confidence is expressed in the midst of the prayer. **For you have heard my vows, O God.** The verb means not only "heard" but "responded to." Prayers were often accompanied by a vow to bring a thank-offering or to render some special service for the Lord. And God had responded. **The heritage of those who fear your name** may be metaphorical language, indicating the blessing that will be surely given to those who honor God. The psalmist exults that he has known such blessing. In the present time of need it is a happy remembrance.

3. God Will Bless His King (61:6-7)

61:6 In 2 Sam 7:16 God promised that the throne of David would be established for ever. In view of such a promise, and in recognition that it would certainly be kept, verses 6 and 7 are not an intrusion into the psalm but a continuance of the confidence already expressed. It is not unfitting that these words be upon the lips of David, as an affirmation of his trust. **Increase the days of the king's life.** Of course the words are a prayer, for no one tells God what he will do. But it is a prayer confidently expressed. **His years for many generations.** That is, he shall be sustained by God and enjoy the privilege of his care. The term translated "many generations" indicates, basically, time in the past so distant that one may not fathom its beginning, or so far in the future as to be lost in infinity. It is such a term as used in the greeting, "O king, live forever!" (Dan 2:4).

61:7 Appoint your love and faithfulness to protect him. How often through the Psalms there is joyful reference to the unfailing love of God (*ḥesed*), present to sustain, whatever the circumstances. The "truth" (*'ĕmeth*, translated as "faithfulness") is that which is firmly established, in this case the unchanging integrity of God, and so, faithfulness. The one whose security is firmly anchored in God is as secure as God is secure.

4. I Will Sing Forever (61:8)

61:8 The psalm that opened with an outcry closes with a song. Indeed, the psalm does not really close, for the song that has arisen in the heart will go on day after day. **Then will I ever sing praise to your name.** To praise God's name is to praise God himself (just as dishonoring that name dishonors him). Through praise God and his sustaining grace are kept in mind. And since his blessings come day by day, one's remembrance of him should be constant, and for ever. The psalm closes with eternity in view, but an eternity that is to be lived one day at a time. It is one's daily walk with the Lord that gives any validity to a professed concern for an eternity with him. **Day after day** — These are the final words of the psalm. "Today, if you hear his voice, do not harden your hearts" (Ps 95:7,8).

B. GOD MY SURE AND CERTAIN HOPE (62:1-12)

Psalm 61 began with a cry of anguish. In contrast, Psalm 62 breathes the atmosphere of patient, unwavering trust in God. Augustine spoke of the restlessness of the human soul until it finds rest in God. This psalm is the testimony of one who has found that rest. He has been lied about and slandered by malicious men seeking his downfall but has remained unshaken. The psalm is not a prayer. It is not a lament. It is a testimony that God alone is worthy of our implicit trust. God, the embodiment of power, abundant in love, and just toward all (vv. 11-12), is all-sufficient as our strength and stay. None can be compared to him, and the schemes and devices that men would substitute for God are doomed to failure. This message the psalmist wants to share (v. 8). His aim is to tell others about God in order that he may challenge them to trust in him also. Except in the closing verse, he does not address God directly, as in a prayer or a lament. He addresses his people as one whose soul is overflowing with good news he wishes to share — God alone is our sure and certain hope, sure because he is not subject to change or failure, and certain because he has demonstrated his willingness and power to save. This certainty is affirmed repeatedly. God is recognized as "rock," "salvation," "fortress," "my salvation and honor," "my mighty rock," and "my refuge."

This testimony (vv. 1-7), is introductory to the instruction that is given in verses 8-12. The didactic nature of these latter verses is readily seen. They could fit quite well in the book of Proverbs. It is not surprising therefore that some would classify the psalm as didactic. Dahood is of the opinion that the wisdom element is not sufficient to justify such a classification. He calls it, simply, "a psalm of trust."[8] Certainly it is that. Confidence in God could scarcely be expressed more dynamically.

There is little in the psalm that would enable us to determine its setting. Verses 3-4, however, suggest that the writer is a person of eminent position in the land; we would assume that he is one who is prominent in public life. In any case, it is evident that his trust in God is basic to his daily existence. But he is opposed by those seeking to bring him down. Masters of deceit through lies and innuendo they would undermine his standing, even while making hypocritical confessions of loyalty. And far from following the lead of this one devoted to God, they would put their trust in the gross national product and in their own ability, through extortion and outright robbery, to satisfy their lust for riches, which have become their god. However, such persons and their schemes are a delusion. Ultimate power belongs to God alone. Knowing this, and knowing also that the Lord is a God of love and justice, the psalmist will continue in his steadfast trust in him. He has found God alone to be sufficient as the refuge of his life.

---

[8]Dahood, *Psalms 51–100*, p. 90.

1. God the Sure Refuge (62:1-4)

62:1-2 My soul finds rest in God alone. The opening word in Hebrew, אַךְ (*'ak*, an adverb, emphatic, meaning, "yea, for no one other than God!" or "Surely") is expressed in our text at the end as "alone." The significance of the verse is seen in the translation of the Jewish Publication Society: "Only for God doth my soul wait in stillness; from Him cometh my salvation."[9] There is none other in whom one could have such quiet confidence. The psalmist could sing, "Be still, my soul" in the assurance that he was in God's care. **He alone is my rock,** etc. The uniqueness of God as savior and the only defense necessary is reiterated. Consequently, there is the calm assurance, **I will never be shaken.** The Hebrew has a qualifying adverb "greatly" (רַבָּה, *rabbāh*, not used in the NIV) indicating that the writer is aware that he may expect assaults against him and that he can expect to feel the pressure of circumstances. But God will enable him to stand; i.e., "I will not be shaken greatly."

62:3-4 In verse 3 he addresses those who threaten him. **How long,** he asks, **will you assault a man?** How long indeed will they attempt to overthrow one who is sustained by God? Is he a **leaning wall,** about to collapse? Perhaps they think so, but their attacks will be futile since God upholds him. Or, the "leaning wall" may be the assailants themselves (KJV), so near to collapse that they are in no position to overthrow another. Just what the adversaries are about is stated specifically in verse 4: **They fully intend to topple him**[10] **from his lofty place,** that one, obviously, being himself. To accomplish their purpose, **they take delight in lies** (smear tactics) to undermine his good name. Hypocritically, **with their mouths they bless,** feigning loyalty (?) **but in their hearts they curse.** Now, however, their hypocrisy has been exposed and the psalmist's trust in God is unshaken.

---

[9]As quoted by Cohen, *The Psalms*, p. 194.

[10]The Hebrew has no stated object of the verb "to topple." To use the third, masculine, singular pronoun "him" is to obscure the meaning since the writer is referring to himself and not another. It is not clear in the NIV if the "him" is referring to the psalmist.

2. A God to Be Trusted by All (62:5-8)

With his faith reconfirmed he now repeats the refrain with which the psalm opened — but with significant variations! There he made the simple assertion, "My soul is in silent expectation before God," or "waits on God." Now with an imperative he commands his soul to continue to trust:

62:5-8a Find rest, O my soul, in God alone. There he affirmed, **my hope comes from him** (God). But he has experienced God's deliverance and now he can say, my expectation is from him, meaning: "I know that my continued trust in him will not bring disappointment." There he had asserted, "I will not be shaken greatly." Now he can say, **I will not be shaken** (period)! "Salvation," "honor," and "mighty rock" are his from God, and so he may say confidently, God is **my refuge.** All of this is his testimony given in order to awaken his people to trust God also and to commit their way to him. **Trust in him at all times, O people.**

If not in God, in whom or in what should one's trust be placed? (Some of the alternatives are mentioned in verses 9-10 and are found to be woefully inadequate. Certainly men without integrity, no matter what else may be said about them, are not to be trusted.) The words "at all times" are significant, for it is quite likely that the person who does not trust God at all times does not trust in him at any time! Note that the people are not asked to believe in God. That would be a superfluous request, since belief in God was universal. One's belief in God makes little difference unless he trusts God. Only when faith is active does God become significant in one's life. And how much greater that significance when he comes to trust him "at all times." The reality of God's presence in one's daily life — it is this that the psalmist would desire for his people.

62:8b Pour out your hearts to him. Let it overflow. Unburden your soul! Do not suppose that God must be addressed only in formal, well articulated prayer. The agonizings of one's heart and spirit are known to him also. We may be sure that the waiting upon God in confident silence, expressed in verse 1, came only after the psalmist had brought his burden to the Lord. Now, he wants the assurance that is his to become that of his people too.

3. God the Incomparable (62:9-12)

62:9-10a The psalmist has given his testimony of what God has done for him. He has called upon his people to put their trust in him. He has intimated that God is not only a refuge but the only refuge that is sure. Now he would show why that is so. First, he comments upon the transitory nature of man. The reference to **lowborn men** and to **the highborn** in the verse signifies all mankind. The former are the common people. They are **but a breath** (so also RSV), "a puff of wind" (NEB), and so are certainly not to take the place of God in one's trust. The latter are men of prominence, whether by reason of position or wealth. But these are **but a lie**, or "a delusion" (RSV). This is not to say that all men of high estate are liars, but it is a delusion to put one's ultimate hope in them. All are, after all, subject to the temptation to deceive, when by doing so they can advance their own cause. But "God is not a man, that he should lie" (Num. 23:19). And God is eternal. However trustworthy human leaders may be, in a moment their life may end, and however great, all have "feet of clay." Such are a temporary refuge at best, and deceptive at their worst. Their "weight" is as nothing compared to the eternal God — they are altogether lighter than breath (NKJV, "vapor"). How far better to trust in God, the Eternal, who is forever faithful.

In every age there is the temptation to make riches the object of one's trust — how few the exceptions! An example is seen in Psalm 30. There the writer made a bold assertion: "'When I felt secure,' I said, 'I will never be shaken'"(v. 6). But he was moved until he found that God was his only sure hope. The fraud and deception in the world where money is worshiped, the graft and bribery in public life, the pandering to the animal appetites in the secular world — all of these are a reflection of a society worshiping at the altar of materialism. To such comes the warning: **Do not trust in extortion or take pride in stolen goods.** Those who do practice extortion, those who embezzle, are actually trusting in their own cleverness at deception. But this is self-deception, a vain trust.

62:10b Though your riches increase, do not set your heart on them. This is not to say that wealth is evil or that it is wrong to possess riches. It does say that to trust in wealth is false security, for all reliance upon earthly possessions must, in the end, prove to be disappointing. In what, then, or in whom, may a person trust with complete confidence? In the One who is *my salvation, my rock, my fortress*; in God, with whom nothing else or no one else may be compared. Two words alone serve the psalmist, in the closing verses, to indicate God's incomparable nature: strength and love.

62:11-12 One thing God has spoken, two things have I heard. The revelation to be made is of such significance as to deserve repetition. **That you, O God, are strong.** Sublime truth! He is the Creator, the Almighty. But even more marvelous is the additional truth that he is also a God of unfailing love. **And that you, O Lord, are loving.** Here again in the Scriptures we have reference to the *ḥesed* of God, to that enduring, unchanging loving-kindness that he offers to those who would enter into covenant with him and respond with a similar love. It is the combination of God's power with his love that is so wonderful in our eyes. In regard to this, the comment of Stewart Perowne is significant to us: "This is the only true representation of God. Power without love is brutality, and love without power is weakness. Power is the strong foundation of love, and love is the beauty and the crown of power."[11] Who would not be moved to call upon such a God as this? The God of love is not capricious, changing toward his creatures according to some whimsical mood. The combination of power and love assures that he will deal justly with all — yea, and with mercy! **Surely you will reward each person according to what he has done.** The power of God makes certain that the outcome of events will be according to his will; the love of God assures that his will is righteous and just and compassionate. The wicked will be brought to account for their wickedness, and those who direct their lives in the ways of righteousness will not go unrewarded. It is on this basis that the appeal is made to all to put their trust in him. He is altogether worthy of such trust. He alone is worthy.

---

[11]Perowne, *The Book of Psalms*, 1:445.

C. A SOUL'S THIRST FOR GOD (63:1-11)

"If only I knew where to find him!" (Job 23:3). The soul's longing for God expressed in this agonizing cry of the patriarch Job has found an echo in the hearts of many. There are occasions when one's acute awareness of his own mortality and of his own weakness thrusts him upon God. Psalm 63 is from one who experiences this and finds his need satisfied. He has known the delight of fellowship with God in the past, especially in worship in the sanctuary in Jerusalem (v. 2). But now he is cut off from the familiar setting. He is in a "dry and weary land" (v. 1), a fugitive from enemies who would destroy him (v. 9). Under these conditions his thirst for God is especially acute. Now in his moment of exile and peril he longs for some demonstration of the power and glory of God he has formerly experienced. Even so, his heart will give way to praise again, so certain he is of God's continued presence with him (v. 3). Accordingly, there is good reason to consider the psalm, from beginning to end, a hymn of thanksgiving.

Differing with the above, some view the psalm as a personal lament of a devout Hebrew in exile. Buttenwieser affirms that "to the exclusion of every other thought," the writer is expressing the "craving of his soul for the life divine."[12] So he would classify the psalm, not as a praise hymn but one continued impassioned prayer, the tenor of which is reflected in his translation of verse 5: "Oh, that the craving of my soul may be satisfied."[13] Mowinckel considers the psalm to be a national lament but not of the ordinary type. Usually such a lament is a response to some great national distress. This psalm, however, he identifies as a lament in view of impending danger, a "protective psalm" designed to ward off the evil. Thus the psalm would serve a cultic purpose. A time of prayer and fasting would be declared by the king, who would lead his people in the presentation of their petition to God.[14]

---

[12]Buttenwieser, *The Psalms*, p. 518. In maintaining his position, Buttenwieser recognizes only verses 1-8 as the original psalm. Weiser, however, views the psalm as a unit, asserting that the various suggestions for transposing or eliminating certain passages are superfluous, (*The Psalms*, p. 434).

[13]Buttenwieser, *The Psalms*, p. 518.

[14]Mowinckel, *Psalms in Israel's Worship*, 1:219.

The very personal nature of the psalm, however, seems rather to refer it to personal experience. Admittedly, the psalm does bear some of the characteristics of a lament. But it is primarily a strong affirmation of faith. To one who says to God, "Your love is better than life" (63:3), lamentation can be only a transitory experience. "Weeping may remain for a night, but rejoicing comes in the morning" (Ps 30:5). This psalm breathes confidence and trust on the part of its author, and there are no compelling reasons why that individual may not have been David, as the heading suggests. At the time of Absalom's rebellion, David was forced to flee Jerusalem to the wilderness of Judah (2 Sam 15:23,28). Thus he found himself cut off from the city and from his familiar surroundings. But he was not cut off from God!

1. God, the Soul's Desire (63:1-4)

63:1a-1b The deep personal feeling of the psalmist toward God is evident in the opening words: **O God, you are my God.** All that is said about God elsewhere in the Psalms is summarized in the simple confession of faith in this chapter. You are my rock, my high tower, my defense, God of all power, God of love, righteous Lord. **Earnestly I seek you.** The verb means, literally, "seek in the morning." (See Isa 26:9.) By extension it means to do a thing as a matter of first importance, or to do "earnestly," thus the NIV translation. For David, this is a matter of first importance. He does seek God earnestly. His whole being, "body and soul," cries out for God — and for nothing else! Only the presence of God in his life can satisfy the longing of his soul.

63:1c-2 In a dry and weary land. These words should be understood as descriptive of the region in which the psalmist finds himself, and not metaphorically, as some view them — thirsting "as if in a dry land." This desolate area is a far cry from the peaceful security he has known in the past. In the sanctuary he had experienced the nearness of God in his power and glory. So now, with greater intensity because of the circumstances, he longs for God anew. Memories of the past have stirred within him the present desire for the divine presence. But also recollections of God's past mercies have rekindled faith and hope, and this calls for praise.

63:3-4 Because your love is better than life, my lips will glorify you. Is David saying, "Why should I worry about life so long as I am assured of your love?" It would seem so. Or, stated conversely, "What would life be worth without that love?" Life in fellowship with God, if only for a moment, would be more to be desired than an eternity without him. Yet David contemplates a continuing relationship with God and will go on blessing the Lord, **as long as I live.**

2. God, the Soul's Satisfaction (63:5-8)

63:5-8 In Psalm 23 the poet wrote, "My cup overflows." Here he says, "I am satisfied as with a rich and sumptuous feast" (v. 5, NEB). From the figure of thirst of verse 1 he moves to that of hunger, only to affirm that the deepest longings of his soul for God have been fully met. His deep satisfaction in the Lord is such as to bring a song of praise and gratitude from his heart to be sounded with **singing lips.** This is followed by three verses that are a unit, including both a confession of the help the psalmist has received from God and a statement of his desire to remain close to the Lord. **On my bed I remember you; I think of you through the watches of the night.** Spurgeon observed: "If day's cares tempt us to forget God, it is well that night's quiet should lead us to remember him. *We see best in the dark if we there see God best*" (italics added).[15] Whether during a sleepless night or in an all night prayer vigil through the three watches of the night (v. 6), the thoughts of the psalmist are upon God. God had been his heart's desire and God is now remembered. More than this, he meditates upon God, and this is of greater significance than the bare remembrance of him. (Joshua was to meditate on the law so that he would be "careful to do everything written in it" (Josh 1:8). The Hebrew term, הָגָה (hāgāh), has a basic meaning of "murmur" or "mutter," as if one were "talking a matter over with himself." Dahood renders the phrase, "Through my vigils [I] muse on you."[16] The result of such meditation has convinced the psalmist of two things: **You are my help**, and **your right**

---

[15]Spurgeon, *Treasury*, II:67.
[16]Dahood, *Psalms 51–100*, p. 95.

hand upholds me. His reaction also has been twofold: **I sing in the shadow of your wings**, and **My soul clings to you,** or "I humbly follow thee with all my heart" (NEB). He has found in God full satisfaction for the longing of his soul.

3. God, the Soul's Defense (63:9-11)

63:9-10 Only now does he give thought to those who are the cause of his present condition as a fugitive from home, those who seek to destroy him. He knows that his life is in jeopardy, but he also knows that God is his defense. With confidence he states the judgment that will fall upon them. They shall go into the lower parts of the earth; that is, into the underworld, the abode of the dead. **They will be given over to the sword.** This indicates that armed combat on the part of the enemy is anticipated. These who would take up the sword would themselves fall on the field of battle, unburied, and thus would **become food for jackals.**

63:11 But the king will rejoice in God. It should not be thought bizarre that David would speak thus of himself in the third person after using the first person "I" throughout the psalm.[17] After all, these enemies are found to be opposing God's anointed king, a king who continues resolutely to trust this same God. He is confident that God will give the victory, that future rejoicing will be his. As for others, **all who swear by God's name will praise him**; that is, everyone who gives his solemn oath in God's name, thereby acknowledging him as true God, shall glory — or, will shout "Halleluia"! The Hebrew root for this latter term is הָלַל (*hālal*). The message is simple; its implication profound. These whose God is the Lord will have abundant reason to **praise him**, "glory" in that relationship (KJV), to "exult" therein (NEB). Expressions of joyful praise and thanksgiving will flow from their lips. By contrast, **the mouths of liars will be silenced.** Such persons have no fear of God

---

[17]Some scholars consider verse 11 to be an intrusion in the text — Gunkel, e.g., who considers it an addition by one who would adapt the Psalm for public worship. Mowinckel, however, recognizes the integrity of the verse as a part of the original psalm. (See Leslie, *The Psalms*, p. 273.)

in their hearts. They do not respect him or his ways but spread lies in order to topple the king. However, the latter is not worried. God is his defense, and God will deal with the treachery of his foes.

D. A SOUL RELIES ON GOD (64:1-10)

Threatened but not dismayed. These words are descriptive of the emotional state of the author of Psalm 64. "The conspiracy of the wicked," though not openly hostile, are secretly scheming evil against him (v. 2). They are vicious and sneaky (vv. 3-4), and, quite certain that their plots will remain undetected (vv. 5-6). But the psalmist is aware that he is in danger and his response is twofold. First of all, there is apprehension, because his foes are seeking his destruction. It is the apprehension that has caused him to bring the matter to God, and the straightforward nature of his appeal indicates that he comes, not as a stranger, but as one who is accustomed to talking with the Lord. Also quite clearly revealed is his assurance that in relying upon God he will not be disappointed. He will be vindicated and he will be delivered.

In view of this clear note of confidence, it seems a bit strained to call the psalm a lament, as it is usually designated.[18] Many have paid respect to the strong note of assurance in the psalm by the way they have qualified their description. Thus William R. Taylor says that it "follows the pattern of a lament"[19] while Artur Weiser says that "the first part . . . is cast in the style of a lament."[20] Claus Westermann says that it is "a lament that has been turned to praise," one of a class of psalms "on the way from petition or supplication and lament" to becoming a psalm of praise.[21] Mowinckel, while retaining the classification of lament, recognizes this as in a subgroup that he designates "protective psalms"; that is, psalms designed to secure divine aid in the face of some impending danger. "The tone of the protective psalm," he says, is "brighter

---

[18]See Rodd, *Psalms 1-72*, p. 117; Eaton, *Psalms*, p. 163
[19]Taylor, *The Book of Psalms*, p. 333.
[20]Weiser, *The Psalms*, p. 457.
[21]Westermann, *Praise and Lament*, p. 80.

than that of the psalms of lamentation. Above all, the confidence and assurance of getting help is more prominent in them."[22] This observation is especially true of Psalm 64.

1. The Assurance of God's Help (64:1-2)

64:1a Hear me, O God, as I voice my complaint. This is the sole request that the psalmist makes of God. Granted this, he is sure that the Lord will respond to his need. But is it necessary to ask God to hear? One cannot prevent him from hearing — he who knows even the innermost thoughts of the heart (Ps 94:11). However, the request for God to hear is an acknowledgment that he is under no obligation to do so. As H.H. Rowley observes: "We come into the presence of God, not as men who know they are bound to be heard, but as men who realize that it is of God's mercy that we are heard. We have no claim on him to the fulfillment of our desires, but present our petitions humbly before him."[23] It is in this vein that the psalmist asks God to hear. And to hear what? "My complaint" (also RSV, NASV). This seems, to the present writer, to be an interpretation on the part of the translator and bears the wrong connotation if it suggests an attitude of complaining. The same may be said of the translation, "my lament" (NEB). Weiser renders the noun as "my trouble,'" without the connotation of complaint: "Hear my voice, O God, in my trouble."[24] Better yet is the suggestion of Kidner, "My troubled thoughts."[25] A neutral translation would be, "my meditation" (NKJV). The psalmist is saying, "Lord, please hear me as I go over this matter." The implication is that once God has heard, he will then make an appropriate response.

64:1b-2 These lines have been translated as petitions! **Protect my life . . . Hide me.** However, following Kirkpatrick and Eerdmans,[26] we would recognize these words as a statement of confidence. The

---

[22]Mowinckel, *The Psalms in Israel's Worship*, 1:220.

[23]Rowley, *Faith of Israel*, p. 172.

[24]Weiser, *The Psalms*, p. 456.

[25]Kidner, *Psalms 1–72*, p. 227.

[26]Kirkpatrick, *The Book of Psalms*, p. 357; Eerdmans, *The Hebrew Book of Psalms*, p. 313.

psalmist is sure that once he has presented the matter to God, he will act on his behalf. "You will protect my life . . . You will hide me."

2. The Arrows of the Wicked (64:3-6)

64:3-4 From this forthright expression of faith, he proceeds to a description of the evil designs of his adversaries. At the outset, it is apparent that their purpose is to destroy him, with words, with malicious slander, misrepresentation or lying accusations. Some would hold that these who are the enemy are resorting to magic, casting spells upon him from which there is no escape. But, as Kidner notes, "It needs no magic to spread havoc with the tongue."[27] Throughout the Scriptures the power for evil that is concentrated in the tongue is specifically noted (see Jas 3:2-10). Here vivid mental images of that power are drawn in the poetic language of the psalmist. He could have said simply that enemies were plotting against him. But he pictures them as having **tongues like swords.** With words like **arrows . . . [t]hey shoot from ambush** and **without fear** since they are careful to stay undetected. Thus with simile and metaphor the picture is drawn.

64:5-6 In verse 5 the figure is changed. The warrior with the sword, the bowman waiting in ambush, have become the hunter of prey who conceals his pitfalls in the pathway of the unsuspecting. **They encourage each other** in an evil manner. They congratulate one another on their cleverness, so certain are they that their schemes will remain undetected. The text of verse 6 is difficult of translation, but the general meaning may be: "They scheme evil things" (saying) 'We have perfected a scheme that is well schemed.'" The concluding line of the verse is a comment of the psalmist indicating that the thinking of such men is beyond our understanding — **Surely the mind and heart of man are cunning.** How could they think that their deeds would remain hidden? God would know! And he would act.

---

[27]Kidner, *Psalms 1-72*, p. 228.

3. The Arrow of God (64:7-9)

64:7-9 With verse 7 the tenor of the psalm changes abruptly. If ever there has been even an inclination toward lament, now it is completely gone. The tables are turned speedily and decisively upon those who plotted evil. If they have arrows drawn ready for a sudden attack from their concealed position, God also has his arrows, and these evil ones are not hidden from him. Suddenly he directs his arrow against them, and they themselves are smitten with the wounds they would have inflicted upon the innocent. Their evil tongues with which they would have destroyed another will be the means of their own downfall. In other psalms in which the psalmist is threatened, he looks to God as his shield, his rock, his strength (e.g., Ps 28:7; 31:2). Here the emphasis is upon the retribution that is certain to fall upon the enemy, rendering him harmless (cf. Ps 7:15,16; 57:6). The evil he has devised against another will fall upon himself instead. This apparently is the meaning of verse 8, which may be translated: "By their (*own*) tongue they will cause it (or, *him*) to fall upon them." If it be *him*, then it is God whom they have caused to send his arrows against them. Or, preferably, they will cause *it*, their punishment, to fall. No antecedent for the pronoun is given nor intended, but *IT* will come. Thus undescribed, the horror of what they are bringing upon themselves is left to the imagination. It will be such, however, that "all that see them shall flee away" (from the dreadful sight). The translation, **will shake their heads** (as in our text, the NIV) is possible, but the reference to fear in verse 9 is more in keeping with the inclination to flee. At times it seems that the wicked continue in their pursuit of evil with impunity. But let the judgment of God fall upon them in such a way that it is recognized as his judgment — and **all mankind will fear.** Not only so, but they will talk about it — **proclaim the works of God and ponder what he has done.** "When your judgments come upon the earth," Isaiah wrote, "the people of the world learn righteousness" (Isa 26:9). Unfortunately, many seem never to learn until then.

4. A Glorious Reality (64:10)

64:10 Let the righteous rejoice, (also RSV), thus is translated the imperfect verb as imperative. But why not render the verb according to the basic significance of the imperfect, namely, that of incomplete, continued action? "The righteous rejoice (and go on rejoicing)." This is a statement of fact. Joy in the Lord is a sublime reality! Skeptics may label even the thought of God a delusion, but the joy is no delusion. "The righteous rejoice and seek refuge in the LORD and all the upright exult" (NEB). They sing *hallelujah*. The psalmist had taken note of this. Furthermore, it was true for him, for he too had exulted in the Lord. And it just might be true for the skeptic if he would make the venture. With this simple statement of the joy of the righteous the psalm closes.

II. THE KING'S RETURN (65:1–66:20)

A. PRAISE BE TO GOD (65:1-13)

The style and development of Psalm 65 parallel to a degree that of a modern-day formula for a persuasive speech. The 5-step formula is simple, logical, and effective. Its aims are to: 1) Get the attention of the audience, 2) Make clear the proposition, 3) Present the proof (the reasons) that establishes the validity of the proposition, 4) Illustrate (give clear examples), and 5) Call for a commitment or other response.

In the psalm the opening verse is the *attention getter* and *proposition* combined into one: "Praise awaits you, O God, in Zion." This statement should arrest the attention of the person who has not been praising God. Here is a debt to his Maker that he has been ignoring! And it will surely strike a responsive chord in the hearts of others who are accustomed to worship.

The remainder of the psalm is given to establish the validity of the proposition. We owe praise to God because he "hear[s] prayer" (v. 2). We owe praise to God because he blots out sin (v. 3). We praise him because he chooses folk to dwell with him (v. 4), and he answers prayer (v. 5). He makes firm the mountains (v. 6). He calms raging seas (v. 7). He causes creation to shout for joy (v. 8). He visits, waters, and enriches the earth, and provides grain (v. 9). He tends the soil like a careful gardener (v. 10). Are these not reasons enough for humankind to praise him?

To illustrate or to cite examples of God's activity on behalf of man, the psalmist will simply direct the eyes of the reader to meadows overflowing with flocks and to valleys covered with grain (v. 13). No call to commitment is issued, but surely one is not needed! The challenge has been given to contemplate the boundless mercies of God that we enjoy daily. If this is not sufficient to bring one to praise God, a formal invitation would be of little value.

Whatever the occasion of the psalm, its concern with the praise of God is unmistakable, a thanksgiving hymn from the lips of a people who know *why* they are praising him. Some believe the psalm to have been prepared for the celebration of a harvest festival. Others, because of the reference to God's stilling "the turmoil of the nations" (v. 7), consider it a praise hymn for deliverance from some national foe. Delitzsch sees it as a combination of praise for deliverance and thanksgiving for a bountiful harvest. He would date the psalm in the reign of Hezekiah, in the third year after Jerusalem had been delivered from almost certain destruction by the Assyrians.[28] It was only by the intervention of God that the city was spared (see Isa 37:36). The invasion by an enemy would have interfered with the cultivation of the land, and there would have been hunger. But two years later, the third year, the seed time and harvest routine would have been reestablished. A plentiful crop now would be especially welcome, a blessing that would indeed be cause for giving praise to God (see Isa 37:30). But whatever the occasion of the psalm when it was written, it will be seen to be quite suitable for use on many occasions when the desire to praise God wells up within one's heart. At such times the psalm gives much to consider in its contemplation of God the redeemer from sin, God the creator and Lord, and God the sustainer of life.

---

[28]Delitzsch, *The Psalms*, 2:225.

1. God Our Redeemer (65:1-4)

The first stanza of the psalm indicates that a throng of worshipers are gathered together to praise God in Jerusalem. Part of their joy is the consciousness that theirs is a special privilege, yet there is also the realization that it is a privilege that is to be extended to all mankind. The people are conscious of their need to be forgiven for sins committed and apparently have been assured of that forgiveness. This makes possible the resumption of fellowship with God and becomes the occasion for their joy and praise.

65:1 Praise awaits you, O God, in Zion. This translation recognizes the second word of the text as being the Hebrew term for "silence": literally, "Praise is silent for you." Is it not true that sometimes silence before God can be more expressive than words? For example, when there is a "quiet time" at the beginning of a time of worship. But an alternate root in this instance seems preferable, a term meaning "to be like" or "befitting."[29] And so, "It is fitting that men praise Thee, O God, in Zion and pay their vows to Thee" (Leupold). Promises, or vows, were often made to God when seeking his help in times of stress. This was not a bargaining with God but an objective means of expressing gratitude. Since God has responded to their prayers (v. 2), their praise, along with the fulfillment of their vows, is most appropriate. It may even be spoken of as praises due to the Lord.

65:2-3 O you who hear prayer, or, "the one hearing prayer" (in distinction from lifeless gods of wood and stone — see Ps 115:4-7). Always with the Hebrews there was the consciousness of God as the one *who is* the *living* God. Only such a God could hear and answer prayer. For this reason, it is to him that all flesh (all humankind) will come. Some would conclude this statement with "on account of sins" (v. 3, RSV). However, this restricts unduly their reason for coming. It is better to retain the verse division of the Hebrew text, with the

---

[29]In Ps 62:1 a similar construction is found (but not identical). There we read, "Truly my soul waits in silence" (RSV). The NIV has: "My soul finds rest in God alone." However, there is a difference in saying "the soul is silent" and "praise is silent," the latter appearing to be a contradiction in terms. It is possible that the choice of the root meaning "silence" for 65:1 was made by some on the basis of 62:1.

meaning that all flesh will come to God for the reason that he is the one hearing prayer. The concern about sin at this point (v. 3) is that of the worshipers themselves, especially of the psalmist as the spokesman, who says: **When we were overwhelmed by sins, you forgave our transgression.** The root of the latter verb is כָּפַר (*kāphar*, "to atone" or "to purge"). It is used of the cleansing of the unclean lips of the prophet (Isa 6:7). A homonym of the term is used in Gen 6:14, both in verb form and as a noun, in reference to Noah's ark. "*Pitch* it within and without with *pitch*." Thus the ark was made unsinkable. May we see here an analogy of God's atoning grace, "within and without," as manifested toward humankind? It should be pointed out, too, that the emphasis in this phrase is on God — **You** (emphatic personal pronoun) **forgave** them (the **transgression**).

65:4 An outburst of joy is reflected in verse 4. **Blessed are those you choose and bring near to live in your courts!** Whether the courts be those of heaven or of the temple in Jerusalem, they signify close fellowship with God, the privilege of those whom God chooses. No one dare think he may stand in God's favor by his own merits, for "all have sinned and fall short of the glory of God" (Rom 3:23). It is God's prerogative, however, to exercise his sovereign will to choose whomever he will, and to extend to them his grace. And who are they? The psalmist would recognize the people of Israel as the chosen of God — chosen, not because they were a great people but because of his mercy toward a people enslaved (as they had been in Egypt) and because of his promise to Abraham (Deut 7:7-8). As his chosen they now share in the **good things of [his] house.** Just to be a part of the people of God was cause enough for rejoicing, but the continuing fellowship in his house with him and with his people filled their cups to overflowing. Here they found their need for divine love, for forgiveness, for cleansing, and for support fully met by God their redeemer.

2. God Our Preserver (65:5-8)

65:5 The nation that was brought to birth through the grace of God owes her continuance to him. He who hears prayer (v. 2) answers prayer, and is addressed as the God of our salvation. The Hebrew verb "to save" has the significance of "rescue," "deliver," "set free." This God had done for Israel time and time again and he was still responsive to their prayers. **You answer us with awesome deeds of righteousness.** From a God who is awesome in majesty, in power, and yes, awesome in love, one would expect awesome deeds. Such had been those by which God had delivered Israel from Sennacherib and the Assyrians. And these were deeds of righteousness in that they were designed to set things right. Only such a God as this can be the confidence, **the hope of all the ends of the earth.** And this he is, whether they realize it or not.

65:6-8 Awesome is the power of God as seen in his creation. It is he who **formed the mountains by [his] power.** Or, we might say, "Who established the tectonic plates and moved the continents about as it pleased him." It is he **who stilled the roaring of the seas.** In ancient mythology the sea was personified as a powerful enemy of humankind and portrayed as a dragon with many heads. But never mind! God in his might is in control. Elsewhere it is recorded of him: "It was you who split open the sea by your power; you broke the heads of the monster in the waters" (Ps 74:13). By that same power it is he who calms the sea of humanity, **the turmoil of the nations.** These manifestations of his power, his deeds of salvation and of judgment, are **wonders,** or signs, that will fill those who dwell in the uttermost parts (of the earth) with awe (or godly fear). At the same time, these evidences of God's control will be cause for joy. **Where morning dawns and evening fades you call forth songs of joy.** There will be rejoicing among all peoples because of these signs of God's power, whether they be people from the distant east or the farthest west.

3. God Our Sustainer and Provider (65:9-13)

65:9 God the Redeemer, God the Preserver of the nation, is also the God who sustains and provides for his people. Attention has been directed in our introductory section to the extensive activity of God on behalf of Israel. Altogether there are nineteen verb forms in the psalm having God as the subject. Five of these appear in verse 9. God visits ("cares for," פָּקַד, *pāqad,* the verb means "to visit for a purpose") the land, he waters it, enriches it, and provides grain. (Here the root is כּוּן, *kûn,* meaning "to establish," "to prepare" and the verb bears overtones of certitude. God does provide food for his creatures — **for so you have ordained it**.) God's provision for seed-time and harvest on earth is firmly established.

65:10 You drench its furrows. The psalmist is not concerned with secondary causes, such as cloud formations and low pressure areas, but recognizes God as the primary giver of the rain and the one making provision for the continuing process of growth and harvest. Verse 10 could be translated as a petition since it contains verb forms that could be identified as imperatives. Thus, "Drench its furrows and level its ridges; soften it with showers and bless its crops." Those who see a cultic use of the psalm view verse 10 as part of the liturgy used in a solemn procession of the ark of the covenant around the temple precincts. As the worshipers advanced, the priests, it is said, would walk alongside the cart that carried the ark, sprinkling holy water, and declaring, "You water the earth, etc." and then voicing their petition: "Water its furrows, etc."[30]

65:11-13 You crown the year with your bounty; that is, "with thy good gifts" (NEB). A year of mercies is now crowned with an abundant harvest. **And your carts overflow with abundance.** The figure, it seems, is that of the farm cart, filled to overflowing. Nor is the abundance limited to the harvest of the field. **The meadows are covered with flocks**, a fitting complement to the valleys, **mantled with grain**. It would appear that all creation is alive and rejoicing as a result of God's goodness: **they shout for joy and sing.**

The psalm has spoken eloquently of the grace of God. How blessed are those whom he has chosen! By his grace he provides atonement for their sins, and cleansing and forgiveness. By it the earth was established, fitted wonderfully to the needs of his creatures. Even the perennial cycle of summer and winter, seedtime and harvest, is evidence of his grace. For not only is God the Creator, the giver of life — and of new life. He continues to be the sustainer and provider of the life he has given. Praise is due to you, O God![31]

---

[30]See Eaton, *Psalms*, p. 165. Eaton does not say that such a ceremony was observed but states a hypothetical case.

[31]How marvelously God prepared the earth for human habitation. He placed the sun in the galaxy we call the Milky Way in a position to keep it

B. THIS IS MY GOD[32] (66:1-20)

Throughout the entirety of Psalm 66 there is sounded clearly a note of thanksgiving. The psalm opens with a call to all the earth to praise God for his awesome deeds (vv. 1-4). This is followed by an account of the blessings of God that brought Israel into existence as a people (vv. 5-7), and then by a reference to the deliverance he has provided from some recent great danger (vv. 8-12). The psalmist, apparently a respected leader, brings offerings of gratitude to God in great number (vv. 13-15), adds his personal testimony of what God has done for him in the answering of his prayer (vv. 16-19), and concludes with a word of praise to God for his unfailing love (v. 20).

Central to the development of the psalm is the deliverance mentioned above. The statement that God "has preserved our lives" (v. 9), indicates that a crisis threatening the death of Israel had developed. The people apparently had been subjected to oppression by others, had been through "fire and water," but God had delivered them (v. 12). It is only by his grace and power that they survived.

The precise occasion for the psalm cannot be determined with certainty. Two proposals are frequently projected. One is the deliverance of Jerusalem from the siege by Sennacherib in 701 B.C. (Isa 36-37). The Assyrians had wrought great desolation in the land, and only by the intervention of God was the city of Jerusalem spared.

---

steady on its course. He supplied it with sufficient hydrogen (82% of its mass) to supply heat for billions of years, we are told — at least as long as God desires. He put the earth in orbit around the sun just at the proper distance to make life as we know it possible. (He did not put us on Venus — much too hot! Nor on Mars — too cold.) He did not make earth a smooth ball, but with high mountains, deep valleys, lakes, and oceans. And he set the earth to spinning at about a thousand miles an hour (at the equator). This variegated surface and the spinning of the earth, with the Coriolis effect, were to make our changing weather patterns possible. And then, as a final touch, God tilted the earth 23° on its axis in relation to the sun, making possible our changes of seasons, and giving longer daylight in summer so crops can mature. How glorious is our God!

[32]With apologies to Herman Wouck for the title. *This Is My God* (Garden City, NY: Doubleday, 1951).

To this end Hezekiah the king had prayed (Isa 37:14-20). If the words of verses 13-20 are from his lips, then we can see their deep significance. The praise and sacrifice offered by the king are not on his own behalf alone but for his people whom God has rescued.

Others consider the psalm to reflect the joy of Israel at the time of her deliverance from Babylonian captivity. The nation had almost died in exile – consider Ezekiel's vision of the "whole house of Israel" as a valley of dry bones! (Ezek 37:11). But God restored her to the homeland. If the psalm is from this period, apparently it would be after the rebuilding of the temple (v. 13). We do not know. But without doubt it is a psalm most suitable to any occasion when the people of God would give thanks for some great deliverance that they have experienced.

The call to worship with which the psalm opens is addressed to all people, thus indicating the universality of God. In verses 8-12 the transition is made to "our God," who "brought us to a place of abundance" (v. 12). Then, beginning with verse 13, the thought progresses to the very personal. Here it is not "God and they" nor even "'God and we" but "God and I," or, more intimately, "I and thou." And so, from the contemplation of God's awesome deeds throughout the earth, to the recollection of his goodness toward his people Israel, the psalmist comes to an acknowledgment of what God has done for him personally. And for this he would bless his name.

1. Their God (66:1-7)

66:1-2 Shout with joy to God, all the earth! Literally, a "shout of joy!" In this fashion all the earth is summoned to praise God. What the psalmist is about to sing about has significance for all nations. He will tell especially what God has done for Israel, believing that others, seeing evidence of his power and mercy, will be drawn to serve and worship him also. He knows, of course, that among the Gentile nations many idols are worshiped. Yet from his viewpoint, since there is only one God, he must be the God of all peoples of the earth. It is with this understanding, then, that we speak of the Lord as *their God*, not in any restricted tribal sense. It is the God of the whole earth who is the object of the praise in the psalm, he who is "King over all the earth" (Ps 47:2).

66:3 Since the psalmist is in Jerusalem (v. 13), the nations are not actually present to hear his call to worship the Lord. Yet in verses 3 and 4 he continues his address to them and gives them words that would be appropriate on their lips. **Say to God,** [or, Say: "O God,][33] **"How awesome [filling with godly fear] are your deeds! So great is your power that your enemies cringe before you."** Other readings for "cringe" are: "submit themselves," or "cower before thee." But these do not convey the full significance of the root כָּחַשׁ (*kāḥaš*). The term has a connotation of deception. The enemies of God may *cringe* before him, or give the appearance of submitting, but it is a deceptive move on their part, hypocritical — they feign allegiance out of fear.

66:4-7 All the earth bows down to you. This may be hyperbole, but this is part of the song and a reference to the homage of Gentiles who have marveled at the awesome deeds of God. He is the universal Lord. Now these are invited to consider especially the mighty acts of God associated with Israel's liberation from Egypt and her entry into the promised land. **Come and see what God has done . . . . He turned the sea into dry land**, and thus made possible the escape of Israel from the grasp of Pharaoh. And upon their arrival at the Jordan (**the waters**) God made it possible for them to cross over on foot. Who would not delight to honor such a God as this?

"Your God is too small!" J.B. Phillips of *New Testament in Modern English* fame maintained, in a book of the same name, that this was true of too many Christians. Certainly it was not true of the author of Psalm 66. His God is no tribal deity, no fetish, nor object of wood or stone. Nor is he a deity who has set the earth in motion and gone off to leave it to its own devices. Marvelous in power and in his concern for his creation, he continues his mighty deeds throughout the earth for the people of all nations to contemplate. This is their God.

---

[33]Instead of "to God" Dahood recognizes the preposition as indicative of the vocative (*Psalms 51–100*, p. 120).

2. Our God (66:8-12)

66:8 It is the God who is above all and who has demonstrated his power over the affairs of men whom the psalmist praises. In his heart he believes that the evidence for such a God is so compelling as to call forth the acclaim even of non-Israelite nations. **Praise our God, O peoples.** It may seem a bit presumptuous to ask other peoples to praise (literally, to bless) our God — but not since he is the living Lord, God over all. God's promise to Abraham was that through his seed (his descendant), all peoples of the earth would be blessed, and this extension of God's mercy should elicit the praise of all. But can man praise or "bless" God? When God is the subject, to bless means to bestow some benefit, or to embue with power, or with his spirit. Obviously man cannot bestow benefits upon God. The remainder of the verse indicates that to bless God means to praise him, to esteem him most highly, or to honor him. One is to do this by the manner of his life, but active participation in the worship of God is called for also — not just a silent honoring of him in the heart — **Let the sound of his praise be heard.** If in his heart one is devoted to God, let that devotion be expressed! (Thank God for the opportunity of corporate worship in the church.)

66:9 The wonders by which Israel was established as a nation were such that all nations could see and marvel at them. No less marvelous in the eyes of the psalmist was God's preservation of his people through many trials. From the tone of verses 9-12 the ordeal through which they had recently come was very great. But God had sustained them and was sustaining them. It is he **who has preserved our lives.** The text has a participle here, from a root meaning "to keep securely" and indicating a present and continuing condition.

66:10-12 In retrospect the psalmist could see that God had been working in the life of his people even in the suffering that they had endured. **For you, O God, tested us.** The affliction they had suffered had enabled them to demonstrate their mettle (and their faith). It had been a means of purification, as silver is purified by the refining process. **You brought us into prison**; that is, permitted us to be ensnared by the enemy. **And laid burdens on our backs.** The KJV translates: "Thou hast caused men to ride over our heads." Captors would sometimes drive their chariots over their fallen foe (see Isa 51:23, a possible meaning here?). **We went through fire and water.** Perhaps not to be taken literally, but as a metaphor of sore trials of diverse kinds. In this it is seen that to have the Lord as one's God is to expect discipline and correction, testing and refining. Can we praise God for that? The psalmist could. Already he has stated that God makes secure the life of his people. Now he adds: **You brought us to a place of abundance.** The verb "brought out" is used often of God's action regarding his people. By his mighty hand he brought Israel out of Egypt (Exod 13:3). By his grace he brings those who are willing out of a life of sin to new life. This he did for Israel. The way may sometimes lead through the wilderness, but the time of refreshing is assured. This is our God.

3. My God (66:13-20)

66:13-15 Beginning with verse 13 the psalm takes an abrupt turn, so abrupt that some would consider it to be the beginning of an altogether separate psalm.[34] Here there is no reference to the people except as they are invited to hear the testimony of the speaker (v. 16). There is no mention of God's deliverance of his people. Instead, here is one who enters the Lord's house to offer sacrifices in accord with vows that he has made. However, if this individual is the king (Hezekiah), and his people have experienced a great deliverance, we may well believe that he has prayed to God for such deliverance and, yes, has made promises to God also. (Just such a prayer was offered to God by Hezekiah when Jerusalem was threatened by Sennacherib's Assyrian armies: "Now, O LORD our God, deliver us from his hand, so that all kingdoms on earth may know that you alone, O LORD, are God" Isa. 37:20). The psalmist testifies that God has answered his prayer (v. 19). And the large number and nature of the sacrifices that he brings would be

---

[34]See Oesterley, for example (*The Psalms*, p. 313). Taylor notes the dissimilarities with what precedes these verses but still considers the psalm to be a unit (*Psalms*, p. 343f.).

appropriate in a time of thanksgiving for national deliverance. Furthermore, for all of the congregation to join in the praise hymn of verses 1-12 would be a fitting introduction to the personal testimony that follows.

66:16-20 Come and listen, all you who fear God. The speaker uses the occasion to give his personal testimony of what God has done. All the earth had been called on to honor God. He would be *their* God. There had been a recital of the wonderful acts of God on behalf of his people, Israel. This is *our* God. But he is also and intimately the God of the individual. This is *my* God! **I cried out to him with my mouth . . . and (he) heard my voice in prayer** (vv. 17a,19b). The deliverance of the nation would also have been the deliverance of the individual, (and this would be an especially appropriate answer to prayer if he were king). Realizing this, the psalmist joyfully testifies to the goodness of God in responding to his petition. It is possible that one may recognize the God who is over all and still stand in a detached and impersonal relationship, regarding him only as *their* God. Or, one may have been frequently in fellowship with the people of God, sharing with them a common faith, and joining with them in service and praise. God is now meaningful in his life as he considers together with others the divine nature and gives thanks for divine blessings. He can delight in the privilege and say, "This is our God." (Did not Jesus teach us to say, when we pray, "Our father"?) That the psalmist rejoiced in what God had done for Israel is evident (vv. 6-18). But not until the general blessing had become his very own in a particular way, not until he had experienced the presence of God and the goodness of God in his own life, could he say, "This is my God." And thus the psalm that began with a call for all the earth to know the Lord ends on a very personal note: **Praise be to God, who has not rejected my prayer or withheld his love from me!**

III. THE KING'S KING (67:1–69:36)

A. MAY THE PEOPLES PRAISE YOU (67:1-7)

Psalm 67 is identified by many as a national psalm of thanksgiving, praising God for a bountiful harvest just realized. Its setting has been said to have been the Feast of Tabernacles, a time of praise and thanksgiving extending over a period of seven days in late autumn (September-October). However, it is significant that no mention is made of a harvest until verse 6, and even here the reference may be to a future yield (v. 6, NIV, also KJV). Also, it is a bit strange, or "puzzling," as Oesterley notes,[35] that a hymn of thanksgiving should open with a *plea* for God's blessing (v. 1). The thanksgiving motif, if present at all, is certainly subdued and does not seem to be typical of the psalm as a whole.

In view of the above, some would classify the psalm as a national lament. But if this be so, it is difficult to determine the occasion for it. Dahood, noting vocabulary and idiom that appear in prayers for rain, considers it to be just that, a prayer for rain to bring relief from a long drought.[36] But, as Stuhlmueller observes, "The tone and spirit of the psalm seem to militate against this interpretation."[37] The principle thrust of the psalm is in a different direction. It opens with a request that "God bless us" and closes on a positive note of assurance that he will bless. But it is the significance that this blessing has for others that receives the focus of attention. It appears that the author has a missionary spirit. Whether this be true or not, he does believe that God's goodness is not restricted to Israel alone and he catches at least a glimpse of Israel's role in making God known to the world, to the end that all peoples would join in the worship of the Lord. God's way, his saving power, have relevance for all nations. This is the theme of the psalm. This it is that gives significance to the refrain in verse 3: "May the peoples praise you, O God," and repeated in verse 5.

That the psalm was intended to be used in public worship seems indicated by the use of the above mentioned refrain. It is a prayer for God to bless (or, to continue to bless) his people, with the realization that such blessing has implications for other peoples, also. (Since God alone is God, it is seen that he is the God of all.) Since no particular blessing is asked for, no particular occasion for the psalm need be sought. It could well become the *daily* prayer of God's people!

---

[35]Oesterley, *The Psalms*, p. 317.
[36]Dahood, *Psalms 51–100*, p. 127.
[37]Stuhlmueller, *Psalms I*, p. 300.

1. Israel Blessed for a Purpose (67:1-2)

67:1 As noted, the psalm does not begin with thoughts of the harvest. Instead, God's mercy and grace are the primary concerns of the worshipers and the subject of their petition. **May God be gracious to us and bless us.** The priestly blessing of Num 6:24-26 may have been the model for the prayer: "The LORD bless you, and keep you; the LORD make his face shine upon you and be gracious to you; the LORD turn his face toward you and give you peace." Instead of LORD (*Yahweh*) the psalm has God (*Elohim*). (This is to be expected since Book 2 of the Psalms shows a preference throughout for *Elohim*.) Those who pray for mercy are acknowledging by the very act that they have no claim upon God. Why, then, do they ask? There is a twofold reason. First, God has proved himself to be gracious to Israel in the past. The entire scope of her history reflects God's concern for and blessing of his people. Understandable, therefore, is their faith that leads them to hope that he will continue to be merciful toward them; that he will **make his face shine upon [them]**; that is, that he will be favorably inclined toward them — that they may know the radiance of his presence.

67:2 But there is another reason for their petition — **That your ways may be known on earth, your salvation among all nations.** They do not ask God's mercy upon themselves alone, but that non-Hebrew nations might also come to a knowledge of God and of his salvation. The way of God with Israel was a witness to the whole world of his goodness and power and thus a challenge to all peoples to recognize him and to seek him.

2. A Call for Universal Praise (67:3-4)

67:3 May the peoples praise you, O God; may all the peoples praise you. If we consider that "all the peoples" embraces all of humankind, and the context suggests this, then the universal nature of this appeal is apparent. But to remove all doubt, the noun is plural — "peoples" — indicating all ethnic groups. "Red and yellow, black and white, they are precious in his sight." To make this unmistakably clear there is the reference in the preceding verse to all nations, and in the following (v. 4) to the clans, or tribes, ("peoples") of the world (a word different in the Hebrew from the nations of verse 2).

But are the peoples of the earth to praise God for what he has done for Israel? Yes, when they recognize that his way is the way that brings blessing and salvation to any people who will acknowledge him and follow him. This, of course, will require faith, but it will be a faith that is based on the evidence before them. God, who promised Abraham that he would make of him a great nation through whom blessing would come to the whole world (Gen 12:2-3), kept that promise. His patience with Israel and his faithfulness to his purpose and to his promise thus become reason indeed why all peoples should praise him.

67:4 May the nations be glad and sing for joy. The praise that is summoned is to be joyful praise, joyful for the reason that God's concern extends to all peoples and because: **you rule the peoples justly.** It is not the great judgment day that is in view here, but God's governance of the world in general. His is a righteous rule; that is, in accordance with what is right, just, or equitable. In addition, God provides guidance: **[You] guide the nations of the earth**, or "You lead"; the verb is the same as that in Psalm 23, "He leads me." It is significant that the root נָחָה (*nāḥāh*, "lead," "guide") is always used in a good sense, never as leading astray or misleading. It signifies conducting one in the right way, toward a predetermined destination, a desired goal. This leadership God provides for the people who are willing to follow his leading.

3. The Blessing That Will Follow (67:5-7)

67:5-6a May the peoples praise you, O God. The repetition of the call to worship emphasizes the fact that the one God of righteousness and mercy, the God who provides the right way and saving power is worthy of the praise of all nations. Here again we see reflected the concern for the participation of the Gentile world in the worship of God. **Then the land will yield its harvest.** This is a good translation. The verb is in the perfect tense, but the context suggests that it is the "perfect of certainty," the anticipated result of the universal acclamation of God. The verse is saying that a world united in the worship of God, a world in harmony with the ways of God, will be a productive world. There is a relationship — close and vital between spiritual good and physical good! (The converse, the close relationship between moral evil and physical evil, is apparent.)

67:6b-7 And God, our God, will bless us. The Hebrew has literally, "God, our God." It is most likely that the original text had "the LORD (Yahweh) our God," and that the change was made to *Elohim* when the psalm was incorporated into Book 2 of the Psalms (the Elohistic Psalter). From beginning to end the psalm would exalt Yahweh as the God who is worthy of the praise of all people, and all have been called to that praise. Now, therefore, Yahweh our God is not just the God of Abraham or the God of the Hebrews; the *our* includes all who have responded. And when it is said that **God will bless us**, it is a promise to all peoples. The blessings that will follow when all the ends of the earth honor and serve God will be worldwide blessings. Understandably, therefore, Jesus taught us to pray: "Your kingdom come, your will be done on earth as it is in heaven" (Matt 6:10). God shall bless us (when) **all the ends of the earth will fear him!**

"May the peoples praise you, O God;
May all the peoples praise you."

B. THE AWESOME GOD (68:1-35)

The grandeur of Psalm 68 is acclaimed by numerous commentators. It is said to be "grand" (Perowne), "magnificent" (Kirkpatrick), "exhilarating" (Kidner), "triumphant" (Leupold), "dramatic" (Ash), "unsurpassed if not unequaled" (MacLaren). At the same time it is recognized as one of the most difficult for the interpreter. The most accomplished Hebrew scholars admit its challenge, both textually and exegetically. The psalm includes a number of words found only here in the OT. (This may be due to its antiquity — apparent to some, questioned by others). Increasing the challenge to interpretation is the fact that the psalm defies classification according to the usual patterns. It contains elements of the praise hymn, of prayer, of thanksgiving; it also contains narration (vv. 7-10) plus an oracle of God (vv. 22-23). There are abrupt changes of thought, accompanied by diverse rhythmic patterns (seven in number!) as well.

In view of the above, some have concluded that we do not have in Psalm 68 a psalm at all, but a collection of fragments of many, a type of anthology or medley — or perhaps a kind of index incorporating lines from as many as thirty poems! Thus Oesterley describes it as "a collection of sentences and phrases taken from a number of different poems, and strung together haphazard [*sic*]."[38] The broad variety of subject matter, the difficulties with syntax, and the inclusion of an unusual number of unique words is cited as evidence for this apparently fragmented condition. It is proposed that the materials were collected to provide a liturgy to be used in a religious drama, perhaps in the celebration of some great victory. Incorporated into such a celebration would be a triumphal procession in the temple compound (vv. 24,25).

Others view the psalm as designed for use in a public celebration, but see in it a much greater unity — a unity of purpose even while literary diversity remains, that purpose being to magnify the Lord as a God of awesome power and goodness. It is a song of jubilation!

The original occasion upon which the song was used must remain a matter of speculation. It would have been fitting for that joyful occasion when David brought the ark of God "from the house of Obed-Edom to the City of David with rejoicing" (2 Sam 6:12). It sings of God's going forth with his people from Sinai, through the wilderness, finally to enter into the "holy place," the sanctuary in Zion. This is history. This God had accomplished, and so great an accomplishment could only foreshadow the ultimate victory of God when all nations would acknowledge his sovereignty. This is the theme of the psalm. The God of Israel, who brought his people from Egyptian bondage, will ultimately be acclaimed by all.

In the development of the theme many names and designations of God are used, including *Elohim*, *Yah* (= *Yahweh*, v. 4), *Shaddai* (the Almighty, v. 14), *Adonai* (Lord, v. 17). These various names, together with the scope of the activities of God that are cited, serve to give a broad perspective of the nature of the deity. He is powerful and

---

[38]Oesterley, *The Psalms*, p. 320.

victorious (vv. 1-3). He is compassionate (vv. 4-6). He is provident respecting the needs of his people (vv. 7-14). He chooses to establish his dwelling among men (vv. 15-18). He provides salvation (vv. 19-23). Consequently, he is praised in Israel (vv. 24-27) and receives the homage of kings (vv. 28-31). Such a God is wholly worthy of universal adoration. Thus the psalm closes with an invitation for all earth's kingdoms to unite in the singing of his praises (vv. 32-35).

1. God Arises Victorious (68:1-3)

68:1-2 At the outset the psalm is reminiscent of the journey of the children of Israel from Sinai through the wilderness on their way to the land of their promised rest. They would be going through hostile territory and they would be opposed. Before starting on the daily march, Moses would position the ark of the covenant at the head of the column and invoke the Lord's blessing as the ark moved forward: "Rise up, O LORD!," he would say, "May your enemies be scattered; may your foes flee before you" (Num 10:35). The psalmist is celebrating God's answer to Moses' prayer, declaring succinctly: **May God arise, may his enemies be scattered.**[39] This is no petition but a statement of fact, that continues: **May his foes flee before him.** God's power is irresistible; his victory is complete. His enemies, like drifting smoke, are driven before him; they become like melted wax; they perish.

68:3 Yet the awesome power that overthrows the wicked poses no threat to the righteous; instead it is, for them, a cause for rejoicing. The same God who is mighty in judgment is mighty to save those who come to him. In either case, the victory is not of man's making but is his.

---

[39]The verbs are the prefixed (imperfect) form, but rather than being imperative, "Let" (KJV, RSV, ASV) or "May" (NIV), they are to be understood as indicating customary behavior, and are so translated by Dahood, Eerdmans, Leupold, and others, including the NEB. The meaning is: "Whenever (or, as often as) the Lord arises, his enemies scatter."

2. God Helps the Unfortunate (68:4-6)

68:4-5 Verses 4-6 introduce one of the abrupt changes of thought that are characteristic of the psalm. From a discussion of the enemies of God the thought turns to orphans and widows and prisoners! The joy of the righteous (v. 3) is not conditioned alone by the overthrow of the enemies of God; there is joy in God's help for the unfortunate. Verse 4 provides a transition, being an invitation to praise God (on both accounts). **Sing to God, sing praise [make music] to his name.** The call to jubilant praise is clear; the remainder of the verse not so clear. Literally, we may translate: "Cast up (or, lift up, extol) the one riding (or, for the one riding) in the desert plains (or, on the clouds) by Yah his name, and exult before him." Parallel with the final "exult before him" we would agree with the NIV, **extol**, thus: "Extol the one riding upon the clouds by his name Yah, and exult (**rejoice**) before him." It is understood that the God who is to be praised is the covenant God of Israel, Yahweh. As a God concerned about his people, he is **a father to the fatherless, a defender of widows.** He helps the unfortunate.

68:6 This verse, though not a recitation of the Exodus experience, is reminiscent of that event. **God sets the lonely in families.** He gives a homeland to Israel. Those who were in bondage are liberated. Yet not all of Israel received the inheritance. **The rebellious live in a sun-scorched land**; just as the rebels against Moses and God, whose lives were lived out to the end in the wilderness (Num 14:26-29).

3. God Acts on Behalf of His People (68:7-14)

68:7-8 When you went out before your people, O God — on the journey of Israel out of Egypt — **when you marched through the wasteland** — on the way to the promised land. The terminology is that of the "Song of Deborah" (Judg 5:4-5). The psalm is citing salvation history as proof of God's victorious power and saving love. **The earth shook, the heavens poured down rain,**[40] **before God!**

---

[40]See Exod 19:16-18.

This latter statement is a bit weak. It is the epiphany itself to which the quaking must be attributed, as reflected in Dahood's rendering, "at the sight of God." The unusual phenomena bear testimony to God's presence and power. Notice the mention of that presence earlier in the psalm. Those who hate God flee from his presence (v. 1). The wicked perish from his presence (v. 2). The righteous rejoice in his presence, or "at the sight of him" (Dahood). In Hebrew the expression is the same in each case except for a change of preposition. If even Sinai quakes at God's presence, who can abide his appearing? No one, except by his grace and mercy. The sudden appearance of God will strike terror in the heart of the wicked; it will bring joy to the righteous.

68:9-10 God provided for the necessities of his people at Sinai and subsequently. In verse 9 he is addressed directly: **You gave abundant showers, O God**, or, "a rain of gifts freely given," signifying perhaps God's gifts of manna, quail, and water during the wilderness wanderings. By these he **refreshed [his] weary inheritance.** Thus were they enabled to dwell in the land, for God had prepared abundantly for his people in their time of need. From the context we gather that this is a reference to the sojourn at Sinai, which continued for about a year (Exod 19:3; Num 10:11). Through this experience the people could gain confidence and thus be prepared for a resumption of their journey, for God would not leave them in the wilderness.

68:11-12 Verses 11-14 speak in summary fashion of what God did for the people of Israel in giving them a land. The time period would be that of Joshua and of the Judges. This much seems to be indicated. Beyond this, the precise interpretation of the verses is quite elusive but they do seem to reflect the victory of Barak and Deborah over Sisera, celebrated in song in Judges 5. **The Lord announced the word.** Here the Lord is *Adonai*, lord and master. He needs but speak a word, and it is done. Here it is a word of victory, of Israel over the kings of Canaan, and a great company of women publish, or proclaim the good news. (The Hebrew has a feminine participle, indicating the ones who are proclaiming.) In Israel, as in other eastern lands, the women would celebrate the news of victory with song and dance (1 Sam 18:6-7). It may be that our text includes fragments of such a victory song: **Kings and armies flee in haste.** Subsequently, "she that tarried at home divided the spoil," (instead of the NIV's **in the camps men divide the plunder**).

68:13-14 The tribe of Reuben sat out the war at home. Instead of aiding their brother tribes in the conflict, they stayed among the sheepfolds, out of harm's way (Judg 5:16). The women dividing the spoil remember. "Never mind," they seem to be saying, "even if they do stay among the sheepfolds" (v. 13, RSV) . . . "see what we have!" The silver dove, then, would be an example of the bounty the women were dividing (see NEB, vv. 11-13). Verse 14, although it has its difficulties, speaks further of the defeat of the kings opposing Israel. **When the Almighty scattered the kings in the land, it was like snow fallen on Zalmon.**

4. God Chooses Zion (68:15-18)

Dear to the heart of the people of Israel was the conviction that God had chosen Jerusalem as his dwelling place among his people. Not that he is some local deity, confined to the borders of this small land, for he is God over all the earth. Nor was Zion, where his abode would be, spectacular for location. It is correctly called the hill of Zion, a very modest mountain, if it may be called that. We do not know just why this particular spot was chosen, but the words of Paul come to mind: "But God chose the weak things of the world to shame the strong" (1 Cor 1:27). Mt. Zion? What is Mount Zion in a world of vast empires and fabulous cities, far more significant when measured by the criteria of size, splendor, and power? But out of Zion would go forth the law of the Lord, and "the word of the LORD from Jerusalem" (Mic 4:2). Weak? Insignificant? From Zion would go forth the living Word of God, a power that would sweep around the world and change the course of history for all ages to come. What would make Jerusalem great? Not her military prowess, not great institutions of learning, not financial wizardry. No, Jerusalem would become great because God would select her to be "the place I have chosen as a dwelling for my Name" (Neh 1:9; see Ps 132:13-18).

68:15-16 Verse 15 identifies the hill of Bashan as a mountain of grandeur: **The mountains of Bashan are majestic mountains.**

Quite likely, the reference is to Mount Hermon to the north of
Israel. But God did not choose Hermon, and this majestic mountain could well be jealous of Zion. **Why gaze in envy, O rugged
mountains, at the mountain where God chooses to reign** (v. 16)?
This seems to be the meaning of the verse although the verb
involved is uncertain as to its precise meaning. (It appears only this
once in the OT.)

68:17-18 The mighty forces at God's disposal are indicated figuratively as the chariots of God. (See 2 Kgs 6:17.) These, with thousands
of angels accompanied God as he brought Israel from Sinai through
the wilderness to Zion and are still at his disposal since he has come
into the holy place. Verse 18 addresses God directly. These words
may be a song of the worshipers in joyful procession (v. 24). **When
you ascended on high**; that is, have ascended holy Mount Zion, **You
led captives in your train.** The figure is that of a conquering king.
You received gifts from men, even from the rebellious. Tribute to
the God of Israel has been sent by many, to the God who has made
Zion his dwelling place! The time would come when peoples around
the world would praise him. Micah and Isaiah both declared that
many nations would say: "Come, let us go up to the mountain of the
LORD, and to the house of the God of Jacob. He will teach us his
ways, so that we may walk in his paths" (Mic 4:2; cf. Isa 2:3). Today
the eyes of many from every corner of the earth are turned toward
the holy city with awe, and with anticipation, as symbolic of the heavenly Jerusalem that shall not pass away.

5. God Provides Salvation (68:19-23)

68:19-20 The relationship of God to his people is a continuing
one. Day by day he makes provision for them. This is the emphasis
of verses 19 and 20. **Praise be to the Lord, to God our Savior, who
daily bears our burdens.** Our daily sustenance is from him.
Moreover, he is the God of our salvation, saving from threatening
death, as verse 20b indicates — **from the Sovereign LORD comes
escape from death.** (Note that escape is plural in the Hebrew, i.e.,
"escapes.")

68:21-22 For the ungodly this is not so. These are called God's
enemies, but they are the enemies of his people as well. For both

reasons they must come under judgment. God shall wound **the head of his enemies.** However, this is no sudden capricious act of God, since these are **the hairy crowns of those who go on in their sins.** Without repentance, they compound their guilt; they continue their defiance of God. And even though they flee to Bashan or to the sea, they shall not escape. The wicked who persist in their wickedness will suffer from their own evil ways. In addition, having rejected his mercy, they will fall under his wrath whose righteousness they have scorned. The deliverance of the oppressed at the hand of God, of necessity, calls for the judgment of the oppressor.

68:23 This verse speaks of the battlefield where the ground literally flows with the blood of those slain in hand-to-hand combat. It is not a pretty picture. War is never pretty. The comment of Derek Kidner on this passage is appropriate. "[It] reeks of blood, but not so certainly of bloodlust – i.e., of killing for the sake of it. There is undisguised joy of victory, and no pretense that victories are anything but gory; but 21b should not be overlooked. This is judgment, not imperialism."[41] After all, it is the guilty upon whom the judgment falls. (See comment on Ps 58:10.)

6. God Receives the Praise of His People (68:24-27)

68:24-25 Verses 24-27 indicate a worship procession making its way to the sanctuary. The victorious God, helper of the unfortunate, benefactor of Israel, who has blessed Zion with his presence and daily has been the God of their salvation – such a one is altogether worthy of praise. And this he receives from a jubilant throng. "They have seen thy goings, O God." This is a literal translation. But since the "going" is into the sanctuary, modern versions use the term "procession," hence the NIV: **Your procession has come into view, O God.** This is certainly justified (see v. 25). However, in the larger context, the "goings" of God may refer to his movements across the pages of Israel's history, for this is what is being celebrated.

68:26-27 Verse 26 may be a song on the lips of the worshipers as they move along. **Praise God in the great congregation.** We

---

[41]Kidner, *Psalms 1–72*, p. 243.

would continue the verse: "(Bless) the Lord, the fountain of Israel."[42] This is in keeping with other Scriptures. Ps 36:9 says of God, "For with you is the fountain of life." And in Jeremiah God is described as "the spring [fountain] of living waters" (Jer 2:13; 17:13). See also Zech 13:1 and John 4:13-14. As the one "from whom all blessings flow," including the blessing of life, God is praised by his people. Verse 27 indicates some of those in the procession, at least as visualized by the psalmist. **There is the little tribe of Benjamin, leading them.** Benjamin and Judah were southern tribes. From the northern part of the country came Zebulon and Naphtali. From the southernmost tribes to the northernmost, the people came to join the joyful worship procession. (Following the battle against the armies of Jabin, the Canaanite king, Zebulun and Naphtali were cited for exceptional bravery – Judg 5:18.)

7. God Will Receive the Homage of Others (68:28-31)

68:28-31 Verse 29 states clearly that kings will bring gifts to God in Jerusalem. Notice Dahood's translation: "Your temple, Most High ('al) is Jerusalem, kings will bring gifts to you."[43] Verses 30-31, however, indicate that Egypt and Ethiopia are recalcitrant. This fact must guide us in our interpretation of this passage. With this in mind, we are led to the following understanding of a difficult text. God will receive gifts from men, However, in view of the resistance of some, he is asked to manifest his might anew. **Summon your power, O God** (v. 28, the power by which you have wrought such

---

[42]Reading "the fountain of Israel" instead of "from the fountain," or even the NIV's "in the assembly of Israel," considering that the preposition *from* in the Hebrew text is a result of dittography, *mimeqor* being written instead of *maqor*. See Kirkpatrick, *The Book of Psalms II*, p. 392 and Briggs, *Psalms* II:110.

[43]Dahood arrives at this simple translation after recognizing the first letter of the verse as *enclitic mem* (*Psalms 51–100*, p. 149). Otherwise, this letter would be the preposition "from." But to say "from thy temple kings will bring gifts to thee" makes little sense. Numerous versions read "because" (from the fact of the presence of the temple) but such a circumlocution seems improbable.

great things for Israel in the past). It needs to be exercised further. **Rebuke the beast among the reeds** (the hippopotamus, perhaps). This is a veiled reference to Egypt, whose great river, in its upper regions, was a habitat of the hippo. **The herd of bulls among the calves of the nations.** The reference eludes us. Leupold would have it indicate "lesser nationalities" (than Egypt) among hostile nations. (So, also, Cohen.) Preferable is Dahood's view that the bulls are the generals of Pharaoh's forces and the calves are the soldiers. The beast among the reeds (including his generals and soldiers) is to be rebuked for trampling peoples "in his lust for silver" (Dahood). It is Egypt (Pharaoh) who has scattered people because he delights in battle.[44] But in spite of Egypt's culpability and need of rebuke, she will join with other nations in bringing gifts to God, as also would Ethiopia (Cush, v. 31).

8. Sing unto God, Earth's Kingdoms (68:32-35)

68:32-35 If the above is the general understanding of verses 28 to 31, then it but demonstrates that even the recalcitrant among the nations would come to acknowledge the Lord. This might be considered unusual (or improbable?). But the reality would testify to the majesty and power of the Lord and be an added reason why all nations should praise him. Add to the above recent developments in the history of the world and the story is still just as amazing in the eastern nations of Europe, in Russia and in China, areas where the worship of God has been suppressed for decades, there are found yet to be thousands upon thousands who praise God. With what good reason, therefore, that we join our voices with those of ancient Israel and say: **Sing to God, O kingdoms of the earth, sing praise to the Lord, Selah.** Blessed be God!

---

[44]See Dahood, *Psalms 51-100*, pp. 149ff.

C. THE PRAYER OF ONE SUFFERING IN GOD'S CAUSE
(69:1-36)

Psalm 69 has about it the aura of great sorrow, helplessness, and despair. The author is deeply troubled and gives free reign to his discordant emotions. He has been smitten of God (v. 26) but of this he does not complain. (He has confessed that he is a sinner, v. 5.) His complaint arises from the unjust suffering he must endure at the hands of enemies. Apparently they have accused him (falsely) of theft (v. 4). Hating him without cause, in great number and with ferocity they attack him, seeking nothing less than his destruction (v. 4). It is not for any wrong that he has done that they do this. "No," he would say to God, "it is for your sake that I have borne reproach" (v. 7). He is suffering in God's cause; he is attacked because of his zeal (v. 9). In modern thought this psalm might be called "The Prayer of a Devout Sufferer"; that is, of one suffering because he is a religious person. When he spends time in fasting he is greeted with scorn (v. 10). And when he seeks to humble himself by wearing sackcloth, he is laughed at (v. 11). In all ages there have been those who would ridicule the devout, and some who would go beyond ridicule to open attack, as in the case of the psalmist. He is suffering, but not for any wrongs he has done. He suffers — for his earnestness in doing the will of God.

Apparently he has interceded with God a long while; his throat is sore from crying out while waiting for God to answer (v. 3). He is fearful of being swept away in the flood of adversity that over-whelms him (vv. 1-2,14-15). Compounding his agony is the realiza-tion that others who trust in God may be humiliated and shamed on account of what is happening to him (v. 6). It appears that he is suffering physically — "my eyes fail" is sometimes descriptive of one who is dying (v. 3) and verse 29 speaks of "pain and distress." He stands in jeopardy of his life (vv. 14-15). Moreover, he suffers the anguish of rejection by his own family (v. 8), and the populace — even the drunks! — deride him (v. 12). He has looked for someone to manifest a measure of pity toward him, to give him a word of comfort, but in vain (v. 20). Instead, all conspire to make his agony worse (v. 21).

His reaction to the unjust assaults of his enemies is a plea to God to destroy them completely, as just retribution (vv. 22-29); and so certain is he that justice will be done, that he closes his psalm with a song of thanksgiving to God, testifying to his continued goodness to his people (vv. 30-36).

In view of the above we would conclude that Psalm 69 was written under circumstances of great suffering, both physical and mental, by one who was unjustly persecuted "for righteousness' sake." In the minds of many the psalm has been associated with Jeremiah. The circumstances and ideas — even the language — resemble those of Jeremiah. Whether or not this resemblance is more than coincidence, it will help immensely in our visualization of the circumstances of the psalmist — and in feeling his heartbeat! — if we view it in the light of the life and experiences of the prophet from Anathoth. Kirkpatrick has indicated numerous points of similarity between the prophet and the psalmist. 1) Both are crushed in spirit because of the unmerited hostility that is shown them (Jer 15:10). 2) In each case the life of the innocent one is threatened (Jer 26:11). 3) "His persecutors are not heathen foreigners but godless fellow-countrymen." 4) "Even his own relations have deserted him" (Jer 12:6). 5) Both pronounce imprecations upon their enemies (Jer 18:20-22). 6) And both give predictions of the restoration of Judah.[45] In our treatment of the text of the psalm we will give attention to the similarities with Jeremiah, and the reader may judge for himself of the relationship of the one to the other.

1. A Sea of Sorrow (69:1-5)

69:1-3 With unrestrained grief the psalmist pours forth the sorrow of his soul. Like a drowning man he utters his plea for help. In metaphorical language he describes his condition as that of one being swept away in a flood, about to perish in the great deep. "The waters have risen up to my neck" (NEB, cf. Jonah 2:5). Death itself is threatening, and he is desperate. I sink in deep mire, or in **the miry depths.** In vain his feet struggle to find a firm support. (At one time Jeremiah was placed in a cistern where "there was no water, but mire" and he sank in the mire — Jer 38:6). I am weary —

---

[45]Kirkpatrick, *The Book of Psalms, Books II–III,* p. 397.

exhausted both physically and emotionally, from incessant crying out to God for relief. (A similar complaint is found in Jer 45:3, although there it falls from the lips of Baruch, Jeremiah's companion: "I am worn out with groaning.") **Looking for my God**, bewildered and frustrated.

69:4 Those who hate me without reason . . . . who seek to destroy me. Their attacks are unjustified, being directed toward an innocent man. These are enemies ("wrongfully") "without reason" — *šeqer*, a noun in Hebrew. But the term indicates more than "Wrong." The verb means "to do falsely," "to lie," "to deceive." In our text the noun is used adverbially. "My enemies," the psalmist is saying, "are destroying me deceitfully;" that is, by resorting to falsehood, to deceit. The RSV would capture this nuance by its rendering: "those who hate me without cause . . . attack me with lies." And this provides a clue to the understanding of the remainder of the verse. The psalmist is charged with theft; and the enemies demand restitution. In "such a case," if animals were involved, the law required that the thief repay four sheep for a sheep (Exod 12:1).If we may use an exclamation point, the response of the psalmist needs no clarification: **I am forced to restore what I did not steal.** (What kind of justice is that?)

69:5 The next sentence is transitional. The psalmist has pleaded innocent of any wrongdoing that would justify the harsh attacks of his enemies. On the other hand, if any of his suffering is due to his own sin or folly, he can accept that. He has not attempted to hide any wrongdoing from God — if that were possible. But his desire to do what is right in the sight of God has brought him added suffering and has served to plunge him more deeply into despair.

2. Suffering in God's Cause (69:6-12)

69:6-7 When a servant of God is made to suffer abuse and ridicule, others who would follow the Lord, especially the immature, are likely to be discouraged, "put to shame," "brought to dishonor" (v. 6, RSV) or as our text states: **disgraced.** This is a concern of the psalmist. But when he prays: **May those who seek you not be put to shame because of me**, or "on my account," it is really a prayer that God will rescue him from his tormentors. This would serve to renew their faith and confidence, for they would know that it was because of his loyalty to God that he had suffered. The extent of that suffering is now indicated.

69:8-12 I am a stranger to my brothers. In a culture where a husband may have had more than one wife, rivalry between the children was not unusual. But the psalmist finds himself even to be an **alien to my own mother's sons.** These are his full blood brothers that are rejecting him, not half-brothers born to another wife of his father. His own immediate family reject him (see Jer 12:6). Would they, perhaps, have accused him of fanaticism? He speaks of his zeal for the temple (v. 9). Is that just reason to be reproached? Perhaps his weeping, his fasting, and his dressing in the sackcloth were signs of concern for the house of God that was neglected or desecrated by frivolous worshipers! In his eyes the things that he had been doing were in keeping with the will of God. Should he, therefore, have to suffer for this? The answer, apparently, is yes! It is not unusual for those who stand firmly for what is right and good to incur the wrath of others.

3. The Prayer (69:13-18)

69:13 The psalmist has admitted weariness in his waiting for God (v. 3). He is perplexed because of the injustice he suffers. But he has not given himself over to despair. Those who "sit in the gate" may lie about him and make him the butt of their jokes (v. 12). **But I pray to you, O LORD, in the time of your favor; in your great love, O God, answer me with your sure salvation.** Here is a strong contrast. I still trust in the steadfast love and loyalty of God, and I appeal to that love. God chooses the time to respond but "respond to me with your firm salvation," that is, a salvation that has been demonstrated as true salvation, not deceptive (cf. Isa 49:8).

69:14-18 Verses 14-15 are a prayer for deliverance from the woes of verses 1-4. The terrors that threaten are recalled: **the mire . . . those who hate me . . . flood waters . . . the depths . . . the pit (the grave?).** Surely the Lord will take pity upon him because his need is so great — this is his plea. And so the prayer continues, dwelling now upon the greatness of God's mercy, his loving-kindness (**love**) and then upon the greatness of the peril threatening him from his enemies. If ever a soul needed deliverance, it is now.

4. The Depths of Anguish (69:19-21)

69:19-20a Many persons have experienced the therapeutic effect of unburdening the soul to another, the experience of "getting it off the chest." This the psalmist has done. And then it occurs to him that God knows all of this already! **You know how I am scorned, disgraced and shamed** (v. 19, cf. Jer 18:23). Even so, again he is moved to give voice to his despair. **Scorn has broken my heart** (v. 20). Jeremiah had a broken heart, also (Jer 23:9). **And has left me helpless.** Just one word in Hebrew, this expression appears only here in the Scriptures, with uncertain meaning. (The RSV has, "I am in despair.") Gesenius recognizes the possibility of a noun ("sickness," or "weakness") and proposes an emendation: "Sickness smites my soul." This provides a parallel structure for the verse: "Reproach has broken my heart, and sickness has smitten my soul."[46] The distress is not just a matter of the emotions; the broken heart is accompanied by bodily suffering.

69:20b-21 I looked for . . . sympathy. The verb means "to look for hopefully," with eager anticipation. But there was no one who would show pity nor compassion toward the grieving. **But there was none.** Instead (!), **They put gall in my food.** The language is figurative, but it does indicate the diabolical treachery of his oppressors. The key to the understanding lies in the word for food. It is not the common term but indicates the meal that is prepared by friends and brought to refresh and to comfort those who are in sorrow upon the death of a loved one.[47] But instead of providing any semblance of comfort, these people would intensify the agony

---

[46]Gesenius, *BDB Lexicon*, p. 633. Dahood would concur as to the syntax, with a slightly different translation: "Abuse has wasted my inmost parts, rank disease crushed my heart" (*Psalms 51–100*, p. 154).

[47]During the fatal illness of the child born to Bathsheba, David would not eat the food his friends provided (2 Sam 12:17). And Jeremiah spoke of a time of such distress that "no one will offer food to comfort those who mourn for the dead" (Jer 16:7).

of the psalmist. They would, figuratively, put gall, bitter herbs or poison, in the meal of comfort, and give him **vinegar** to drink, not alleviating but intensifying his thirst.

5. The Imprecation (69:22-29)

The psalmist is at a decided disadvantage in dealing with persons unscrupulously wicked, at least it would seem so. As a servant of God, he cannot stoop to the mean tricks they practice. Furthermore, God has said, "It is mine to avenge; I will repay" (Deut 32:35). Yet the Scriptures are not silent on the matter of retribution. (Consider the fate of Haman, who was hanged on the gallows that he had built for Mordecai, Esth 5:14; 7:9-10.) The psalmist is concerned that the way of the righteous be vindicated in the eyes of the world, for the unbroken reign of evil would intimate that God is indifferent to the injustices on earth.

69:22-25 Such concerns as these should inform our understanding of verses 22-28, which Leupold designates: "A prayer for the total overthrow of ungodly enemies."[48] The psalmist is saying, in effect: "Lord, demonstrate your power, execute justice; the matter is in your hands." May their eyes be darkened. This would render them completely impotent to harass the innocent any more. **Pour out your wrath on them.** Much as some may think otherwise, the wrath of God against evil is a well-defined biblical doctrine, and "When he is angry, the earth trembles" (Jer 10:10). Other Scriptures may state, "You set aside all your wrath" (Ps 85:3). But that is for those who have sought God's forgiveness (Ps 85:2). The psalmist sees no inclination at all toward repentance on the part of his enemies. His reasoning is: The wicked are doomed by the wrath of God; let doom fall upon them!

69:26-28 For they persecute those you wound. The psalmist has suffered (illness, perhaps) which he considers as discipline from God. Yet he has acknowledged his guilt (v. 8), and we may conclude that he has repented (vv. 10-11). He has not abandoned the way of the Lord but has remained zealous in his service (v. 9). For

---

[48]Leupold, *The Psalms*, p. 506.

this loyalty, he suffers at the hands of others. So, **charge them with crime upon crime**, he cries (v. 27), or "punishment to punishment;" meaning "Give them the punishment their sin deserves" (v. 27, NEB). **Do not let them share in your salvation.** The psalmist, having confessed himself to be a sinner, knows that a sinner may hope to be forgiven, vindicated, and restored to the fellowship of God. This is what it means to "share in your salvation." But these persist in their wickedness against others. Therefore, **may they be blotted out of the book of life.** It is those who seek and fear God who will be found in the book of the living (Amos 5:4; Mal 3:16), those who do good and not evil (Amos 5:14), who turn away from wickedness (Ezek 18:31). The judgment of God is called upon these who do not seek God, who do not do good, and who persist in evil. If he is vindictive, we can understand. But the basic desire of the psalmist is to see an open demonstration of righteous judgment.

69:29 I am in pain and distress or "afflicted and in pain." This verse is transitional. The writer's attention here returns to his own immediate condition, to his own need. He has pleaded his case. He will leave his enemies in the hands of God, looking to the Lord for deliverance from them. **May your salvation, O God,** (your saving power) **protect me,** from the reach of my enemies.

6. The Song of Assurance (69:30-36)

69:30a The psalm closes on a jubilant note, reflecting the confidence of the psalmist that God has heard his petition. **I will praise God's name in song.** To praise the "name" of God is to recognize and to honor the person of God, the presence of God, and his character as God. True praise is not the fulfillment of an obligation or the obedience to a command. Indeed, it cannot be. It is a spontaneous overflow of the heart of one who is thrilled to know God for who he is, for what he is, and for what he does.

69:30b-31 One who continues through life without a conscious knowledge of God, of his nature and of his works, will feel no particular urge to sing his praises. But, to know him is to love him and to praise him. One might seek to honor God, or to gain his favor(?) by bringing a sacrifice. But a song of praise (a שִׁיר, šîr) that is the

466

overflow of a thankful heart brings more honor to God than an ox
(a שׁוֹר, *šôr*) brought in sacrifice (vv. 30-31). This is no repudiation of
the place of sacrifice in the worship of God. It is the recognition
that God will accept the praises of a sincere heart even when not
accompanied by a sacrifice. (See Ps 40:6.)

69:32-33 The psalmist had been concerned that what had happened to him would bring discouragement to others (v. 6). Now he
knows that his deliverance will strengthen others who may have lost
heart. **The poor** (the humble, the oppressed) **will see and be glad.**
They will be encouraged to see that the Lord does hear **the needy,**
that he is concerned for **his captive people.** Reference to captives
("his prisoners," KJV; "his own that are in bonds," RSV) could refer
to those taken to Babylonia during the reign of Jehoiachin, king of
Judah, among whom were Daniel (Dan 1:1-6) and Ezekiel (2 Kgs
24:14-17). (In Jeremiah's vision of two baskets of figs, the good figs
are the exiles in Babylon and the bad figs are the residue of Israel
left in Jerusalem — Jer 24:1-3.) The same term "prisoners" or "captives" appears in Ps 68:6. There the reference is to the Israelites who
were in bondage to Egypt. Some believe that God's "captives" in
verse 33 are those "bound to his service" (NEB); that is, figuratively
prisoners or captives. However, it seems that actual bondage is indicated. If one questions what effect a victory for a servant of God in
Jerusalem could have on the exiles in Babylon, it should be noted
that Jeremiah was in contact with the elders of the exile (Jer 29:1ff.).

69:34-36 Let heaven and earth praise him. How decidedly the
mood of the Psalmist has changed! The implication is that in some
way he has been rescued from the sea of despair that would carry
him to destruction. Or else he is so confident of God's deliverance
that he proceeds as though it were an accomplished fact. He has
said that "the LORD hears the needy; he does not despise his captive
people" (v. 33). This in itself is reason enough for heaven and earth
to praise him. But, more than this, **God will save Zion, and rebuild
the cities of Judah.** On one occasion Jeremiah asked the question
of God, "Have you rejected Judah completely? Do you despise
Zion?" (Jer 14:19). That, too, would have been in a moment of
despair. But elsewhere the prophet states: "In the towns of Judah,
flocks will again pass under the hand of the one who counts them"
(Jer 33:13). God would "restore health" to Zion.

IV. THE KING'S PLAN (70:1–72:20)

A. MAKE HASTE, O GOD, TO HELP (70:1-5)

Psalm 70, except for a few slight but significant textual variations, is identical to Ps 40:13-17. Was it drawn from that source for some particular use? Or were these verses an originally independent poem combined with another to form Psalm 40? We believe the former to be the case, that Psalm 40 is a unit — see the discussion on that psalm — and that Psalm 70 was drawn from Psalm 40 to be used as a prayer for deliverance in a time of pressing need. The particular occasion for this use of the psalm we have no way of knowing, but the urgency of the situation is unmistakable. Hence our title, *Make Haste, O God!*[49]

Since these verses have already been considered in the treatment of Psalm 40, the remarks here will be confined to a discussion of textual matters. This, it is believed, will serve to indicate the note of urgency that we associate with this psalm. It should also give some insight relative to the changes a text might experience in the course of its transmission and in its usage.

A noticeable difference is seen in the variety of names or designations used for God. In verse 1a and in verse 4 *Elohim* is used instead of *Yahweh* (as in Psalm 40). But in verse 1b *Yahweh* is retained (as in 40:13). *Elohim* also appears in verse 5 instead of *Adonai* (Lord) of 40:17. But *Elohim* of 40:17 ("O my God") becomes *Yahweh* in 70:5b! The reasons for this wide variety of changes eludes us.

Other differences may be noted. The text of Ps 40:13 has, "Be pleased, O LORD (Yahweh) to save me." But "be pleased" is omitted from 70:1. The "confounded together" of 40:14 is simply "confounded" in 70:2 (KJV only, the NIV does not reveal the drop of a

---

[49]Wm. R. Taylor, in his treatment of this psalm, does not detect a note of urgency at all, chiefly because there is no definitive statement of any situation requiring urgency. Rather, he identifies the underlying mood of the psalm to be impatience on the part of the poet, who has no propensity for waiting on God! But is not the threat of death (v. 2) urgent? (See Wm. R. Taylor, *The Book of Psalms*, pp. 369ff.)

word "together", יַחַד, *yaḥad*), and the "seek after my soul to destroy it" is reduced to "seek after my soul," (again only in KJV, the NIV translates both places as **all who desire my ruin**, combining two Hebrew words into one English thought: "desire my ruin"; the KJV is a literal translation of the Hebrew.)

Again, in 40:15 we find "that say unto me" but in 70:3 the "unto me" is omitted. (Once again only in KJV, the NIV "smooths" out the text in 70:3 by supplying "to me" from 40:15.) All of these changes represent a shortening of the text, and thus a quickening of the pace at which the psalm moves. Such brevity, as Kidner notes, "gives a stronger sense of urgency to the prayer" (as compared to Psalm 40).[50]

Following the word order of the Hebrew, we may translate: "O God, deliver me! O LORD, save me! Hasten!" Actually, the verse has two infinitives and a verb imperative: "O God, to deliver me – O LORD, to help me – Hasten!" The emphasis upon haste is heightened by the use of this same imperative (חוּשָׁה, *ḥûšah*) in the closing verse of the psalm, constituting an inclusio. In verses 2-3 the psalmist makes mention of those responsible for the threat against his life, and verse 4 refers to the joy that comes to the people of God because of God's salvation. The closing statement then is an acknowledgment of God as **my help and my deliverer** with a third and final appeal for haste – **do not delay!** Thus, has a part of Psalm 40 been utilized in a time of distress as a vehicle for the expressing of one's urgent need for God's help.

B. THE PRAYER OF AN AGED SAINT (71:1-24)

Psalm 71 has the distinction of having been written by a person of mature years, one who has grown old in the Lord's fellowship. Faithful to God since childhood, through the years he has trusted the Lord, and still trusts, although at the present time he is growing feeble of body (v. 16), perhaps already with "one foot in the grave" (v. 20), and he is beset by enemies, wicked and cruel (vv. 4,10). But he is well prepared for this hour, for he has weathered many

---

[50]Kidner, *Psalms 1-72*, p. 249.

storms of life. God, he said, "made me see troubles, many and bitter" (v. 20). But always God had brought him through, and thus his faith had been strengthened. Now, although he does cry out to God for deliverance — that he not be forsaken in his old age — it is with confidence that he does so, a confidence nurtured through the years by God's teaching (v. 17). Consequently, the psalm is devoid of any note of self-pity or despair. Instead, the dominant chord throughout is one of jubilation.

The psalm is commonly classified as an individual lament. Certainly it seems to be the words of an individual, a resume of the spiritual pilgrimage of one whom God has sustained "from birth" (v. 6). Yet, for all the personal references, Briggs considers it to be a prayer of the congregation,[51] and Buttenwieser would classify it as a communal lament.[52] Oesterley concludes, however, that to interpret the many personal references in a collective sense is "to put a forced and unnatural meaning on many passages, and to misunderstand the entire spirit and purpose of the psalm."[53]

One having a familiarity with the content and phraseology of the Psalms will note that Psalm 71 is composed, to a great extent, of portions of others, especially of those found in Book 1. Verses 1-3 are, with slight changes, the same as Ps 31:1-3. The thought of verses 5-6 is found in 22:9-10, and verse 13 is like 35:4. In addition, there are numerous thoughts and expressions throughout the psalm that find a counterpart elsewhere. This very obvious fact led Kirkpatrick to describe the psalm as "little more than a mosaic of fragments and reminiscences of other psalms," but testifying: "it possesses a singular beauty and tenderness of its own."[54] It would be a mistake, however, to consider the psalm to be a composite of others in the sense of a scissors and paste operation. Rather, we have here a very personal — and original! — prayer. It comes readily and directly from the heart of an aged saint who for years has lived with the Psalms, until it has become second nature for him to express himself in the familiar and well-loved phrases.

[51]Briggs, *Psalms*, 2:124.
[52]Buttenwieser, *The Psalms*, p. 572.
[53]Oesterley, *The Psalms*, p. 333.
[54]Kirkpatrick, *Psalms*, p. 409.

The psalm does contain a note of distress. The writer has enemies who would take advantage of his advanced years. (Why they bear enmity toward him we are not told.) And there is a plea for help. But from the outset the prayer reflects a confidence that continues to sustain him, a confidence that is born of reflection upon God's past mercies, and that is demonstrated by the words of praise with which the psalm ends.

1. A Plea for Deliverance (71:1-13)

71:1-2 The psalm opens with a plea for God's help, but the very first words express faith and assurance. **In you, O LORD, I have taken refuge.** This is a literal translation. **Deliver me in your righteousness**; that is, in accord with your righteous nature which shows itself in your faithfulness to those who are devoted to you. (It is a thought similar to that expressed elsewhere in the phrase "for your name's sake." (See Ps 31:1,3.) This righteousness of God includes his fidelity in regard to his servant and is emphasized by the psalmist as the basis of his appeal, for in the Hebrew verse 2 opens with these words: "In your righteousness deliver me and rescue me." In verses 15, 16, and 24 the righteousness of God becomes the subject of the psalmist's testimony "all day long" and it is extolled in verse 19.

71:3-13 Be my rock of refuge . . . my rock and my fortress (v. 3). These words extend the thought of verse 1. The one who would "flee for refuge" to God would find that refuge to be most adequate and he delights in multiplying words expressive of that security — strong habitation, rock, fortress. He has need for such protection because at the present time he finds himself in danger at the hands of enemies, **wicked, evil**, and **cruel.** This is the occasion for his prayer, and his plea is for deliverance. We cannot discern the nature of their assaults, but apparently they consider his physical condition as evidence that **God has forsaken him**; he is free game. His plea is that God will continue to show himself to be the righteous one that he is: **Do not cast me away when I am old . . . . come quickly . . . to help me.** He is confident that his prayer will be heard. From his youth he has trusted God (v. 5), and he has not been disappointed.

From birth I have relied on you. The verb נִסְמַכְתִּי (*nismaktî*, from סָמַךְ, *sāmak*, "to lean") is reflexive and as such most expressive: "I have leaned myself, braced myself, upon you." What a picture of a life of trust, a life sustained in the fellowship and by the power of God! It is reflection upon this that gives hope to the psalmist in his present time of need and emboldens him to pray: **May my accusers perish in shame; may those who want to harm me be covered with scorn and disgrace.**

2. A Confidence Born of Experience (71:14-21)

71:14 In whatever way God may respond, on his part the psalmist will go on trusting in him. This is the significance of verse 14. The verse begins with an emphatic **But as for me**, and continues, **I will always have hope.** Such is his confidence in God. The verb (יָחַל, *yāḥal*) has the basic meaning "to wait," but with a dual connotation of patience plus confident expectation, thus to anticipate that which is sure to come. The basis for such hope lies in the past experiences of the psalmist.

71:15 The psalmist here indicates that the occasions of God's righteous acts and of his saving deeds on behalf of his aged servant have been almost without number. The verse opens with a verb meaning "to enumerate, to number," and closes with a noun from the same root. **My mouth will tell of your righteousness** [your faithful deeds], **of your** [acts of] **salvation all day long, though I know not its measure** [their number]. So many have been the righteous acts of God in the past that to recall them fully justifies patience for the present and confidence for the future.

71:16-20 From his youth God has taught him by **marvelous deeds** and **troubles, many and bitter** (!), which he has weathered (v. 20). So he will continue even now to go in the strength of the LORD and make mention of (God's) righteousness (v. 16). It is his desire to share with others the great good news of God's saving acts. This he has done in the past — **and to this day I declare your marvelous deeds.** And he is confident that, although his years may be declining, God will continue to sustain him **till I declare your power to the next generation.** So great is his trust in God's great-

ness and faithfulness — **Who, O God, is like you?** — that he anticipates that those whom he evangelizes will respond and will also
become the recipients of God's grace. This is indicated by verse 20,
the Hebrew text of which has the pronouns in the plural: **Though
you have made me [us] see troubles, many and bitter, you will
restore my [our] life again.** (The Hebrew text seems to be defective
at this point and thus should be read as singular.) From the contemplation of his own experience with God, and from his declaration of God's greatness to others, he has moved to the logical conclusion that they also will experience renewal. This is not
inconsistent with verse 21, where his thought reverts to his own situation.

71:21 You will increase my honor. The noun גְּדוּלָּה (gᵉdûllāh)
signifies the honor, sense of worth, or esteem, accruing to a person
because of who he is, the position he holds, the wealth he has accumulated, etc. Its opposite would be "disgrace." One of the aims of
the enemies of the psalmist apparently was the defamation of his
character (v. 10). He is not now boasting that God will make him
great, but that he will restore his respect, show him to be a man of
honor![55] **God will comfort me once again**, or, better, "encircle me
with comfort." This is the meaning of the Hebrew text and should
be retained.[56] (The translation "comfort me again" of some versions
is based on the LXX.) In spite of all that his enemies may do, they
cannot deprive him of the comfort that is his from God whom he
has known and served so many years.

3. Praise for God's Faithfulness (71:22-24)

71:22-24 The psalm opened with a strong affirmation of trust: "In
you, O LORD, I have taken refuge." It closes with an affirmation that
this trust has been vindicated: **Those who wanted to harm me have
been put to shame and confusion.** This does not necessarily mean
that the conflict with the enemies has been resolved. It may mean
that so certain is the psalmist of the outcome that he speaks as

---

[55]See the discussion of gᵉdhullāh in *TDOT*, 2:400.
[56]See Dahood, *Psalms 51-100*, p. 400.

though it has already transpired. In either case his faith in God remains unshaken. And this is cause for celebration, cause for praise!

The reflection of great joy, this praise arises from a heart over-flowing with the awareness of God's greatness and goodness. The whole person of the psalmist is involved, that he may exult in God to the utmost. He enhances his worship by the use of musical instruments, thus employing his fingers (v. 22). With his lips he praises God in song (v. 23). With his **tongue** he talks of **God's righteous acts.** His worship of God involves the whole soul (v. 23). Such is all true worship. A feeling of the greatness of God, alone and unexpressed, is not worship. The voicing of praises to God, without the inner confirmation of the spirit, is not worship. Worship is both the *feeling* and the *expression* of adoration to God, a subjective feeling given an objective expression. And one may know that he has worshiped God when the loyalty and devotion that he has expressed to the Lord are reflected in his life. In this way he may know certainly — and others will know — that he has been with God.

With confidence the psalmist voices his prayer to God for deliverance. He has contemplated the years that he has spent in God's fellowship and care — he has "leaned on God" from childhood. The result has been the assurance that God's faithfulness may be depended upon. And this realization has so stirred his emotions that he must praise God. The joy in his soul must be, and is, openly expressed. And this is the culmination of what began as a lament! Praise be to God!

C. A PRAYER FOR A KING (72:1-20)

A truth of the utmost importance to humankind is deeply embedded in the consciousness of the author of Psalm 72 and from this consciousness the psalm arises. Simply stated, it is this: The justice and righteousness of God constitute the perfect standard for human government and the enabling power by which that standard may operate. As one reads the psalm, so significant a truth should not be overlooked. But it may be, because it is not even mentioned. However, by implication it is clearly indicated, and this principle is basic to the understanding of the psalm.

The psalm is a prayer for a king, a very simple prayer, that he may rule with justice and righteousness in accord with the just and righteous standards of God. This standard is right for man, not because God *says* so, but because he *is* so, and he would have his people be as he is (Matt 5:48). "He is the Rock, his works are perfect, and all his ways are just. A faithful God who does no wrong, upright and just is he" (Deut 32:4). This is not to say that God himself is subject to some established norm to which he would conform; he *is* the norm, in his own holiness and righteousness! This standard is shown to be right for man, not only because it is God's standard, but because it works. In the words of Cyril Rodd, God "is the source of both moral righteousness and material prosperity."[57] The way of peace, life, and happiness the world around is to live by his standard of justice. This is the doctrine, the theology, and the wisdom underlying Psalm 72. It is this that makes the prayer so significant.

That the psalm is a prayer for a king is clearly indicated in the opening verse. The desire is that through him the justice of God may go forth with its accompanying blessings. The identity of the king is not revealed. The superscription, "of," or "to" or "for" Solomon, reflects the view of the ancient Jewish fathers that the psalm pertains to that son of David (v. 1, "the royal son"). The author is not identified, but the words would be appropriate on the lips of David on behalf of his son. The prophet Nathan had spoken to David of God's promise: "Your house and your kingdom will endure forever before me; your throne will be established forever" (2 Sam 7:16). And before his death David advised Solomon to be faithful in the ways of God, "so that you may prosper in all you do and wherever you go" (1 Kgs 2:3). The psalm envisions the righteous rule of God's servant, the king, and the prosperity that will result from righteous rule.

It so happens that the ideal here presented was never realized by Solomon nor by any other who sat upon the throne of David. Was the psalmist then engaged in wishful thinking? Or was he using hyperbole, not intending to be taken literally in every statement? Some would say that this is the case. W. Stewart McCullough, for

---

[57]Rodd, *Psalms 1–72*, p. 134.

example, identifies as hyperbole the reference to "the longevity of the king, vs.5; the extent of his dominion, vss.8-11; the durability of his fame, vs.17."[58] There is no reason why the psalmist might not use hyperbole. This is clearly the case in Ps 119:136. And as his contemporaries read the psalm, or used it for a coronation (?), they would not hesitate to voice such exalted expectations.

Nevertheless, Jewish tradition recognized the psalm as having messianic implications. In the Targum the opening verse is given: "O God, give the precepts of thy judgment to King Messiah and thy righteousness to the son of King David." In accordance with this, Moses Buttenwieser states categorically that "the psalm is messianic throughout."[59] Buttenwieser posits a late date for the psalm, shortly after 301 B.C. This necessitates the messianic interpretation since there were no kings in Israel at this time.[60] Others, however, noting that there is no mention of Psalm 72 in the NT, do not consider it messianic. Leslie, for example, states that it "has nothing to do with the messianic ruler, but is concerned solely with the earthly monarch."[61] In the view of the present writer, the psalm was not written with messianic intent, nor was it so understood in the contemporary circle. However, since the reign it envisions is patently beyond the capabilities of ordinary humankind, and since the ideal found fulfillment in the Christ, it would certainly seem to be, if not a prophecy, then a foreshadowing of Jesus the Messiah — righteous and just (v. 2), concerned for the poor (v. 4), with universal dominion (v. 8), receiving the gifts of kings (vv. 10-11), a compassionate Lord (vv. 12-14), with his name enduring forever (v. 17). This is the king that the psalmist visualizes, that David (?) visualizes, as he prays for his son Solomon, who would succeed him on the throne. It would remain, however, for a future son of David — "great David's greater Son" — to become that universal, just and righteous, Lord and King.

[58]McCullough, *The Book of Psalms*, *(IB)*, p. 379.
[59]Buttenwieser, *The Psalms*, p. 781.
[60]Dahood says, "Of course, the psalm is pre-exilic" and calls attention to the archaic nature of some of the language (*Psalms 51–100*, p. 179).
[61]Leslie, *The Psalms*, p. 94.

1. The Prayer for Righteousness and Justice (72:1)

72:1 By the measure of faith, the distinction between "may it be" and "it will be" is only a matter of degree. In the view of the present writer, the faith of the psalmist was such that, after his initial prayer to God on behalf of the king, he could say, and did say, "It will be." Only the first verb is imperative (so in the Hebrew): "Give," (**Endow**). Those that follow are the prefixed form ("imperfect") and may be rendered as simple future. That is, these words are an assertion of what will result when God answers the initial request. This understanding of the text is clearly indicated in our text, the NIV, as well as others.[62] For example, "He will judge your people in righteousness" (v. 2). "The mountains will bring prosperity" (v. 3), etc.

The supreme desire of the psalmist on behalf of the king is expressed in the first verse: **Endow the king with your justice, O God, the royal son with your righteousness.** This will equip him, the royal son who is now king, for a reign both just and prosperous. The justice the king executes is to be in accord with God's judgments, not according to any man-made appraisal of values or system of ethics. And his own righteousness is to reflect the righteousness of God. This says that, essential to the success of any government and absolutely necessary to the welfare of the nation, the king (or national leaders) of that nation must govern by right principles, namely, by God's standard. Clearly expressed, "The welfare of the nation depends on the morality that is practiced within it."[63]

---

[62]The KJV follows the Geneva Bible of 1560 in rendering the verbs in this manner. The same is true of the Douay-Rheims (Catholic) version, the ASV, the NIV, and the NKJV. On the other hand, the Emphasized Bible (1897) translates most of the verbs as petitions. So also James Moffatt (1922), the RSV, the Good News Bible, and Mitchell Dahood, Moses Buttenwieser, and Carrol Stuhlmueller. Also the NASB (a change from the ASV). The NEB (1970) expresses a petition in verses 1,3,8, otherwise employing the future indicative. The New American Bible (Catholic, 1970) has the petition in verses 1,5,8, and An American Translation (Wm. F. Beck, Lutheran, 1976) in verses 1,3 only. The present writer is in basic agreement with the KJV, the ASV, and the NIV on this matter.

[63]Cyril S. Rodd, *Psalms 1–72*, p. 134.

God's standard and the human are set in sharp contrast in Jer 22:13-17. The prophet has just informed Jehoiakim, king in Jerusalem, that his brother will never return from Egypt. A paraphrase of the remarks to the king may indicate their relevance to the present.

> Shame on the man who uses government office to serve his own interests and to satisfy his greed, to build a huge estate by fraud and deception, who sells his vote and influence to the highest bidder, with absolutely no concern that justice is done. Do you think that such crookedness proves you to be a great statesman? Consider Josiah, your father. He did not go hungry! Yet he did do what is right and just, and all went well with him. He dispensed justice to the poor and lowly. Is this not what it means to know God — to be guided in the discharge of the duties of your office by God's standard of what is right and good and just?

It may appear strange to some that in the prayer of the psalmist there is not included a request for wisdom on behalf of the king. As a matter of fact, Solomon himself prayed: "So give your servant a discerning heart to govern your people and to distinguish between right and wrong" (1 Kgs 3:9). But when the psalmist prays "Give . . . justice and righteousness," it is the very essence of wisdom that he asks! (See Ps 114:10 and our discussion of Psalm 1, *Wisdom and Folly*.) He would ask God to endow the king with knowledge of the divine standards of justice and righteousness. This, he knows, is the only foundation for a beneficent rule.

2. The Anticipated Results (72:2-7)

Such a king, walking in the ways of God, could expect God's blessings upon his land, blessings many and varied. These would include the following.

72:2 *A Righteous Reign.* **He will judge your people in righteousness.** Notice the pronoun "your"; it is significant. The king will not say, "These are *my* people and I will rule them as I please." They are *your* people (God's), and thus are to be treated fairly and with respect — all of them, including the poor and the lowly. The verb

דִּין (*dîn*, "judge") is broad in scope, inclusive of the entire range of governmental activity. It could be translated "rule" or "govern." In every area of government under a righteous rule, justice and right will prevail.

72:3 *Peace and Prosperity.* **The mountains will bring prosperity to the people.** What a promise! The word "prosperity," although appropriate, does not cover the breadth of meaning of the Hebrew *shalom.* It is a "peace" that includes a condition of harmony, of well-being, of fulfillment, and of plenty. Some would visualize the mountains as terraced to the summit with productive fields, but the language is better taken as figurative. By the mercy of God the very hills and mountains of the land would be productive of peace and plenty in this land where righteousness reigns. Indeed, it is by righteousness that this happy result will be achieved: "The mountains will bring peace and prosperity . . . by means of righteousness." God had promised Israel: "If you follow my decrees and are careful to obey my commands, I will send you rain in its season, and the ground will yield its crops and the trees of the field their fruit. . . . and live in safety in your land" (Lev 26:3-6).

The righteousness that is in harmony with God's righteousness will always be productive of good. Thus wrote the prophet Isaiah: "The fruit of righteousness will be peace; the effect of righteousness will be quietness and confidence forever" (Isa 32:17). These are the results when God endows the king with his justice and righteousness. Pray that it may be so! (And for the converse, see the daily newspaper!)

72:4 *Care for the Poor and the Oppressed.* **He will defend the afflicted among the people and save the children of the needy; he will crush the oppressor.** Justice is for all. The poor will not be shown favoritism in court just because they are poor (Exod 23:3). But neither will they be denied fairness (Exod 23:6). They will be saved (or delivered) from those who would abuse them and the oppressor will be crushed. The breadth of meaning of שָׁפַט, (*šāphat*, "to judge") is evident in this verse. It is to dispense justice, to rescue, defend, or save the innocent, and to put down the oppressor. When considered in connection with the righteousness of God, it has a further dimension, that of "salvation," of "redemption," yes, of "justification"! God would make possible the rehabilitation of the offender. The justice of God includes concern that the evildoer be restored. The oppressor must be crushed. But God's justice makes room for repentance and renewal for those who seek it. "Turn! Turn from your evil ways!" God calls, "Why will you die?" (Ezek 33:11).[64]

72:5 *Reverence for God.* When people have experienced righteous rule, when they have seen the peace and prosperity that result, when the poor and oppressed are delivered, when even evildoers are redeemed and restored, is it not reasonable that the people will have reverence for the God from whom such blessings have come? Addressing his remarks to God, the psalmist says: **He will endure as long as the sun, as long as the moon, through all generations**. Generation after generation will delight to honor such a God. (Note that a variant reading of the LXX suggests the NIV's translation. The Hebrew text has: "They will fear you," instead of "And he will endure (or live)." It is a matter of confusing *yods* and *waws* by a copyist which is easily done!)[65]

72:6-7 *A Refreshing Shower.* Too many peoples of the world have suffered at the hands of despotic rulers and from venal government officeholders. God's righteous ruler, by contrast, will be like a refreshing shower, **like rain falling on a mown field**, revitalizing the soil after the grass is harvested. In his last recorded words David expressed a similar thought: "When one rules over men in righteousness, when he rules in the fear of God, he is . . . like the brightness after rain that brings the grass from the earth" (2 Sam 23:3-4). **In his days the righteous will flourish.** It is the righteous, or just man, who often suffers the greatest abuse from wicked

---

[64]See W.F. Lofthouse, "The Righteousness of Yahveh," *The Expository Times*, vol. 50 (1939): 341-345.

[65]"They will fear you" is a simple translation of the unaltered Hebrew text and is similar to that found in the ASV, the NASB, and the NKJV. The text is treated in a comparable fashion by Eerdmans (*The Hebrew Book of Psalms*, p. 341), Cohen (*The Psalms*, p. 228), Dahood (*Psalms 51–100*, p. 178), and Leupold (*The Psalms*, p. 517). Others, however, following the LXX, translate: "May he live" (or, "he shall live") "while the sun endures" (instead of "They will fear you." (Cf. RSV, NEB, NIV, NAB, et. al.) While this suggests eternal life on the part of the king and is appealing in its messianic reference, the present writer sees no overwhelming reason for rejecting the Hebrew text with its verb meaning "to revere him."

rulers. But such will live and flourish when the justice and right-eousness of God are the foundation on which a nation is founded and by which it is governed.

3. The Prayer for Universal Reign (72:8)

72:8 The imperative verb of verse 1 is followed by verbs in the imperfect without conjunctions, and so are translated as simple declaratives. In verse 8, however, the conjunction appears with the verb. Considering this to be the connecting link, we relate this verb to the initial verb of the psalm. Thus, "Give the king your justice" (v. 1), "and let him have dominion also from sea to sea" (v. 8). This verse, then, we recognize as the second petition of the psalm on behalf of the king. It would seem to be both natural and appropriate to add this prayer to the original request. The enjoyment of the blessings of the righteous rule inspired of God should not be limited to one country alone. Is it not desirable to pray that the reign of righteousness be extended **to the ends of the earth**? This is not a prayer for conquest or for domination, but that righteous rule, under God and in accord with his all-righteous will, may be the heritage of all the earth.

4. The Anticipated Results (72:9-14)

The answer to the prayer of verse 1 would be a righteous reign, prosperity, care for the poor, reverence for God, and general refreshing for the land. God's answer to the prayer for a universal reign would also have its consequences, as follows.

72:9-11 *Homage from Far and Near.* **The desert tribes will bow before him.** These are the desert tribes, nomadic people, who traditionally resist any system of control. But even these will delight to offer homage to this upright ruler. The same may be said even of his enemies. They too come to acclaim him in an act of homage described as **lick[ing] the dust.** These all bow before him, not because they have been overwhelmed in battle and brought cringing to his feet, but because they have been overwhelmed by his goodness, his justice and righteousness, his concern for the poor, the weak, the oppressed. All kings, all nations will serve him **for he will deliver the needy** . . . etc. "When a man's ways are pleasing to the Lord, he makes even his enemies live at peace with him" (Prov 16:7).

72:12-14 *Help for the Needy and the Oppressed.* It is significant that these verses open with the conjunction "for" (or "because"), in Hebrew כִּי (kî). Here are stipulated the reasons for the worldwide acclaim accorded to God's righteous king, acclaim that is his, as Rotherham says, "because he deserves it"! The forgotten masses and those suffering oppression and violence are no longer ignored. Their cries are heard and answered. **He will rescue them from oppression and violence.** The verb גָּאַל (gāʼal, "redeem, avenge, ransom") describes the action of the kinsman-redeemer on the part of a blood relative. In some circles "Life is cheap." But every life is of concern to the righteous king, who can look upon the destitute even as near-of-kin. **Precious is their blood in his sight.** Help for the last, the least, and the lost will be abundantly provided in his kingdom.

5. The Prayer for Long Life (72:15)

72:15 The psalmist has asked for a just and righteous rule, for a reign universal in its scope. Now he prays that it may be of long duration. Thus verse 15 is interpreted by many. *Long may he live!*[66] The conjunction (in the Hebrew text) with the verb may indicate once again that this is a petition, "May he live." Compare this with "Long live the king," or "Live forever, O king!" Who would not wish this for such a one and be most willing to continue to bring him gifts, to pray for him, and to praise him daily?

6. The Anticipated Results (72:16-17)

72:16 As the justice and righteousness of God become the norm for humankind, the fruits of righteousness, including material

---

[66]Others consider that *he*, the poor man whom the king has helped, shall live, receive a gift of gold, and respond by praying for the king and praising him. It seems, rather, that this verse is a petition for life on the part of the king.

blessings, will become evident. **Let grain abound throughout the land; on the tops of the hills may it sway. Let its fruit flourish like Lebanon; let it thrive like the grass of the field.** The waving of the fields of grain is like the stirring of the wind among the cedars of Lebanon, an indication of abundance of grain.

72:17 As for the one who has implemented such a reign upon the earth, through the endowment that God has provided, **His name** [shall] **endure forever.** In royal circles it was understood that a king's name was preserved when his son ascended the throne after him, and would continue so long as his dynasty should last. Here is envisioned a reign that shall continue forever. And **all nations will be blessed through him** — not just men of Israel, but all nations **will call him blessed**, in view of his just and righteous rule.

7. The Doxology and the Colophon (72:18-20)

72:18-19 These verses constitute a doxology. Since each of the five books of Psalms closes in such a fashion, it is understood that these were added to each book at the time of its compilation. Probably that is the case. But even so, verses 18 and 19 constitute a very fitting close to Psalm 72. Beyond question the psalm has been discussing **marvelous deeds** and a "Blessed be Yahweh" is most appropriate. And the prayer, **May the whole earth be filled with his glory**, accompanied by its **Amen, and Amen**, would anticipate the time when the ideal reign upon earth by the ideal King would become a reality.

72:20 The final verse, beyond doubt, was a subscript to the collection of Davidic Psalms that appear in Books 1 and 2. Book 3 begins with a group of Psalms by Asaph, but it and Books 4 and 5 also contain other Psalms of David.